D1369135

EVERYMAN, I will go with thee,

and be thy guide,

In thy most need to go by thy side

The Golden Treasury of Longer Poems

SELECTED AND EDITED BY
ERNEST RHYS

DENT: LONDON, MELBOURNE AND TORONTO
EVERYMAN'S LIBRARY
DUTTON: NEW YORK

No. 746   Hardback ISBN 0 460 00746 7
No. 1746   Paperback ISBN 0 460 01746 2

INTRODUCTION
TO THE ORIGINAL EDITION

THIS volume of longer poems is the natural successor to
the two anthologies of songs and lyrics and the ballad book
in the same library. It does not apply too rigidly its measure
of length, being intended to take up the line of English
verse at the point where the others paused, to maintain
the record and make it of a piece with the rest. There are
poems that are still lyrical, like Drayton's 'Agincourt', and
others, like Chaucer's 'Knightes Tale', which show the
sustained narrative power of English verse. Again there are
poems, like Parnell's 'Hermit', which knit up afresh the
old ballad tradition of 'Chevy Chase' and 'Clerk Saunders'.
There are noble elegies, too, and tributes of poet to poet—
'Adonais' and Ben Jonson's lines to the Beloved Memory of
Shakespeare, while the English love of place and of Nature
is heard again and again in its pages. In all this variety, the
main purpose is to show the great succession of the English
poets who wrote, as Coleridge says, with

> A light in sound, a soundlike power in light,
> Rhythm in all thought, and joyance everywhere.

It keeps on the whole close to the recognized track. It
does not forget the great prose writers, like Swift and Dr
Johnson, who influenced verse. But chiefly it upholds the
princely line, in which Chaucer, Spenser, Marvell, Milton,
Ben Jonson, Crashaw, Henry Vaughan, Pope, Goldsmith,
Burns, Wordsworth, Coleridge, Byron, Shelley and Keats
are the masters and the great maintainers. In the shadow

of their greater fame stand other poets worthy of remembrance, on whom as it were the true tradition took hold— men who were not great poets but who yet contributed to the rich store. Such were Thomas Warton, whose 'Grave of King Arthur' is rescued from comparative forgetfulness, and Shenstone, whose 'Schoolmistress' is the reminder of an old and pleasant mode of rural art. In other cases there is a question of poems that influenced the world and in a sense became part not only of the dialect of their own time, but of the permanent language of verse; and these too have not been forgotten. In a few instances items have been omitted because they are already printed in the poetry-books of the series: e.g. 'Chevy Chase', 'Robin Hood' and 'John Gilpin'. For space is precious and every poem has jealously to be considered, in the claim of the many that must be omitted.

On the modern side, the book stops short with the close of last century, where the personal glamour, as we may call it, and the deceptive contemporary estimate, enters the list. Who of us can tell what the last value is going to prove of some of those younger poets, under whose spell we may have willingly enough fallen?—in whose poetry,

> As in a mansion like their proper home
> Even forms and substances are circumfused . . .
> And through the turnings intricate of verse
> Present themselves as objects recognized,
> In flashes, and with glory not their own.

We have only included then from the later pieces some of those which have already lasted a generation, and worn well, and stood the test of a change of generations and fashions.

For permission to use copyright verses acknowledgment is due and is hereby made; to Mr Robert Bridges and Mr John Murray for 'The Summer-House on the Mound'; to Mrs Meynell for 'A Letter from a Girl to Her Own Old Age'; to Mr Wilfrid Meynell for Francis Thompson's 'The Hound of Heaven'; to Mr William Watson for 'Wordsworth's Grave'; and to Mr W. B. Yeats for 'The Death of Cuchulain'.

1921   E. R.

PUBLISHER'S NOTE

In 1950 the publishers decided to extend the scope of this volume by including poets later than Robert Bridges, with whom it had hitherto ended. Accordingly, in the reprint of that year poems by Gibson, Chesterton, Brooke, Blunden, Bottomley, de la Mare, Lawrence and Binyon were added.

In 1954 the volume was further enlarged by the inclusion of poems by Kipling, Masefield, Armstrong and Day Lewis, and the following statement of the sources of all the new poems, and acknowledgments, was included:

For permission to use these copyright verses acknowledgments are made: to Mrs George Bambridge, Methuen & Co. Ltd, and the Macmillan Company of Canada Ltd for 'The Rhyme of the Three Sealers' by Rudyard Kipling; to the trustees of the Hardy estate and Macmillan & Co. Ltd for 'The Dead Quire' by Thomas Hardy; to the executors of Rupert Brooke and Sidgwick & Jackson Ltd for 'The Old Vicarage, Granchester' from the *Collected Poems* of Rupert Brooke; to Gordon Bottomley and Constable & Co. Ltd for 'The Maid of Arc'; to Mrs Laurence Binyon and the Society of Authors for an extract from *The Sirens* by Laurence Binyon; to Wilfrid Gibson and Macmillan & Co. Ltd for 'Flannen Isle' from *Collected Poems (1905–1925)*; to Edmund Blunden for 'The Silver Bird of Herndyke Mill'; to the executrix of G. K. Chesterton for 'Lepanto' from the *Collected Poems* of G. K. Chesterton; to Mrs Frieda Lawrence and W. Heinemann Ltd for 'Snake' by D. H. Lawrence; to Dr John Masefield and W. Heinemann Ltd for 'Spanish Waters' from the *Collected Poems* of John Masefield; to Martin Secker Ltd for 'Miss Thompson Goes Shopping' by Martin Armstrong; to Walter de la Mare and Faber & Faber Ltd for 'The Old Angler'; to C. Day Lewis and the Hogarth Press Ltd for 'Sing we the two Lieutenants' from 'A Time to Dance' included in the *Collected Poems* of C. Day Lewis.

PUBLISHER'S NOTE

In 1950, the publishers decided to extend the scope of this volume by including poems later than Robert Bridges, with whom it had hitherto ended. Accordingly, in this reprint of that anthology by Gibson, Chesterton, Brooke, Flecker, Bottomley, de la Mare, Lawrence, and Binyon were added. In 1962 the volume was further enlarged by the inclusion of poems by Yeats, Masefield, Armstrong, and Day Lewis, and the following statement of the sources of all the new poems and acknowledgements was included:

The publishers wish to thank the owners of the copyright poems and others named for permission to use the poems. [remainder illegible]

CONTENTS

CONTENTS

GEOFFREY CHAUCER

THE KNIGHTES TALE[1]

WHILOM, as olde stories tellen us,
Ther was a duk y-namèd Theseus;
Of Athens he was lord and governoúr,
And in his tyme such a conqueroúr,
That gretter was ther non under the sonne.
Ful many a riche contree had he wonne;
That with his wisdom and his chivalrie
He conquered al the realme of Femynye,
That whilom was i-clepèd Scythia;
And wedded hath the queen Hippolyta,
And brought her home with him to his contree,
With moche glorie and gret solemnitee,
And eek her younge sister Emelye.
And thus with victorie and with melodye
Let I this noble duk to Athens ryde,
And al his host, in armes him biside.
And certes, were it not too long to heere,
I wolde have told you fully the manére,
How wonnen was the realm of Femenye
By Theseus, and by his chivalrye;
And of the grete bataille for the nonce
Bytwix Athénes and the Amazons;
And how besiegèd was Hippolyta,
The faire hardy queen of Scythia;
And of the feste that was at her weddynge,
And of the tempest at her home comynge;

---

[1] In this version by Arthur Burrell, M.A., the spelling has been slightly modernised, and some difficulties of vocabulary have been cleared away. Some care has been taken to preserve Chaucer's melody. The italic " e " is to be very lightly sounded, so lightly that the sound is hinted at, rather than heard.

But al that thing I most as now forbere.
I have, God wot, through a large feeld to fare,
And weake be the oxen in my plough,
The remnaunt of the tale is long inough;
I wol not stop a man of al this rowte.
Lat every felawe telle his tale aboute,
And lat see now who shal the soper wynne,
And where I lafte, I wolde agayn begynne.

This duk, of whom I make mencioún,
When he was comen almost unto the toun,
In al his wealth and in his moste pryde,
He was war, as he cast his eye aside,
Wher that ther knelèd in the hye weye
A companye of ladies, tweye and tweye,
Ech like the other, clad in clothes blake;
But such a cry and such a wo they make,
That in this world no creätúre lyvýnge,
Hath herde such another lámentynge,
And of that cry stinten they never wolde,
Til they the reynes of his bridel holde.
" What folk be ye that at myn hom comynge
Perturben so my feste with cryénge? "
Quoth Theseus, " have ye so gret envýe
To myn honoúr, that thus compleyne and crie?
Or who hath you injúrèd, or offendid?
Nay tell it me if it may be amendid;
And why that ye be clad thus al in blak? "
The oldest lady of them alle spak,
When she hadde swownèd with a dedly chere,
That it was pity for to see or heere;
And seyde: " Lord, to whom Fortune hath geven
Victorie, and as a conquerour to lyven,
Noughte greveth us youre glorie and honoúr;
But we beseechen mercy and socoúr.
Have mercy on oure wo and oure distresse.
Som drope of pitee, thurgh youre gentilnesse,
Uppon us wretchede wommen lat thou falle.
For certes, lord, ther is noon of us alle,
That hath not been a duchesse or a queene;
Now be we caytifs, as it is wel seene:
Thankèd be Fortune, and her false wheel,
That no estat assureth to be weel.
And certes, lord, to abiden youre presénce

Here in the temple of the goddesse Clemence
We have ben waytynge al this fourtenight;
Now helpe us, lord, since it is in thy might.
I wretche, which that wepe and waylle thus,
Was whilom wyf to kyng Capaneus,
That died at Thebes, cursèd be that day,
And alle we that be in this array,
And maken alle this lamentacioun,
We leften alle oure housbondes at the toun,
Whil that the siege ther aboute lay.
And yet the olde Creon, welaway!
That lord is now of Thebes the citee,
Fulfilde of ire and of iniquitee,
He for despyt, and for his tyrannýe,
To do the deede bodyes vilonýe,
Of alle oure lordes, which that be i-slawe,
Hath alle the bodies on an heep y-drawe,
And will not suffre them by no assent
Neither to be y-buried nor i-brent,
But maketh houndes ete them in despite."
And with that word, withoute more respite,
They fillen flat, and criden piteously,
"Have on us wretched wommen som mercy,
And lat oure sorrow synken in thyn herte."
This gentil duk doun from his courser sterte
With herte piteous, when he herde them speke.
Him thoughte that his herte wolde breke,
Whan he saw them so piteous and so poor,
That whilom weren of so gret honoúr.
And in his armes he them alle up hente,
And them confórteth in ful good entente;
And swor his oth, as he was trewe knight,
He wolde do for them as wel he might
And on the tyraunt Creon vengeance take,
That al the people of Grece sholde speke
How Creon was of Theseus y-served,
As one that hath his deth right wel deserved.
And right anon, withoute more delaye
His baner he desplayeth, and took his waye
To Thebes-ward, and al his host bysyde;
Nor near Athenes wolde he go nor ryde,
Nor take his ese fully half a day,
But onward on his way that nyght he lay;

And sente anon Hippolyta to go,
And Emelye hir yonge sister too,
Unto the toun of Athenes for to dwelle;
And forth he rode; ther is no more to telle.

The red statúe of Mars with spere and targe
So shyneth in his white baner large,
That alle the feeldes gliter up and doun;
And by his baner was borne his pennón
Of gold ful riche, in which was set to view
The Minatour which that in Crete he slew.
Thus rode this duk, thus rode this conqueroúr,
And in his host of chevalrie the flour,
Til that he cam to Thebes, and alighte
Fayre in a feeld wher as he thoughte to fighte.
But shortly for to speken of this thing,
With Creon, which that was of Thebes kyng,
He faught, and slew him manly as a knight
In plain bataille, and putte his folk to flight;
And by assault he wan the citee after,
And rente doun bothe wal, and sparre, and rafter;
And to the ladies he restored agayn
The bones of their housbondes that were slayn,
To do exéquies, as was then the guise.
But it were al too long for to devyse
The grete clamour and the lámentynge
Which that the ladies made at the brennynge
Of the bodyes and the grete honoúr
That Theseus the noble conqueroúr
Doth to the ladyes, when they from him wente.
But shortly for to telle is myn entente.
Whan that this worthy duk, this Theseus,
Hath Creon slayn, and Thebes wonne thus,
Stille in the feelde he took al night his reste,
And dide with al the contree as he list.

To ransake in the heap of bodyes dede
Them for to strip of harness and of wede,
The searchers diden businesse and cure,
After the bataile and discomfiture,
And so bifel, that in the heap they founde,
Thurgh pierced with many a grevous blody wounde,
Two yonge knightes lying by and by,
Both in one coat of arms wrought richely;
Of whiche two, Arcite hight the one,

And the other knight was naméd Palamon.
Not fully quyk, nor fully deed they were,
But by their coat armure, and by their gear,
Heraldes knewe them wel in special,
As knights that weren of the blood royál
Of Thebes, and of sistren tuo i-born.
Out of the heap the searchers have them torn,
And have them caried softe unto the tente
Of Theseus, and ful sone he them sente
To Athenes, for to dwellen in prisoun
Perpetuelly, he wolde no ransom.
And this duk when he hadde thus i-doon,
He took his host, and hom he rode anon
With laurel crownèd as a conqueroúr;
And there he lyveth in joye and in honoúr
Al through his lyf; what wille ye wordes mo?
And in a tour, in angwishe and in wo,
Dwell evermo wher gold may profit none
This Arcite and his felawe Palamon.
Thus passeth yeer by yeer, and day by day,
Til it fel once upon a morn of May
That Emelie, far fairer to be seene
Than is the lilie on her stalke grene,
And fressher than the May with floures newe—
For with the rose colour strove her hewe,
I know not which was fairer of them two—
Ere it was day, as she was wont to do,
She was arisen, and al redy dight;
For May wil have no sloggardye a nyght.
The sesoun priketh every gentil herte,
And maketh him out of his sleepe sterte,
And seith, " Arise, and do thin óbservance."
This makèd Emelye have rémembrance
To do honoúr to May, and for to ryse.
I-clothèd was she fressh for to devyse.
Her yellow hair was braided in a tresse,
Byhynde her bak, a yerde long I gesse.
And in the gardyn as the sonne upriste
She walketh up and doun wher as she liste.
She gathereth floures, party whyte and red,
To make a subtle gerland for her hed,
And as an angel hevenly she song.
The grete tour, that was so thikke and strong,

Which of the castel was the cheef dongeoún,
(Ther as this knightes weren in prisoún,
Of which I tolde yow, and telle shal)
Was evene joynging to the garden wal,
Where as this Emely hadde her pleyynge,
Bright was the sonne, and cleer was the mornyng,
And Palamon, this woful prisoner,
As was his wont, by leve of his gayler
Was risen, and roamèd in a chambre on high,
Where he could al the noble citee espye,
And eek the garden, ful of braunches grene,
In which that Emelye the fresshe and shene
Was in her walk, and romèd up and doun.
This sorweful prisoner, this Palamon,
Goth in the chambre roamyng to and fro,
And to himself compleynyng of his wo;
That he was born; ful ofte he seyd, alas!
And so byfel, by áventure or case,
That thurgh a wyndow thikke and many a barre
Of iren greet and square as eny sparre,
He cast his eyen upon Emelya,
And therwithal he blinked and cryèd, a!
As that he stongen were unto the herte.
And with that crye Arcite anon up sterte,
And seyde, " Cosyn myn, what eyleth thee,
That art so pale and deedly for to see?
Why criedest thou? who hath thee doon offence?
For Goddes love, tak al in pacience
Oure prisoun, for it may non other be;
Fortune hath geven us this adversitee.
Som wikked aspéct or disposicioún
Of Saturne, by sum constellacioún,
Hath geven us this, though gainst it we had sworn;
So stood the heven when that we were born;
We moste endure it: this is the short and pleyn."
    This Palamon answered, and seyde ageyn,
" Cosyn, for-sothe, of this opynyoún.
Thou hast a veyn imaginacioún.
This prisoun causèd me not for to crye.
But I was hurt right now thorough myn eye
Into myn herte, that wil my bane be.
The fairnesse of the lady that I see
Yonde in the gardyn roming to and fro,

Is cause of al my cryying and my wo.
I know not whether womman or goddesse;
But Venus is it, sothly as I gesse."
And therwithal on knees adoun he fel,
And seyd*e*: " Venus, if it be youre wil
You in this gardyn thus to transfigúre,
Bifore me sorrowful wretched creätúre,
Out of this prisoun help that we may scape.
And if so be oure destynee be shape,
By word eterne to die in this prisoún,
On our lineáge have sum compassioún,
That is so lowe y-brought by tyrannye."
And with that word Arcit*e* gan espye
Where that this lady roamèd to and fro.
And with that sight her beauty hurt him so,
That if that Palamon was wounded sore,
Arcite is hurt as moche as he, or more.
And with a sigh he seyd*e* piteously:
" The fressh*e* beauty sleeth me suddenly
Of her that roameth yonder in the place;
And save I have her mercy and her grace
That I may see her beauty day by day,
I am but deed; ther is no more to seye."
This Palamon, whan he those word*e*s herde,
Dispiteously he lokèd, and answérede:
" Whether sayst thou in ernest or in pley? "
" Nay," quoth Arcite, " in ernest in good fey.
God helpe me so, ful loth am I to pleye."
This Palamon gan knytte his brow*e*s tweye:
" It would not be to thee a gret honoúr,
For to be false, and for to be traytoúr
To me, that am thy cosyn and thy brother
I-sworn ful deepe, and each of us to other,
That never even for death and for his paine,
Til lif*e* shal depart*e* from us twayne,
Neyther of us in love to hynder other,
Nor in no other case, my dear*e* brother;
But that thou shuldest trewly further me
In every case, and I shal further thee.
This was thyn othe, and myn also certáyn;
I wot right wel, thou darst it not withsayn.
Thus art thou sworn to help me out of doute.
And now thou woldest falsely be aboute

To love my lady, whom I love and seek,
And ever shal, until myn herte break.
Now certes, false Arcite, thou shalt not so.
I loved her first, and tolde thee my woe
That thou shouldst help me as my brother sworn
To further me, as I have told biforn.
For which thou art i-bounden as a knight
To helpe me, if it lay in thy might,
Or else thou art false, I dare wel sayn."
To this Arcite ful proudly spake agayn.
" Thou shalt," quoth he, " be rather false than I.
But thou art false, I telle thee utterly.
For *par amour* I loved her first ere thou.
What wilt thou sayn? thou knewest not yet now
Whether she be a woman or goddésse.
Thyn is affectioun for holynesse,
And myn is love, as for a creatúre;
For which I tolde thee myn áventúre
As to my cosyn, and my brother sworn.
Suppose, that thou lovedest her biforn;
Knowest thou not wel the olde clerkes saw,
That none shal geve a lover any lawe,
Love is grettere lawe, by my pan,
Than may be given to any erthly man?
Therfore posityf lawe, and such decree,
Is broke alway for love in each degree.
A man must needes love when al is said.
He may nought flee it, though he shulde be deed,
Be she a mayde, or be she widewe or wyf.
And eke it is not likely al thy lyf
To standen in her grace, no more shal I;
For wel thou knowest thyself in verity,
That thou and I be damnèd to prisoún
Perpetuelly, us gayneth no ransóm.
We stryve, as do the houndes for the bone,
They foughte al day, and yet their part was none;
Ther came a kyte, while that they were wrothe,
And bare away the bone betwixt them bothe.
And therefore at the kynges court, my brother,
Eache man is for himself, ther is no other.
Love if thou list; for I love and ay shal;
And sothly, deare brother, this is al.
Here in this prisoun muste we endure.

And each of us must take his áventúre."
Gret was the stryf and long bytwixe them tweye,
If that I hadde leisure for to seye;
But to the effect. It happèd on a day,
(To telle it you as shortly as I may)
A worthy duk that highte Peirithous,
That felaw was to the duk Theseus
Since that same day that they were children lyte,
Was come to Athénes, his felawe to visíte,
And for to pley, as he was wont to do,
For in this world he lovèd noman so:
And he loved him as tenderly agayn.
So wel they loved, as olde bookes sayn,
That whan the oon was deed, sothly to telle,
His felawe wente and sought him doun in helle;
But of that story lyst me nought to write.
Duk Peirithous lovèd wel Arcite,
And hadde him known at Thebes yeer by yeer,
And fynally at réqueste and prayér
Of Peirithous, withouten any ransóm
Duk Theseus him let out of prisoún,
Frely to go, wher that he list to dwell,
In such a gyse, as I shal pleynly tell.
This was the covenaunt, playnly to endite,
Betwixe Theseus and this Arcite:
That if so were, that Arcite were founde
Evere in his lyf, on any place or grounde,
In eny contree of this Theseus,
And he were caught, it was recorded thus,
That with a swerde sharpe he sholde dye;
Withouten any other remedy,
He took his leeve, and homward he him spedde;
Let him be war, in daunger lieth his head.
  How gret a sorrow suffreth now Arcite.
The deth he feleth thorugh his herte smyte;
He weepeth, weyleth, cryeth piteously;
To slay himself he wayteth privily.
He seyde, " Allas the day that I was born!
Now is my prisoun werse than was biforn;
Now am I doomed eternally to dwelle
Not only in purgatorie, but in helle.
Allas! that ever I knewe Peirithous!
For else I had y-dwelt with Theseus

I-fetered in his prisoun for ever mo.
Than had I been in bliss, and not in woe.
Only the sight of her, whom that I serve,
Though that her grace I may not even deserve
Wold have sufficèd right ynough for me.
O dere cosyn Palamon," quoth he,
" Thyn is the victorie of this áventúre,
Ful blisfully in prisoun to endure ;
In prisoun? nay, certes in paradys !
Wel hath fortune y-tornèd thee the dice,
That hath the sight of her, and I the absénce.
For possible is, since thou hast her presénce,
And art a knight, a worthi and an able,
That by som case, since fortune is chaungáble,
Thou maist to thy desir somtyme atteyne.
But I that am exilèd, and barrén
Of alle grace, am in so gret despeir,
That neither water, erthe, nor fyr, nor air,
Nor creätúre, that of them makèd is,
May ever helpe or comfort me in this.
Wel ought I die in wanhope and distresse ;
Farwel my lyf and al my jolynesse.
Allas ! why blamen folk so in comúne
The providence of God, or else fortúne,
That giveth them ful ofte in many a gyse
Wel better than they can themselves devyse ?
One man desireth for to have richésse,
That cause is of his murder or gret seeknésse.
And one man wolde out of his prisoun fayn,
That in his hous is by his servants slayn.
Infínite harmes be in this matére ;
We never know what thing we prayen here.
We fare as he that dronke is as a mouse.
A dronke man wot wel he hath an hous,
But he not knoweth which the way is thider,
And to a dronke man the wey is slider,
And certes in this world so faren we.
We seeken faste after felicitee,
But we go wrong ful ofte trewely.
Thus may we see alle day, and namely I,
That thought I had a gret opinioún,
That if I mighte skape fro prisoún,
Then had I been in joye and perfyt health,

And now I am exilèd fro my wealth.
Since that I may not see you, Emelye,
 Iam but deed; ther is no remedye."
 Uppon that other syde Palamon,
When that he wiste that Arcite had gone,
Such sorrow maketh, that the grete tour
Resowneth of his yellying and clamoúr.
The very feteres of his legges grete
Were of his bitter salte teres wete.
" Allas!" quoth he, " Arcita, cosyn myn,
Of al oure strif, God wot, the fruyt is thin.
Thow walkest now in Thebes at thi large,
And of my woe thou makest litel charge.
Thou maiste, since thou hast wysdom and mannede,
Assemble al the folk of oure kyndred,
And make a werre so sharpe in this citee,
That by som áventure, or by som trety,
Thou mayst her wynne to lady and to wyf,
For whom that I must needes lose my lyf.
For as by wey of possibilitee,
Since thou art at thi large of prisoun free,
And art a lord, gret is thy ávantage,
More than in myn, that sterve here in a cage.
For I must weepe and weyle, whil that I lyve,
With al the woe that prisoun may me give,
And eek with peyne that love me giveth also,
That doubleth al my torment and my woe."
Therwith the fire of jelousye upsterte
Withinne his brest, and caught him by the herte
So madly, that he like was to byholde
The box-tree, or the asshen deed and colde.
Then seyde: " O goddes cruel, that govérne
This world with byndyng of your word eterne,
And written in the table of adamant
Is all your will and youre eterne graunte,
How is mankynde more by you held
Than is the sheep, that lieth in the field?
For slayn is man right as another beste,
And dwelleth eek in prisoun and arreste,
And hath seknesse, and greet adversitee,
And ofte tymes gilteles, pardé.
What governaunce is in youre prescience,
That gilteles tormenteth innocence?

And yet encreaseth this al my penaúnce,
That man is bounden to this óbservaúnce
For Goddes sake to conquer al his wille,
When every beste may al his lust fulfille.
And when a beste is deed, he hath no peyne;
But man after his deth must wepe and pleyne,
Though in this world he have care and woe.
Withouten doute he shall have peynes mo.
The answer of this I leve to divinis,
But wel I wot, that in this world gret pyne is.
Allas! I see a serpent or a theef,
That unto many a man hath done mescheef,
Go at his large, and where him lust may turne.
But I muste be in prisoun through Saturne,
And eek through Juno, jealous and eke wood,
That hath destroyèd wel nigh al the blood
Of Thebes, with his waste walles wyde.
And Venus sleeth me on that other syde
For jelousye, and fere of him—Arcyte."
  Now wol I stynte of Palamon a lite,
And lete him in his prisoun stille dwelle,
And of Arcita forth then wil I telle.
The somer passeth, and the nightes longe
Encreasen double wise the peynes stronge
Bothe of the lover and the prisoner.
I know not which one is the wofuller.
For shortly for to sey, this Palamoun
Perpetuelly is damnèd in prisoún,
In cheynes and in feteres to be deed;
And Arcite is exiled upon his hed
For evere mo as out of that contree,
And nevere mo shal he his lady see.
Now loveres axe I you this question,
Who hath the worse, Arcite or Palamon?
That one may see his lady day by day,
But in prisoun he muste dwelle alway.
That other where him luste may ryde or go,
But see his lady shal he never mo.
Now deem it as you liste, ye that can,
For I wil telle forth as I bigan.
  When that Arcite to Thebes come was,
Ful oft a day he moaned and seyd alas!
For see his lady shal he never mo.

And shortly to concluden al his woe,
So moche sorrow had never creätúre,
That is or shal be while the world may dure.
His sleep, his mete, his drynk is him byraft,
That lene he waxeth, and drye as eny shaft.
His eyen hollow, grisly to biholde;
His hewe yellow, and pale as asshen colde,
And solitary he was, and ever alone,
And waillyng al the night, making his mone.
And if he herde song or instrument,
Then wolde he wepe, he might not be silent;
So feble were his spirits, and so lowe,
And chaungèd so, that no man coulde knowe
His speche nor his vois, though men it herde.
And in his look, for al the world he fared
Naught only lyke the lovers heaviness
Of Cupido, but rather lik madnesse,
Engendred of humoúr melancolýk,
In his forehead and braine fántastic.
And shortly turnèd was all up-so-doun
Bothe habit and eek disposicioun
Of him, this woful lovere Dan Arcite.
What shulde I alway of his woe endite?
When he endurèd had a yeer or tuo
This cruel torment, and this peyne and woe,
At Thebes, in his contree, as I seyde,
Upon a night in sleep as he him leyde,
Him thought that how the wingèd god Mercúrie
Byforn him stood, and bad him to be merry.
His slepy staff in hond he bar upright;
An hat he wered upon his heres bright.
Arrayèd was this god (as he took keepe)
As he was when he Argus laid to sleep;
And seyde thus: " To Athenes shalt thou wende;
There is y-shapen of thy woe an ende."
And with that word Arcite woke and sterte.
" Now trewely how sore that me smerte."
Quoth he, " to Athenes right now wil I fare;
And for the drede of deth shal I not spare
To see my lady, that I love utterlie;
In her presénce I reck not if I die."
And with that word he caught a gret myroúr,
And saw that chaungèd was al his coloúr,

And saw his visage was in another kynde.
And right anon it ran him into mynde,
That since his face was so dísfigúred
Of maladie the which he had endured,
He mighte wel, if that he kept him lowe,
Lyve in Athénes ever more unknowe,
And see his lady wel nigh day by day.
And right anon he chaungèd his aray,
And clothèd him as a pore laborer.
And al alone, save only one squyer,
That knew his counsel well and al his case,
Which was disgysèd poorely as he was,
To Athenes is he gone the nexte way.
And to the court he went upon a day,
And at the gate he profred his servýse,
To dragge and drawe, what-so men wolde devyse
And shortly on this matter for to seyn,
He fel in office with a chamberleyn,
The which that dwellyng was with Emelye.
For he was wys, and coulde sone aspye
Of every servaunt, which that servèd there.
Wel coulde he hewe woode, and water bere,
For he was yonge and mighty for the nonce,
And also he was long and bygge of bones
To do what eny wight can him devyse.
A yeer or two he was in this servýse,
Page of the chambre of Emelye the bright;
And Philostrate he told men that he hight.
But half so wel byloved a man as he
There never was in court of his degree.
He was so gentil of his condicioún,
That throughout al the court was his renoun.
They seyde that it were a charitee
That Theseus would advancen his degree
And putten him in honourable servýse,
Ther where he might his vertu exercise.
And thus withinne a while his name spronge
Bothe of his dedes, and his goode tonge,
That Theseus hath taken him so neer
That of his chambre he made him be squyer,
And gaf him gold to mayntene his degree;
And eek men brought him out of his countree
Fro yeer to yeer ful pryvyly his rente;

But honestly and shyly he it spente,
That no man wondred how that he it hadde.
And thre yeer in this wise his lyf he ladde,
And bare him so in pees and eek in warre,
Ther was no man that Theseus loveth more.
And in this blisse let I now Arcite,
And speke I wil of Palamon a lyte.

In derknes orrible and strong prisoún
This seven yeer hath livèd Palamoun,
All pinèd, what for woe and for distresse.
Who feleth double sorrow and hevynesse
But Palamon? that love constreyneth so,
That quite out of his witt he goth for woe;
And eek therto he is a prisoner
Perpetuelly, nat only for a yeer.
Who coude ryme in English properly
His martirdom? for-sothe it am not I;
Therefore I passe as lightly as I may.
It fel that in the seventhe yeer in May
The thridde night, (as olde bookes seyn,
That al this storie tellen more pleyn)
Were it by áventure or destinee,
(As, when a thing is shapen, it shal be,)
That soone after the mydnyght, Palamoun
By helpyng of a freend brak his prisoún,
And fleeth the citee fast as he may go,
For he had given drinke his gayler so
Of a spicerie and of a certeyn wyn,
With narcotykes and opie of Thebes fyn,
That al that night though that men wolde him shake,
The gayler sleep, he mighte nought awake.
And thus he fleeth as fast as ever he may.
The night was short, and sone cam the day,
That at all needs he most himselven hyde,
And to a grove faste ther besyde
With fearful foot then stalketh Palamoun.
For shortly this was his opynyoun,
That in that grove he wolde him hyde al day,
And in the night then wolde he take his way
To Thebes-ward, and pray his frendes alle
On Theseus to helpe him to battaile.
And shortely, or he wolde lose his lyf,
Or wynnen Emelye unto his wyf.

This is theffect of his intente playn.
Now wil I torne unto Arcite agayn,
That litel wiste how near him was his care,
Til that fortúne hath brought him in the snare.
    The busy larke, messager of day,
Saluteth in her song the morning gray;
And fyry Phebus ryseth up so bright,
That al the orient laugheth with the light,
And with his stremes dryeth in the greves
The silver dropes, hongyng on the leeves.
And Arcite, that is in the cours royál
With Theseus, his squyer principal,
Is risen, and loketh on the mery day,
And for to do his óbservance to May
Remembryng all the poynt of his desire,
He on his courser, proud as is the fire,
Is riden to the feeldes him to pleye,
Out of the court, were it a myle or tweye.
And to the grove, of which that I you tolde,
By áventure his wey he gan to holde,
To maken him a garland for the morn,
Were it of woodbyn or of hawe-thorn,
And lowde he song against the sonne sheene:
" May, with al thy floures and thy greene,
Welcome be thou, thou faire fresshe May!
I hope that I som grene gete may."
And fro his courser, with a lusty herte,
Into the grove ful lustily he sterte,
And in a pathe he romèd up and doun,
Whereas by áventure this Palamoun
Was in a bushe, that no man might him see.
Ful sore aferèd of his deth was he,
And nothing knew he that it was Arcite:
God wot he wolde have trowèd it ful lite.
For soth it hath been seyd ful many yeres,
That feeldes have eyen, and the woode hath eeres.
It is ful wise to bear an evene minde,
At everich hour the foe his foe may finde.
Ful litel wot Arcite of his feláwe,
That was so nigh to herken all his sawe,
For in the busche he sitteth now ful stille.
Whan that Arcite had romèd al his fille,
And songen al the roundel lustily,

Into a studie he fel sodeynly,
As do these lovers in there queynt manére,
Now in the toppe, now lying in the mire,
Now up, now doun, as boket in a welle.
Right as the Friday, sothly for to telle,
Now it shyneth, and now reyneth faste,
Right so gan fickel Venus overcaste
The hertes of her folk, right as her day
Is fickel, right so chaungeth her aray.
Seldom is Friday like each other day.
Whan that Arcite hadde songe, he gan to stay.
And sette him doun withouten eny more:
" Alas! " quoth he, " that day that I was bore!
How longe Juno, thurgh thy crueltee
Wilt thou destroyen Thebes the citee?
Allas! i-brought is to confusioún
The blood royál of Cadme and Amphioun:
Of Cadmus, which that was the firste man
That Thebes built, or first the toun bygan,
And of that citee first was crownèd kyng,
Of his lynáge am I, and his ofspring
By verray lyne, and of his stock royál:
And now I am so caytyf and so thral,
That he that is my mortal enemy,
I serve him as his squyer poorely.
And yet doth Juno me far more shame,
For I dare nought byknowe myn owne name,
But ther as I was wont to be Arcite,
Now am I Philostrate, nought worth a myte.
Allas! thou felle Mars, alas! Juno,
Thus hath youre ire owre lynage all fordo,
Save only me, and wretched Palamoun,
That Theseus hath martyred in prisoún.
And over al this, to slay me utterly,
Love hath his fyry dart so brennyngly
I-stickèd thurgh my trewe careful herte,
That shapen was my deth before my shirte.
Ye slay me with youre eyen, Emelye;
Ye be the cause wherfore that I dye.
Of al the remenant of myn other care
Ne sette I nought the value of a tare,
So that I coude do ought to youre pleasaúnce."
And with that word he fel doun in a traunce

A longe tyme; and aftirward upsterte
This Palamon, that thoughte thurgh his herte
He felt a cold sword suddenly to glyde;
For ire he quaked, he wolde no longer abyde.
And when that he hath herd Arcites tale,
As he were mad, with face deed and pale,
He sterte him up out of the busshes thikke,
And seyd: " Arcyte, false traitour wikke,
Now art thou caught, that lovest my lady so,
For whom that I have al this peyne and woe,
And art my blood, and to my counseil sworn,
As I ful ofte have told thee here byforn,
And has deceivèd here duk Theseus,
And falsely chaungèd hast thy name thus;
I wil be deed, or else thou shalt dye.
Thou shalt not love my lady Emelye,
But I wil love hire only and no mo;
For I am Palamon thy mortal fo.
And though that I no wepen have in this place,
But out of prisoun am y-stert by grace,
I drede not that either thou shalt dye,
Or that thou never shalt love Emelye.
Choose which thou wilt, for thou shalt not departe."
This Arcita, with ful despiteous herte,
Whan he him knew, and had his tale herde,
As fierce as lyoun pulleth out a swerde,
And seide thus: " By God that sitteth above,
Were it not thou art sike and mad for love,
And eek that thou no wepen hast in this place,
Thou sholdest never out of this grove pace,
Thou sholdest deyen of myn owen hond.
For I defye the suretee and the bond
Which that thou seyst that I have maad to thee.
For, very fool, know well that love is free,
And I will love hire yet for al thy might.
But, for thou art a gentil perfight knight,
And woldest fighten for her by batayle,
Have heere my trothe, tomorrow I wil not fayle,
Withouten wityng of eny other wight,
That heer I will be founden as a knight,
And bryngen harneys right inough for thee;
And choose the best, and leave the worst for me.
And mete and drynke this night wil I bryng

Inough for thee, and cloth for thy beddynge.
And if so be that thou my lady wynne,
And sle me in this wood that I am inne,
Thou maist wel have thy lady as for me."
This Palamon answereth, " I graunt it thee."
And thus they be depart til morning light,
Whan ech of them had pledged his feith to fight.
　　O Cupide, foe of alle charitee!
O King, that wolt no felaw have with thee,
Ful soth is seyde, that love and eek lordshipe
Wol not, for aught, have any fellowship.
Wel fynden that Arcite and Palamoun.
Arcite is ridden anon unto the toun,
And on the morrow, ere it were day light,
Ful prively two armours hath he dight,
Bothe suffisaunt and mete for to do
The batayl in the feeld betwix them two.
And on his hors, alone as he was borne,
He caryed al this armour him biforn;
And in the grove, at tyme and place i-sette,
This Arcite and this Palamon be mette.
Then changen gan their colour in their face.
Right as the hunter in the land of Trace
That stondeth in the gappe with a spere,
When honted is the lyoun or the bere,
And hereth him com rushing in the greves,
And breking both the bowes and the leves,
And thenketh, " Here cometh my mortel enemy,
Withoute faile, he must be deed or I;
For eyther I must slay him at the gappe,
Or he must slee me, if it me myshappe: "
Se ferden they, in changyng of their hew,
As fer as eyther of them other knew.
Ther was no good day, ne no salutyng;
But streyt withouten word or réhersyng,
Eche one of them helpeth to arm the other,
As friendly as he were his owen brother;
And thenne with their sharpe speres stronge
They thrusten eche at other wonder longe.
And then it semede that this Palamoun
In his fightyng were as a mad lyoun,
And as a cruel tygre was Arcite:
As wilde boores they began to smyte,

That frothen white as fome, in anger wood.
Up to the ancle they fought in there blood.
And in this wise I lete them fightyng welle;
And forthere wil I of duk Theseus telle.

The destinee mynistre general,
That executeth truly over all
The events, that God hath seen and seide byforn;
So strong it is, that though the world had sworn
The contrary of a thing by yea or nay,
Yet som tyme it shal falle upon a day
What falleth nought within a thousand yeere.
For certeynly oure appetites here,
Be it of war, or peace, or hate, or love,
Al is it rulèd by the sight above.
This mene I now by mighty Theseus,
That for to hunten is so désirous,
And namely the grete hert in May,
That in his bed ther dawneth him no day,
He is not clad, and redy for to ryde
With hunt and horn, and houndes him byside.
For in his huntyng hath he such delyt,
That it is al his joye and appetyt
To be himself the grete hertes bane,
For after Mars he serveth now Dyane.

Cleer was the day, as I have told ere this,
And Theseus, with alle joye and bliss,
With his Hippolyta, the fayre queene,
And Emelye, clothèd al in greene,
On huntyng be thay riden royally.
And to the grove, that stood ther faste by,
In which ther was an hert as men him tolde,
Duk Theseus the streyte wey hath holde.
And to the place he rydeth him ful right,
Where was the hert y-wont to have his flight,
And over a brook, and so forth in his weye.
This duk wil have of him a cours or tweye
With houndes, such as he can best comaunde.
And whan this duk was come into the ground,
Under the sonne he loketh, and right anon
Was war of Arcite and of Palamon,
That foughten fierce, as it were bores tuo;
The brighte swerdes wente to and fro
So hideously, that with the leste strook

It seemeth as it wolde felle an oak;
But what they were, nothing did he ween.
This duk his hors smot with his spores sheen,
And at a stert he was betwixt them tuo,
And pulled out a swerd and crièd, " Hoo! "
Nomore, on peyne of losyng of your hed.
By mighty Mars, anon he shal be ded,
That smyteth eny strook, that I may see!
But telle me what maner men ye be,
That be so hardy for to fighten here
Withoute judge or other officere,
As it were in a lyste royally? "
This Palamon answerede hastily,
And seyde: " Sir, what nedeth wordes mo?
We have the deth deservèd bothe tuo.
Tuo woful wretches be we, and caytyves,
That be encombred of oure owne lyves;
And as thou art a rightful lord and judge,
Give neither eny mercy nor refúge.
And sle me first, for seynte charitee;
But sle my felaw eek as wel as me.
Or sle him first; for, look that thou know him right,
This is thy mortal fo, this is Arcite,
That fro thy lond by thee is banishèd,
For which he hath deservèd to be ded.
For this is he that came to thi gate
And seyd, that he was clepèd Philostrate.
Thus hath he cheated thee ful many a yer,
And thou hast made of him thy cheef squyer.
And this is he that loveth Emelye.
For since the day is come that I shal dye,
I make pleynly my confessioún,
That I am he, the woful Palamoun,
That hath thi prisoun broke wikkedly.
I am thy mortal fo, and it am I
That loveth so hot Emely the bright,
That I wil dye present in his sight.
Therefore I aske deeth and my justíce;
But slee my felaw in the same wyse,
For bothe we have deservèd to be slayn."
    This worthy duk answered anon agayn,
And seide: " This in a short conclusioún:
Your owne mouth, by your owne confessioún,

Hath damned you bothe, and I wil it recorde.
It needeth nought to hang yow with the corde.
Ye shal be deed by mighty Mars the red!"
The queen anon for very wommanhede
Gan for to wepe, and so ded Emelye,
And alle the ladies in the companye.
Great pitee was it, as it thought them alle,
That evere such a chaunce shulde falle;
For gentil men they were and of gret estate,
And nothing but for love was this debate.
And saw their bloody woundes wyde and sore;
And alle they cryden, bothe less and more,
" Have mercy, Lord, upon us wommen alle! "
And on there bare knees anon they falle,
And wolde have kissed his feet right as he stood.
Til at the laste aslakèd was his mood;
For pitee runneth sone in gentil herte.
And though he first for ire quaked and sterte
He hath it al considered in a clause,
The trespas of them bothe, and eek the cause:
And although that his ire there gylt accused,
Yet he, in his resoún, them bothe excused;
And thus he thought that every maner man
Wil help himself in love if that he can,
And eek delyver himself out of prisoún.
And in his hert he had compassioún
Of wommen, for they wepen ever as one;
And in his gentil hert he thought anon,
And sothly he to himself he seyde: " Fy
Upon a lord that wil have no mercy,
But be a lyoun both in word and dede,
To them that be in répentaúnce and drede,
As wel as to a proud dispiteous man,
That wol maynteyne what he first bigan.
That lord hath litel of discrecioún,
That in such case knows no divisioún;
But wayeth pride and humblenesse as one."
And shortly, whan his ire is over-gon,
He gan to loke on them with lighter eye,
And spak these same wordes in charity.
" The god of love, a! benedicite,
How mighty and how gret a lord is he!
Agaynst his might there standeth no obstácles,

He may be cleped a god for his mirácles;
For he can maken at his owen gyse
Of every herte, al that he wil devyse.
Lo here is Arcite and here Palamoun,
That freely weren out of my prisoún,
And might have lyved in Thebes royally,
And know I am their mortal enemy.
And that there deth lieth in my might also
And yet hath love, for al their eyen tuo,
I-brought them hider bothe for to dye.
Now looke ye, is nat that an high folye?
Who may not be a foole, if that he love?
Byholde for Goddes sake that sitteth above,
See how they blede. Be they nought wel arrayed?
Thus hath their lord, the god of love, them payed
Their wages and their fees for their servise.
And yet they wenen for to be ful wise,
That serven love, for ought that may bifalle.
But this is yet the beste game of alle,
That she, for whom they have this jelousye,
Can them therfore as moche thank as me.
She wot no more of al this hote fare,
By God, than wot a cuckow or an hare.
But al must be assayèd hot or colde;
A man must be a fool or yong or olde;
I wot it by myself ful yore agon:
For in my tyme a lover was I one.
And since that I knewe well of loves peyne,
And wot how sore it can a man destreyne,
As he that hath ben oft caught in his trap,
I you forgeve wholly this myshappe,
At réquest of the queen that kneleth here,
And eek of Emely, my sister deere.
And ye shal bothe anon unto me swere,
That never ye shal harm my contree deere,
Nor make werre on me by night or day,
But be my freendes in alle that ye may.
I will forgeve this trespas every whit."
And they him swore his axyng faire and fit,
And him for lordship and for mercy prayde,
And he them graunted mercy, and thus he sayde:
" To speke of royal lynage and richés
Though that she were a queen or a pryncess,

Ech of yow both is worthy doutéless
To weddé when tyme is, but nontheles
I speke as for my sister Emelye,
For whom ye have this stryf and jelousye,
Ye wot youreself she may not weddé two
At once, although ye faughten ever mo:
That one of yow, whether he be loth or lief,
He may go play uppon an ivy leef;
This is to say, she may nought havé bothe,
Al be ye never so jelous, or so lothe.
Therefore I put you bothe in this degree,
That ech of you shal have his destynee,
As him is shape, and herken in what wyse;
Lo here the ende of that I shal devyse.
My wil is this, for playn conclusioun,
Withouten eny repplicacioun,
If that you liketh, tak it for the best,
That ech of you shall go wherever he list
Frely withouten raunsom or dangér;
And this day fyfty weekés, fer or near,
Ech of you then shal bryng an hundred knightés,
Armèd for lystés here in all our sightés
Al redy to contest her by batayle.
And thus commaunde I you withouten fayle
Upon my trothe, and as I am a knight,
That which of yow two bothé that hath might,
This is to sey, that whethir he or thou
May with his hundred, as I spak of now,
Slay his contráry, or out of lystés dryve,
Him shal I geve faire Emelye to wyve
To whom that fortune geveth so fair a grace.
The lystés shal I make here in this place,
And God so wisly on my sowle have ruth,
As I shal even judgé be in truth.
Ye shul no othir endé with me make,
That one of yow shal either be ded or take.
And if you thinketh this is wel i-sayde,
Say youré say, and hold yow wel apaydé.
This is youre ende and youre conclusioun."
Who loketh lightly now but Palamoun?
Who spryngeth up for joyé but Arcite?
Who couldé telle, or who coude wel endite,
The joyé that is made in al this place

Whan Theseus hath don so fair a grace?
But down on knees wente every maner wight,
And thanked him with al their hertes miht,
And namely these two Thebans of his grace.
And thus with good hope and with mery face
They take their leve, and hom-ward bothe they ryde
To Thebes-ward, with olde walles wyde.

I trowe men wold deme it necligence,
If I forgete to telle the dispence
Of Theseus, that goth so busily
To maken up the lystes royally.
And such a noble theatre to see,
I dar say in this world shal never be.
The circuite of it was a myle aboute,
Wallèd of stoon, and dychèd al withoute.
Round was the shape, in maner of compáss,
Ful of degrees, the height of sixty pace,
That when a man was set in one degree
He stayèd nought his felaw for to see.

Est-ward ther stood a gate of marbul whit,
West-ward another such in opposit.
And shortly to conclude, such a place
Was non in erthe within so litel space.
In al the lond ther was no craftesman
That géométry or arithmétic can,
Nor portreyour, nor kerver of ymáges,
That Theseus gave not his mete and wages
The theatre for to maken and devyse.
And for to do his rite and sacrifise,
His est-ward hath upon the gate above,
In worship of Venús, goddéss of love,
Don make an altar and an oratory;
And westward in the mynde and memory
Of Mars, he hath i-makèd a temple hy
That coste of gold and silver largely.
And northward, in a toret on the walle,
Of alabaster whit and red corálle
An oratory riche for to see,
To clene Dyane, goddess of chastitee,
Hath Theseus i-wrought in noble wise.
But yit had I forgeten to devyse
The nobil kervyng, and the portretures,
The shape, and countenaunce of the figúres,

That weren in these oratories three.
   First in the temple of Venus thou may see
Wrought in the wal, ful piteous to byholde,
The broken slepes, and the sighes colde;
The sacred teeres, and the lámentyng;
The fyry strokes and the désiryng,
That loves servaunts in this lyf enduren;
The othes that their covenants assuren.
Plesánce and hope, desyr, fool-hardynesse,
Beautee and youthe, lecherie and richesse,
Charmes and sorcery, lesynges and flatery,
Dispense, busynes, and jelousy,
That wered of yelow goldes a gerland,
And a cukkowe sittyng on her hand;
Festes, and instruments, carols, and daunces,
Lust and array, and al the circumstaunces
Of love, which I rekned and reken shal,
Ech by the other were peynted on the wal.
And mo than I can make of mencioun.
For sothly al the mount of Citheroun,
Where Venus hath her principal dwellyng,
Was shewèd on the wal in portrayyng
With alle the gardyn, and al the lustynes.
Nought was forgot; the porter Idelnesse,
And Narcisus the fayr of long agon,
And al the foly of kyng Salomon,
And al the grete strengthe of Hercules,
Thenchauntements of Medea and Cerces,
And of Turnús the hard fyry coráge,
The riche Cresus caytif in serváge.
Thus may we see, that wisdom and riches,
Beautee and sleighte, strengthe and hardynes,
May not with Venus holde comparisoún,
For as she liste she turneth up or doun.
Lo, al this folk i-caught were in her trace,
Til they for wo ful often sayde allas.
Sufficeth this ensample one or tuo,
Although I rekon coud a thousend mo.
The statu of Venus, glorious for to see,
Was naked flotyng in the large see,
And from the navel doun al covered was
With waves grene, and bright as eny glas.
In her right hand a harpe hadde she,

And on her hed, ful semely for to see,
A rose garland swete and wel smellyng,
Above her heed her doves were flickering.
Bifore hir stood hir sone Cupido,
Upon his shuldres were wynges two;
And blynd he was, as it is often seene;
A bowe he bare and arrows fair and keene.
Why shuld I not as wel telle you alle
The portraiture, that was upon the walle
Within the temple of Mars of mighty strength?
Al peynted was the wal in bredth and length
Like to the halles of the grisly place,
Y-callèd the gret temple of Mars in Thrace,
Within that colde and frosty regioún,
Where Mars hath built his sovereyn mansioún.
First on the wal was peynted a foréste,
In which ther dwellède neyther man nor beste,
With knotty knarry bareyn treës olde
With stubbes sharpe and hideous to beholde;
In which ther ran a rumble and a moan,
As though a storme shulde tear the branches down:
And downward wher the hil to the plaine is bent,
Ther stood the temple of Mars armypotent,
Wrought al of burnèd steel, of which the entry
Was long and streyt, and ghastly for to see.
And therout came a blast in suche wise,
That it made al the gates for to rise.
The northern light in at the dore shone,
For wyndow on the walle was ther none,
Through which men might the light of day discerne.
The dores wer alle adamant eterne,
Y-clenchèd overthwart and endelong
With iron tough; and, for to make it strong,
Every pillar the temple to sustaine
Was round and greet, of iron bright and sheene.
Ther saw I first the dark imagining
Of felony, and al the compassyng;
The cruel wrath, as eny furnace red;
The pickepurs, and eke the pale Dread;
The smyler with the knyf under his cloke:
The stables burnyng with the blake smoke;
The tresoun of the murtheryng in the bed;
The open warres, with woundes al y-bled;

Conflict with bloody knyf, and sharp menáce.
Al ful of shriekyng was that sory place.
The slayer of himself yet saw I ther,
His herte blood hath bathèd al his hair;
The nayl y-dryven in the skull at nyght;
The colde deth, with mouth gapyng upright.
In midst of al the temple sat Meschaunce,
With sory comfort and evil countynaúnce.
Ther I saw Madness laughyng in his rage;
Armèd complaint, alarm and fierce outráge.
The body in the bushe, with throte y-bled:
A thousand slayne, and none of sickness dead;
The tiraunt, with the prey bi force y-refte;
The toune distroyèd, there was no thing lefte.
Ther burnt the shippes daunsyng up and doun;
Ther dyed the hunter by the wilde lión:
The sowe eatyng the child right in the cradel;
The cook y-skalded, for al his longe ladel.
Nought was forgot the ill-fortúne of Mart;
The carter over-ridden by his cart,
Under the wheel ful lowe he lay adoun.
Ther wer also in Mars his regioún,
The barbour, and the butcher, and the smyth
That forgeth sharpe swordes on his stith.
And al above y-peynted in a tour
Saw I Conquest sittyng in grete honoúr,
The scharpe swerde hangyng over his hed
Y-fastened by a slender twines thread.
Y-peynted was the slaughter of Julius,
Of grete Nero, and of Antonius;
Al be that at that tyme they were unborn,
Yet was their deth y-peynted ther beforn,
By menacyng of Mars, each ones figúre,
So was it shewèd in the pourtretúre
As is y-peynted in the sterres above,
Who shal be slayn or who shal dye for love.
Sufficeth one example in stories olde,
I may not reken them alle, though I wolde.

    The statue of Mars upon a carte stood,
Armèd, and lokèd grym and red as blood;
And over his hed ther shyneth two figúres
Of sterres, that be clepèd in scriptúres,
The one Puella, that other Rubius.

This god of armes was arrayèd thus.
A wolf ther stood byforn him at his feet
With eyen red, and of a man he ate;
With subtil pencel peynted was this storie,
In honouring of Mars and of his glorie.

   Now to the temple of Dyane the chaste
As shortly as I can I wil me haste,
To telle you al the descripcioún.
Depeynted be the walles up and doun,
Of huntyng and of shamefast chastitee.
Ther saw I how woful Calystopé,
When that Dyane was agreved with her,
Was turnèd from a womman to a bere,
And after was she made the lode-sterre;
Thus was it peynted, I can say no more;
Her son is eek a star, as men may see.
Ther saw I Dyane turned intil a tree,
I mene nought the hy goddés Dyane,
But Peneus doughter, the whiche highte Dane.
Ther saw I Atheon an hert i-makèd,
For vengeance that he saw Dyane al naked;
I saw how that his houndes have him caught
And eten him, for that they knew him naught.
Yit peynted was a litel forthermore.
How Atthalaunce huntyd the wilde bore,
And Melyagre, and many another mo,
For which Dyane wrought them care and wo.
Ther saw I eek ful many another story,
The which me list not drawe in memory.
This goddess on an hert ful hy she sat,
With smale houndes al aboute her feet,
And undernethe her feet she had the moone,
Wexyng it was, and shulde wane soone,
In gaude greene her statue clothèd was,
With bowe in hande, and arrows in a case.
Her eyen caste she ful lowe adoun,
Where Pluto hath his derke regioún.
A womman travailyng was her biforn,
But for her child so longe was unborn
Ful piteously Lucyna gan she calle,
And seyde, " Help, for thou mayst best of alle."
Wel coude he peynten lyf-like that it wrought,
With many a floren he the hewes bought.

Now be these listes made, and Theseus
That at his grete cost arrayèd thus
The temples and the theatres to see,
When it was don, it liked him wonderly.
But stynt I wil of Theseus a lite,
And speke of Palamon and of Arcite.
   The day approcheth of their tourneying,
That eche shuld an hundred knightes brynge,
The batail to maintain, as I you tolde,
And to Athenes, their covenant to holde,
Hath eche of them brought out an hundred knightes
Wel armèd for the werre at alle rights.
And certeynly ther trowèd many a man
That never, since the day this world bigan,
To speke of knighthod or of high degree,
As fer as God hath makèd land or sea,
Came, from so fewe, so good a company.
For every wight that loveth chyvalry,
And wolde seek to have a noble name
Hath preyèd that he might be of that game;
Wel was to him, that therto chosen was.
For if ther felle to morrow such a case,
I knowe wel, that every lusty knight
That loveth his lady, and that hath his might,
Were it in Engelond, or elleswhere,
They wolde longen douteless to be there.
To fighte for a lady; *bencité!*
It were a lusty sighte for to see.
And right so journeyed they with Palamon.
With him ther wente knyghtes many a oon;
Some will be armèd in an armour stout,
In a brest-plat and in a lighte cote;
And som wold have a peyre of plates large;
And som wold have a Pruce shield, or targe;
Som wil be armèd on their legges weel,
And have an ax, and eek a mace of steel.
Ther is no newe gyse, that is not old.
Armèd were they, as I have now you told,
Eche at his pleasure and opinioun.
   There mayst thou see comyng with Palamoun
Ligurge himself, the grete kyng of Thrace;
Blak was his berd, and manly was his face.
The circles of his eyen in his hed

They glowéden bytwixe yellow and red,
And lik a griffoun lokèd he aboute,
With shaggy heres on his browes stoute;
His lymes greet, his brawnes hard and stronge,
His shuldres brood, his armes rounde and longe.
And as the gyse was in his contree,
Ful heye upon a car of gold stood he,
With foure white bulls in the traces.
In stede of cote armoúr on his harness,
He had a bere skyn, cole-blak and old,
With nailes yelwe, and bright as eny gold.
His longe heer y-kempt byhynd his bak,
As eny raven fether it shone for blak.
A wrethe of gold arm-great, and huge of weight,
Upon his hed, set ful of stones bright,
Of fyne rubies and of dyamaunts.
Aboute his car ther wenten white hounds,
Twenty and mo, as grete as eny steer,
To hunten at the lyoun or the bere,
And followed him, with muzzle fast i-bounde,
Collared with golde, and ringes fylèd rounde.
An hundred lordes had he in his route
Armèd ful wel, with hertes stern and stoute.

    With Arcite, as in stories ye shal finde,
The gret Emetreus, the kyng of Ynde,
Uppon a steede bay, trappèd in steel,
Covered with cloth of gold dyápred wel,
Cam rydyng lyk the god of armes, Mars.
His cote armour was of a cloth of Tars,
Broided with perles whyte, round and grete.
His sadil was of burnt gold newe y-bete;
A mantelet upon his shuldre hangyng
Brim-ful of rubies red, as fire sparklyng.
His crispe hair all into ringes dight,
And that was yelwe, and gliteryng as the light.
His nose was high, his eyen bright and keen,
His lippes rounde, his colour was sangwyn,
A fewe frekles in his face y-sprinkled,
Betwixe yelwe and blak somewhat y-mingled,
And as a lyoun he his lokyng caste.
Of fyve and twenty yeer his age I caste.
His berd was wel bygonne for to sprynge;
His voys was as a trumpe thunderynge.

Upon his hed he werèd laurel grene
A garlond fresch and lusty for to sene.
Upon his hond he bar for his delyt
An egle tame, as eny lylie whyt.
An hundred lordes had he with him ther,
Al armèd save their hedes in their gear,
Ful richely in alle maner thinges.
For truste wel, that dukes, erles, kynges,
Were gadred in this noble companye,
For love, and for encrease of chivalrye.
Aboute the kyng ther ran on every part
Ful many a tame lyoun and lepard.
And in this wise these lordes alle and some
Be on the Sonday to the citee come
Aboute prime, and in the toun alight.
This Theseus, this duk, this worthy knight,
Whan he had brought them into this citee,
And innèd them, eche one at his degree
He festeth them, and doth so gret laboúr
To lodge them, and do them al honoúr,
That yit men thinketh that no mannes wyt
Of non estat coude aught amenden it.
The mynstralcye, the servyce at the feste,
The grete giftes to the most and leste,
The riche aray of Theseus palace,
And who sat first and last upon the dais,
What ladies fayrest be or best daunsyng,
Or which of them can harpen best or syng,
And who most felyngly speketh of love;
What haukes sitten on the perche above,
What houndes lyen in the floor adoun,
Of al this make I now no mencioun;
But of theffect; that thinketh me the beste;
Now comth the poynt, and herken if you leste.
   The Sonday night, ere day bigan to springe,
Whan Palamon the larke herde synge,
Although it were nought day by houres tuo,
Yit sang the larke, and Palamon also
With holy herte, and with an high coráge
He rose, to wenden on his pilgrymage
Unto the blisful Cithera benigne,
I mene Venus, honorable and digne.
And in her hour he walketh forth a pace

Unto the lystes, where hir temple was,
And doun he kneleth, and, with humble cheer
And herte sore, he seide as ye shal heer.
  " Fairest of faire, o lady myn Venús,
Doughter of Jove, and spouse to Vulcanus,
Thou gladder of the mount of Citheroun,
For that great love thou haddest to Adon
Have pitee on my bitter teeres smerte,
And tak myn humble prayer to thin herte.
Allas! I have no langage for to telle
Theffectes or the torments of myn helle;
Myn herte may myn harmes not betray;
I am so confus, that I may not seye.
But mercy, lady bright, that knowest wel
My thought, and felest what harm that I feel,
Consider al this, have ruth upon my sore,
And wisely shal I now for evermore
With all my might thi trewe servant be,
And holde werre alway with chastitee;
That make I myn avow, so ye me helpe.
I care not of armes for to yelpe,
Nor do I aske to-morn to have victórie,
Or rénoun in this case, or veyne glorie
Of pris of armes, blowyng up and doun,
But I wolde have the ful possessioun
Of Emelye, and dye in thi servise;
Fynd thou the maner how, and in what wyse.
I recche nat, if it may better be,
To have victorie of him, or he of me,
So that I have my lady in myn armes.
For though so be that Mars be god of armes,
And ye be Venus, the goddéss of love,
Youre vertu is so gret in heven above,
Thy temple wil I worshipe evermo,
And on thin altar, whether I ryde or go,
I wil do sacrifice, and fyres light.
And if ye wil nat so, my lady bright,
Then pray I thee tomorrow with a darte
That fiers Arcite may pierce me to the herte.
Thenne rekke I not, when I have lost my lyf,
Though that Arcita have hir to his wyf.
This is theffect and ende of my prayére;
Gif me my love, thou blisful lady deere."

Whan the orisoun was don of Palamon,
His sacrifice he dede, and that anon
Ful piteously, with alle circumstances,
Though telle I nat as now his óbservánces.
But at the last the statu of Venus shook,
And made a signe, wherby that he took
That his prayér accepted was that day.
For though the signe shewèd a delay,
Yet wist he wel that graunted was his boone;
And with glad herte he went him hom ful soone.
    The third hour inequál that Palamon
Bigan to Venus temple for to goon,
Up rose the sonne, and up rose Emelye,
And to the temple of Dian gan she hye.
Hir maydens, that she with hir thider ladde,
Ful redily with them the fyr they hadde,
The incense, the clothes, and the remnant al
That to the sacrifice longen shal;
The hornes ful of mead, as is the gyse;
Ther lakketh nought to do their sacrifise.
Smokyng the temple, ful of clothes faire.
This Emelye with herte debonaire
Hir body wessh with watir of a welle;
But how she dide her rite I dare nat telle,
Save it be eny thing in general;
And yet it were a game to here it al;
To him that meneth wel it were no wrong:
But it is good a man sholde kepe his tong.
Hir brighte hair was kempt, untressèd al;
A corone of a grene oak cerial
Upon hir heed was set ful fair and bright.
Tuo fyres on the alter gan she light,
And did al thinges, as men may biholde
In Stace of Thebes and the bokes olde.
Whan kyndled was the fyr, with piteous cheere
Unto Dyan she spak, as ye may heere.
    " O chaste goddes of the woodes greene,
By whom bothe heven and erthe and see is seene,
Queen of the regne of Pluto derk and lowe,
Goddes of maydenes, that myn hert has knowe
Ful many a yeer, ye wot what I desire,
So keep me fro the vengeance and the ire,
That Atheon did suffer trewely:

O chaste goddesse, wel knowest thou that I
Desire to be a mayden al my lyf,
Nor never wil I be no love nor wyf.
I am yit, thou knowest, of thi company,
A mayden, and love huntyng and venery,
And for to walken in the woodes wylde,
And nought to be a wyf, and be with chylde.
Nought wil I knowe the company of man.
Now helpe me, lady, since ye may and kan,
For the three formes that thou hast in the.
And Palamon, that hath such love to me,
And eek Arcite, that loveth me so sore,
This grace I praye thee withouten more,
And sende love and pees betwix them two;
And fro me torne awey their hertes so,
That al their hote love, and their desire,
And al their torment, and their busy fyre
Be quensht, or turnèd in another place.
And if so be thou wolt do me no grace,
Or if my destynee be shapid so,
That I shal needes have one of them two,
So send me him that most desireth me.
Biholde, goddes of clene chastitee,
The bitter teeres that on my cheekes falle.
Since thou art mayde, and keper of us alle,
My maydenhode thou keep and wel conserve,
And whil I lyve a mayde I wil thee serve."
    The fyres burn upon the alter cleer,
Whil Emelye was thus in hir preyér;
But sodeinly she saw a sighte queynt,
For right anon one of the fyres did faint,
And glowed agayn, and after that anon
That other fyr was quensht, and al agon;
And as it quensht, it made a whistelyng,
As doth a wete brand in his burning.
And at the brandes end out ran anon
As it were bloody dropes many a one;
For which so sore agast was Emelye,
That she wel nigh mad was, and gan to crie,
For she ne wiste what it signifyed;
But all alone for feere thus she cryed,
And wepte, that it was pitee to heere.
And therewithal Dyane gan appeere,

With bow in hond, right as a hunteresse,
And seyd " A ! doughter, stynt thyn hevynesse.
Among the goddes hye it is affermed,
And by eterne word writ and confermed,
Thou shalt be wedded unto one of those,
That have for thee so many cares and woes;
But unto which of them may I nat telle.
Farwel, for I may here no lenger dwelle.
The fyres which that on myn alter burn
Shal thee declare, ere that thou homward turn,
Thyn áventure of love, and in this place."
And with that word, the arrows in the case
Of the goddesse clatren faste and rynge,
And forth she went, and made a vanysshynge,
For which this Emelye astoneyd was,
And seide, " What amounteth this, allas !
I put me under thy proteccioún,
Dyane, and in thi disposicioún."
And hom she goth anon the nexte way.
This is theffect, ther is no more to say.

The houre nexte of Mars that folowed this,
Arcite unto the temple walkyd is,
To fyry Mars to do his sacrifise,
With al the rightes of his pagan wise.
With piteous herte and hy devocioún,
Right thus to Mars he sayd his orisoún:
" O stronge god, that in the countree colde
Of Trace honoúred and lord art thou y-hold,
And hast in every realm and every land
Of armes al the bridel in thy hand,
And guidest al as thou dost wel devyse,
Accept of me my piteous sacrifise.
If so be that my youthe may deserve,
And that my might be worthi for to serve
Thy godhed, that I may be one of thine,
Then pray I thee have pity on my pyne,
For that same peyne, and that for hote fyr,
In which whilom thou burnedst for desyre,
Whan that thou didst obtaine the gret beautee
Of faire Venus, that is so fressh and free,
And haddest hir in armes at thy wille;
Though on a tyme mischeef thee bifel,
When Vulcan caught thee in his nette wide,

And fand thee liggyng by his wyfes side
For that same sorwe that was in thin herte,
Have pity too upon my peynes smerte.
I am yong and unkonnyng, as thou knowst,
And, as I trowe, with love offendid most,
That ever was eny lyve creätúre;
For she, that doth me al this wo endure,
Ne rekketh never whether I synke or live.
And wel I wot, ere she me mercy give,
I must with strengthe wyn hir in the place;
And wel I wot, withouten help or grace
Of thee, my strengthe may nought a whit avayle.
Then help me, lord, tomorrow in my batayle,
For that same fyr that whilom burnèd the,
Right so this fyre now it burneth me;
Make now tomorrow I have the victorie.
Myn be the travail, al thin be the glorie.
Thy soverein tempul wol I most honoúren
Of any place, and alway most laboúren
In thy pleasure and in the craftes stronge.
And in thy tempul I wil my baner hong,
And alle the armes of my companye,
And ever more, unto that day I dye,
Eterne fyr I wol bifore thee fynde.
And eek to this avow I wil me bynde:
My beard, myn heer that hangeth longe adoun
That never yit has felt offensioún
Of rasour or of shere, I wil thee give,
And be thy trewe servaunt whiles I lyve.
Lord, have thou pity uppon my sorrows sore,
Gif me the victorie, I aske no more."

The preyer ended of Arcite the strang,
The rynges on the tempul dore that hang,
And eek the dores, clatereden ful fast,
Of which Arcita somwhat was agast.
The fires brenden on the alter bright,
That it gan al the tempul for to light;
A swete smel anon the ground did give,
Anon his hond Arcita did upheave,
And more encens into the fyr yet cast,
With othir rites, and than atte last
The statu of Mars bigan his hauberk rynge,
And with that soun he herd a murmurynge

Ful lowe and dym, and sayde thus, " Victorie."
For which he gaf to Mars honoúr and glorie.
And thus with joye, and hope wel to win,
Arcite anon is gon unto his inne,
As fayn as bird is of the brighte sonne.
And right anon such stryf there is bygonne
For that same grauntyng, in the heven above,
Bitwixe Venus the goddés of love,
And Mars the sterne god armypotent,
That Jupiter was busy it to stent;
Til that the pale Saturnus the colde,
That knew so many áventures olde,
Found in his old experiens an art,
That he ful sone hath plesyd every part.
As soth is sayd, eld hath gret ávantage,
In eld is bothe wisdom and uságe;
Men may out-runne but not out-counselle age.
Saturne anon, to stynte stryf and rage,
Although to do thys be agaynst his mind,
Of al this stryf he can a remedy fynde.
" My deere doughter Venus," quoth Saturne,
" My cours, that hath so wyde for to turne,
Hath more power than wot eny man.
Myn is the drowning in the see so wan;
Myn is the prisoun in the derke ward;
Myn is the stranglyng and hangyng by the cord;
The murmur, and the cherles rébellyng;
The gronyng, and the privy enpoysonyng,
I make vengeance and ful correctioun,
Whiles dwellyng in the signe of the lyoun.
Myn is the ruin of the hye halles,
The fallyng of the toures and the walles
Upon the mynour or the carpenter.
I slew Samson in shakyng the piler:
And myne be the maladies colde,
The derke tresoun, and the plottes olde;
Myn eye is the fadir of pestilens.
Now wepe nomore, I shal do my diligence,
That Palamon, that is myn own servaunt,
Shal have his lady, as thou didst him graunt.
Though Mars shal kepe his knight, yet nevertheles
Bitwixe you ther must som tyme be pees;
Al be ye nought of one complexioún,

That every day causeth divisioún.
I am thi fadirs fadir, at thy wille;
Wepe thou nomore, I wil thi lust fulfille."
Now wil I stinten of the goddes above,
Of Mars, and of Venús goddéss of love,
And telle you, as pleinly as I can,
The grete effecte for which that I bigan.

Gret was the fest in Athenes on that day.
And eek the lusty sesoun of that May
Made every wight to be in such plesaunce
That al the Monday jousten they and daunce,
And spenden it in Venus high servise.
But by the cause that they shal arise
Erly amorrow for to see that fight,
Unto their reste wente they at nyght,
And on the morrow whan the day gan spryng,
Of hors and harness noyse and clateryng
Ther was in al the hostelryes aboute;
And to the paleys rode ther many a route
Of lordes, upon steedes and palfréys.
Ther mayst thou see devysing of harness
So uncouth and so riche wrought and wel
Of goldsmithry, of broidery, and steel;
The sheldes bright, the helmets, and trappings;
Gold-beten helmes, hauberks, and cote armings;
Lordes in clothes riche on their coursers,
Knightes of retenu, and eek squyers
Nailing the speres, and helmes buckelyng,
Girdyng of sheeldes, with the thongs lacyng;
Where the need was, there they were nothing ydel;
Ther fomen steedes, on the golden bridel
Gnawyng, and faste the armurers also
With fyle and hamer prikyng to and fro;
Yeomen on foot, and knaves many a one
With shorte staves, as thikke as they may goon;
Pypes, and trompes, drums, and clariounes,
That in the batail blewe bloody sownes;
The paleys ful of pepul up and doun,
Heer three, ther ten, holdyng their questioun,
Dyvynyng of these Thebans knightes two.
Som seyden thus, some seyd it shal be so;
Som held with him that hath the blake berd,
Som with the bald, some with the thikke haired:

Som sayd he lokèd grym and woldè fight;
He hath an ax of twenti pound of wight.
Thus was the hallè ful of dévynyng,
Long after that the sonnè gan to springe.
The gret Theseus that of his sleep is wakèd
With menstralcy and noysè that was makèd,
Kept yit the chambre of his paleys rare,
Til that the Thebanes knyghtes bothè were
Honoúrèd, and into the paleys go.
Duk Theseus was set at a wyndow,
Arayèd right as he were god on throne.
The pepul preseth thider-ward ful sone
Him for to see, and do him reverence,
And eek herken his hest and his sentence.
An herauld on a skaffold made a hoo,
Til al the noyse of the pepul was i-do;
And whan he saw the pepul of noyse al stille,
Thus shewèd he the mighty dukes wille.

" The lord hath of his hy discrecioun
Considered, that it were destruccioun
To gentil blood, to fighten in this wise
In mortal batail in this enterprise;
Wherfor to shapen that they shuld not dye,
He wil his firstè purpos modifye.
No man therfore, on peyne of los of lyf,
No maner shot, nor pollax, nor schort knyf
Into the lystes sende, or thider brynge;
Nor schortè swerd to stick with poynt bytyng
No man shal drawe, or berè by his side.
And noman shal agayns his felawe ryde
But one cours, with a sharpe y-grounden spere;
If eny fall he shal on foote fight there.
And he that is the loser, shal be take,
And not slayn, but be brought unto the stake,
That shal be fixèd hy on eyther syde;
But thider he shal by force, and ther abyde.
And if so falle, a chieftayn shuldè go
Unto the stake, or elles slay his fo,
No lenger shal the fight betwixe them laste.
God spedè you; go forth and ley on faste.
With long swerd and with macè fight your fille.
Go now your way; this is the lordes wille."
The voices of the pepul touch the sky,

So lowde crièd thei with jollitee:
" God save such a lord that is so good,
He willeth no destruccioun of blood! "
Up go the trompes and the melodye.
And to the lystes ryde the companye
By ordynaunce, throughout the citee large,
Hangyng with cloth of gold, and not with serge.
Ful lik a lord this nobul duk can ryde,
And these two Theban knightes on eyther side;
And after rode the queen, and Emelye,
And after, of ladyes another companye,
And after, comunes al in there degree.
And thus they passéden thurgh that citee,
   And to the lystes come thei by tyme.
It was not of the day yet fully pryme,
When sette was duk Theseus riche and hye,
Hippolyta the queen and Emelye,
And other ladyes in there degrees aboute.
Unto the seates presseth al the route;
And westeward, thorugh the gates of Mart,
Arcite, and eek the hundred of his part,
With baners red ys entred right anon;
And at that same moment Palamon
Is, under Venus, est-ward in that place,
With baner whyt, and hardy cheer and face.
   In al the world, to seeken up and doun,
So even withoute doute or question
Ther never were suche companyes tweye.
For ther was non so wys that coude seye,
That any had of the other ávantage
In worthines, or state or in viságe,
So evene were they chosen for to gesse.
And in two rankes faire they them dresse.
And when there names i-rad were everyone,
That in there nombre guile was ther non,
Then were the gates shut, and crièd lowde:
" Do now your devoir, yonge knightes proude! "
The heralds laft there prikyng up and doun;
Now ryngede out the tromp and clarioun;
Ther is nomore to say, but est and west
In go the speres ful surely in the rest;
In goth the sharpe spur into the side.
Ther see men who can juste, and who can ryde;

Ther shiver shaftes upon shuldres thyk;
He feeleth thurgh the navel the sharpe prik.
Up sprengen speres twenty foot on hight;
Out go the swerdes as the silver bright.
The helmes they to-hewen and to-shred;
Out brast the blood, with runnyng stremes red,
With mighty maces the bones thay to-burst.
He thurgh the thikkest of the throng gan thrust,
Ther stomble steedes strong, and doun gan falle,
He rolleth under foot as doth a balle.
He fighteth on his foot with a tronchoun,
And hurleth the other with his hors adoun.
He thurgh the body hurt is, and is take
Will he or no, and brought unto the stake,
As covenant was, right where he must abyde.
Another lad is on that other syde.
And Theseus doth make them al to reste,
Them to refressche, and drinke it so them list.
Ful oft a-day these knights, these Thebans two
Togider met, and wrought his felaw wo;
Unhorsèd hath ech other of them tweye.
Ther was no tygyr in the vale of Galgopheye,
Whan that her whelp is stole, whan it is lite,
So cruel on the hunt, as is Arcite
For jelous hert upon this Palamon:
Nor in Belmary ther is no fell lion,
That hunted is, or is for hunger wood,
Nor of his prey desireth so the blood,
As Palamon to slay his fo Arcite.
The jelous strokes on their helmes byte;
Out renneth blood on bothe their sides red.
Som tyme an ende ther is of every deed;
For ere the sonne unto his reste went,
The strange king Emetreus gan hent
This Palamon, as he faught with Arcite,
And deep into his flessh his swerd did byte;
And by the force of twenti he is take
Unyielded, and y-drawn unto the stake.
And in the rescue of this Palamoun
The stronge kyng Ligurg is born adoun;
And kyng Emetreus for al his strengthe
Is borne out of his sadel his swerdes lengthe,
So hit him Palamon ere he were take;

But al for nought, he brought was to the stake.
His hardy herte might him helpe nought;
He most abyde when that he was caught,
By force, and eek by composicioun.
Who sorroweth now but woeful Palamoun,
That may nomore go agayn to fight?
And when that Theseus had seen that sight,
He cryèd, " Ho! nomore, for it is don!
And non shal longer unto his felaw goon.
I wol be trewe judge, and no partýe.
Arcyte of Thebes shal have Emelýe,
That hath her by his fortune now i-wonne."
Anon ther is a noyse of people begun
For joye of this, so loude and heye withalle,
It semèd that the very listes wolde falle.
What can now fayre Venus do above?
What seith she now? what doth this queen of love?
But wepeth so, for wantyng of her wille,
Til that her teeres in the lystes fill;
She seyde: " I am ashamèd douteless."
Saturnus seyd: " O daughter, hold thy peace.
Mars hath his wille, his knight hath all his boon,
And by myn heed thou shalt be esèd soone."
The trompes with the lowde mynstralcy,
The heraldes, that ful lowde yelle and cry,
Been merry in there joye for Dan Arcyte.
But herk to me, and stay but yet a lite,
For there bifel a miracle anon.
This Arcyte fiercely hath put his helm adoun,
And on his courser for to shewe his face,
He prikèd up and down the large place,
Lokyng upward upon his Emelye;
And she agayn him cast a frendly eye,
(For wommen, for to speke as in comune,
Thay follow alle the favour of fortúne)
And was alle his in cheer, and in his herte.
Out of the ground a fyr infernal stert,
From Pluto sent, at réquest of Satúrne,
For which his hors for feere gan to turne,
And leep asyde, and foundred as he leep;
And ere that Arcyte may of this take keep,
He pight him on the pomel of his hed,
That in that place he lay as he were ded,

His brest to-broken, with his sadil bowe.
As blak he lay as eny coal or crowe,
So was the blood y-ronnen in his face.
Anon he was y-born out of the place
With herte sore, to Theseus paleys.
Then was he carven out of his harnéys,
And in a bed ful fair and soft y-brought,
For yit he was in memory and thought,
And alway crying after Emelye.
Duk Theseus, and al his companye,
Is comen hom to Athenes his citee,
With alle bliss and gret solemnitee.
Al be it that this áventure was falle,
He wolde nought discómforten them alle.
Men seyd eek, that Arcita schuld nought dye,
He shal be helèd of his maladye.
And of another thing they were as fayn,
That of them alle ther was non y-slayn,
Al were they sore hurt, and namely one,
That with a spere was piercèd his brest bone.
To other woundes, and to-broken armes,
Some hadden salves, and some hadden charmes,
Drugges of herbes and sage the doctours gave
To drinken, for they wolde their lyves save.
And eek this noble duk, as he wel can,
Comfórteth and honoúreth every man,
And made revel al the longe night,
Unto the straunge lordes, as it was right.
Nor ther was holden no discomfytyng,
But as at justes or at a tourneyinge;
For sothly ther was no discomfiture,
For fallynge doun is but an áventure.
And to be led with fors unto the stake
Unyielden, and with twenty knightes take,
A person allone, withouten helpers moo,
And draggèd forth by arme, foot, and toe,
And eke his steede dryven forth with staves,
With footemen, bothe yeomen and eke knaves,
It was not counted him no vilonye,
Nor any man held it for cowardye.
  For which duk Theseus loud anon let crie,
To stynten al rancoúr and al envýe,
The prize was wel on one syde as on other,

And every side lik, as others brother;
And gaf them giftes after there degree,
And fully held a feste dayes three;
And convoyèd the knightes worthily
Out of his toun a journee largely.
And hom went every man the righte way.
Ther was no more, but " Farwel, have good day! "
Of this batayl I wol no more endite,
But speke of Palamon and of Arcyte.

Swelleth the brest of Arcyte, and the sore
Encreaseth at his herte more and more.
The clothred blood, for all the leche-craft,
Corrumpith, and is in his body left,
That neither veyne blood, ne any cutting,
Ne drynk of herbes may be his helpyng.
The vertu expulsif, or animal,
From thilke vertu clepèd natural,
May not the venym voyde, nor expelle.
The pypes of his lunges gan to swelle,
And every muscle in his brest adoun
Is filled with venym and corrupcioun.
There holp him neither, for to get his lyf,
Vomyt up-ward, ne doun-ward laxatif;
Al is to-broken thilke regioún;
Nature hath now no dominacioún.
And certeynly where nature wil not wirche,
Farwel phisik; go bere the man to chirche.
This is the end, that Arcyte moste dye.
For which he sendeth after Emelye,
And Palamon, that was his cosyn deere.
Than seyd he thus, as ye shal after heere.

" Naught may the woful spirit in myn herte
Declare a poynt of all my sorrows smerte
To you, my lady, that I love most;
But I byquethe the service of my ghost
To you aboven every creätúre,
Since that my lyf may now no longer dure.
Allas, the wo! allas, the peynes stronge,
That I for you have suffred, and so longe!
Allas, the deth! alas, myn Emelye!
Allas, departyng of our companye!
Allas, myn hertes queen! allas, my wyf!
Myn hertes lady, ender of my lyf!
What is this world? what asken men to have?

Now with his love, now in his colde grave
Allone withouten eny companye.
Farwel, my swete! farwel, myn Emelye!
And softe take me in your armes tweye,
For love of God, and herk to what I seye.
I have heer with my cosyn Palamon
Had stryf and rancour many a day i-gon,
For love of you, and eek for jelousie.
And Jupiter have on my soul pitye,
To speken of a lover proprely,
With alle circumstances trewely,
That is to seyn, truthe, honour, and knighthede,
Wysdom, humblesse, estate, and high kindrede,
Fredom, and al that longeth to that art,
So Jupiter have of my soule part,
As in this world right now I knowe non
So worthy to be loved as Palamon,
That serveth you, and wil do al his lyf.
And if that ye shal ever be a wyf,
Forget not Palamon, that gentil man."
And with that word his speche faile gan;
For from his herte up to his brest was come
The cold of deth, that him had overcome.
And yet moreover in his armes two
The vital strength is lost, and al i-go.
At last the intellect, withouten more,
That dwellèd in his herte sik and sore,
Gan fayle, when the herte felte death,
Duskèd his eyen two, and fayled his breth.
But on his lady yit he cast his eye;
His laste word was, " Mercy, Emelye! "
His spiryt chaungèd was, and wente there,
As I cam never, I can not tellen where.
Therefore I stynte, I am no dyvynistre;
Of soules fynde I not in this regístre,
Nor list I those opynyouns to telle
Of them, though that they knowen where they dwelle.
Arcyte is cold, let Mars his soule take;
Now will I of the storie further speke.

  Shrieked Emely, and howlèd Palamon,
And Theseus his sistir took anon
Swoonyng, and bare hir fro the corps away.
What helpeth it to tarye forth the day,

To tellen how she weep bothe eve and morrow?
For in such case wommen can have such sorrow,
When that there housbonds be from them ago,
That for the more part they sorrow so,
Or elles fallen in such maladye,
That atte laste certeynly they dye.
Infýnyt been the sorrows and the teeres
Of olde folk, and folk of tendre yeeres;
So gret a wepyng was ther none certayn,
Whan Ector was i-brought, al fressh i-slayn,
As that ther was for deth of this Theban;
For sorrow of him weepeth child and man
At Thebes, allas! the pitee that was there,
Scratching of cheekes, rending eek of hair.
" Why woldist thou be ded," the wommen crye,
" And haddest gold enow—and Emelye? "
No man mighte gladd the herte of Theseus,
Savyng his olde father Egeus,
That knew this worldes transmutacioún,
As he hadde seen it tornen up and doun,
Joye after woe, and woe aftir gladnesse:
And shewèd him ensample and likenesse.

" Right as ther deyde never man," quoth he,
" That livèd not in erthe in som degree,
So yet there lyvede never man," he seyde,
" In all this world, that som tyme was not deyde.
This world is but a thurghfare ful of woe,
And we be pilgryms, passyng to and fro;
Deth is an ende of every worldly sore."
And over al this yet seide he moche more
To this effect, ful wysly to exhorte
The peple, that they shulde him récomfórte.

Duk Theseus, with al his busy care,
Cast now about where that the sepulture
Of good Arcyte may best y-makèd be.
And eek most honourable in his degré.
And atte last he took conclusioún,
That where at first Arcite and Palamon
Hadden for love the batail them bytwene,
That in the same grove, swete and greene,
There when he hadde his amorous desires,
His cómpleynt, and for love his hote fyres,
He wolde make a fyr, in which the office

Of funeral he might al áccomplice;
And gave comaunde anon to hakke and hewe
The okes old, and lay them on a rowe,
In hepes wel arrayèd for to burn.
His officers with swifte foot they runne,
And ryde anon at his comaundement.
And after this, Theseus hath men i-sent
After a bier, and it al overspredde
With cloth of golde, the richest that he hadde.
And in the same suit he clad Arcyte;
Upon his hondes were his gloves white;
Eke on his heed a croune of laurel grene;
And in his hond a swerd ful bright and kene.
He leyde him with bare visage on the biere,
Therwith he weep that pity was to heere.
And for the peple shulde see him alle,
Whan it was day he brought them to the halle,
That roreth with the cry and with the sound.
Then cam this woful Theban Palamoun,
With flotery berd, and ruggy asshy heeres,
In clothis blak, y-droppèd al with teeres,
And, passyng all in wepyng, Emelye,
The rewfullest of al the companye.
And in as moche as the service shuld be
The more noble and riche in his degree,
Duk Theseus let forth three steedes bryng.
That trappèd were in steel al gliteryng,
And covered with the armes of Dan Arcyte.
Upon the steedes, that weren grete and white,
Ther seten folk, of which one bar his sheeld,
Another his spere up in his hondes held;
The thridde bar with him his bowe Turkeys,
Of brend gold was the case and eek the harness;
And riden forth a pace with sorrowful chere
Toward the grove, as ye shal after heere.
The nobles of the Grekes that ther were
Upon there shuldres carieden the beere,
With slake pace, and eyen red and wete,
Thurghout the citee, by the maister streete,
That spred was al with blak, and up on hy
With blak the houses are covered utterly.
Upon the right hond went olde Egeus,
And on that other syde duk Theseus,

With vessels in there hand of gold wel fyn,
As ful of hony, mylk, and blood, and wyn;
Eke Palamon, with a gret companye;
And after that com woful Emelye,
With fyr in hond, as was that time the gyse,
To do the office of funeral servise.

   High labour, and ful gret apparailyng
Was at the service and at the fyr makyng,
That with his grene top reachèd the sky,
And twenty fathom broad the okes lie;
This is to seyn, the bowes were so brode.
Of straw first was ther leyd ful many a lode.
But how the fyr was makyd up on highte,
And eek the names how the trees highte,
As ook, fir, birch, asp, aldir, holm, popler,
Wilw, elm, plane, assh, box, chestnut, laurer,
Mapul, thorn, beech, hasil, ew, wyppyltree,
How they were felde, shal nought be told for me;
Ne how the goddes ronnen up and doun,
Disheryted of habitacioun,
In which they long had dwelt in rest and pees,
Nymphes and Faunes, and Hamadryades;
Nor how the beestes and the briddes alle
Fledden for feere, when the woode was falle;
Nor how the ground agast was of the light,
That was not wont to see no sonne bright;
Nor how the fyr was laid with straw below,
And thenne with drye stykkes cloven in two,
And thenne with grene woode and spicerie,
And thenne with cloth of gold and jewelry,
And gerlandes hangyng with ful many a flour,
The myrre, the incense with al so sweet odour;
Nor how Arcyte lay among al this,
Nor what richesse aboute his body is;
Nor that how Emely, as was the gyse,
Putt in the fyr of funeral servise;
Nor how she swownèd when she made the fyre,
Nor what she spak, nor what was hir desire;
Nor what jewels men in the fire cast,
When that the fyr was gret and brente fast;
Nor how sum caste their sheeld, and summe their spere,
And of their vestiments, which that they were,
And cuppes ful of wyn, and mylk, they had,

Unto the fyr, that brent as it were mad;
Nor how the Grekes with an huge route
Thre tymes ryden al the fyr aboute
Upon the lefte hond, with an high shoutyng,
And thries with there speres clateryng;
And thries how the ladyes gan to crye;
Nor how that home-ward led was Emelye;
Nor how Arcyte is brent to ashen colde;
Nor howe that liche-wake was y-holde
Al that same night, nor how the Grekes pleye
The wake-playes, care I nat to seye;
Who wrastleth best naked, with oyle enoynt,
Nor who that bar him best at every point.
I wil not telle eek how that they be gon
Hom to Athénes when the pley is don.
But shortly to the poynt now wil I wende,
And maken of my longe tale an ende.

By proces and by lengthe of certeyn yeres
Al styntyd is the mournyng and the teeres
Of alle Grekes, by general assent.
Then semèd me ther was a parlement
At Athenes, on a certeyn poynt and case;
Among the whiche poyntes spoken was
To have with certeyn contrees álliaunce,
And have fully of Thebans óbeissance.
For which this noble Theseus anon
Let senden after gentil Palamon,
Unwist of him what was the cause and why;
But in his blake clothes sorrowfully
He cam at his comaundement in hye.
Then sente Theseus for Emelye.
When they were sette, and husht was al the place,
And Theseus abyden hadde a space
Ere eny word cam fro his breste wyse,
His eyen set he where he did devyse,
And with a sad viságe he sighèd stille,
And after that right thus he seide his wille.

"The firste movere of the cause above,
Whan he first made the fayre cheyne of love,
Gret was the effect, and high was his entente;
Wel wist he why, and what therof he mente;
For with that faire cheyne of love he bound
The fyr, the watir, the air, and eek the lond

In certeyn boundes, that they may not flee;
That same prynce and movere eek," quoth he,
" Hath stabled, in this wretched world adoun,
Som certeyn dayes and duracioún
To alle that are engendrid in this place,
Beyond the whiche day they may nat pace,
Though that they yit may wel there dayes abridge;
Ther needeth no auctorité to allege;
For it is provèd by experience,
But that I will declaren my sentence.
Than may men wel by this ordre discerne,
That the same movere stable is and eterne.
Wel may men knowe, but it be a fool,
That every part deryveth from his whole.
For nature hath not take his bygynnyng
Of no partye nor morsel of a thing,
But of a thing that parfyt is and stable,
Descendyng, til it be corumpable.
And therfore of his wyse providence
He hath so wel biset his ordenaunce,
That kinds of thinges and progressioúns
Shallen endure by their successioúns,
And not eterne be withoute lye:
This maistow understand and se with eye.
" Lo, see the ook, that hath long norisschyng
Fro tyme that it gynneth first to springe,
And hath so long a lyf, as we may see,
Yet atte laste wasted is the tree.
" Considereth eek, how that the harde stoon
Under oure foot, on which we trede and goon,
Yit wasteth, as it lieth by the weye.
The brode ryver som tyme wexeth dreye.
The grete townes see we wane and wende.
Then may I see that al thing hath an ende.
" Of man and womman see we wel also,
They liven all in oon of termes two,
That is to seyn, in youthe or elles in age,
All must be deed, the kyng as shal a page;
Som in his bed, som in the deepe see,
Som in the large feeld, as men may see.
Ther helpeth naught, al goth the same weye,
Thenne may I see wel that al thing shal deye.
What maketh this but Jupiter the kyng?

The which is prynce and cause of alle thing,
Convertyng al unto his propre wille,
From which he is deryvèd, soth to telle.
And against this no creätúre alive
Of no degree avayleth for to stryve.
　" Then is it wisdom, as it thenketh me,
To maken vertu of necessitee,
And take it wel, what we can nat eschewe,
And namely what to alle of us is due.
And who-so murmureth aught, he doth folye,
And rebel is to him that is on high.
And certeynly a man hath most honoúr
To deyen in his excellence and flour,
Whan he is certeyn of his goode name.
Then hath he don his freend, nor himself no shame,
And glader ought his freend be of his deth,
When with honoúr is yielden up the breth,
Thanne whan his name all feeble is for age,
And al forgeten is his great coráge.
Thenne is it best, as for a worthi fame,
To dye whan a man is best in name.
The contrary of al this is wilfulnesse.
Why murmur we? why have we hevynesse,
That good Arcyte, of chyvalry the flour,
Departed is, with worship and honoúr
Out of this foule prisoun of this lyf?
Why murmureth heer his cosyn and his wyf
At his welfare, that loven him so wel?
Can he them thank? nay, God wot, not at all,
They bothe his soule and eek themselves offende,
And yet they may their sorrow nat amende.
　" How shal I then conclude verrily,
But after woe to counsel jolitee,
And thanke Jupiter for al his grace?
And ere that we departe fro this place,
I counsel that we make, of sorrows two,
One parfyt joye lastyng ever mo:
And loke now wher most sorrow is her-inne,
Ther wil we first amenden and bygynne.
　" Sistyr," quoth he, " this is my ful assent,
With al the advice heer of my parlement,
That gentil Palamon, your owne knight,
That serveth you with herte, wil, and might,

And ever hath don, since fyrst tyme ye him knewe,
That ye shal of your grace pity show.
And take him for your housbond and your lord:
Lend me youre hand, for this is oure acord,
Let see now of your wommanly pity.
He is a kynges brothirs son, pardee;
And though he were a pore bachiller,
Since he hath servèd you so many a yeer,
And had for you so gret adversitee,
Hit moste be considered, trust to me.
For gentil mercy greter is than right."
Than seyde he thus to Palamon ful right;
" I trowe ther needeth litel sermonyng
To maken you assente to this thing.
Com neer, and tak your lady by the hond."
Betwix them was i-made anon the bond,
That highte matrimoyn or mariáge,
By alle the counseil of the baronage.
And thus with bliss and eek with melodye
Hath Palamon i-wedded Emelye.
And God, that al this wyde world hath wrought,
Send him his love, that hath it deere i-bought.
For now is Palamon in al his wealth,
Lyvynge in blisse, richesse, and in health,
And Emely him loveth so tendirly,
And he hir serveth al so gentilly,
That never was ther word bitweene them two
Of jelousy, nor of non othir woe.
Thus endeth Palamon and Emelye;
And God save al this fayre companye! Amen!

GEOFFREY CHAUCER.

LONDON LICKPENNY

To London once my steps I bent,
   Where truth in nowise should be faint;
To Westminster-ward I forthwith went,
   To a Man of Law to make complaint,
   I said " For Mary's love, that holy saint,
   Pity the poor that would proceed! "
But for lack of Money I could not speed.

And as I thrust the press among,
  By froward chance my hood was gone,
Yet for all that I stayed not long
  Till to the King's Bench I was come.
  Before the Judge I kneel'd anon,
  And pray'd him for God's sake to take heed.
  But for lack of Money I might not speed.

Beneath them sat clerks a great rout,
  Which fast did write by one assent,
There stood up one and cried about
  " Richard, Robert, and John of Kent! "
  I wist not well what this man meant,
  He crièd so thickly there indeed.
  But he that lacked Money might not speed.

Unto the Common Pleas I yode[1] tho,
  Where sat one with a silken hood;
I did him reverence, for I ought to do so,
  And told my case as well as I could,
  How my goods were defrauded me by falsehood.
  I got not a mum of his mouth for my meed,
  And for lack of Money I might not speed.

Unto the Rolls I gat me from thence,
  Before the clerkes of the Chancerie,
Where many I found earning of pence,
  But none at all once regarded me.
  I gave them my plaint upon my knee;
  They likèd it well when they had it read,
  But lacking Money I could not be sped.

In Westminster Hall I found out one
  Which went in a long gown of ray,[2]
I crouchèd and kneeled before him anon,
  For Marye's love of help I him pray.
  " I wot not what thou mean'st," gan he say;
  To get me thence he did me bede,
  For lack of money I could not speed.

Within this Hall, neither rich nor yet poor
  Would do for me aught although I should die.
Which seeing, I got me out of the door
  Where Flemings began on me for to cry,

---

[1] Went.   [2] Striped cloth.

" Master, what will you copen[1] or buy?
Fine felt hats, or spectacles to read?
Lay down your silver, and here you may speed."

Then to Westminster Gate I presently went,
  When the sun was at highé prime;
Cookés to me they took good intent,
  And proffered me bread with ale and wine,
  Ribs of beef, both fat and full fine;
A fairé cloth they gan for to sprede,
But wanting Money I might not speed.

Then unto London I did me hie,
  Of all the land it beareth the prise.
" Hot peascodés ! " one began to cry,
  " Strawberry ripe ! " and " Cherries in the rise ! "
  One bade me come near and buy some spice,
Pepper and saffroné they gan me bede[2],
But for lack of Money I might not speed.

Then to the Cheap I began me drawn,
  Wheré much people I saw for to stand;
One offered me velvuet, silk, and lawn,
  Another he taketh me by the hand,
  " Here is Paris thread, the fin'st in the land ! "
I never was used to such things indeed,
And wanting Money I might not speed.

Then went I forth by London Stone,
  Throughout all Can'wick Street.[3]
Drapers much cloth me offered anon;
  Then comes me one cried, " Hot sheep's feet ! "
One criede " Mackerel ! " " Rushes green ! " another
    gan greet;[4]
  One bade me buy a hood to cover my head,
But for want of Money I might not be sped.

Then I hied me into East Cheap;
  One cries " Ribs of beef," and many a pie;
Pewter pottés they clatter'd on a heap,
  Theré was harpé, pipe, and minstrelsie.

[1] (Dutch " koopen "), buy.   [2] Bid.
[3] Candlewick *Street*, where Cannon Street now runs.   [4] Cry.

" Yea, by cock! " " Nay, by cock! " some began cry;
Some sung of Jenkin and Julian for their meed,
But for lack of Money I might not speed.

Then into Cornhill anon I yode,
  Where was much stolen gear among;
I saw where hung mine owné hood
    That I had lost among the throng:
    To buy my own hood I thought it wrong;
  I knew it well as I did my Creed,
  But for lack of Money I could not speed.

The taverner took me by the sleeve,
  " Sir," saith he, " will you our wine assay? "
I answered, " That cannot much me grieve,
    A penny can do no more than it may."
    I drank a pint, and for it I did pay.
  Yet soon ahungered from thence I yede,
  And wanting Money I could not speed.

Then hied I me to Billingsgate,
  And one cried, " Hoo! Go we hence! "
I prayèd a barge man, for God'ses sake,
    That he would sparé me my expence.
    " Thou scrap'st not here," quoth he, " under two pence;
  I list not yet bestow any alms deed."
  Thus lacking Money I could not speed.

Then I conveyéd me into Kent;
  For of the law would I meddle no more,
Becausé no man to me took intent,
  I dight me to do as I did before.
  Now Jesus, that in Bethlehem was bore,
  Save London, and send true lawyers their meed!
  For whoso wants Money with them shall not speed.

                                    JOHN LYDGATE.

ROBIN HOOD'S END

" Hast thou ony greencloth,
  That thou wylte sell to me? "
" Yea, fore God," sayd Robyn,
  " Thirty yerdes and three."

" Robyn," sayd our kynge,
  " Now pray I thee
To sell me some of that cloth,
  To me and my meyné."

" Yes, fore God," then sayd Robyn,
  " Or elles I were a fool;
Another day ye wyll me clothe,
  I trowe, ayenst the Yule."

The kynge cast off his coat then,
  A grene garment he did on,
And every knyght did so, i-wys,
  They clothed them full soon.
Whan they were clothed in Lincoln green,
  They kest away their gray.
Now we shall to Notyngham,
  All thus our kynge gan say.
Their bowes bent, forth they went,
  Shotynge all in-fere,
Toward the town of Notyngham,
  Outlaws as they were.

Our kynge and Robyn rode togyder,
  For sooth as I you say,
And they shot pluck-buffet,
  As they went by the way;
And many a buffet our kynge wan,
  Of Robyn Hode that day:
And nothing spared good Robyn
  Our kynge in his pay.
" So God me helpe," sayd our kynge,
  " Thy name is nought to lere,
I sholde not get a shot of thee,
  Though I shot all this yere."

All the people of Notyngham
    They stode and behelde,
They saw nothyng but mantels of grene
    They covered all the felde;
Than every man to other gan say,
    I drede our kynge be slone;
Come Robyn Hode to the towne, i-wys,
    On lyve he leaveth not one.
Full hastily they began to flee,
    Both yeomen and knaves,
And olde wyves that myght evyll goo,
    They hopped on theyr staves.

The kynge laughe full fast,
    And commanded theym agayne;
When they see our comly kynge,
    I-wys they were full fayne.
They ete and drank, and made them glad
    And sang with notes hye.
Than bespake our comly kynge
    To syr Rycharde at the Lee:
He gave hym there his londe again,
    A good man he bad hym be.
Robyn thanked our comely kynge,
    And set hym on his knee.

Had Robyn dwelled in the kynges courte
    But twelve monethes and three
That he had spent an hondred pounde,
    And all his mennes fee.
In every place where Robyn came,
    Ever more he layde down,
Both for knyghtes and squyres,
    To gete hym grete renown.
By than the year was all agone,
    He had no man but twayn
Lytell Johan and good Scathelocke,
    Wyth hym all for to gone.
Robyn sawe yonge men shoot,
    Full fayre upon a day,
" Alas!" than sayd good Robyn,
    " My welthe is went away.
Sometyme I was an archer good,

A stiff and eke a stronge,
  I was committed the best archer,
    That was in mery Englonde.
Alas! " then sayd good Robyn,
  " Alas and well a day!
Yf I dwell lenger with the kynge,
  Sorrow wyll me slay! "

Forth than went Robyn Hode,
  Tyll he came to our kynge:
" My lorde the kynge of Englonde,
  Graunte me myn askynge.
I made a chapell in Bernysdale,
  That semely is to see
It is of Mary Magdalene,
  And thereto would I be;
I might never in this seven night,
  No tyme to sleep ne wynke,
Nother all these seven dayes,
  Nother ete ne drynke.
Me longeth sore to Bernysdale,
  I may not be therfro,
Barefote and wolwarde I have hyght
  Thither for to go. "

" Yf it be so," then sayd our kynge,
  " It may no better be;
Seven nyght I give thee leave,
  No lengre, to dwell fro me. "

" Gramercy, lorde," then sayd Robyn
  And set hym on his kne;
He toke his leave full courteysly,
  To grene wode then went he.
Whan he came to grene wode,
  In a mery mornynge,
There he herde the notes small
  Of byrdes mery syngynge.
" It is ferre gone," sayd Robyn
  " That I was last here,
Me lyste a lytell for to shote
  At the dun deere. "
Robyn slewe a full grete harte,

His horne than gan he blow,
That all the outlawes of that forest,
  That horne could they know,
And gathered them together,
  In a lytell throw,
Seven score of wight yonge men,
  Came ready in a row;
And fayre dyde off theyr hoods,
  And set them on theyr knee:
" Welcome," they sayd, " our mayster,
  Under this grenewood tree! "

Robyn dwelled in grenewood,
  Twenty yere and two,
For all drede of Edwarde our kynge,
  Agayne wolde he not goo.
Yet he was begyled, I wys,
  Through a wycked woman,
The pryoresse of Kyrkesly,
  That nye was of his kynne,
For the love of a knyght,
  Syr Roger of Donkesley,
That was her fere, speciall
  Full evyll mote they thee.

They toke together their counsell
  Robyn Hode for to sle,
And how they myght best do that deed,
  His ill death for to be.
Than bespake good Robyn,
  In place where as he stode,
To morow I must to Kyrkesley,
  Craftely to be leten blode.
Syr Roger of Donkestere,
  By the Pryoresse he lay,
And there they betrayed good Robyn Hode,
  Through their false play.
Cryst have mercy on his soule,
  That dyed on the rood!
For he was a good outlawe,
  And did poor men moch good.

                                        ANON.

THE RESTLESS STATE OF A LOVER

THE sun hath twice brought forth his tender green,
And clad the earth in lively lustiness:
Once have the winds the trees despoiled clean,
And new again begins their cruelness,
Since I have hid under my breast the harm
That never shall recover healthfulness.
The winters hurt recovers with the warm:
The parched green restored is with the shade.
What warmth (alas) may serve for to disarm
The frozen heart that mine in flame hath made?
What cold again is able to restore
My fresh green years, that wither thus and fade?
Alas, I see, nothing hath hurt so sore,
But time in time reduceth a return:
In time my harm increaseth more and more,
And seems to have my cure always in scorn.
Strange kinds of death, in life that I do try,
At hand to melt, far off in flame to burn.
And like as time list to my cure apply,
So doth each place my comfort clean refuse.
All thing alive, that seeth the heavens with eye,
With cloak of night may cover, and excuse
It self from travail of the day's unrest,
Save I, alas, against all others use,
That then stir up the torments of my breast,
And curse each star as causer of my fate.
And when the sun hath eke the dark opprest,
And brought the day, it doth nothing abate
The travails of mine endless smart and pain,
For then, as one that hath the light in hate,
I wish for night, more covertly to plain,
And me withdraw from every haunted place,
Lest by my cheer my chance appear too plain:
And in my mind I measure pace by pace,
To seek the place where I my self had lost,
That day that I was tangled in the lace,
In seeming slack that knitteth ever most:
But never yet the travail of my thought
Of better state could catch a cause to boast.

For if I found sometime that I have sought,
Those stars by whom I trusted of the port,
My sails do fall, and I advance right nought,
As anchored fast, my spirits do all resort
To stand agazed, and sink in more and more
The deadly harm which she doth take in sport.
Lo, if I seek, how I do find my sore:
And if I flee I carry with me still
The venom'd shaft, which doth his force restore
By haste of flight, and I may plain my fill
Unto my self, unless this careful song
Print in your heart some parcel of my tene;
For I, alas, in silence all too long
Of mine old hurt yet feel the wound but green.
Rue on my life; or else your cruel wrong
Shall well appear, and by my death be seen.

EARL OF SURREY.

ON THE DEATH OF SIR THOMAS WYATT

WYATT resteth here, that quick could never rest:
    Whose heavenly gifts increasèd by disdain;
And virtue sank the deeper in his breast:
    Such profit he by envy could obtain.

A head, where wisdom mysteries did frame;
    Whose hammers beat still in that lively brain,
As on a stithy where that some work of fame
    Was daily wrought, to turn to Britain's gain.

A visage stern, and mild; where both did grow
    Vice to contemn, in virtue to rejoice:
Amid great storms, whom grace assured so,
    To live upright, and smile at fortune's choice.

A hand, that taught what might be said in rhyme
    That reft Chaucér the glory of his wit.
A mark, the which (unperfected for time)
    Some may approach, but never none shall hit.

A tongue, that served in foreign realms his king;
    Whose courteous talk to virtue did inflame
Each noble heart; a worthy guide to bring
    Our English youth by travail unto fame.

An eye, whose judgment none affect could blind,
    Friends to allure, and foes to reconcile;
Whose piercing look did represent a mind
    With virtue fraught, reposèd, void of guile.

A heart, where dread was never so imprest
    To hide the thought that might the truth advance!
In neither fortune loft, nor yet represt,
    To swell in wealth, or yield unto mischance.

A valiant corpse, where force and beauty met:
    Happy, alas! too happy, but for foes,
Livèd, and ran the race that nature set;
    Of manhood's shape, where she the mould did lose.

But to the heavens that simple soul is fled,
    Which left, with such as covet Christ to know,
Witness of faith, that never shall be dead;
    Sent for our health, but not received so.

Thus for our guilt this jewel have we lost;
The earth his bones, the heavens possess his ghost.
                    EARL OF SURREY.

OF THE COURTIER'S LIFE

(TO JOHN POINS)

MINE own John Poins, since ye delight to know
    The causes why that homeward I me draw,
    And flee the press of Courts, whereso they go,
Rather than to live thrall under the awe

Of lordly looks; wrappèd within my cloak,
To will and lust learning to set a law:
It is not that, because I scorn or mock
The power of them to whom fortúne hath lent
Charge over us, of right to strike the stroke;
But true it is, that I have always meant
Less to esteem them than the common sort
Of outward things that judge in their intent,
Without regard what inward doth resort.
I grant sometime of glory that the fire
Doth touch my heart. Me list not to report
Blame by honour, and honour to desire.
But how may I this honour now attain,
That cannot dye the colour black a liar?
My Poins, I cannot frame my tongue to feign;
To cloke the truth for praise, without desert,
Of them that list all vice for to retain.
I cannot honour them that set their part
With Venus and Bacchús all their life long;
Nor hold my peace of them, although I smart.
I cannot crouch nor kneel to such a wrong,
To worship them like God on earth alone,
That are as wolves these sely lambs among.
I cannot with my words complain and moan,
And suffer nought; nor smart without complaint;
Nor turn the word that from my mouth is gone.
I cannot speak and look like as a saint;
Use wiles for wit, and make deceit a pleasure;
And call craft, counsel; for lucre still to paint.
I cannot wrest the law to fill the coffer,
With innocént blood to feed my self fat,
And do most hurt, where that most help I offer.
I am not he that can allow the state
Of high Cæsár, and damn Cato to die,
That with his death did scape out of the gate
From Cæsar's hands, if Livy doth not lie,
And would not live where liberty was lost:
So did his heart the common wealth apply.
I am not he, such eloquence to boast,
To make the crow in singing as the swan;
Nor call the lion of coward beasts the most,
That cannot take a mouse, as the cat can;
And he that dieth for hunger of the gold,

Call him Aléxander; and say that Pan
Passeth Apollo in music many fold;
 Praise Sir Thopas for a noble tale,
 And scorn the story that the Knight told;
Praise him for counsel that is drunk of ale;
 Grin when he laughs that beareth all the sway,
 Frown when he frowns, and groan when he is pale;
On others' lust to hang both night and day.
 None of these points would ever frame in me:
 My wit is nought, I cannot learn the way.
And much the less of things that greater be;
 That asken help of colours to devise
 To join the mean with each extremity;
With nearest virtue aye to cloke the vice;
 And, as to purpose likewise it shall fall,
 To press the virtue that it may not rise.
As, drunkenness good fellowship to call;
 The friendly foe, with his fair double face,
 Say he is gentle and courteous therewithal;
Affirm that favel hath a goodly grace
 In eloquence; and cruelty to name
 Zeal of justice, and change in time and place;
And he that suffereth offence without blame,
 Call him pitiful; and him true and plain
 That raileth reckless unto each man's shame;
Say he is rude, that cannot lie and feign;
 The lecher, a lover; and tyranny
 To be the right of a prince's reign.
I cannot, I, no, no! it will not be.
 This is the cause that I could never yet
 Hang on their sleeves that weigh, as thou mayst see,
A chip of chance more than a pound of wit.
 This maketh me at home to hunt and hawk,
 And in foul weather at my book to sit,
In frost and snow, then with my bow to stalk,
 No man doth mark whereso I ride or go.
 In lusty leas at liberty I walk;
And of these news I feel nor weal nor woe,
 Save that a clog doth hang yet at my heel.
 No force for that; for it is ordered so
That I may leap both hedge and dike full wele.
 I am not now in France to judge the wine,
 With savoury sauce the delicates to feel;

Nor yet in Spain, where one must him incline
    Rather than to be, outwardly to seem.
    I meddle not with wits that be so fine.
Nor Flanders cheer lets not my sight to deem
    Of black and white, nor takes my wit away
    With beastliness; such do those beasts esteem.
Nor I am not where truth is given in prey
    For money, poison, and treasón, of some
    A common practice, usèd night and day.
But I am here in Kent and Christendom,
    Among the Muses, where I read and rhyme:
    Where if thou list, mine own John Poins, to come,
Thou shalt be judge how I do spend my time.

SIR THOMAS WYATT.

PROTHALAMION

" A Spousall Verse, made by Edm. Spenser, in honour of the double mariage of the two honorable and vertuous ladies, the Ladie Elizabeth, and the Ladie Katherine Somerset, daughters to the right honourable the Earle of Worcester, and espoused to the two worthie gentlemen M. Henry Gilford and M. William Peter Esquyers," 1596.

CALME was the day, and through the trembling ayre
Sweete-breathing Zephyrus did softly play
A gentle spirit, that lightly did delay
Hot Titans beames, which then did glyster fayre;
When I, (whom sullein care,
Through discontent of my long fruitlesse stay
In Princes Court, and expectation vayne
Of idle hopes, which still doe fly away,
Like empty shaddowes, did afflict my brayne,)
Walkt forth to ease my payne
Along the shoare of silver streaming Themmes;
Whose rutty Bancke, he which his River hemmes
Was paynted all with variable flowers,
And all the meades adornd with daintie gemmes
Fit to decke maydens bowres,
And crowne their Paramours
Against the Brydale day, which is not long:
    Sweete Themmes! runne softly, till I end my Song.

There, in a Meadow, by the Rivers side,
A Flocke of Nymphes I chaunced to espy,

All lovely Daughters of the Flood thereby,
With goodly greenish locks, all loose untyde,
As each had bene a Bryde;
And each one had a little wicker basket,
Made of fine twigs, entrayled curiously,
In which they gathered flowers to fill their flasket,
And with fine Fingers cropt full feateously
The tender stalkes on hye.
Of every sort, which in that Meadow grew,
They gathered some; the Violet, pallid blew,
The little Dazie, that at evening closes,
The virgin Lillie, and the Primrose trew,
With store of vermeil Roses,
To decke their Bridegromes posies
Against the Brydale day, which was not long:
  Sweete Themmes! runne softly, till I end my Song.

With that I saw two Swannes of goodly hewe
Come softly swimming downe along the Lee;
Two fairer Birds I yet did never see;
The snow, which doth the top of Pindus strew,
Did never whiter shew,
Nor Jove himselfe, when he a Swan would be,
For love of Leda, whiter did appeare;
Yet Leda was (they say) as white as he,
Yet not so white as these, nor nothing neare;
So purely white they were,
That even the gentle streame, the which them bare,
Seem'd foule to them, and bad his billowes spare
To wet their silken feathers, least they might
Soyle their fayre plumes with water not so fayre,
And marre their beauties bright,
That shone as heavens light,
Against their Brydale day, which was not long:
  Sweete Themmes! runne softly, till I end my Song.

Eftsoones the Nymphes, which now had Flowers their
    fill,
Ran all in haste to see that silver brood,
As they came floating on the Christal Flood;
Whom when they sawe, they stood amazed still,
Their wondring eyes to fill;
Them seem'd they never saw a sight so fayre,

Of Fowles, so lovely, that they sure did deeme
Them heavenly borne, or to be that same payre
Which through the Skie draw Venus silver Teeme;
For sure they did not seeme
To be begot of any earthly Seede,
But rather angels, or of Angels breede:
Yet were they bred of Somers-heat, they say,
In sweetest Season, when each Flower and weede
The earth did fresh aray;
So fresh they seem'd as day,
Even as their Brydale day, which was not long:
   Sweete Themmes! runne softly, till I end my Song.

Then forth they all out of their baskets drew
Great store of Flowers, the honour of the field,
That to the sense did fragrant odours yield,
All which upon those goodly Birds they threw
And all the Waves did strew,
That like old Peneus Waters they did seeme,
When downe along by pleasant Tempes shore
Scattred with Flowers, through Thessaly they streeme,
That they appeare, through Lillies plenteous store,
Like a Brydes Chamber flore.
Two of those Nymphes, meane while, two Garlands bound
Of freshest Flowres which in that Mead they found,
The which presenting all in trim Array.
Their snowie Foreheads therewithall they crownd,
Whil'st one did sing this Lay,
Prepar'd against that Day,
Against their Brydale day, which was not long:
   Sweete Themmes! runne softly, till I end my Song.

" Ye gentle Birdes! the worlds faire ornament,
And heavens glorie, whom this happie hower
Doth leade unto your lovers blisfull bower,
Joy may you have, and gentle hearts content
Of your loves couplement;
And let faire Venus, that is Queene of love,
With her heart-quelling Sonne upon you smile,
Whose smile, they say, hath vertue to remove
All Loves dislike, and friendships faultie guile
For ever to assoile.

Let endlesse Peace your steadfast hearts accord,
And blessed Plentie wait upon your bord;
And let your bed with pleasures chast abound,
That fruitfull issue may to you afford,
Which may your foes confound,
And make your joyes redound
Upon your Brydale day, which is not long:
   Sweete Themmes! runne softlie, till I end my Song."

So ended she; and all the rest around
To her redoubled that her undersong,
Which said their brydale daye should not be long:
And gentle Eccho from the neighbour ground
Their accents did resound.
So forth those joyous Birdes did passe along,
Adowne the Lee, that to them murmurde low,
As he would speake, but that he lackt a tong,
Yet did by signes his glad affection show,
Making his streame run slow.
And all the foule which in his flood did dwell
Gan flock about these twaine, that did excell
The rest, so far as Cynthia doth shend
The lesser starres. So they, enranged well,
Did on those two attend,
And their best service lend
Against their wedding day, which was not long:
   Sweete Themmes! run softly, till I end my Song.

At length they all to mery London came,
To mery London, my most kyndly Nurse,
That to me gave this Lifes first native sourse,
Though from another place I take my name,
An house of auncient fame:
There when they came, whereas those bricky towres
The which on Themmes brode aged backe doe ryde,
Where now the studious Lawyers have their bowers,
There whylome wont the Templer Knights to byde,
Till they decayd through pride:
Next whereunto there standes a stately place,
Where oft I gayned giftes and goodly grace
Of that great Lord, which therein wont to dwell,
Whose want too well now feeles my freendles case;
But ah! here fits not well

Olde woes, but joyes, to tell
Against the bridale daye, which is not long:
 Sweete Themmes! runne softly, till I end my Song.

Yet therein now doth lodge a noble Peer,
Great Englands glory, and the Worlds wide wonder,
Whose dreadfull name late through all Spaine did
  thunder,
And Hercules two pillors standing neere
Did make to quake and feare:
Faire branch of Honor, flower of Chevalrie!
That fillest England with thy triumphes fame,
Joy have thou of thy noble victorie,
And endlesse happinesse of thine owne name
That promiseth the same;
That through thy prowesse, and victorious armes,
Thy country may be freed from forraine harmes;
And great Elisaes glorious name may ring
Through al the world, fil'd with thy wide Alarmes,
Which some brave muse may sing
To ages following.
Upon the Brydale day, which is not long:
 Sweete Themmes! runne softly, till I end my Song.

From those high Towers this noble Lord issuing,
Like Radiant Hesper, when his golden hayre
In th' Ocean billowes he hath bathed fayre,
Descended to the Rivers open vewing,
With a great traine ensuing.
Above the rest were goodly to bee seene
Two gentle Knights of lovely face and feature,
Beseeming well the bower of anie Queene,
With gifts of wit, and ornaments of nature,
Fit for so goodly stature,
That like the twins of Jove they seem'd in sight,
Which decke the Bauldricke of the Heavens bright;
They two, forth pacing to the Rivers side,
Received those two faire Brides, their Loves delight;
Which, at th' appointed tyde,
Each one did make his Bryde
Against their Brydale day, which is not long:
 Sweete Themmes! runne softly, till I end my Song.
        EDMUND SPENSER.

THE IMAGE OF DEATH

I LOATHE that I did love,
    In youth that I thought sweet,
As time requires for my behove
    Methinks they are not meet.

My longings do me leave,
    My fancies all are fled,
And tract of time begins to weave
    Grey hairs upon my head.

For Age with stealing steps
    Hath clawed me with his crutch,
And lusty Life away she leaps
    As there had been none such.

My Muse doth not delight
    Me as she did before;
My hand and pen are not in plight,
    As they have been of yore.

For Reason me denies
    This youthly idle rhyme;
And day by day to me she cries,
    " Leave off these toys in time."

The wrinkles in my brow,
    The furrows in my face,
Say, limping Age will lodge him now,
    Where Youth must give him place.

The harbinger of Death,
    To me I see him ride;
The cough, the cold, the gasping breath
    Doth bid me to provide

A pickaxe and a spade,
    And eke a shrouding sheet,
A house of clay for to be made
    For such a guest most meet.

Methinks I hear the clerk,
　　That knolls the careful knell,
And bids me leave my woeful work,
　　Ere Nature me compel.

My keepers knit the knot
　　That Youth did laugh to scorn,
Of me that clean shall be forgot,
　　As I had not been born.

Thus must I youth give up,
　　Whose badge I long did wear;
To them I yield the wanton cup
　　That better may it bare.

Lo, here the barèd skull,
　　By whose bald sign I know,
That stooping Age away shall pull
　　Which youthful years did sow.

For Beauty with her band
　　These crooked cares hath wrought,
And shippèd me into the land
　　From whence I first was brought.

And ye that bide behind,
　　Have ye none other trust:
As ye of clay were cast by kind,
　　So shall ye waste to dust.

　　　　　　　　　　　　　LORD VAUX.

AGINCOURT

FAIR stood the wind for France,
When we our sails advance,
Nor now to prove our chance
　　Longer will tarry;
But putting to the main
At Kaux, the mouth of Seine,
With all his martial train
　　Landed King Harry.

And taking many a fort
Furnish'd in warlike sort,
Marcheth towards Agincourt
    In happy hour;
Skirmishing day by day
With those that stopp'd his way
Where the French Gen'ral lay
    With all his power.

Which in his height of pride
King Henry to deride,
His ransom to provide
    To the King sending;
Which he neglects the while
As from a nation vile,
Yet with an angry smile
    Their fall portending.

And turning to his men
Quoth our brave Henry then:
"Though they to one be ten,
    Be not amazed:
Yet have we well begun,
Battles so bravely won
Have ever to the sun
    By fame been raised.

" And for myself (quoth he)
This my full rest shall be,
England ne'er mourn for me
    Nor more esteem me:
Victor I will remain
Or on this earth lie slain,
Never shall she sustain
    Loss to redeem me.

" Poitiers and Cressy tell,
When most their pride did swell.
Under our swords they fell:
    No less our skill is
Than when our grandsire great,
Claiming the regal seat,
By many a warlike feat
    Lopp'd the French Lilies."

The Duke of York so dread
The eager vaward led;
With the main Henry sped
    Amongst his henchmen;
Exeter had the rear,
A braver man not there,—
O Lord, how hot they were
    On the false Frenchmen!

They now to fight are gone:
Armour on armour shone,
Drum now to drum did groan,—
    To hear was wonder.
That with the cries they make
The very earth did shake;
Trumpet to trumpet spake,
    Thunder to thunder.

Well it thine age became,
O noble Erpingham,
Which did'st the signal aim
    To our hid forces;
When from a meadow by,
Like a storm suddenly,
The English archery
    Struck the French horses,

With Spanish yew so strong,
Arrows a cloth-yard long,
That like to serpents stung
    Piercing the weather;
None from his fellow starts,
But playing manly parts,
And like true English hearts,
    Stuck close together.

When down their bows they threw
And forth their bilboes drew
And on the French they flew,
    Not one was tardy;
Arms were from shoulders sent,
Scalps to the teeth were rent,
Down the French peasants went,
    Our men were hardy.

Thus while our noble King,
His broad-sword brandishing,
Down the French host did ding,
    As to o'erwhelm it;
And many a deep wound lent,
His arms with blood besprent,
And many a cruel dent
    Bruised his helmet.

Gloster, that Duke so good,
Next of the Royal blood,
For famous England stood
    With his brave brother;
Clarence, in steel so bright,
Though but a maiden knight,
Yet in that furious fight
    Scarce such another.

Warwick in blood did wade,
Oxford the foe invade,
And cruel slaughter made
    Still as they ran up:
Suffolk his axe did ply,
Beaumont and Willoughby
Bare them right doughtily,
    Ferrers and Fanhope.

Upon Saint Crispin's day
Fought was this noble fray
Which fame did not delay
    To England to carry:
O when shall English men
With such acts fill a pen,
Or England breed again
    Such a King Harry!

               MICHAEL DRAYTON.

MUSIC'S DUEL

Now westward Sol had spent the richest beams
Of Noon's high glory, when hard by the streams
Of Tiber, on the scene of a green plat,
Under protection of an oak, there sate
A sweet Lute's-master; in whose gentle airs
He lost the day's heat, and his own hot cares.
    Close in the covert of the leaves there stood
A nightingale, come from the neighbouring wood:
(The sweet inhabitant of each glad tree,
Their Muse, their Syren—harmless Syren she!)
There stood she list'ning, and did entertain
The music's soft report, and mould the same
In her own murmurs, that whatever mood
His curious fingers lent, her voice made good:
The man perceiv'd his rival, and her art;
Dispos'd to give the light-foot lady sport,
Awakes his lute, and 'gainst the fight to come
Informs it in a sweet preludium
Of closer strains, and ere the war begin,
He lightly skirmishes on every string,
Charg'd with a flying touch: and straightway she
Carves out her dainty voice as readily,
Into a thousand sweet distinguish'd tones,
And reckons up in soft divisions,
Quick volumes of wild notes; to let him know
By that shrill taste, she could do something too.
    His nimble hands' instinct then taught each string
A cap'ring cheerfulness; and made them sing
To their own dance; now negligently rash
He throws his arm, and with a long-drawn dash
Blends all together; then distinctly trips
From this to that; then quick returning skips
And snatches this again, and pauses there.
She measures every measure, everywhere
Meets art with art; sometimes as if in doubt
Not perfect yet, and fearing to be out
Trails her plain ditty in one long-spun note,
Through the sleek passage of her open throat,
A clear unwrinkled song; then doth she point it
With tender accents, and severely joint it

By short diminutives, that being rear'd
In controverting warbles evenly shar'd,
With her sweet self she wrangles.   He amaz'd
That from so small a channel should be rais'd
The torrent of a voice, whose melody
Could melt into such sweet variety,
Strains higher yet; that tickled with rare art
The tatling strings (each breathing in his part)
Most kindly do fall out; the grumbling base
In surly groans disdains the treble's grace;
The high-perch't treble chirps at this and chides,
Until his finger (Moderator) hides
And closes the sweet quarrel, rousing all,
Hoarse, shrill at once; as when the trumpets call
Hot Mars to th' harvest of Death's field, and woo
Men's hearts into their hands; this lesson too
She gives him back; her supple breast thrills out
Sharp airs, and staggers in a warbling doubt
Of dallying sweetness, hovers o'er her skill,
And folds in wav'd notes with a trembling bill
The pliant series of her slippery song;
Then starts she suddenly into a throng
Of short, thick sobs, whose thund'ring volleys float
And roll themselves over her lubric throat
In panting murmurs, 'still'd out of her breast,
That ever-bubbling spring; the sugared nest
Of her delicious soul, that there does lie
Bathing in streams of liquid melody;
Music's best seed-plot, whence in ripen'd airs
A golden-headed harvest fairly rears
His honey-dropping tops, ploughed by her breath,
Which there reciprocally laboureth
In that sweet soil; it seems a holy choir
Founded to th' name of great Apollo's lyre,
Whose silver-roof rings with the sprightly notes
Of sweet-lipp'd angel-imps, that swill their throats
In cream of morning Helicon, and then
Preferre soft-anthems to the ears of men,
To woo them from their beds, still murmuring
That men can sleep while they their matins sing:
(Most divine service) whose so early lay,
Prevents the eye-lids of the blushing Day!
There you might hear her kindle her soft voice,

In the close murmur of a sparkling noise,
And lay the ground-work of her hopeful song,
Still keeping in the forward stream, so long,
Till a sweet whirl-wind (striving to get out)
Heaves her soft bosom, wanders round about,
And makes a pretty earthquake in her breast,
Till the fledg'd notes at length forsake their nest,
Fluttering wanton shoals, and to the sky
Wing'd with their own wild echoes, prattling fly.
She opes the floodgate, and lets loose a tide
Of streaming sweetness, which in state doth ride
On the wav'd back of every swelling strain,
Rising and falling in a pompous train.
And while she thus discharges a shrill peal
Of flashing airs; she qualifies their zeal
With the cool epode of a graver note,
Thus high, thus low, as if her silver throat
Would reach the brazen voice of War's hoarse bird
Her little soul is ravish'd: and so pour'd
Into loose ecstasies, that she is plac'd
Above herself, Music's Enthusiast.

    Shame now and anger mix'd a double stain
In the Musician's face; " yet once again
(Mistress) I come; now reach a strain, my lute.
Above her mock, or be for ever mute;
Or tune a song of victory to me,
Or to thyself, sing thine own obsequie."
So said, his hands, sprightly as fire, he flings
And with a quivering coyness tastes the strings.
The sweet-lip'd sisters, musically frighted,
Singing their fears, are fearfully delighted,
Trembling as when Apollo's golden hairs
Are fann'd and frizzled, in the wanton airs
Of his own breath: which married to his lyre
Doth tune the spheres, and make Heaven's self look higher.
From this to that, from that to this he flies,
Feels Music's pulse in all her arteries;
Caught in a net which there Apollo spreads,
His fingers struggle with the vocal threads.
Following those little rills, he sinks into
A sea of Helicon; his hand does go
Those paths of sweetness which with nectar drop,
Softer than that which pants in Hebe's cup.

The humorous strings expound his learnèd touch.
By various glosses; now they seem to grutch,
And murmur in a buzzing din, then jingle
In shrill-tongue'd accents: striving to be single.
Every smooth turn, every delicious stroke
Gives life to some new grace; thus doth h' invoke
Sweetness by all her names; thus, bravely thus
(Fraught with a fury so harmonious)
The lute's light genius now does proudly rise,
Heav'd on the surges of swoll't rapsodies,
Whose flourish (meteor-like) doth curl the air
With flash of high-born fancies: here and there
Dancing in lofty measures, and anon
Creeps on the soft touch of a tender tone;
Whose trembling murmurs melting in wild airs
Runs to and fro, complaining his sweet cares,
Because those precious mysteries that dwell
In Music's ravish'd soul, he dares not tell,
But whisper to the world: thus do they vary
Each string his note, as if they meant to carry
Their Master's blest soul (snatch'd out at his ears
By a strong ecstasy) through all the spheres
Of Music's heaven; and seat it there on high
In th' empyræan of pure harmony.
At length (after so long, so loud a strife
Of all the strings, still breathing the best life
Of blest variety, attending on
His fingers' fairest revolution
In many a sweet rise, many as sweet a fall)
A full-mouth'd diapason swallows all.
  This done, he lists what she would say to this,
And she (although her breath's late exercise
Had dealt too roughly with her tender throat),
Yet summons all her sweet powers for a note.
Alas! in vain! for while (sweet soul!) she tries
To measure all those wild diversities
Of chattering strings, by the small size of one
Poor simple voice, rais'd in a natural tone;
She fails, and failing grieves, and grieving dies.
She dies; and leaves her life the Victor's prize
Falling upon his lute: O, fit to have
(That liv'd so sweetly) dead, so sweet a grave!
                              RICHARD CRASHAW.

FORTUNE AND VIRTUE

I

FORTUNE smiles! Cry holiday:
  Dimples on her cheek do dwell.
Fortune frowns! cry well-a-day:
  Her love is Heaven, her hate is Hell.
Since Heaven and Hell her power obey,
When she smiles cry holiday!
    Holiday! with joy we cry,
    And bend, and bend, and merrily
    Sing hymns to Fortune's deity:
    Sing hymns to Fortune's deity.

Let us sing, merrily, merrily, merrily!
  With our song let heaven resound!
  Fortune's hands our heads have crown'd!
Let us sing, merrily, merrily, merrily!

II

Virtue's branches wither, Virtue pines.
  O pity, pity, and alack the time!
Vice doth flourish, Vice in glory shines,
  Her gilded boughs above the cedar climb.
Vice hath golden cheeks, O pity, pity!
  She in every land doth monarchise.
Virtue is exiled from every city,
  Virtue is a fool, Vice only wise.
  O pity, pity! Virtue weeping dies.
Vice laughs to see her faint. Alack the time!
  This sinks; with painted wings the other flies.
Alack, that best should fall, and bad should climb!
  O pity, pity, pity! mourn, not sing!
Vice is a saint, Virtue an underling.
Vice doth flourish, Vice in glory shines:
Virtue's branches wither, Virtue pines.

III

All loudly cry, Virtue the victory!
Virtue the victory! For joy of this,
Those self-same hymns which you to Fortune sung
Let them be now in Virtue's honour rung:

Virtue smiles. Cry holiday:
  Dimples on her cheek do dwell.
Virtue frowns! Cry well-a-day:
  Her love is Heaven, her hate is Hell.
Since Heaven and Hell obey her power,
Tremble when her eyes do lower.
Since Heaven and Hell her power obey,
Where she smiles, cry holiday!
    Holiday! with joy we cry,
    And bend, and bend, and merrily
    Sing hymns to Virtue's deity:
    Sing hymns to Virtue's deity.
              THOMAS DEKKER.

TO THE MEMORY OF MY BELOVED
MASTER WILLIAM SHAKESPEARE

AND WHAT HE HATH LEFT US

To draw no envy, SHAKESPEARE, on thy name,
Am I thus ample to thy book and fame;
While I confess thy writings to be such,
As neither Man nor Muse can praise too much.
'Tis true, and all men's suffrage. But these ways
Were not the paths I meant unto thy praise;
For seeliest ignorance on these may light,
Which, when it sounds at best, but echoes right;
Or blind affection, which doth ne'er advance
The truth, but gropes, and urgeth all by chance;
Or crafty malice might pretend this praise,
And think to ruin where it seemed to raise.
These are, as some infámous bawd or whore
Should praise a matron; what could hurt her more?
But thou art proof against them, and, indeed,
Above the ill fortune of them, or the need.
I therefore will begin: Soul of the age!
The applause! delight! the wonder of our stage!
My SHAKESPEARE rise! I will not lodge thee by
Chaucer, or Spenser, or bid Beaumont lie
A little further, to make thee a room:

Thou art a monument without a tomb,
And art alive still while thy book doth live
And we have wits to read, and praise to give.
That I not mix thee so my brain excuses,
I mean with great, but disproportioned Muses:
For if I thought my judgment were of years,
I should commit thee surely with thy peers,
And tell how far thou didst our Lyly outshine,
Or sporting Kyd, or Marlowe's mighty line.
And though thou hadst small Latin and less Greek,
From thence to honour thee, I would not seek
For names: but call forth thund'ring Æschylus,
Euripides, and Sophocles to us,
Pacuvius, Accius, him of Cordova dead,
To life again, to hear thy buskin tread
And shake a stage: or when thy socks were on,
Leave thee alone for the comparison
Of all that insolent Greece or haughty Rome
Sent forth, or since did from their ashes come.
Triumph, my Britain, thou hast one to show,
To whom all Scenes of Europe homage owe.
He was not of an age, but for all time!
And all the Muses still were in their prime,
When, like Apollo, he came forth to warm
Our ears, or like a Mercury to charm!
Nature herself was proud of his designs,
And joyed to wear the dressing of his lines!
Which were so richly spun, and woven so fit,
As, since, she will vouchsafe no other wit.
The merry Greek, tart Aristophanes,
Neat Terence, witty Plautus, now not please;
But antiquated and deserted lie,
As they were not of Nature's family.
Yet must I not give Nature all; thy Art,
My gentle Shakespeare, must enjoy a part.
For though the poet's matter nature be,
His art doth give the fashion: and, that he
Who casts to write a living line, must sweat,
(Such as thine are) and strike the second heat
Upon the Muses' anvil: turn the same,
And himself with it, that he thinks to frame;
Or for the laurel he may gain a scorn;
For a good poet's made, as well as born.

And such wert thou! Look how the father's face
Lives in his issue, even so the race
Of Shakespeare's mind and manners brightly shines
In his well turned and true filed lines:
In each of which he seems to shake a lance,
As brandisht at the eyes of ignorance.
Sweet Swan of Avon! what a sight it were
To see thee in our waters yet appear,
And make those flights upon the banks of Thames,
That so did take Eliza, and our James!
But stay, I see thee in the hemisphere
Advanced, and made a constellation there!
Shine forth, thou Star of Poets, and with rage,
Or influence, chide or cheer the drooping stage,
Which, since thy flight from hence, hath mourned like night,
And despairs day but for thy volume's light.

BEN JONSON.

ODE ON LEAVING THE GREAT TOWN

Come, spur away,
I have no patience for a longer stay,
    But must go down
    And leave the chargeable noise of this great town:
I will the country see
Where old simplicity
    Tho' hid in grey,
    Doth look more gay
Than foppery in plush and scarlet clad.
    Farewell you city wits, that are
    Almost at civil war;
'Tis time that I grow wise when all the world grows mad.

More of my days
I will not spend to gain an idiot's praise:
    Or to make sport
    For some slight puny of the inns of court.
Then, worthy Stafford, say,
How shall we spend the day?
    With what delights
    Shorten the nights

When from this tumult we are got secure;
    Where mirth with all her freedom goes,
      Yet shall no finger lose
Where every word is thought, and every thought is pure.

    There, from the tree
    We'll cherries pluck, and pick the strawberry;
      And every day
      Go see the wholesome country girls make hay,
Whose brown hath lovelier grace
Than any painted face
      That I do know
      Hyde Park can show;
Where I had rather gain a kiss, than meet
      (Though some of them, in greater state,
      Might court my love with plate)
The beauties of the Cheape, and wives of Lombard Street.

    But think upon
    Some other pleasures, these to me are none.
      Why do I prate
      Of women, that are things against my fate?
I never mean to wed
That torture to my bed.
      My muse is she
      My love shall be:
Let clowns get wealth and heirs!—when I am gone,
      And the great bugbear, grisly death,
      Shall take this idle breath,
If I a poem leave, that poem is my son.

    Of this no more—
    We'll rather taste the bright Pomona's store;
      No fruit shall 'scape
      Our palates, from the damson to the grape.
Then full, we'll seek a shade,
And hear what music's made;
      How Philomel
      Her tale doth tell,
And how the other birds do fill the quire,
      The thrush and blackbird lend their throats,
      Warbling melodious notes,
We will all sports enjoy, which others but desire.

Ours is the sky
Where, at what fowl we please, our hawks shall fly.
  Nor will we spare
    To hunt the crafty fox, or tim'rous hare;
But let our hounds run loose
In any ground they choose:
  The buck shall fall,
  The stag and all.
Our pleasures must from their own warrants be.
  For to my muse, if not to me,
  I am sure all game is free;
Heav'n, earth, are all but parts of her great royalty.

And when we mean
To taste of Bacchus' blessings now and then,
  And drink by stealth
    A cup or two to noble Barkley's health,
I'll take my pipe and try
The Phrygian melody,
  Which he that hears
  Lets through his ears
A madness to distemper all the brain.
  Then I another pipe will take,
  And Doric music make,
To civilise with graver notes our wits again.

THOMAS RANDOLPH.

THE NYMPH ON THE DEATH
OF HER FAWN

THE wanton troopers riding by
Have shot my fawn, and it will die.
Ungentle men! They cannot thrive
Who killed thee. Thou ne'er didst, alive,
Them any harm; alas! nor could
Thy death to them do any good.
I'm sure I never wished them ill,
Nor do I for all this; nor will:
But, if my simple pray'rs may yet
Prevail with Heaven to forget

Thy murder, I will join my tears
Rather than fail. But O my fears!
It cannot die so. Heaven's king
Keeps register of everything,
And nothing may we use in vain;
Ev'n beasts must be with justice slain;
Else men are made their deodands.
Though they should wash their guilty hands
In this warm life-blood, which doth part
From thine, and wound me to the heart,
Yet could they not be clean; their stain
Is dyed in such a purple grain,
There is not such another in
The world to offer for their sin.

Inconstant Sylvio, when yet
I had not found him counterfeit,
One morning, I remember well,
Tied in this silver chain and bell,
Gave it to me: nay, and I know
What he said then—I'm sure I do.
Said he: " Look how your huntsman here
Hath taught a fawn to hunt his deer."
But Sylvio soon had me beguiled:
This waxed tame, while he grew wild,
And, quite regardless of my smart,
Left me his fawn, but took his heart.

Thenceforth I set myself to play
My solitary time away
With this; and very well content
Could so mine idle life have spent;
For it was full of sport, and light
Of foot and heart, and did invite
Me to its game: it seemed to bless
Itself in me. How could I less
Than love it? Oh, I cannot be
Unkind to a beast that loveth me!

Had it lived long, I do not know
Whether it, too, might have done so
As Sylvio did; his gifts might be

Perhaps as false, or more, than he.
For I am sure, for aught that I
Could in so short a time espy,
Thy love was far more better than
The love of false and cruel man.

With sweetest milk and sugar first
I it at mine own fingers nursed;
And as it grew so every day,
It waxed more white and sweet than they.
It had so sweet a breath! and oft
I blushed to see its foot more soft,
And white, shall I say? than my hand—
Than any lady's of the land!

It was a wondrous thing how fleet
'Twas on those little silver feet.
With what a pretty skipping grace
It oft would challenge me the race;
And when 't had left me far away,
'Twould stay, and run again, and stay;
For it was nimbler much than hinds,
And trod as if on the four winds.

I have a garden of my own,
But so with roses overgrown,
And lilies, that you would it guess
To be a little wilderness;
And all the spring-time of the year
It loved only to be there.
Among the beds of lilies I
Have sought it oft, where it should lie
Yet could not, till itself would rise,
Find it, although before mine eyes;
For in the flaxen lilies' shade,
It like a bank of lilies laid.
Upon the roses it would feed,
Until its lips ev'n seemed to bleed;
And then to me 'twould boldly trip,
And print those roses on my lip.
But all its chief delight was still
On roses thus itself to fill;

And its pure virgin lips to fold
In whitest sheets of lilies cold.
Had it lived long, it would have been
Lilies without, roses within.

ANDREW MARVELL.

ON THE MORNING OF CHRIST'S NATIVITY
Composed 1629

I

THIS is the month, and this the happy morn,
Wherein the Son of Heaven's Eternal King,
Of wedded maid and virgin mother born,
Our great redemption from above did bring;
For so the holy sages once did sing,
    That he our deadly forfeit should release,
And with his Father work us a perpetual peace.

II

That glorious form, that light unsufferable,
And that far-beaming blaze of majesty,
Wherewith he wont at Heaven's high council-table
To sit the midst of Trinal Unity,
He laid aside, and, here with us to be,
    Forsook the courts of everlasting day,
And chose with us a darksome house of mortal clay.

III

Say, Heavenly Muse, shall not thy sacred vein
Afford a present to the Infant God?
Hast thou no verse, no hymn, or solemn strain,
To welcome him to this his new abode,
Now while the heaven, by the Sun's team untrod,
    Hath took no print of the approaching light,
And all the spangled host keep watch in squadrons bright?

IV

See how from far upon the eastern road
The star-led wizards haste with odours sweet!
Oh! run; prevent them with thy humble ode,

And lay it lowly at his blessed feet;
Have thou the honour first thy Lord to greet,
   And join thy voice unto the Angel Quire,
From out his secret altar touched with hallowed fire.

THE HYMN

I

   It was the winter wild,
   While the heaven-born child
All meanly wrapt in the rude manger lies;
   Nature, in awe of him,
   Hath doffed her gaudy trim,
With her great Master so to sympathise:
It was no season then for her
To wanton with the Sun, her lusty paramour.

II

   Only with speeches fair
   She woos the gentle air
To hide her guilty front with innocent snow,
   And on her naked shame,
   Pollute with sinful blame,
The saintly veil of maiden white to throw;
Confounded, that her Maker's eyes
Should look so near upon her foul deformities.

III

   But he, her fears to cease,
   Sent down the meek-eyed Peace:
She, crowned with olive green, came softly sliding
   Down through the turning sphere,
   His ready harbinger,
With turtle wing the amorous clouds dividing;
And, waving wide her myrtle wand,
She strikes a universal peace through sea and land.

IV

   No war, or battle's sound,
   Was heard the world around;
The idle spear and shield were high uphung;

The hookèd chariot stood,
Unstained with hostile blood;
The trumpet spake not to the armèd throng;
And kings sat still with awful eye,
As if they surely knew their sovran Lord was by.

V

But peaceful was the night
Wherein the Prince of Light
His reign of peace upon the earth began.
The winds, with wonder whist,
Smoothly the waters kissed,
Whispering new joys to the mild Oceán,
Who now hath quite forgot to rave,
While birds of calm sit brooding on the charmèd wave.

VI

The stars, with deep amaze,
Stand fixed in steadfast gaze,
Bending one way their precious influence,
And will not take their flight,
For all the morning light,
Or Lucifer that often warned them thence;
But in their glimmering orbs did glow.
Until their Lord himself bespake, and bid them go.

VII

And, though the shady gloom
Had given day her room,
The Sun himself withheld his wonted speed,
And hid his head for shame,
As his inferior flame
The new-enlightened world no more should need:
He saw a greater Sun appear
Than his bright throne or burning axletree could bear.

VIII

The shepherds on the lawn,
Or ere the point of dawn,
Sat simply chatting in a rustic row;
Full little thought they than
That the mighty Pan

Was kindly come to live with them below:
Perhaps their loves, or else their sheep,
Was all that did their silly thoughts so busy keep.

IX

When such music sweet
Their hearts and ears did greet
As never was by mortal finger strook,
Divinely-warbled voice
Answering the stringed noise,
As all their souls in blissful rapture took:
The air, such pleasure loth to lose,
With thousand echoes still prolongs each heavenly close.

X

Nature, that heard such sound
Beneath the hollow round
Of Cynthia's seat the Airy region thrilling,
Now was almost won
To think her part was done,
And that her reign had here its last fulfilling:
She knew such harmony alone
Could hold all Heaven and Earth in happier union.

XI

At last surrounds their sight
A globe of circular light,
That with long beams the shamefaced Night arrayed;
The helmèd cherubim
And sworded seraphim
Are seen in glittering ranks with wings displayed,
Harping in loud and solemn quire,
With unexpressive notes, to Heaven's new-born Heir.

XII

Such music (as 'tis said)
Before was never made,
But when of old the Sons of Morning sung,
While the Creator great
His constellations set,
And the well balanced World on hinges hung,

And cast the dark foundations deep,
And bid the weltering waves their oozy channel keep.

XIII

Ring out, ye crystal spheres!
Once bless our human ears,
If ye have power to touch our senses so;
And let your silver chime
Move in melodious time;
And let the bass of heaven's deep organ blow;
And with your ninefold harmony
Make up full consort to the angelic symphony.

XIV

For, if such holy song
Enwrap our fancy long,
Time will run back and fetch the Age of Gold;
And speckled Vanity
Will sicken soon and die;
And leprous Sin will melt from earthly mould;
And Hell itself will pass away,
And leave her dolorous mansions to the peering day.

XV

Yea, Truth and Justice then
Will down return to men,
Orbed in a rainbow; and, like glories wearing,
Mercy will sit between,
Throned in celestial sheen,
With radiant feet the tissued clouds down steering;
And Heaven, as at some festival,
Will open wide the gates of her high palace-hall.

XVI

But wisest Fate says No,
This must not yet be so;
The Babe yet lies in smiling infancy
That on the bitter cross
Must redeem our loss,
So both himself and us to glorify:
Yet first, to those ychained in sleep,
The wakeful trump of doom must thunder through the deep.

XVII

With such a horrid clang
As on Mount Sinai rang,
While the red fire and smouldering clouds outbrake:
The aged Earth, agast,
With terror of that blast,
Shall from the surface to the centre shake,
When, at the world's last session,
The dreadful Judge in middle air shall spread his throne.

XVIII

And then at last our bliss
Full and perfect is,
But now begins; for from this happy day
The Old Dragon under ground,
In straiter limits bound,
Not half so far casts his usurpèd sway,
And, wroth to see his kingdom fail,
Swinges the scaly horror of his folded tail.

XIX

The Oracles are dumb;
No voice or hideous hum
Runs through the archèd roof in words deceiving.
Apollo from his shrine
Can no more divine,
With hollow shriek the steep of Delphos leaving.
No nightly trance, or breathèd spell,
Inspires the pale-eyed priest from the prophetic cell.

XX

The lonely mountains o'er,
And the resounding shore,
A voice of weeping heard and loud lament;
From haunted spring, and dale
Edged with poplar pale,
The parting Genius is with sighing sent;
With flower-inwoven tresses torn
The Nymphs in twilight shade of tangled thickets mourn.

XXI

In consecrated earth,
And on the holy hearth,
The Lars and Lemures moan with midnight plaint
In urns, and altars round,
A drear and dying sound
Affrights the flamens at their service quaint;
And the chill marble seems to sweat,
While each peculiar Power forgoes his wonted seat.

XXII

Peor and Baälim
Forsake their temples dim,
With that twice-battered God of Palestine;
And moonèd Ashtaroth,
Heaven's queen and mother both,
Now sits not girt with tapers' holy shine:
The Libyc Hammon shrinks his horn;
In vain the Tyrian maids their wounded Thammus mourn.

XXIII

And sullen Moloch, fled,
Hath left in shadows dread
His burning idol all of blackest hue;
In vain with cymbal's ring
They call the grisly king,
In dismal dance about the furnace blue;
The brutish gods of Nile as fast,
Isis, and Orus, and the dog Anubis, haste.

XXIV

Nor is Osiris seen
In Memphian grove or green,
Tramping the unshowered grass with lowings loud;
Nor can he be at rest
Within his sacred chest;
Nought but profoundest Hell can be his shroud;
In vain, with timbrelled anthems dark,
The sable-stolèd sorcerers bear his worshipped ark.

XXV

He feels from Juda's land
The dreaded Infant's hand;
The rays of Bethlehem blind his dusky eyn;
Nor all the gods beside
Longer dare abide,
Not Typhon huge ending in snaky twine:
Our Babe, to show his Godhead true,
Can in his swaddling bands control the damnèd crew.

XXVI

So, when the sun in bed,
Curtained with cloudy red,
Pillows his chin upon an orient wave,
The flocking shadows pale
Troop to the infernal jail,
Each fettered ghost slips to his several grave,
And the yellow-skirted fays
Fly after the night-steeds, leaving their moon-loved maze.

XXVII

But see! the Virgin blest
Hath laid her Babe to rest.
Time is our tedious song should here have ending:
Heaven's youngest-teemèd star
Hath fixed her polished car,
Her sleeping Lord with handmaid lamp attending;
And all about the courtly stable
Bright-harnessed Angels sit in order serviceable.

JOHN MILTON.

THE CHRONICLE

MARGARITA first possess'd,
If I remember well, my breast,
Margarita, first of all;
But when awhile the wanton maid
With my restless heart had play'd,
Martha took the flying ball.

Martha soon did it resign
To the beauteous Catherine.
  Beauteous Catherine gave place
(Tho' loth and angry she to part
With the possession of my heart)
  To Eliza's conquering face.

Eliza to this hour might reign,
Had she not evil counsels ta'en:
  Fundamental laws she broke,
And still new favourites she chose,
Till up in arms my passions rose,
  And cast away her yoke.

Mary then, and gentle Ann,
Both to reign at once began,
  Alternately they sway'd;
And sometimes Mary was the fair,
And sometimes Ann the crown did wear,
  And sometimes both I obey'd.

Another Mary then arose,
And did rigorous laws impose;
  A mighty tyrant she!
Long, alas, should I have been,
Under that iron-scepter'd queen,
  Had not Rebecca set me free.

When fair Rebecca set me free,
'Twas then a golden time for me,
  But soon those pleasures fled:
For the gracious princess died,
In her youth and beauty's pride,
  And Judith reigned in her stead.

One month, three days, and half an hour,
Judith held the sov'reign pow'r,
  Wondrous beautiful her face;
But so weak and small her wit,
That she to govern was unfit,
  And so Susannah took her place.

But when Isabella came,
Arm'd with a resistless flame,
   And th' artillery of her eye;
While she proudly march'd about
Greater conquests to find out,
   She beat out Susan by the bye.

But in her place I then obey'd
Black-ey'd Bess, her viceroy maid,
   To whom ensued a vacancy;
Thousand worse passions then possess'd
The interregnum of my breast;
   Bless me from such an anarchy!

Gentle Henrietta then,
And a third Mary next began;
   Then Joan, and Jane, and Audria,
And then a pretty Thomasine,
And then another Catharine,
   And then a long et cætera.

But should I now to you relate
The strength and riches of their state,
   The powder, patches, and the pins,
The ribands, jewels, and the rings,
The lace, the paint, and warlike things,
   That make up all their magazines:

If I should tell the politic arts
To take and keep men's hearts;
   The letters, embassies, and spies,
The frowns, the smiles, and flatteries,
The quarrels, tears, and perjuries,
   Numberless, nameless mysteries!

And all the little lime-twigs laid
By Machiavel, the waiting maid;
   I more voluminous should grow
(Chiefly if I, like them, should tell
All change of weather that befel)
   Than Holinshed or Stow.

But I will briefer with them be,
Since few of them were long with me;
    An higher and a nobler strain
My present emperess does claim,
Eleonora, first o' the name,
    Whom God grant long to reign.

ABRAHAM COWLEY.

THE NEW YEAR

HARK! the cock crows, and yon bright star
Tells us the day himself's not far;
And see where, breaking from the night,
He gilds the western hills with light.
With him old Janus doth appear,
Peeping into the future year,
With such a look as seems to say,
The prospect is not good that way.
Thus do we rise ill sights to see,
And 'gainst ourselves to prophesy;
When the prophetic fear of things
A more tormenting mischief brings,
More full of soul-tormenting gall,
Than direct mischiefs can befall.
But stay! but stay! methinks my sight,
Better inform'd by clearer light,
Discerns sereneness in that brow,
That all contracted seem'd but now.
His revers'd face may show distaste,
And frown upon the ills are past;
But that which this way looks is clear,
And smiles upon the New-born Year.
He looks too from a place so high,
The Year lies open to his eye;
And all the moments open are
To the exact discoverer.
Yet more and more he smiles upon
The happy revolution.
Why should we then suspect or fear
The influences of a year,
So smiles upon us the first morn,

And speaks us good so soon as born?
Plague on 't! the last was ill enough,
This cannot but make better proof;
Or, at the worst, as we brush'd through
The last, why so we may this too:
And then the next in reason should
Be superexcellently good:
For the worst ills (we daily see)
Have no more perpetuity,
Than the best fortunes that do fall;
Which also bring us wherewithal
Longer their being to support,
Than those do of the other sort:
And who has one good year in three,
And yet repines at destiny,
Appears ungrateful in the case,
And merits not the good he has.
Then let us welcome the New Guest
With lusty brimmers of the best;
Mirth always should Good Fortune meet,
And render e'en Disaster sweet:
And though the Princess turn her back,
Let us but line ourselves with sack,
We better shall by far hold out,
Till the next Year she face about.

CHARLES COTTON.

THE WORLD

I saw Eternity the other night,
Like a great ring of pure and endless light,
    All calm, as it was bright;
And round beneath it, Time, in hours, days, years,
    Driven by the spheres,
Like a vast shadow moved; In which the world
    And all her train were hurl'd.

The doting Lover in his quaintest strain
    Did there complain;
Near him, his lute, his fancy, and his slights,[1]
    Wit's sour[2] delights;

---

[1] Sleights, tricks.   [2] Perhaps, unsatisfying.

With gloves and knots,[1] the silly snares of pleasure;
　　Yet his dear treasure
All scatter'd lay, while he his eyes did pour
　　Upon a flower.

The darksome Statesman[2] hung with weights and woe,
Like a thick midnight-fog, moved there so slow,
　　He did not stay, nor go;
Condemning thoughts—like sad eclipses—scowl
　　Upon his soul,
And clouds of crying witnesses without
　　Pursued him with one shout;
Yet digg'd the mole, and lest his ways be found,
　　Work'd under ground,
Where he did clutch his prey; but One did see
　　That policy;
Churches and altars fed him; perjuries
　　Were gnats and flies;
It rain'd about him blood and tears, but he
　　Drank them as free.

The fearful Miser on a heap of rust
Sate pining all his life there; did scarce trust
　　His own hands with the dust;
Yet would not place one piece above, but lives
　　In fear of thieves:
Thousands there were as frantic as himself,
　　And hugg'd each one his pelf.
The down-right Epicure placed heaven in sense,
　　And scorn'd pretence;
While others, slipt into a wide excess,
　　Said little less;
The weaker sort, slight, trivial wares enslave,
　　Who think them brave;[3]
And poor, despisèd Truth sat counting by
　　Their victory.

Yet some, who all this while did weep and sing,
And sing, and weep, soar'd up into the ring;
　　But most would use no wing.

[1] Ribbons.
[2] Pym's career, with O. Cromwell's by poetic insight, is here (1650) unquestionably photographed.
[3] Magnificent.

O fools—said I—thus to prefer dark night
  Before true light!
To live in grots, and caves, and hate the day
  Because it shews the way:—
The way, which from this dead and dark abode
  Leads up to GOD;
A way where you might tread the Sun, and be
  More bright than he!
But as I did their madness so discuss,
  One whisper'd thus,—
This ring the Bride-groom did for none provide,
  But for His Bride.

        HENRY VAUGHAN.

HOME

WHAT is House and what is Home,
Where with freedom thou hast room,
And may'st to all tyrants say,
This you cannot take away?
'Tis no thing with doors and walls,
Which at every earthquake falls;
No fair towers, whose princely fashion
Is but Plunder's invitation;
No stout marble structure, where
Walls Eternity do dare;
No brass gates, no bars of steel,
Tho' Time's teeth they scorn to feel:
Brass is not so bold as Pride,
If on Power's wings it ride;
Marble's not so hard as Spite
Arm'd with lawless Strength and Might.
Right and just Possession, be
Potent names, when Laws stand free:
But if once that rampart fall,
Stoutest thieves inherit all:
To be rich and weak's a sure
And sufficient forfeiture.

 Seek no more abroad, say I,
House and Home, but turn thine eye

Inward, and observe thy breast;
There alone dwells solid Rest.
That's a close immurèd tower
Which can mock all hostile power.
To thyself a tenant be,
And inhabit safe and free.
Say not that this House is small,
Girt up in a narrow wall:
In a cleanly sober mind
Heaven itself full room doth find
Th' Infinite CREATOR can
Dwell in it; and may not Man?
Here content make thy abode
With thyself and with thy GOD.
Here in this sweet privacy
May'st thou with thyself agree,
And keep House in peace, tho' all
Th' Universe's fabric fall.
No disaster can distress thee,
Nor no Fury dispossess thee:
Let all war and plunder come,
Still may'st thou dwell safe at Home.

Home is everywhere to thee,
Who can'st thine own dwelling be;
Yea, tho' ruthless Death assail thee,
Still thy lodging will not fail thee;
Still thy Soul's thine own; and she
To an House removed shall be;
An eternal House above,
Wall'd, and roof'd, and paved with Love.
There shall these mud-walls of thine,
Gallantly repair'd, out-shine
Mortal Stars;—No Stars shall be
In that Heaven but such as Thee.

JOSEPH BEAUMONT.

THE HERMIT

FAR in a wild, unknown to public view,
From youth to age a reverend Hermit grew,
The moss his bed, the cave his humble cell,
His food the fruits, his drink the crystal well,
Remote from man, with God he pass'd his days,
Prayer all his business, all his pleasure praise.

A life so sacred, such serene repose,
Seem'd Heaven itself, till one suggestion rose—
That vice should triumph, virtue vice obey;
This sprung some doubt of Providence's sway:
His hopes no more a certain prospect boast,
And all the tenor of his soul is lost.
So when a smooth expanse receives imprest
Calm nature's image on its watery breast,
Down bend the banks, the trees depending grow,
And skies beneath with answering colours glow;
But if a stone the gentle sea divide,
Swift rushing circles curl on every side,
And glimmering fragments of a broken sun:
Banks, trees, and skies, in thick disorder run.

To clear this doubt, to know the world by sight,
To find if books, or swains report it right
(For yet by swains alone the world he knew,
Whose feet came wandering o'er the nightly dew),
He quits his cell: the pilgrim-staff he bore,
And fix'd the scallop in his hat before,
Then with the sun a rising journey went,
Sedate to think, and watching each event.

The morn was wasted in the pathless grass,
And long and lonesome was the wild to pass:
But when the southern sun had warm'd the day,
A youth came posting o'er a crossing way;
His raiment decent, his complexion fair,
And soft in graceful ringlets wav'd his hair;
Then near approaching, " Father, hail ! " he cried;
And " Hail, my son ! " the reverend sire replied:
Words follow'd words, from question answer flow'd,
And talk of various kind deceiv'd the road;
Till each with other pleas'd, and loth to part,
While in their age they differ, join in heart.

Thus stands an aged elm in ivy bound,
Thus youthful ivy clasps an elm around.
  Now sunk the sun; the closing hour of day
Came onward, mantled o'er with sober grey;
Nature in silence bid the world repose:
When near the road a stately palace rose:
There, by the moon, thro' ranks of trees they pass,
Whose verdure crown'd their sloping sides of grass.
It chanc'd the noble master of the dome
Still made his house the wandering stranger's home;
Yet still the kindness, from a thirst of praise,
Prov'd the vain flourish of expensive ease.
The pair arrive: the liveried servants wait;
Their lord receives them at the pompous gate.
The table groans with costly piles of food,
And all is more than hospitably good.
Then, led to rest, the day's long toil they drown,
Deep sunk in sleep, and silk, and heaps of down.
  At length 'tis morn, and at the dawn of day
Along the wide canals the zephyrs play;
Fresh o'er the gay parterres the breezes creep,
And shake the neighbouring wood to banish sleep.
Uprise the guests, obedient to the call;
An early banquet deck'd the splendid hall;
Rich luscious wine a golden goblet grac'd,
Which the kind master forc'd the guests to taste.
Then, pleas'd and thankful, from the porch they go:
And, but the landlord, none had cause of woe:
His cup was vanish'd; for in secret guise
The younger guest purloin'd the glittering prize.
As one who spies a serpent in his way,
Glistening and basking in the summer ray,
Disorder'd stops to shun the danger near,
Then walks with faintness on, and looks with fear;
So seem'd the sire, when far upon the road
The shining spoil his wily partner show'd.
He stopp'd with silence, walk'd with trembling heart,
And much he wish'd, but durst not ask, to part:
Murmuring he lifts his eyes, and thinks it hard
That generous actions meet a base reward.
  While thus they pass, the sun his glory shrouds,
The changing skies hang out their sable clouds;
A sound in air presag'd approaching rain,

And beasts to covert scud across the plain.
Warn'd by the signs, the wandering pair retreat
To seek for shelter at a neighbouring seat:
'Twas built with turrets on a rising ground,
And strong, and large, and unimprov'd around;
Its owner's temper, timorous and severe,
Unkind and griping, caus'd a desert there.
As near the miser's heavy doors they drew,
Fierce rising gusts with sudden fury blew;
The nimble lightning mix'd with showers began,
And o'er their heads loud rolling thunder ran.
Here long they knock, but knock or call in vain,
Driv'n by the wind, and batter'd by the rain.
At length some pity warm'd the master's breast
('Twas then his threshold first receiv'd a guest:)
Slow creeking turns the door with jealous care,
And half he welcomes in the shivering pair;
One frugal faggot lights the naked walls,
And nature's fervor thro' their limbs recals:
Bread of the coarsest sort with meagre wine,
(Each hardly granted) serv'd them both to dine;
And when the tempest first appear'd to cease,
A ready warning bid them part in peace.

    With still remark the pondering Hermit view'd,
In one so rich, a life so poor and rude;
And why should such (within himself he cried)
Lock the lost wealth a thousand want beside?
But what new marks of wonder soon take place
In every setting feature of his face,
When from his vest the young companion bore
That cup the generous landlord own'd before,
And paid profusely with the precious bowl
The stinted kindness of this churlish soul!

    But now the clouds in airy tumult fly;
The sun emerging opes an azure sky;
A fresher green the smelling leaves display,
And glittering as they tremble, cheer the day:
The weather courts them from the poor retreat,
And the glad master bolts the wary gate.

    While hence they walk, the Pilgrim's bosom wrought
With all the travail of uncertain thought;
His partner's acts without their cause appear;
'Twas there a vice, and seem'd a madness here:

Detesting that, and pitying this, he goes,
Lost and confounded with the various shows.
　Now night's dim shades again involve the sky,
Again the wanderers want a place to lie;
Again they search, and find a lodging nigh.
The soil improv'd around, the mansion neat,
And neither poorly low, nor idly great,
It seem'd to speak its master's turn of mind,
Content, and not for praise but virtue kind.
　Hither the walkers turn with weary feet,
Then bless the mansion, and the master greet.
Their greeting fair, bestow'd with modest guise,
The courteous master hears, and thus replies:
　" Without a vain, without a grudging heart,
To him who gives us all, I yield a part;
From him you come, for him accept it here,
A frank and sober, more than costly cheer."
He spoke, and bid the welcome table spread,
Then talk'd of virtue till the time of bed;
When the grave household round his hall repair,
Warn'd by a bell, and close the hours with prayer.
At length the world, renew'd by calm repose,
Was strong for toil; the dappled morn arose;
Before the pilgrims part, the younger crept,
Near the clos'd cradle, where an infant slept
And writh'd his neck; the landlord's little pride,
O strange return! grew black, and gasp'd, and died.
Horror of horrors! what! his only son!
How look'd our Hermit when the fact was done!
Not hell, tho' hell's black jaws in sunder part,
And breathe blue fire, could more assault his heart.
　Confus'd and struck with silence at the deed,
He flies; but, trembling, fails to fly with speed.
His steps the youth pursues; the country lay
Perplex'd with roads; a servant show'd the way:
A river cross'd the path; the passage o'er
Was nice to find; the servant trod before:
Long arms of oak an open bridge supplied,
And deep the waves beneath the bending branches glide.
The youth, who seem'd to watch a time to sin,
Approach'd the careless guide and thrust him in:
Plunging he falls, and rising lifts his head:
Then flashing turns, and sinks among the dead,

Wild flashing rage inflames the father's eyes;
He bursts the bands of fear, and madly cries,
" Detested wretch! "—But scarce his speech began,
When the strange partner seem'd no longer man:
His youthful face grew more serenely sweet:
His robe turn'd white, and flow'd upon his feet;
Fair rounds of radiant points invest his hair;
Celestial odours breathe thro' purpled air;
And wings, whose colours glitter'd on the day,
Wide at his back their gradual plumes display,
The form etherial bursts upon his sight,
And moves in all the majesty of light.

Tho' loud at first the Pilgrim's passion grew,
Sudden he gaz'd, and wist not what to do;
Surprise in secret chains his words suspends,
And in a calm his settling temper ends.
But silence here the beauteous angel broke
(The voice of music ravish'd as he spoke:)

" Thy prayer, thy praise, thy life to vice unknown,
In sweet memorial rise before the throne:
These charms success in our bright region find,
And force an angel down to calm thy mind;
For this commission'd, I forsook the sky—
Nay, cease to kneel!—thy fellow-servant I.

" Then know the truth of government Divine,
And let these scruples be no longer thine.

" The Maker justly claims that world he made,
In this the right of Providence is laid;
Its sacred majesty thro' all depends
On using second means to work his ends;
'Tis thus, withdrawn in state from human eye,
The Power exerts his attributes on high;
Your actions uses, nor controls your will,
And bids the doubting sons of men be still.

' What strange events can strike with more surprise,
Than those which lately struck thy wondering eyes?
Yet, taught by these, confess the Almighty just;
And, where you can't unriddle, learn to trust.

" The great, vain man, who far'd on costly food,
Whose life was too luxurious to be good;
Who made his ivory stands with goblets shine,
And forc'd his guests to morning draughts of wine;
Has, with the cup, the graceless custom lost,

And still he welcomes, but with less of cost.
"The mean suspicious wretch, whose bolted door
Ne'er mov'd in pity to the wandering poor,
With him I left the cup to teach his mind
That Heaven can bless, if mortals will be kind.
Conscious of wanting worth, he views the bowl,
And feels compassion touch his grateful soul.
Thus artists melt the sullen ore of lead,
With heaving coals of fire upon its head;
In the kind warmth the metal learns to glow,
And, loose from dross, the silver runs below.
"Long had our pious friend in virtue trod,
But now the child half-wean'd his heart from God;
(Child of his age) for him he liv'd in pain,
And measur'd back his steps to earth again.
To what excesses had his dotage run!
But God, to save the father, took the son.
To all but thee in fits he seem'd to go;
And 'twas my ministry to deal the blow.
The poor fond parent, humbled in the dust,
Now owns in tears the punishment was just.
"But how had all his fortunes felt a wrack,
Had that false servant sped in safety back!
This night his treasur'd heaps he meant to steal,
And what a fund of charity would fail!
Thus heaven instructs thy mind: this trial o'er,
Depart in peace, resign, and sin no more."
On sounding pinions here the youth withdrew!
The sage stood wondering as the seraph flew.
Thus look'd Elisha, when to mount on high,
His master took the chariot of the sky:
The fiery pomp ascending left the view;
The prophet gaz'd, and wish'd to follow too.
The bending Hermit here a prayer begun:
Lord! as in heaven, on earth thy will be done.
Then, gladly turning, sought his ancient place,
And pass'd a life of piety and peace.

THOMAS PARNELL.

PROTOGENES AND APELLES

When poets wrote and painters drew,
As nature pointed out the view;
Ere Gothic forms were known in Greece,
To spoil the well-proportioned piece;
And in our verse ere monkish rhymes
Had jangled their fantastic chimes;
Ere on the flowery lands of Rhodes,
Those knights had fixed their dull abodes,
Who knew not much to paint or write,
Nor cared to pray, nor dared to fight:
Protogenes, historians note,
Lived there, a burgess, scot and lot;
And as old Pliny's writings shew,
Apelles did the same at Co.
Agreed these points of time and place,
Proceed we in the present case.
Piqued by Protogenes's fame,
From Co to Rhodes Apelles came,
To see a rival and a friend,
Prepared to censure, or commend;
Here to absolve, and there object,
As art with candour might direct.
He sails—he lands—he comes—he rings;
His servants follow with the things:
Appears the governante of th' house,
For such in Greece were much in use
If young or handsome, yea or no,
Concerns not me or thee to know.
    "Does Squire Protogenes live here?"
"Yes, sir," says she, with gracious air
And curtsy low; "but just called out
By lords peculiarly devout,
Who came on purpose, sir, to borrow
Our Venus for the feast to-morrow,
To grace the church; 'tis Venus' day:
I hope, sir, you intend to stay,
To see our Venus? 'tis the piece
The most renowned throughout all Greece;
So like th' original, they say:

But I have no great skill that way.
But, sir, at six—'tis now past three—
Dromo must make my master's tea:
At six, sir, if you please to come,
You'll find my master, sir, at home."

    " Tea," says a critic big with laughter,
" Was found some twenty ages after;
Authors, before they write, should read."
'Tis very true; but we'll proceed.

    " And, sir, at present would you please
To leave your name."—" Fair maiden, yes.
Reach me that board."   No sooner spoke
But done.   With one judicious stroke,
On the plain ground Apelles drew
A circle regularly true:
" And will you please, sweetheart," said he,
" To show your master this from me?
By it he presently will know
How painters write their names at Co."
He gave the panel to the maid.
Smiling and curtseying, " Sir," she said,
" I shall not fail to tell my master:
And, sir, for fear of all disaster,
I'll keep it my own self: safe bind,
Says the old proverb, and safe find.
So, sir, as sure as key or lock—
Your servant, sir—at six o'clock."

    Again at six Apelles came,
Found the same prating civil dame.
" Sir, that my master has been here,
Will by the board itself appear.
If from the perfect line be found
He has presumed to swell the round,
Or colours on the draught to lay,
' 'Tis thus '—he ordered me to say—
' Thus write the painters of this isle;
Let those of Co remark the style.' "

    She said, and to his hand restored
The rival pledge, the missive board.
Upon the happy line were laid
Such obvious light and easy shade,
The Paris' apple stood confessed,
Or Leda's egg, or Chloe's breast.

Apelles viewed the finished piece;
"And live," said he, "the arts of Greece!
Howe'er Protogenes and I
May in our rival talents vie;
Howe'er our works may have expressed
Who truest drew, or coloured best,
When he beheld my flowing line,
He found at least I could design:
And from his artful round, I grant,
That he with perfect skill can paint."

    The dullest genius cannot fail
To find the moral of my tale;
That the distinguished part of men,
With compass, pencil, sword, or pen,
Should in life's visit leave their name
In characters which may proclaim
That they with ardour strove to raise
At once their arts and country's praise;
And in their working, took great care
That all was full, and round, and fair.

                        MATTHEW PRIOR.

BAUCIS AND PHILEMON

[IMITATED FROM THE EIGHTH BOOK OF OVID]

IN ancient times, as story tells,
The saints would often leave their cells,
And stroll about, but hide their quality,
To try good people's hospitality.
    It happened on a winter night—
As authors of the legend write—
Two brother-hermits, saints by trade,
Taking their tour in masquerade,
Disguised in tattered habits, went
To a small village down in Kent;
Where, in the strollers' canting strain,
They begged from door to door in vain;
Tried every tone might pity win,
But not a soul would let them in.

Our wandering saints in woful state,
Treated at this ungodly rate,
Having through all the village past,
To a small cottage came at last,
Where dwelt a good old honest yeoman,
Called in the neighbourhood Philemon,
Who kindly did the saints invite
In his poor hut to pass the night.
And then the hospitable sire
Bid Goody Baucis mend the fire,
While he from out the chimney took
A flitch of bacon off the hook,
And freely from the fattest side
Cut out large slices to be fried;
Then stepped aside to fetch them drink,
Filled a large jug up to the brink,
And saw it fairly twice go round;
Yet—what was wonderful—they found
'Twas still replenished to the top,
As if they ne'er had touched a drop.
The good old couple were amazed,
And often on each other gazed:
For both were frighted to the heart,
And just began to cry: " What art? "
Then softly turned aside to view
Whether the lights were burning blue.
The gentle pilgrims, soon aware on 't,
Told them their calling and their errant:
" Good folks, you need not be afraid,
We are but saints," the hermits said;
" No hurt shall come to you or yours;
But, for that pack of churlish boors,
Not fit to live on Christian ground,
They and their houses shall be drowned:
While you shall see your cottage rise,
And grow a church before your eyes."

They scarce had spoke, when fair and soft,
The roof began to mount aloft;
Aloft rose every beam and rafter,
The heavy wall climbed slowly after.

The chimney widened, and grew higher,
Became a steeple with a spire.

The kettle to the top was hoist,

And there stood fastened to a joist;
But with the up-side down, to shew
Its inclination for below:
In vain; for some superior force,
Applied at bottom, stops its course;
Doomed ever in suspense to dwell,
'Tis now no kettle, but a bell.

A wooden jack, which had almost
Lost by disuse the art to roast,
A sudden alteration feels,
Increased by new intestine wheels:
And, what exalts the wonder more,
The number made the motion slower;
The flier, which, thought 't had leaden feet,
Turned round so quick, you scarce could see 't.
Now, slackened by some secret power,
Can hardly move an inch an hour.
The jack and chimney, near allied,
Had never left each other's side:
The chimney to a steeple grown,
The jack would not be left alone;
But, up against the steeple reared,
Became a clock, and still adhered:
And still its love to household cares,
By a shrill voice at noon, declares;
Warning the cook-maid not to burn
That roast meat, which it cannot turn.

The groaning chair was seen to crawl,
Like a huge snail, half up the wall;
There stuck aloft in public view,
And, with small-change, a pulpit grew.

The porringers, that in a row
Hung high, and made a glittering show,
To a less noble substance changed,
Were now but leathern buckets ranged.

The ballads pasted on the wall,
Of Joan of France, and English Moll,
Fair Rosamond, and Robin Hood,
The Little Children in the Wood,
Now seemed to look abundance better,
Improved in picture, size, and letter;
And high in order placed, describe
The heraldry of every tribe.

A bedstead of the antique mode,
Compact of timber many a load;
Such as our grandsires wont to use,
Was metamorphosed into pews;
Which still their ancient nature keep,
By lodging folk disposed to sleep.

The cottage, by such feats as these,
Grown to a church by just degrees;
The hermits then desire their host
To ask for what he fancied most.
Philemon, having paused a while,
Returned them thanks in homely style;
Then said: " My house is grown so fine,
Methinks I still would call it mine:
I'm old, and fain would live at ease;
Make me the parson, if you please."
He spoke, and presently he feels
His grazier's coat fall down his heels:
He sees, yet hardly can believe,
About each arm a pudding sleeve:
His waistcoat to a cassock grew,
And both assumed a sable hue;
But, being old, continued just
As threadbare and as full of dust.
His talk was now of tithes and dues;
Could smoke his pipe and read the news:
Knew how to preach old sermons next,
Vamped in the preface and the text:
At christenings well could act his part,
And had the service all by heart:
Wished women might have children fast,
And thought whose sow had farrowed last:
Against dissenters would repine,
And stood up firm for right divine:
Found his head filled with many a system,
But classic authors—he ne'er missed them.

Thus having furbished up a parson,
Dame Baucis next they played their farce on:
Instead of homespun coifs, were seen
Good pinners, edged with Colberteen:
Her petticoat, transformed apace,
Became black satin flounced with lace.
Plain Goody would no longer down;

'Twas Madam, in her grogram gown.
Philemon was in great surprise,
And hardly could believe his eyes
Amazed to see her look so prim;
And she admired as much at him.

Thus, happy in their change of life,
Were several years the man and wife:
When on a day, which proved their last,
Discoursing o'er old stories past,
They went by chance, amidst their talk,
To the churchyard to fetch a walk;
When Baucis hastily cried out:
" My dear, I see your forehead sprout!"
" Sprout," quoth the man, " what's this you tell us?
I hope you don't believe me jealous?
But, yet, methinks, I feel it true;
And really yours is budding too——
Nay—— Now I cannot stir my foot;
It feels as if 'twere taking root."

Description would but tire my Muse;
In short, they both were turned to yews.

Old Goodman Dobson, of the green,
Remembers he the trees hath seen;
He'll talk of them from noon to night,
And goes with folks to shew the sight;
On Sundays, after evening-prayer,
He gathers all the parish there;
Points out the place of either yew,
Here Baucis, there Philemon grew.
'Till once a parson of our town,
To mend his barn, cut Baucis down;
At which, 'tis hard to be believed,
How much the other tree was grieved;
Grew scrubby, died a-top, was stunted;
So the next parson stubbed and burnt it.

JONATHAN SWIFT.

THE SECOND EPISTLE OF THE ESSAY ON MAN

ARGUMENT.—I. The business of man not to pry into God, but to study himself. His middle nature; his powers and frailties, ver. 1–19. The limits of his capacity, ver. 19, etc.—II. The two principles of man, self-love and reason, both necessary, ver. 53, etc. Self-love the stronger, and why, ver. 67, etc. Their end the same, ver. 81, etc.—III. The passions, and their use, ver. 93–130. The predominant passion, and its force, ver. 132–160. Its necessity, in directing men to different purposes, ver. 165, etc. Its providential use, in fixing our principle, and ascertaining our virtues, ver. 177.—IV. Virtue and vice joined in our mixed nature; the limits near, yet the things separate and evident: What is the office of reason, ver. 202–216.—V. How odious vice in itself, and how we deceive ourselves into it, ver. 217.—VI. That, however, the ends of Providence and general good are answered in our passions and imperfections, ver. 238, etc. How usefully these are distributed to all orders of men, ver. 241. How useful they are to society, ver. 251. And to individuals, ver. 263. In every state, and every age of life, ver. 273, etc.

I. Know then thyself, presume not God to scan;
The proper study of mankind is man.
Placed on this isthmus of a middle state,
A being darkly wise, and rudely great:
With too much knowledge for the sceptic side,
With too much weakness for the stoic's pride,
He hangs between; in doubt to act, or rest;
In doubt to deem himself a god, or beast;
In doubt his mind or body to prefer;
Born but to die, and reasoning but to err;
Alike in ignorance, his reason such,
Whether he thinks too little, or too much:
Chaos of thought and passion, all confused;
Still by himself abused, or disabused;
Created half to rise, and half to fall;
Great lord of all things, yet a prey to all;
Sole judge of truth, in endless error hurled:
The glory, jest, and riddle of the world!

Go, wondrous creature! mount where science guides,
Go, measure earth, weigh air, and state the tides;
Instruct the planets in what orbs to run,
Correct old time, and regulate the sun;
Go, soar with Plato to the empyreal sphere,
To the first good, first perfect, and first fair;
Or tread the mazy round his followers trod,
And quitting sense call imitating God;[1]

[1] The new platonics taught by Ammonius Saccas towards the end of the second century.

As eastern priests in giddy circles run,
And turn their heads to imitate the sun.
Go, teach eternal wisdom how to rule—
Then drop into thyself, and be a fool!

Superior beings, when of late they saw
A mortal man unfold all nature's law,
Admired such wisdom in an earthly shape,
And showed a Newton as we show an ape.

Could he, whose rules the rapid comet bind,
Describe or fix one movement of his mind?
Who saw its fires here rise, and there descend,
Explain his own beginning, or his end?
Alas, what wonder! man's superior part
Unchecked may rise, and climb from art to art;
But when his own great work is but begun,
What reason weaves, by passion is undone.

Trace science then, with modesty thy guide;
First strip off all her equipage of pride;
Deduct what is but vanity, or dress
Or learning's luxury, or idleness;
Or tricks to show the stretch of human brain,
Mere curious pleasure, or ingenious pain;
Expunge the whole, or lop the excrescent parts
Of all our vices have created arts;
Then see how little the remaining sum,
Which served the past, and must the times to come!

II. Two principles in human nature reign;
Self-love, to urge, and reason, to restrain;
Nor this a good, nor that a bad we call,
Each works its end, to move or govern all:
And to their proper operation still,
Ascribe all good; to their improper, ill.

Self-love, the spring of motion, acts[1] the soul;
Reason's comparing balance rules the whole.
Man, but for that, no action could attend,
And but for this, were active to no end:
Fixed like a plant on his peculiar spot,
To draw nutrition, propagate, and rot;
Or, meteor-like, flame lawless through the void,
Destroying others, by himself destroyed.

Most strength the moving principle requires;
Active its task, it prompts, impels, inspires.

[1] Used for " actuates."

Sedate and quiet the comparing lies,
Formed but to check, deliberate, and advise.
Self-love still stronger, as its object's nigh;
Reason's at distance, and in prospect lie:
That sees immediate good by present sense;
Reason, the future and the consequence.
Thicker than arguments, temptations throng,
At best more watchful this, but that more strong.
The action of the stronger to suspend,
Reason still use, to reason still attend.
Attention, habit and experience gains;
Each strengthens reason, and self-love restrains.

Let subtle schoolmen teach these friends to fight,
More studious to divide than to unite;
And grace and virtue, sense and reason split,
With all the rash dexterity of wit.
Wits, just like fools, at war about a name,
Have full as oft no meaning, or the same.
Self-love and reason to one end aspire,
Pain their aversion, pleasure their desire;
But greedy that, its object would devour,
This taste the honey, and not wound the flow'r;
Pleasure, or wrong or rightly understood,
Our greatest evil, or our greatest good.

II. Modes of self-love the passions we may call
'Tis real good, or seeming, moves them all:
But since not ev'ry good we can divide,
And reason bids us for our own provide;
Passions, though selfish, if their means be fair,
List under reason, and deserve her care;
Those, that imparted, court a nobler aim,
Exalt their kind, and take some virtue's name.

In lazy apathy let stoics boast
Their virtue fixed; 'tis fixed as in a frost;
Contracted all, retiring to the breast;
But strength of mind is exercise, not rest:
The rising tempest puts in act the soul,
Parts it may ravage, but preserves the whole.
On life's vast ocean diversely we sail,
Reason the card,[1] but passion is the gale;
Nor God alone in the still calm we find,

[1] The "card" on which the points of the mariner's compass are marked, signifies of course the compass itself.

He mounts the storm, and walks upon the wind.
　Passions, like elements, though born to fight,
Yet, mixed and softened, in His work unite:
These 'tis enough to temper and employ;
But what composes man, can man destroy?
Suffice that reason keep to nature's road,
Subject, compound them, follow her and God.
Love, hope, and joy, fair pleasure's smiling train,
Hate, fear, and grief, the family of pain,
These mixed with art, and to due bounds confined,
Make and maintain the balance of the mind:
The lights and shades, whose well-accorded strife
Gives all the strength and colour of our life.
　Pleasures are ever in our hands or eyes;
And when in act they cease, in prospect rise;
Present to grasp, and future still to find,
The whole employ of body and of mind.
All spread their charms, but charm not all alike;
On diff'rent senses diff'rent objects strike;
Hence diff'rent passions more or less inflame,
As strong or weak the organs of the frame;
And hence one master passion in the breast,
Like Aaron's serpent, swallows up the rest.
　As man, perhaps, the moment of his breath,
Receives the lurking principle of death;
The young disease, that must subdue at length,
Grows with his growth, and strengthens with his strength:
So, cast and mingled with his very frame,
The mind's disease, its ruling passion came;
Each vital humour which should feel the whole,
Soon flows to this, in body and in soul:
Whatever warms the heart, or fills the head,
As the mind opens, and its functions spread,
Imagination plies her dang'rous art,
And pours it all upon the peccant part.
　Nature its mother, habit is its nurse;
Wit, spirit, faculties, but make it worse;
Reason itself but gives it edge and power;
As heaven's blest beam turns vinegar more sour.
　We, wretched subjects, though to lawful sway,
In this weak queen some fav'rite still obey:
Ah! if she lent not arms, as well as rules,
What can she more than tell us we are fools?

Teach us to mourn our nature, not to mend,
A sharp accuser, but a helpless friend!
Or from a judge turn pleader, to persuade
The choice we make, or justify it made:
Proud of an easy conquest all along,
She but removes weak passions for the strong:
So, when small humours gather to a gout,
The doctor fancies he has driven them out.

Yes, nature's road must ever be preferred:
Reason is here no guide, but still a guard:
'Tis hers to rectify, not overthrow,
And treat this passion more as friend than foe:
A mightier pow'r the strong direction sends,
And sev'ral men impels to sev'ral ends:
Like varying winds, by other passions tost,
This drives them constant to a certain coast.
Let power or knowledge, gold or glory, please,
Or (oft more strong than all) the love of ease;
Through life 'tis followed, even at life's expense;
The merchant's toil, the sage's indolence,
The monk's humility, the hero's pride,
All, all alike, find reason on their side.

The Eternal Art educing good from ill,
Grafts on this passion our best principle:
'Tis thus the mercury of man is fixed,
Strong grows the virtue with his nature mixed;
The dross cements what else were too refined,
And in one int'rest body acts with mind.

As fruits, ungrateful to the planter's care,
On savage stocks inserted learn to bear;
The surest virtues thus from passions shoot,
Wild nature's vigour working at the root.
What crops of wit and honesty appear
From spleen, from obstinacy, hate, or fear!
See anger, zeal and fortitude supply;
Even avarice, prudence; sloth, philosophy;
Lust, through some certain strainers well refined,
Is gentle love, and charms all womankind;
Envy, to which the ignoble mind's a slave,
Is emulation in the learned or brave;
Nor virtue, male or female, can we name,
But what will grow on pride, or grow on shame.

Thus nature gives us (let us check our pride)

The virtue nearest to our vice allied:
Reason the bias turns to good from ill,
And Nero reigns a Titus, if he will.
The fiery soul abhorred in Catiline,
In Decius charms, in Curtius is divine:[1]
The same ambition can destroy or save,
And makes a patriot as it makes a knave.

  This light and darkness in our chaos joined,
What shall divide? The God within the mind:[2]

  Extremes in nature equal ends produce,
In man they join to some mysterious use;
Though each by turns the other's bound invade,
As, in some well-wrought picture, light and shade,
And oft so mix, the diff'rence is too nice
Where ends the virtue, or begins the vice.

  Fools! who from hence into the notion fall,
That vice or virtue there is none at all.
If white and black blend, soften, and unite
A thousand ways, is there no black or white?
Ask your own heart, and nothing is so plain;
'Tis to mistake them, costs the time and pain.

  Vice is a monster of so frightful mien,
As, to be hated, needs but to be seen:
Yet seen too oft, familiar with her face,
We first endure, then pity, then embrace.
But where the extreme of vice, was ne'er agreed:
Ask where's the north? at York, 'tis on the Tweed;
In Scotland, at the Orcades; and there,
At Greenland, Zembla, or the Lord knows where.
No creature owns it in the first degree,
But thinks his neighbour further gone than he;
Even those who dwell beneath its very zone,
Or never feel the rage, or never own;
What happier natures shrink at with affright,
The hard inhabitant contends is right.

  Virtuous and vicious ev'ry man must be,
Few in the extreme, but all in the degree;

---

[1] Decius, who devoted himself to the infernal gods, and rushed to
his death in battle because he had learned in a vision that the army
would be victorious whose generals should fall. Curtius leaped into a
gulf which had opened in the Roman Forum, and could not be closed
till the most valuable thing to Rome had been cast in. It was a warrior
on his horse and in his armour.

[2] Conscience; a sublime expression of Plato's.

The rogue and fool by fits is fair and wise;
And even the best, by fits, what they despise,
'Tis but by parts we follow good or ill;
For, vice or virtue, self directs it still;
Each individual seeks a sev'ral goal;
But Heav'n's great view is one, and that the whole.
That counter-works each folly and caprice;
That disappoints the effect of every vice;
That, happy frailties to all ranks applied,
Shame to the virgin, to the matron pride,
Fear to the statesman, rashness to the chief,
To kings presumption, and to crowds belief;
That, virtue's ends from vanity can raise,
Which seeks no int'rest, no reward but praise;
And build on wants, and on defects of mind,
The joy, the peace, the glory of mankind.
    Heav'n forming each on other to depend,
A master, or a servant, or a friend,
Bids each on other for assistance call,
Till one man's weakness grows the strength of all.
Wants, frailties, passions, closer still ally
The common interest, or endear the tie.
To these we owe true friendship, love sincere,
Each home-felt joy that life inherits here;
Yet from the same we learn, in its decline,
Those joys, those loves, those interests to resign;
Taught half by reason, half by mere decay,
To welcome death, and calmly pass away.
    Whate'er the passion, knowledge, fame, or pelf,
Not one will change his neighbour with himself.
The learned is happy nature to explore,
The fool is happy that he knows no more;
The rich is happy in the plenty giv'n,
The poor contents him with the care of heav'n.
See the blind beggar dance, the cripple sing,
The sot a hero, lunatic a king;
The starving chemist in his golden views[1]
Supremely blest, the poet in his muse.
    See some strange comfort ev'ry state attend,
And pride bestowed on all, a common friend;
See some fit passion ev'ry age supply.
Hope travels through, nor quits us when we die.

[1] The alchemist in search of the Philosopher's Stone.

Behold the child, by Nature's kindly law,
Pleased with a rattle, tickled with a straw:
Some livelier play-thing gives his youth delight,
A little louder, but as empty quite:
Scarfs, garters, gold, amuse his riper stage,
And beads and prayer-books are the toys of age:
Pleased with this bauble still, as that before;
'Till tired he sleeps, and life's poor play is o'er.
  Meanwhile opinion gilds with varying rays
Those painted clouds that beautify our days;
Each want of happiness by hope supplied,
And each vacuity of sense by pride:
These build as fast as knowledge can destroy;
In folly's cup still laughs the bubble, joy;
One prospect lost, another still we gain;
And not a vanity is given in vain,
Even mean self-love becomes, by force divine,
The scale to measure others' wants by thine.
See! and confess, one comfort still must rise,
'Tis this, Though man's a fool, yet God is wise.

POPE.

A NOCTURNAL REVERIE

In such a Night, when every louder Wind
Is to its distant Cavern safe confin'd;
And only gentle Zephyr fans his Wings,
And lonely Philomel, still waking, sings;
Or from some Tree, fam'd for the Owl's delight;
She, hollowing clear, directs the Wand'rer right:
In such a Night, when passing Clouds give place,
Or thinly veil the Heav'ns mysterious Face;
When in some River, overhung with Green,
The waving Moon and trembling Leaves are seen;
When freshen'd Grass now bears it self upright,
And makes cool Banks to pleasing Rest invite,
Whence springs the Woodbine, and the Bramble-Rose,
And where the sleepy Cowslip shelter'd grows;
Whilst now a paler Hue the Foxglove takes,
Yet checquers still with Red the dusky brakes:
When scatter'd Glow-worms, but in Twilight fine,
Shew trivial Beauties watch their Hour to shine;

Whilst Salisb'ry stands the Test of every Light,
In perfect Charms, and perfect Virtue bright:
When Odours, which declin'd repelling Day,
Thro' temp'rate Air uninterrupted stray;
When darken'd Groves their softest Shadows wear,
And falling Waters we distinctly hear;
When thro' the Gloom more venerable shows
Some ancient Fabric, awful in Repose,
While Sunburnt Hills their swarthy Looks conceal,
And swelling Haycocks thicken up the Vale:
When the loos'd Horse now, as his Pasture leads,
Comes slowly grazing thro' th' adjoining Meads,
Whose stealing pace, and lengthen'd Shade we fear,
Till torn up Forage in his Teeth we hear:
When nibbling Sheep at large pursue their Food,
And unmolested Kine rechew the Cud;
When Curlews cry beneath the Village-walls,
And to her straggling Brood the Partridge calls;
Their shortliv'd Jubilee the Creatures keep,
Which but endures, whilst Tyrant-Man do's sleep:
When a sedate Content the Spirit feels,
And no fierce Light disturbs, whilst it reveals;
But silent Musings urge the Mind to seek
Something, too high for Syllables to speak;
Till the free Soul to a compos'dness charm'd,
Finding the Elements of Rage disarm'd,
O'er all below a solemn Quiet grown,
Joys in th' inferior World, and thinks it like her Own:
In such a Night let Me abroad remain,
Till Morning breaks, and All's confus'd again;
Our Cares, our Toils, our Clamours are renew'd,
Or Pleasures, seldom reach'd, again pursu'd.

COUNTESS OF WINCHILSEA.

GRONGAR HILL

SILENT Nymph! with curious eye,
Who the purple ev'ning lie
On the mountain's lonely van,
Beyond the noise of busy man,
Painting fair the form of things,

While the yellow linnet sings,
Or the tuneful nightingale
Charms the forest with her tale;
Come, with all thy various hues,
Come, and aid thy sister Muse;
Now, while Phœbus, riding high,
Gives lustre to the land and sky,
Grongar Hill invites my song,
Draw the landscape bright and strong;
Grongar! in whose mossy cells,
Sweetly musing, Quiet dwells;
Grongar! in whose silent shade,
For the modest Muses made,
So oft I have, the ev'ning still,
At the fountain of a rill
Sat upon a flow'ry bed,
With my hand beneath my head,
While stray'd my eyes o'er Towy's flood,
Over mead and over wood,
From house to house, from hill to hill,
Till Contemplation had her fill.
 About his chequer'd sides I wind,
And leave his brooks and meads behind,
And groves and grottoes where I lay,
And vistas shooting beams of day.
Wide and wider spreads the vale,
As circles on a smooth canal:
The mountains round, unhappy fate!
Sooner or later, of all height,
Withdraw their summits from the skies,
And lessen as the others rise:
Still the prospect wider spreads,
Adds a thousand woods and meads;
Still it widens, widens still,
And sinks the newly-risen hill.
 Now I gain the mountain's brow,
What a landscape lies below!
No clouds, no vapours, intervene;
But the gay the open scene
Does the face of Nature show
In all the hues of heav'n's bow,
And, swelling to embrace the light,
Spreads around beneath the sight.

Old castles on the cliffs arise,
Proudly tow'ring in the skies;
Rushing from the woods, the spires
Seem from hence ascending fires;
Half his beams Apollo sheds
On the yellow mountain heads,
Gilds the fleeces of the flocks,
And glitters on the broken rocks.
Below me trees unnumber'd rise,
Beautiful in various dyes;
The gloomy pine, the poplar blue,
The yellow beech, the sable yew,
The slender fir, that taper grows,
The sturdy oak with broad-spread boughs,
And beyond the purple grove,
Haunt of Phyllis, queen of love!
Gaudy as the op'ning dawn,
Lies a long and level lawn,
On which a dark hill, steep and high,
Holds and charms the wand'ring eye:
Deep are his feet in Towy's flood,
His sides are cloth'd with waving wood,
And ancient towers crown his brow,
That cast an awful look below;
Whose ragged walls the ivy creeps,
And with her arms from falling keeps;
So both a safety from the wind
On mutual dependence find.
'Tis now the raven's bleak abode;
'Tis now th' apartment of the toad;
And there the fox securely feeds,
And there the pois'nous adder breeds,
Conceal'd in ruins, moss, and weeds;
While, ever and anon, there falls
Huge heaps of hoary moulder'd walls.
Yet Time has seen, that lifts the low,
And level lays the lofty brow,
Has seen this broken pile complete,
Big with the vanity of state:
But transient is the smile of Fate!
A little rule, a little sway,
A sunbeam in a winter's day,
Is all the proud and mighty have

Between the cradle and the grave.
     And see the rivers how they run
Thro' woods and meads, in shade and sun!
Sometimes swift, sometimes slow,
Wave succeeding wave, they go
A various journey to the deep,
Like human life to endless sleep!
Thus is Nature's vesture wrought,
To instruct our wand'ring thought;
Thus she dresses green and gay,
To disperse our cares away.
     Ever charming, ever new,
When will the landscape tire the view!
The fountain's fall, the river's flow,
The woody valleys warm and low;
The windy summit, wild and high,
Roughly rushing on the sky!
The pleasant seat, the ruin'd tow'r,
The naked rock, the shady bow'r;
The town and village, dome and farm,
Each give each a double charm,
As pearls upon an Ethiop's arm.
     See on the mountain's southern side,
Where the prospect opens wide,
Where the ev'ning gilds the tide,
How close and small the hedges lie!
What streaks of meadows cross the eye!
A step, methinks, may pass the stream,
So little distant dangers seem;
So we mistake the future's face,
Ey'd thro' Hope's deluding glass;
As yon' summits soft and fair,
Clad in colours of the air,
Which, to those who journey near,
Barren, brown, and rough appear;
Still we tread the same coarse way;
The present's still a cloudy day.
     O may I with myself agree,
And never covet what I see!
Content me with an humble shade,
My passions tam'd, my wishes laid;
For while our wishes wildly roll,
We banish quiet from the soul:

'Tis thus the busy beat the air,
And misers gather wealth and care.
　　Now, ev'n now, my joys run high,
As on the mountain-turf I lie;
While the wanton Zephyr sings,
And in the vale perfumes his wings;
While the waters murmur deep;
While the shepherd charms his sheep;
While the birds unbounded fly,
And with music fill the sky,
Now, ev'n now, my joys run high.
　　Be full, ye Courts! be great who will;
Search for Peace with all your skill:
Open wide the lofty door,
Seek her on the marble floor:
In vain you search, she is not there;
In vain ye search the domes of Care!
Grass and flow'rs Quiet treads,
On the meads and mountain-heads,
Along with Pleasure close ally'd,
Ever by each other's side,
And often, by the murm'ring rill,
Hears the thrush, while all is still,
Within the groves of Grongar Hill.

JOHN DYER.

THE PASSIONS

AN ODE FOR MUSIC[1]

WHEN Music, heavenly maid, was young,
While yet in early Greece she sung,
The passions oft, to hear her shell,
Thronged around her magic cell,
Exulting, trembling, raging, fainting,
Possest beyond the muse's painting:
By turns they felt the glowing mind
Disturbed, delighted, raised, refined;
Till once, 'tis said, when all were fired,
Filled with fury, rapt, inspired,
From the supporting myrtles round
They snatched her instruments of sound;

---

[1] Performed at Oxford, with Hayes' music, in 1750.

And, as they oft had heard apart
Sweet lessons of her forceful art,
Each (for madness ruled the hour)
Would prove his own expressive power.

First Fear, his hand, its skill to try,
  Amid the chords bewildered laid,
And back recoiled, he knew not why,
  Even at the sound himself had made.

Next Anger rushed; his eyes on fire,
  In lightnings owned his secret stings:
In one rude clash he struck the lyre,
  And swept, with hurried hand, the strings.

With woeful measures wan Despair
  Low, sullen sounds his grief beguiled;
A solemn, strange, and mingled air;
  'Twas sad by fits, by starts 'twas wild.

But thou, O Hope, with eyes so fair,
  What was thy delightful measure?[1]
Still it whispered promised pleasure,
  And bade the lovely scenes at distance hail!
Still would her touch the strain prolong;
  And from the rocks, the woods, the vale,
She called on Echo still, through all the song;
  And, where her sweetest theme she chose,
  A soft responsive voice was heard at every close,
And hope enchanted smiled, and waved her golden hair.

And longer had she sung;—but, with a frown,
  Revenge impatient rose:
He threw his blood-stained sword, in thunder, down;
    And with a withering look,
  The war-denouncing trumpet took,
And blew a blast so loud and dread,
Were ne'er prophetic sounds so full of woe!
    And, ever and anon, he beat
    The doubling drum, with furious heat;
And though sometimes, each dreary pause between,

[1] In some renderings: What was thy delighted measure?

Dejected Pity, at his side,
  Her soul-subduing voice applied,
Yet still he kept his wild unaltered mien,
While each strained ball of sight seemed bursting from his
      head.
  Thy numbers, Jealousy, to naught were fixed;
    Sad proof of thy distressful state;
  Of differing themes the veering song was mixed;
    And how it courted love, now raving called on hate.

With eyes upraised, as one inspired,
Pale Melancholy sat retired;
And, from her wild sequestered seat,
In notes by distance made more sweet,
Poured through the mellow horn her pensive soul:
  And, dashing soft from rocks around,
  Bubbling runnels joined the sound;
Through glades and glooms the mingled measure stole,
  Or, o'er some haunted stream, with fond delay,
    Round an holy calm diffusing,
    Love of peace, and lonely musing,
  In hollow murmurs died away.
But O! how altered was its sprightlier tone,
When Cheerfulness, a nymph of healthiest hue,
  Her bow across her shoulder flung,
  Her buskins gemmed with morning dew,
Blew an inspiring air, that dale and thicket rung,
  The hunter's call, to faun and dryad known!
The oak-crowned sisters, and their chaste-eyed queen,
  Satyrs and sylvan boys, were seen,
  Peeping from forth their alleys green:
Brown Exercise rejoiced to hear;
  And Sport leapt up, and seized his beechen spear.
Last came Joy's ecstatic trial:
He, with viny crown advancing,
  First to the lively pipe his hand addrest;
But soon he saw the brisk awakening viol,
  Whose sweet entrancing voice he loved the best;
They would have thought who heard the strain
  They saw, in Tempe's vale, her native maids,
  Amidst the festal sounding shades,
To some unwearied minstrel dancing,
While, as his flying fingers kissed the strings,

Love framed with mirth a gay fantastic round:
Loose were her tresses seen, her zone unbound;
And he, amidst his frolic play,
As if he would the charming air repay,
Shook thousand odours from his dewy wings.

O Music! sphere-descended maid,
Friend of pleasure, wisdom's aid!
Why, goddess! why, to us denied,
Lay'st thou thy ancient lyre aside?
As, in that loved Athenian bower,
You learned an all-commanding power,
Thy mimic soul, O nymph endeared,
Can well recall what then it heard;
Where is thy native simple heart,
Devote to virtue, fancy, art?
Arise, as in that elder time,
Warm, energetic, chaste, sublime!
Thy wonders, in that godlike age,
Fill thy recording sister's page—
'Tis said, and I believe the tale,
Thy humblest reed could more prevail,
Had more of strength, diviner rage,
Than all which charms this laggard age;
E'en all at once together found,
Cecilia's mingled world of sound—
O bid our vain endeavours cease;
Revive the just designs of Greece:
Return in all thy simple state!
Confirm the tales her sons relate!

WILLIAM COLLINS.

LONDON

Tho' grief and fondness in my breast rebel,
When injur'd Thales bids the town farewel,
Yet still my calmer thoughts his choice commend,
(I praise the hermit, but regret the friend,)
Resolv'd at length, from vice and London far,
To breathe in distant fields a purer air,
And, fix'd on Cambria's solitary shore,
Give to St. David one true Briton more.

For who woud leave, unbrib'd, Hibernia's land,
Or change the rocks of Scotland for the Strand?
There none are swept by sudden fate away,
But all whom hunger spares with age decay:
Here malice, rapine, accident, conspire,
And now a rabble rages, now a fire;
Their ambush here relentless ruffians lay,
And here the fell attorney prowls for prey;
Here falling houses thunder on your head,
And here a female atheist talks you dead.

While Thales waits the wherry that contains
Of dissipated wealth the small remains,
On Thames's banks in silent thought we stood,
Where Greenwich smiles upon the silver flood;
Struck with the seat that gave Eliza birth,
We kneel, and kiss the consecrated earth;
In pleasing dreams the blissful age renew,
And call Britannia's glories back to view:
Behold her cross triumphant on the main,
The guard of commerce and the dread of Spain,
Ere masquerades debauch'd, excise oppress'd,
Or English honour grew a standing jest.

A transient calm the happy scenes bestow,
And for a moment lull the sense of woe.
At length awaking, with contemptuous frown
Indignant Thales eyes the neighb'ring town.

Since worth, he cries, in these degen'rate days
Wants ev'n the cheap reward of empty praise;
In those curs'd walls, devote to vice and gain,
Since unrewarded science toils in vain;
Since hope but sooths to double my distress,
And ev'ry moment leaves my little less;
While yet my steady steps no staff sustains,
And life still vig'rous revels in my veins,
Grant me, kind heaven, to find some happier place,
Where honesty and sense are no disgrace;
Some pleasing bank where verdant osiers play,
Some peaceful vale with nature's paintings gay,
Where once the harass'd Briton found repose,
And safe in poverty defy'd his foes;
Some secret cell, ye pow'rs, indulgent give.
Let —— live here, for —— has learn'd to live.
Here let those reign, whom pensions can incite

To vote a patriot black, a courtier white;
Explain their country's dear-bought rights away,
And plead for pirates in the face of day;
With slavish tenets taint our poison'd youth,
And lend a lie the confidence of truth.

    Let such raise palaces, and manors buy,
Collect a tax, or farm a lottery;
With warbling eunuchs fill our silenc'd stage,
And lull to servitude a thoughtless age.

    Heroes, proceed! what bounds your pride shall hold?
What check restrain your thirst of pow'r and gold?
Behold rebellious virtue quite o'erthrown,
Behold our fame, our wealth, our lives your own.
To such the plunder of a land is giv'n,
When publick crimes inflame the wrath of heav'n;
But what, my friend, what hope remains for me,
Who start at theft, and blush at perjury?
Who scarce forbear, tho' Britain's court he sing,
To pluck a titled poet's borrow'd wing;
A statesman's logic unconvinc'd can hear,
And dare to slumber o'er the Gazetteer;
Despise a fool in half his pension dress'd,
And strive in vain to laugh at Clodio's jest?

    Others, with softer smiles and subtler art,
Can sap the principles, or taint the heart;
With more address a lover's note convey,
Or bribe a virgin's innocence away.
Well may they rise, while I, whose rustick tongue
Ne'er knew to puzzle right, or varnish wrong,
Spurn'd as a beggar, dreaded as a spy,
Live unregarded, unlamented die.

    For what but social guilt the friend endears?
Who shares Orgilio's crimes, his fortune shares.
But thou, should tempting villany present
All Marlb'rough hoarded, or all Villiers spent,
Turn from the glitt'ring bribe thy scornful eye,
Nor sell for gold, what gold could never buy,
The peaceful slumber, self-approving day,
Unsullied fame, and conscience ever gay.

    The cheated nation's happy fav'rites see!
Mark whom the great caress, who frown on me!
London, the needy villain's gen'ral home,
The common sewer of Paris and of Rome,

With eager thirst, by folly or by fate,
Sucks in the dregs of each corrupted state.
Forgive my transports on a theme like this,
I cannot bear a French metropolis.

Illustrious Edward! from the realms of day,
The land of heroes and of saints survey;
Nor hope the British lineaments to trace,
The rustick grandeur, or the surly grace,
But, lost in thoughtless ease and empty show,
Behold the warrior dwindled to a beau;
Sense, freedom, piety, refin'd away,
Of France the mimick, and of Spain the prey.

All that at home no more can beg or steal,
Or like a gibbet better than a wheel,
Hiss'd from the stage, or hooted from the court,
Their air, their dress, their politicks import;
Obsequious, artful, voluble, and gay,
On Britain's fond credulity they prey.
All sciences a fasting Monsieur knows,
And bid him go to hell, to hell he goes.

Ah! what avails it, that, from slav'ry far,
I drew the breath of life in English air;
Was early taught a Briton's right to prize,
And lisp the tale of Henry's victories;
If the gull'd conqueror receives the chain,
And flattery prevails when arms are vain?

Studious to please and ready to submit,
The supple Gaul was born a parasite:
Still to his int'rest true, where'er he goes,
Wit, brav'ry, worth, his lavish tongue bestows;
In ev'ry face a thousand graces shine,
From ev'ry tongue flows harmony divine.
These arts in vain our rugged natives try,
Strain out with fault'ring diffidence a lie,
And get a kick for awkward flattery.

Besides, with justice this discerning age
Admires their wond'rous talents for the stage:
Well may they venture on the mimick's art,
Who play from morn to night a borrow'd part;
Practis'd their master's notions to embrace,
Repeat his maxims, and reflect his face;
With ev'ry wild absurdity comply,
And view each object with another's eye;

To shake with laughter ere the jest they hear,
To pour at will the counterfeited tear,
And as their patron hints the cold or heat,
To shake in dog days, in December sweat,
How, when competitors like these contend,
Can surly virtue hope to fix a friend?
Slaves that with serious impudence beguile,
And lie without a blush, without a smile;
Can Balbo's eloquence applaud, and swear
He gropes his breeches with a monarch's air.

For arts like these preferr'd, admir'd, caress'd
They first invade your table, then your breast;
Explore your secrets with insidious art,
Watch the weak hour, and ransack all the heart;
Then soon your ill-plac'd confidence repay,
Commence your lords, and govern or betray.

By numbers here from shame or censure free
All crimes are safe, but hated poverty.
This, only this, the rigid law pursues;
This, only this, provokes the snarling muse.
The sober trader at a tatter'd cloak
Wakes from his dream, and labours for a joke;
With brisker air the silken courtiers gaze,
And turn the varied taunt a thousand ways,
Of all the griefs that harass the distress'd,
Sure the most bitter is a scornful jest;
Fate never wounds more deep the gen'rous heart,
Than when a blockhead's insult points the dart.

Has heaven reserv'd, in pity to the poor,
No pathless waste, or undiscover'd shore?
No secret island in the boundless main?
No peaceful desert yet unclaim'd by Spain?
Quick let us rise, the happy seats explore,
And bear oppression's insolence no more.
This mournful truth is ev'ry where confess'd,
SLOW RISES WORTH, BY POVERTY DEPRESS'D:
But here more slow, where all are slaves to gold,
Where looks are merchandise, and smiles are sold;
Where won by bribes, by flatteries implor'd,
The groom retails the favours of his lord.

But hark! th' affrighted crowd's tumultuous cries
Roll through the streets, and thunder to the skies:
Rais'd from some pleasing dream of wealth and pow'r,

Some pompous palace, or some blissful bow'r,
Aghast you start, and scarce with aching sight
Sustain the approaching fire's tremendous light;
Swift from pursuing horrors take your way,
And leave your little ALL to flames a prey;
Then thro' the world a wretched vagrant roam,
For where can starving merit find a home?
In vain your mournful narrative disclose,
While all neglect, and most insult your woes.

Should heaven's just bolts Orgilio's wealth confound,
And spread his flaming palace on the ground,
Swift o'er the land the dismal rumour flies,
And publick mournings pacify the skies;
The laureat tribe in venal verse relate
How virtue wars with persecuting fate;
With well-feign'd gratitude the pension'd band
Refund the plunder of the beggar'd land.
See! while he builds, the gaudy vassals come,
And crowd with sudden wealth the rising dome;
The price of boroughs and of souls restore;
And raise his treasures higher than before:
Now bless'd with all the baubles of the great,
The polish'd marble, and the shining plate,
Orgilio sees the golden pile aspire,
And hopes from angry heav'n another fire.

Could'st thou resign the park and play, content,
For the fair banks of Severn or of Trent;
There might'st thou find some elegant retreat,
Some hireling senator's deserted seat,
And stretch thy prospects o'er the smiling land,
For less than rent the dungeons of the Strand;
There prune thy walks, support thy drooping flow'rs,
Direct thy rivulets, and twine thy bow'rs,
And, while thy grounds a cheap repast afford,
Despise the dainties of a venal lord:
There ev'ry bush with nature's musick rings,
There ev'ry breeze bears health upon its wings;
On all thy hours security shall smile,
And bless thine evening walk and morning toil.

Prepare for death, if here at night you roam,
And sign your will before you sup from home.
Some fiery fop, with new commission vain,
Who sleeps on brambles till he kills his man,

Some frolick drunkard, reeling from a feast,
Provokes a broil, and stabs you for a jest.
    Yet ev'n these heroes, mischievously gay,
Lords of the street, and terrors of the way,
Flush'd as they are with folly, youth, and wine,
Their prudent insults to the poor confine;
Afar they mark the flambeau's bright approach,
And shun the shining train and golden coach.
    In vain, these dangers past, your doors you close,
And hope the balmy blessings of repose:
Cruel with guilt, and daring with despair,
The midnight murd'rer bursts the faithless bar;
Invades the sacred hour of silent rest,
And leaves, unseen, a dagger in your breast.
    Scarce can our fields, such crowds at Tyburn die,
With hemp the gallows and the fleet supply.
Propose your schemes, ye senatorian band,
Whose *ways* and *means* support the sinking land,
Lest ropes be wanting in the tempting Spring,
To rig another convoy for the king.
    A single gaol in Alfred's golden reign
Could half the nation's criminals contain;
Fair Justice then, without constraint ador'd,
Held high the steady scale, but sheath'd the sword,
No spies were paid, no special juries known:
Blest age! but, ah! how diff'rent from our own!
    Much could I add,—but see! the boat at hand,
The tide returning, calls me from the land:
Farewell!—When, youth and health and fortune spent,
Thou fly'st for refuge to the wilds of Kent,
And tir'd, like me, with follies and with crimes,
In angry numbers warn'st succeeding times;
Then shall thy friend—nor thou refuse his aid—
Still foe to vice, forsake his Cambrian shade;
In virtue's cause once more exert his rage,
Thy satire point, and animate thy page.

                                    SAMUEL JOHNSON.

THE SCHOOLMISTRESS

Ah me! full sorely is my heart forlorn,
To think how modest worth neglected lies;
While partial fame doth with her blasts adorn
Such deeds alone as pride and pomp disguise;
Deeds of ill sort, and mischievous emprise;
Lend me thy clarion, goddess! let me try
To sound the praise of merit ere it dies;
Such as I oft have chancëd to espy,
Lost in the dreary shades of dull obscurity.

In every village marked with little spire,
Embowered in trees, and hardly known to fame,
There dwells, in lowly shed, and mean attire,
A matron old, whom we schoolmistress name;
Who boasts unruly brats with birch to tame:
They grieven sore, in piteous durance pent,
Awed by the power of this relentless dame;
And oft-times, on vagaries idly bent,
For unkempt hair, or task unconned, are sorely shent.

And all in sight doth rise a birchen tree,
Which learning near her little dome did stow;
Whilome a twig of small regard to see,
Though now so wide its waving branches flow,
And work the simple vassals mickle woe;
For not a wind might curl the leaves that blew,
But their limbs shuddered, and their pulse beat low;
And as they looked, they found their horror grew,
And shaped it into rods, and tingled at the view.

Near to this dome is found a patch so green,
On which the tribe their gambols do display;
And at the door imprisoning board is seen,
Lest weakly wights of smaller size should stray;
Eager, perdie, to bask in sunny day!
The noises intermixed, which thence resound,
Do learning's little tenement betray;
Where sits the dame, disguised in look profound,
And eyes her fairy throng, and turns her wheel around.

Her cap, far whiter than the driven snow,
Emblem right meet of decency does yield:
Her apron dyed in grain, as blue, I trow,
As is the harebell that adorns the field;
And in her hand, for sceptre, she does wield
Tway birchen sprays; with anxious fear entwined,
With dark distrust, and sad repentance filled;
And steadfast hate, and sharp affliction joined,
And fury uncontrolled, and chastisement unkind.

A russet stole was o'er her shoulders thrown;
A russet kirtle fenced the nipping air;
'Twas simple russet, but it was her own;
'Twas her own country bred the flock so fair!
'Twas her own labour did the fleece prepare;
And, sooth to say, her pupils ranged around,
Through pious awe, did term it passing rare;
For they in gaping wonderment abound,
And think, no doubt, she been the greatest wight on ground.

Albeit ne flattery did corrupt her truth,
Ne pompous title did debauch her ear;
Goody, good woman, gossip, n'aunt, forsooth,
Or dame, the sole additions she did hear;
Yet these she challenged, these she held right dear;
Ne would esteem him act as mought behove,
Who should not honoured eld with these revere;
For never title yet so mean could prove,
But there was eke a mind which did that title love.

One ancient hen she took delight to feed,
The plodding pattern of the busy dame;
Which, ever and anon, impelled by need,
Into her school, begirt with chickens, came;
Such favour did her past deportment claim;
And, if neglect had lavished on the ground
Fragment of bread, she would collect the same;
For well she knew, and quaintly could expound,
What sin it were to waste the smallest crumb she found.

Herbs, too, she knew, and well of each could speak,
That in her garden sipped the silvery dew;
Where no vain flower disclosed a gaudy streak,

But herbs for use and physic, not a few,
Of gray renown, within those borders grew:
The tufted basil, pun-provoking thyme,
Fresh balm, and marigold of cheerful hue:
The lowly gill, that never dares to climb;
And more I fain would sing, disdaining here to rhyme.

Here oft the dame, on Sabbath's decent eve,
Hymnèd such psalms as Sternhold forth did mete;
If winter 'twere, she to her hearth did cleave,
But in her garden found a summer-seat:
Sweet melody! to hear her then repeat
How Israel's sons, beneath a foreign king,
While taunting foemen did a song entreat,
All, for the nonce, untuning every string,
Uphung their useless lyres—small heart had they to sing.

For she was just, and friend to virtuous lore,
And passed much time in truly virtuous deed;
And in those elfins' ears would oft deplore
The times, when truth by popish rage did bleed,
And tortuous death was true devotion's meed;
And simple faith in iron chains did mourn,
That nould on wooden image place her creed;
And lawny saints in smouldering flames did burn:
Ah! dearest Lord, forefend thilk days should e'er return!

In elbow-chair (like that of Scottish stem,
By the sharp tooth of cankering eld defaced,
In which, when he receives his diadem,
Our sovereign prince and liefest liege is placed)
The matron sat; and some with rank she graced,
(The source of children's and of courtiers' pride!)
Redressed affronts—for vile affronts there passed;
And warned them not the fretful to deride.
But love each other dear, whatever them betide.

Right well she knew each temper to descry,
To thwart the proud, and the submiss to raise;
Some with vile copper-prize exalt on high,
And some entice with pittance small of praise;
And other some with baleful sprig she 'frays:
Even absent, she the reins of power doth hold,

While with quaint arts the giddy crowd she sways;
Forewarned, if little bird their pranks behold,
'Twill whisper in her ear, and all the scene unfold.

Lo! now with state she utters her command;
Eftsoons the urchins to their tasks repair,
Their books of stature small they take in hand,
Which with pellucid horn secured are,
To save from finger wet the letters fair:
The work so gay, that on their back is seen,
St. George's high achievements does declare;
On which thilk wight that has y-gazing been,
Kens the forthcoming rod—unpleasing sight, I ween!

Ah! luckless he, and born beneath the beam
Of evil star! it irks me whilst I write;
As erst the bard by Mulla's silver stream,[1]
Oft, as he told of deadly dolorous plight,
Sighed as he sung, and did in tears indite;
For brandishing the rod, she doth begin
To loose the brogues, the stripling's late delight;
And down they drop; appears his dainty skin,
Fair as the furry coat of whitest ermilin.

O ruthful scene! when, from a nook obscure,
His little sister doth his peril see,
All playful as she sat, she grows demure;
She finds full soon her wonted spirits flee;
She meditates a prayer to set him free;
Nor gentle pardon could this dame deny—
If gentle pardon could with dames agree—
To her sad grief that swells in either eye,
And wrings her so that all for pity she could die.

No longer can she now her shrieks command;
And hardly she forbears, through awful fear,
To rushen forth, and, with presumptuous hand,
To stay harsh justice in its mid career.
On thee she calls, on thee her parent dear;
(Ah! too remote to ward the shameful blow!)
She sees no kind domestic visage near,
And soon a flood of tears begins to flow,
And gives a loose at last to unavailing woe.

[1] Spenser.

But ah! what pen his piteous plight may trace?
Or what device his loud laments explain—
The form uncouth of his disguised face—
The pallid hue that dyes his looks amain—
The plenteous shower that does his cheek distain?
When he, in abject wise, implores the dame,
Ne hopeth aught of sweet reprieve to gain;
Or when from high she levels well her aim,
And, through the thatch, his cries each falling stroke proclaim.

But now Dan Phœbus gains the middle sky,
And liberty unbars her prison door;
And like a rushing torrent out they fly;
And now the grassy cirque han covered o'er
With boisterous revel rout and wild uproar;
A thousand ways in wanton rings they run.
Heaven shield their short-lived pastimes I implore;
For well may freedom erst so dearly won
Appear to British elf more gladsome than the sun.

Enjoy, poor imps! enjoy your sportive trade,
And chase gay flies, and cull the fairest flowers;
For when my bones in grass-green sods are laid,
O never may ye taste more careless hours
In knightly castles or in ladies' bowers.
O vain to seek delight in earthly thing!
But most in courts, where proud ambition towers;
Deluded wight! who weens fair peace can spring
Beneath the pompous dome of kaiser or of king.

See in each sprite some various bent appear!
These rudely carol must incondite lay;
Those sauntering on the green, with jocund leer
Salute the stranger passing on his way;
Some builden fragile tenements of clay;
Some to the standing lake their courses bend,
With pebbles smooth at duck and drake to play;
Thilk to the huxter's savoury cottage tend,
In pastry kings and queens the allotted mite to spend.

Here as each season yields a different store,
Each season's stores in order ranged been;
Apples with cabbage-net y-covered o'er,
Galling full sore the unmoneyed wight, are seen,

And gooseb'rie clad in livery red or green;
And here, of lovely dye, the catherine pear,
Fine pear! as lovely for thy juice, I ween;
O may no wight e'er penniless come there,
Lest, smit with ardent love, he pine with hopeless care.

See, cherries here, ere cherries yet abound,
With thread so white in tempting posies tied,
Scattering, like blooming maid, their glances round,
With pampered look draw little eyes aside;
And must be bought, though penury betide.
The plum all azure, and the nut all brown;
And here each season do those cakes abide,
Whose honoured names[1] the inventive city own,
Rendering through Britain's isle Salopia's praises known.

Admired Salopia! that with venial pride
Eyes her bright form in Severn's ambient wave,
Famed for her loyal cares in perils tried,
Her daughters lovely, and her striplings brave:
Ah! midst the rest, may flowers adorn his grave
Whose art did first these dulcet cates display!
A motive fair to learning's imps he gave,
Who cheerless o'er her darkling region stray;
Till reason's morn arise, and light them on their way.

WILLIAM SHENSTONE.

ELEGY WRITTEN IN A COUNTRY CHURCH-YARD

The curfew tolls the knell of parting day,
    The lowing herd wind slowly o'er the lea,
The ploughman homeward plods his weary way,
    And leaves the world to darkness and to me.

Now fades the glimmering landscape on the sight,
    And all the air a solemn stillness holds,
Save where the beetle wheels his droning flight,
    And drowsy tinklings lull the distant folds;

[1] Shrewsbury Cakes.

Save that from yonder ivy-mantled tower
  The moping owl does to the moon complain
Of such as, wand'ring near her secret bower,
  Molest her ancient solitary reign.

Beneath those rugged elms, that yew-tree's shade,
  Where heaves the turf in many a mould'ring heap,
Each in his narrow cell for ever laid,
  The rude Forefathers of the hamlet sleep.

The breezy call of incense-breathing Morn,
  The swallow twitt'ring from the straw-built shed,
The cock's shrill clarion, or the echoing horn,
  No more shall rouse them from their lowly bed.

For them no more the blazing hearth shall burn,
  Or busy housewife ply her evening care;
No children run to lisp their sire's return,
  Or climb his knees the envied kiss to share.

Oft did the harvest to their sickle yield,
  Their furrow oft the stubborn glebe has broke;
How jocund did they drive their team afield!
  How bowed the woods beneath their sturdy stroke!

Let not Ambition mock their useful toil,
  Their homely joys, and destiny obscure;
Nor Grandeur hear, with a disdainful smile,
  The short and simple annals of the poor.

The boast of heraldry, the pomp of power,
  And all that beauty, all that wealth e'er gave,
Awaits alike th' inevitable hour.
  The paths of glory lead but to the grave.

Nor you, ye Proud, impute to these the fault,
  If Mem'ry o'er their tomb no trophies raise,
Where thro' the long-drawn aisle and fretted vault
  The pealing anthem swells the note of praise.

Can storied urn or animated bust
  Back to its mansion call the fleeting breath?
Can Honour's voice provoke the silent dust,
  Or Flatt'ry soothe the dull cold ear of Death?

Perhaps in this neglected spot is laid
  Some heart once pregnant with celestial fire;
Hands, that the rod of empire might have swayed,
  Or waked to ecstasy the living lyre.

But Knowledge to their eyes her ample page
  Rich with the spoils of time did ne'er unroll;
Chill Penury repressed their noble rage,
  And froze the genial current of the soul.

Full many a gem, of purest ray serene,
  The dark unfathomed caves of ocean bear;
Full many a flower is born to blush unseen,
  And waste its sweetness on the desert air.

Some village-Hampden, that with dauntless breast
  The little tyrant of his fields withstood;
Some mute inglorious Milton here may rest,
  Some Cromwell guiltless of his country's blood.

Th' applause of list'ning senates to command,
  The threats of pain and ruin to despise,
To scatter plenty o'er a smiling land,
  And read their history in a nation's eyes,

Their lot forbad; nor circumscribed alone
  Their growing virtues, but their crimes confined;
Forbad to wade through slaughter to a throne,
  And shut the gates of mercy on mankind,

The struggling pangs of conscious truth to hide,
  To quench the blushes of ingenuous shame,
Or heap the shrine of Luxury and Pride
  With incense kindled at the Muse's flame.

Far from the madding crowd's ignoble strife,
   Their sober wishes never learned to stray;
Along the cool sequestered vale of life
   They kept the noiseless tenor of their way.

Yet ev'n these bones from insult to protect
   Some frail memorial still erected nigh,
With uncouth rhymes and shapeless sculpture decked,
   Implores the passing tribute of a sigh.

Their name, their years, spelt by th' unlettered Muse,
   The place of fame and elegy supply;
And many a holy text around she strews,
   That teach the rustic moralist to die.

For who, to dumb Forgetfulness a prey,
   This pleasing anxious being e'er resigned,
Left the warm precincts of the cheerful day,
   Nor cast one longing ling'ring look behind?

On some fond breast the parting soul relies,
   Some pious drops the closing eye requires;
Ev'n from the tomb the voice of Nature cries,
   Ev'n in our ashes live their wonted fires.

For thee, who mindful of th' unhonoured Dead
   Dost in these lines their artless tale relate;
If chance, by lonely contemplation led,
   Some kindred spirit shall inquire thy fate,

Haply some hoary-headed swain may say,
   "Oft have we seen him at the peep of dawn
Brushing with hasty steps the dews away
   To meet the sun upon the upland lawn.

"There at the foot of yonder nodding beech,
   That wreaths its old fantastic roots so high,
His listless length at noontide would he stretch,
   And pore upon the brook that babbles by.

" Hard by yon wood, now smiling as in scorn,
  Mutt'ring his wayward fancies he would rove,
Now drooping, woeful wan, like one forlorn,
  Or crazed with care, or crossed in hopeless love.

" One morn I missed him on the customed hill,
  Along the heath and near his fav'rite tree;
Another came; nor yet beside the rill,
  Nor up the lawn, nor at the wood was he;

" The next with dirges due in sad array
  Slow thro' the church-way path we saw him borne.
Approach and read (for thou canst read) the lay
  Graved on the stone beneath yon aged thorn."

THE EPITAPH

Here rests his head upon the lap of Earth
  A Youth to Fortune and to Fame unknown.
Fair Science frowned not on his humble birth,
  And Melancholy marked him for her own.

Large was his bounty, and his soul sincere,
  Heav'n did a recompense as largely send;
He gave to Misery all he had, a tear,
  He gained from Heav'n ('twas all he wished) a friend.

No farther seek his merits to disclose,
  Or draw his frailties from their dread abode,
  (There they alike in trembling hope repose,)
  The bosom of his Father and his God.

THE GRAVE OF KING ARTHUR[1]

STATELY the feast, and high the cheer:
Girt with many an armed peer,
Cilgarran, in thy castle hall,
And canopied with golden pall,
Sublime in formidable state,
And warlike splendour, Henry sate;
Prepared to stain the briny flood
Of Shannon's lakes with rebel blood.
    Illumining the vaulted roof,
A thousand torches flam'd aloof:
From massy cups, with golden gleam
Sparkled the red metheglin's stream:
To grace the gorgeous festival,
Along the lofty-window'd wall,
The storied tapestry was hung:
With minstrelsy the rafters rung
Of harps, that with reflected light
From the proud gallery glitter'd bright:
While gifted bards, a rival throng,
(From distant Mona, nurse of song,
From Teivi, fring'd with umbrage brown,
From Elvy's vale, and Cader's crown,
From many a shaggy precipice
That shades Ierne's hoarse abyss,

[1] King Henry the Second, having undertaken an expedition into
Ireland, to suppress a rebellion raised by Roderick, King of Connaught,
commonly called O Connor Dun, or the brown monarch of Ireland,
was entertained, in his passage through Wales, with the songs of the
Welsh Bards. The subject of their poetry was King Arthur, whose
history had been so long disguised by fabulous inventions, that the
place of his burial was in general scarcely known or remembered.
But in one of these Welsh poems sung before Henry, it was recited,
that King Arthur, after the battle of Camlan in Cornwall, was interred
at Glastonbury Abbey, before the high altar, yet without any external
mark or memorial. Afterwards Henry visited the abbey, and com-
manded the spot, described by the Bard, to be opened: when digging
near twenty feet deep, they found the body, deposited under a large
stone, inscribed with Arthur's name. This is the ground-work of
the following Ode: but for the better accommodation of the story
to our present purpose, it is told with some slight variations from the
Chronicle of Glastonbury. The castle of Cilgarran, where this discovery
is supposed to have been made, now a most romantic ruin, stands on
a rock descending to the river Teivi in Pembrokeshire: and was built
by Roger Montgomery, who led the van of the Normans at Hastings.

And many a sunless solitude
Of Radnor's inmost mountains rude,)
To crown the banquet's solemn close,
Themes of British glory chose;
And to the strings of various chime
Attemper'd thus the fabling rime.

   " O'er Cornwall's cliffs the tempest roar'd,
High the screaming sea-mew soar'd;
On Tintaggel's[1] topmost tower
Darksom fell the sleety shower;
Round the rough castle shrilly sung
The whirling blast, and wildly flung
On each tall rampart's thundering side
The surges of the tumbling tide:
When Arthur rang'd his red-cross ranks
On conscious Camlan's crimson'd banks:
By Mordred's faithless guile decreed
Beneath a Saxon spear to bleed!
Yet in vain a paynim foe
Arm'd with fate the mighty blow;
For when he fell, an elfin queen,
All in secret, and unseen,
O'er the fainting hero threw
Her mantle of ambrosial blue;
And bade her spirits bear him far,
In Merlin's agate-axled car,
To her green isle's enamel steep,
In the navel of the deep.
O'er his wounds she sprinkled dew
From flowers that in Arabia grew:
On a rich, inchanted bed,
She pillow'd his majestic head;
O'er his brow, with whispers bland,
Thrice she wav'd an opiate wand;
And, to soft music's airy sound,
Her magic curtains clos'd around.
There, renew'd the vital spring,
Again he reigns a mighty king;
And many a fair and fragrant clime,

[1] Tintaggel, or Tintadgel Castle, where King Arthur is said to have been born, and to have chiefly resided. Some of its huge fragments still remain, on a rocky peninsular cape, of a prodigious declivity towards the sea, and almost inaccessible from the land side, on the northern coast of Cornwall.

Blooming in immortal prime,
By gales of Eden ever fann'd,
Owns the monarch's high command:
Thence to Britain shall return,
(If right prophetic rolls I learn)
Borne on Victory's spreading plume,
His ancient sceptre to resume;
Once more, in old heroic pride,
His barbèd courser to bestride;
His knightly table to restore,
And the brave tournaments of yore."
They ceas'd: when on the tuneful stage
Advanc'd a bard, of aspect sage;
His silver tresses, thin-besprent,
To age a graceful reverence lent;
His beard, all white as spangles frore
That cloth Plinlimmon's forests hoar,
Down to his harp descending flow'd;
With Time's faint rose his features glow'd;
His eyes diffus'd a soften'd fire,
And thus he moved the warbling wire.

" Listen, Henry, to my rede!
Not from fairy realms I lead
Bright-rob'd Tradition, to relate
In forgèd colours Arthur's fate;
Tho' much of old romantic lore
On the blest theme I keep in store:
But boastful Fiction should be dumb,
Where Truth the strain might best become.
If thine ear may still be won
With songs of Uther's glorious son;
Henry, I a tale unfold,
Never yet in rime enroll'd,
Nor sung nor harp'd in hall or bower;
Which in my youth's full early flower,
A minstrel, sprung of Cornish line,
Who spoke of kings from old Locrine,
Taught me to chant, one vernal dawn,
Deep in a cliff-encircled lawn,
What time the glistening vapours fled
From cloud-envelop'd Glyder's[1] head;
And on its sides the torrents gray

[1] A mountain in Caernarvonshire.

Shone to the morning's orient ray.
   When Arthur bow'd his haughty crest,
No princess, veil'd in azure vest,
Snatch'd him, by Merlin's potent spell,
In groves of golden bliss to dwell;
Where, crown'd with wreaths of mistletoe,
Slaughter'd kings in glory go:
But when he fell, with winged speed,
His champions, on a milk-white steed,
From the battle's hurricane,
Bore him to Joseph's towered fane,
In the fair vale of Avalon:[1]
There, with chanted orison,
And the long blaze of tapers clear,
The stolèd fathers met the bier;
Through the dim aisles, in order dread
Of martial woe, the chief they led,
And deep intomb'd in holy ground,
Before the altar's solemn bound.
Around no dusky banners wave,
No mouldering trophies mark the grave:
Away the ruthless Dane has torn
Each trace that Time's slow touch had worn;
And long, o'er the neglected stone,
Oblivion's veil its shade has thrown:
The faded tomb, with honour due,
'Tis thine, O Henry, to renew!
Thither, when Conquest has restor'd
Yon recreant isle, and sheath'd the sword,
When Peace with palm has crown'd thy brows,
Haste thee, to pay thy pilgrim vows.
There, observant of my lore,
The pavement's hallow'd depth explore;
And thrice a fathom underneath
Dive into the vaults of death.
There shall thine eye, with wild amaze,
On his gigantic stature gaze;
There shalt thou find the monarch laid,
All in warrior-weeds array'd:
Wearing in death his helmet-crown,
And weapons huge of old renown.

[1] Glastonbury Abbey, said to be founded by Joseph of Arimathea; in a spot, anciently called the island, or valley, of Avalonia.

Martial prince, 'tis thine to save
From dark oblivion Arthur's grave!
So may thy ships securely stem
The western frith: thy diadem
Shine victorious in the van,
Nor heed the slings of Ulster's clan:
Thy Norman pike-men win their way
Up the dun rocks of Harald's bay:[1]
And from the steeps of rough Kildare
Thy prancing hoofs the falcon scare:
So may thy bow's unerring yew
Its shafts in Roderick's heart embrew."[2]
    Amid the pealing symphony
The spicèd goblets mantled high,
With passions new the song impress'd
The listening king's impatient breast:
Flash the keen lightnings from his eyes;
He scorns awhile his bold emprise;
Ev'n now he seems, with eager pace,
The consecrated floor to trace;
And ope, from its tremendous gloom,
The treasures of the wondrous tomb:
Ev'n now, he burns in thought to rear,
From its dark bed, the ponderous spear,
Rough with the gore of Pictish kings:
Ev'n now fond hope his fancy wings,
To poise the monarch's massy blade,
Of magic-temper'd metal made;
And drag to day the dinted shield
That felt the storm of Camlan's field.
O'er the sepulchre profound
Ev'n now, with arching sculpture crown'd,
He plans the chantry's choral shrine,
The daily dirge, and rites divine.

THOMAS WARTON.

[1] The Bay of Dublin. Harald, or Har-fager, the Fair-haired, King of Norway, is said, in the Life of Gryffudh ap Conan, prince of North Wales, to have conquered Ireland, and to have founded Dublin.

[2] Henry is supposed to have succeeded in this enterprise, chiefly by the use of the long-bow, with which the Irish were entirely unacquainted.

AN EXCELENTE BALADE OF CHARITIE

(AS WROTEN BIE THE GODE PRIEST, THOMAS ROWLEY, 1464)

In Virgine the sweltry sun 'gan sheene,
  And hot upon the mees did cast his ray;
The apple ripened from its paly green,
  And the soft pear did bend the leafy spray;
  The pied chelándre sung the livelong day;
'Twas now the pride, the manhood of the year,
And eke the ground was dressed in its most neat aumere.

The sun was gleaming in the midst of day,
  Dead-still the air, and eke the welkin blue,
When from the sea arose in drear array
  A heap of clouds of sable sullen hue,
  The which full fast unto the woodland drew,
Hiding at once the sunnis beauteous face,
And the black tempest swelled, and gathered up apace.

Beneath a holm, fast by a pathway-side,
  Which did unto Saint Godwin's convent led,
A hapless pilgrim moaning did abide,
  Poor in his view, ungentle in his weed,
  Long filled with the miseries of need.
Where from the hailstone could the beggar fly?
He had no houses there, nor any convent nigh.

Look in his clouded face, his sprite there scan;
  How woe-begone, how withered, sapless, dead!
Haste to thy church-glebe-house, accursed man!
  Haste to thy kiste, thy only sleeping bed.
  Cold as the clay which will grow on thy head
Is charity and love among high elves;
Knightis and barons live for pleasure and themselves.

The gathered storm is ripe; the big drops fall,
  The sun-burnt meadows smoke, and drink the rain;
The coming ghastness do the cattle 'pall,
  And the full flocks are driving o'er the plain;
  Dashed from the clouds, the waters fly again;
The welken opes; the yellow lightning flies,
And the hot fiery steam in the wide lowings dies.

List! now the thunder's rattling noisy sound
  Moves slowly on, and then embollen clangs,
Shakes the high spire, and lost, expended, drowned,
  Still on the frighted ear of terror hangs;
  The winds are up; the lofty elmen swangs;
Again the lightning and the thunder pours,
And the full clouds are burst at once in stony showers.

Spurring his palfrey o'er the watery plain,
  The Abbot of Saint Godwin's convent came;
His chapournette was drented with the rain,
  And his pencte girdle met with mickle shame;
  He backwards told his bede-roll at the same
The storm increases, and he drew aside,
With the poor alms-craver near to the holm to bide.

His cloak was all of Lincoln cloth so fine,
  With a gold button fastened near his chin,
His autremete was edged with golden twine,
  And his shoe's peak a loverde's might have been;
  Full well it shewn he thoughten cost no sin.
The trammels of his palfrey pleased his sight,
For the horse-milliner his head with roses dight.

"An alms, sir priest!" the drooping pilgrim said,
  "Oh! let me wait within your convent-door,
Till the sun shineth high above our head,
  And the loud tempest of the air is o'er.
  Helpless and old am I, alas! and poor.
No house, no friend, no money in my pouch,
All that I call my own is this my silver crouche."

"Varlet!" replied the Abbot, "cease your din;
  This is no season alms and prayers to give,
My porter never lets a beggar in;
  None touch my ring who not in honour live."
  And now the sun with the black clouds did strive,
And shedding on the ground his glaring ray;
The abbot spurred his steed, and eftsoon rode away.

Once more the sky was black, the thunder rolled,
  Fast running o'er the plain a priest was seen;
Not dight full proud, nor buttoned up in gold,

His cope and jape were grey, and eke were clean;
    A limitour he was of order seen;
And from the pathway-side then turned he,
Where the poor beggar lay beneath the elmen tree.

" An alms, sir priest! " the drooping pilgrim said,
    " For sweet Saint Mary and your order sake."
The limitour then loosened his pouch-thread,
    And did thereout a groat of silver take:
    The needy pilgrim did for haline shake,
" Here, take this silver, it may ease thy care,
We are God's stewards all, naught of our own we bear.

" But ah! unhappy pilgrim, learn of me.
    Scathe any give a rent-roll to their Lord;
Here, take my semi-cope, thou'rt bare, I see,
    'Tis thine; the saints will give me my reward."
    He left the pilgrim, and his way aborde.
Virgin and holy saint, who sit in gloure,
Or give the mighty will, or give the good man power.

                 THOMAS CHATTERTON.

THE SHIPWRECK

But now Athenian mountains they descry,
And o'er the surge Colonna frowns on high.
Beside the cape's projecting verge is placed
A range of columns long by time defaced;
First planted by devotion to sustain,
In elder times, Tritonia's sacred fane.
Foams the wild beach below with maddening rage,
Where waves and rocks a dreadful combat wage.
The sickly heaven, fermenting with its freight,
Still vomits o'er the main the feverish weight:
And now, while winged with ruin from on high,
Through the rent cloud the ragged lightnings fly,
A flash quick glancing on the nerves of light,
Struck the pale helmsman with eternal night:
Rodmond, who heard a piteous groan behind,
Touched with compassion, gazed upon the blind;

And while around his sad companions crowd,
He guides the unhappy victim to the shroud,
" Hie thee aloft, my gallant friend," he cries;
" Thy only succour on the mast relies."
The helm, bereft of half its vital force,
Now scarce subdued the wild unbridled course;
Quick to the abandoned wheel Arion came,
The ship's tempestuous sallies to reclaim.
Amazed he saw her, o'er the sounding foam
Upborne, to right and left distracted roam.
So gazed young Phaëton, with pale dismay,
When, mounted on the flaming car of day,
With rash and impious hand the stripling tried
The immortal coursers of the sun to guide.
The vessel, while the dread event draws nigh,
Seems more impatient o'er the waves to fly:
Fate spurs her on. Thus, issuing from afar,
Advances to the sun some blazing star;
And, as it feels the attraction's kindling force,
Springs onward with accelerated force.

With mournful look the seamen eyed the strand,
Where death's inexorable jaws expand;
Swift from their minds elapsed all dangers past,
As, dumb with terror, they beheld the last.
Now on the trembling shrouds, before, behind,
In mute suspense they mount into the wind.
The genius of the deep, on rapid wing,
The black eventful moment seemed to bring.
The fatal sisters, on the surge before,
Yoked their infernal horses to the prore.
The steersmen now received their last command
To wheel the vessel sidelong to the strand.
Twelve sailors, on the foremast who depend,
High on the platform of the top ascend:
Fatal retreat! for while the plunging prow
Immerges headlong in the wave below,
Down-pressed by watery weight the bowsprit bends,
And from above the stem deep crashing rends.
Beneath her beak the floating ruins lie;
The foremast totters, unsustained on high;
And now the ship, fore-lifted by the sea,
Hurls the tall fabric backward o'er her lee;
While, in the general wreck, the faithful stay

Drags the maintop-mast from its post away.
Flung from the mast, the seamen strive in vain
Through hostile floods their vessel to regain.
The waves they buffet, till, bereft of strength,
O'erpowered, they yield to cruel fate at length.
The hostile waters close around their head,
They sink for ever, numbered with the dead!

Those who remain their fearful doom await,
Nor longer mourn their lost companions' fate.
The heart that bleeds with sorrows all its own,
Forgets the pangs of friendship to bemoan.
Albert and Rodmond and Balemon here,
With young Arion, on the mast appear;
Even they, amid the unspeakable distress,
In every look distracting thoughts confess;
In every vein the refluent blood congeals,
And every bosom fatal terror feels.
Enclosed with all the demons of the main,
They viewed the adjacent shore, but viewed in vain. * *

And now, lashed on by destiny severe,
With horror fraught the dreadful scene drew near!
The ship hangs hovering on the verge of death,
Hell yawns, rocks rise, and breakers roar beneath!
In vain, alas! the sacred shades of yore,
Would arm the mind with philosophic lore;
In vain they'd teach us, at the latest breath,
To smile serene amid the pangs of death.
Even Zeno's self, and Epictetus old,
This fell abyss had shuddered to behold.
Had Socrates, for godlike virtue famed,
And wisest of the sons of men proclaimed,
Beheld this scene of frenzy and distress,
His soul had trembled to its last recess!
O yet confirm my heart, ye powers above,
This last tremendous shock of fate to prove!
The tottering frame of reason yet sustain!
Nor let this total ruin whirl my brain!

In vain the cords and axes were prepared,
For now the audacious seas insult the yard;
High o'er the ship they throw a horrid shade,
And o'er her burst, in terrible cascade.
Uplifted on the surge, to heaven she flies,
Her shattered top half buried in the skies,

Then headlong plunging thunders on the ground,
Earth groans, air trembles, and the deeps resound!
Her giant bulk the dread concussion feels,
And quivering with the wound, in torment reels;
So reels, convulsed with agonising throes,
The bleeding bull beneath the murderer's blows.
Again she plunges; hark! a second shock
Tears her strong bottom on the marble rock!
Down on the vale of death, with dismal cries,
The fated victims shuddering roll their eyes
In wild despair; while yet another stroke,
With deep convulsion, rends the solid oak:
Till, like the mine, in whose infernal cell
The lurking demons of destruction dwell,
At length asunder torn her frame divides,
And crashing spreads in ruin o'er the tides.

WILLIAM FALCONER.

THE DESERTED VILLAGE

SWEET Auburn! loveliest village of the plain,
Where health and plenty cheer'd the labouring swain,
Where smiling spring its earliest visit paid,
And parting summer's lingering blooms delay'd:
Dear lovely bowers of innocence and ease,
Seats of my youth,[1] when every sport could please,
How often have I loiter'd o'er thy green,
Where humble happiness endear'd each scene;
How often have I paus'd on every charm,
The shelter'd cot, the cultivated farm,
The never-failing brook, the busy mill,
The decent church that topp'd the neighbouring hill,
The hawthorn bush, with seats beneath the shade,
For talking age and whispering lovers made;
How often have I bless'd the coming day,
When toil remitting lent its turn to play,
And all the village train, from labour free,
Led up their sports beneath the spreading tree:

[1] Some of the details of the picture are borrowed from Lissoy, the
little hamlet in Westmeath where the author spent his younger days.

While many a pastime circled in the shade,
The young contending as the old survey'd;
And many a gambol frolick'd o'er the ground,
And sleights of art and feats of strength went round;
And still as each repeated pleasure tir'd,
Succeeding sports the mirthful band inspir'd;
The dancing pair that simply sought renown,
By holding out to tire each other down!
The swain mistrustless of his smutted face,
While secret laughter titter'd round the place;
The bashful virgin's side-long looks of love,
The matron's glance that would those looks reprove:
These were thy charms, sweet village; sports like these,
With sweet succession, taught even toil to please;
These round thy bowers their cheerful influence shed,
These were thy charms—But all these charms are fled.

Sweet smiling village, loveliest of the lawn,
Thy sports are fled, and all thy charms withdrawn;
Amidst thy bowers the tyrant's hand is seen,
And desolation saddens all thy green;
One only master grasps the whole domain,
And half a tillage stints thy smiling plain:
No more thy glassy brook reflects the day,
But chok'd with sedges, works its weedy way.
Along thy glades, a solitary guest,
The hollow-sounding bittern guards its nest;
Amidst thy desert walks the lapwing flies,
And tires their echoes with unvaried cries.
Sunk are thy bowers, in shapeless ruin all,
And the long grass o'ertops the mouldering wall;
And, trembling, shrinking from the spoiler's hand,
Far, far away, thy children leave the land.

Ill fares the land, to hastening ills a prey,
Where wealth accumulates, and men decay:
Princes and lords may flourish, or may fade;
A breath can make them, as a breath has made;
But a bold peasantry, their country's pride,
When once destroy'd, can never be supplied.

A time there was, ere England's griefs began,
When every rood of ground maintain'd its man;

For him light labour spread her wholesome store,
Just gave what life requir'd, but gave no more:
His best companions, innocence and health;
And his best riches, ignorance of wealth.

But times are alter'd; trade's unfeeling train
Usurp the land and dispossess the swain;
Along the lawn, where scatter'd hamlets rose,
Unwieldy wealth, and cumbrous pomp repose;
And every want to opulence allied,
And every pang that folly pays to pride.
Those gentle hours that plenty bade to bloom,
Those calm desires that ask'd but little room,
Those healthful sports that grac'd the peaceful scene,
Liv'd in each look, and brighten'd all the green;
These, far departing, seek a kinder shore,
And rural mirth and manners are no more.

Sweet AUBURN! parent of the blissful hour
Thy glades forlorn confess the tyrant's power.
Here as I take my solitary rounds,
Amidst thy tangling walks, and ruin'd grounds,
And, many a year elaps'd, return to view
Where once the cottage stood, the hawthorn grew,
Remembrance wakes with all her busy train,
Swells at my breast, and turns the past to pain.[1]

In all my wanderings round this world of care,
In all my griefs—and GOD has given my share—
I still had hopes my latest hours to crown,
Amidst these humble bowers to lay me down;
To husband out life's taper at the close,
And keep the flame from wasting by repose.
I still had hopes, for pride attends us still,
Amidst the swains to show my book-learn'd skill,
Around my fire an evening group to draw,
And tell of all I felt, and all I saw;
And, as an hare, whom hounds and horns pursue,
Pants to the place from whence at first she flew,
I still had hopes, my long vexations pass'd,
Here to return—and die at home at last.

[1] There is no satisfactory evidence that Goldsmith ever revisited
Ireland after he left it in 1752.

O blest retirement, friend to life's decline,
Retreats from care, that never must be mine,
How happy he who crowns in shades like these,
A youth of labour with an age of ease;
Who quits a world where strong temptations try,
And since 'tis hard to combat, learns to fly!
For him no wretches, born to work and weep,
Explore the mine, or tempt the dangerous deep;
No surly porter stands in guilty state
To spurn imploring famine from the gate;
But on he moves to meet his latter end,
Angels around befriending Virtue's friend;
Bends to the grave with unperceiv'd decay,
While Resignation gently slopes the way;
And, all his prospects brightening to the last,
His Heaven commences ere the world be pass'd![1]

Sweet was the sound, when oft at evening's close
Up yonder hill the village murmur rose;
There, as I pass'd with careless steps and slow,
The mingling notes came soften'd from below;
The swain responsive as the milkmaid sung,
The sober herd that low'd to meet their young;
The noisy geese that gabbled o'er the pool,
The playful children just let loose from school;
The watchdog's voice that bay'd the whisp'ring wind,
And the loud laugh that spoke the vacant mind;
These all in sweet confusion sought the shade,
And fill'd each pause the nightingale had made.
But now the sounds of population fail,
No cheerful murmurs fluctuate in the gale,
No busy steps the grass-grown footway tread,
For all the bloomy flush of life is fled.
All but yon widow'd, solitary thing,
That feebly bends beside the plashy spring;
She, wretched matron, forc'd in age, for bread,
To strip the brook with mantling cresses spread,
To pick her wintry faggot from the thorn,
To seek her nightly shed, and weep till morn;

[1] Under the title of *Resignation*, Reynolds in 1771 dedicated a print of an old man to Goldsmith as " expressing the character " sketched in this paragraph.

She only left of all the harmless train,
The sad historian of the pensive plain.[1]

Near yonder copse, where once the garden smil'd,
And still where many a garden flower grows wild;
There, where a few torn shrubs the place disclose,
The village preacher's modest mansion rose.[2]
A man he was to all the country dear,
And passing rich with forty pounds a year;
Remote from towns he ran his godly race,
Nor e'er had chang'd, nor wished to change his place;
Unpractis'd he to fawn, or seek for power,
By doctrines fashion'd to the varying hour;
Far other aims his heart had learn'd to prize,
More skill'd to raise the wretched than to rise.
His house was known to all the vagrant train,
He chid their wanderings, but reliev'd their pain;
The long remember'd beggar was his guest,
Whose beard descending swept his aged breast;
The ruin'd spendthrift, now no longer proud,
Claim'd kindred there, and had his claims allow'd;
The broken soldier, kindly bade to stay,
Sat by his fire, and talk'd the night away;
Wept o'er his wounds, or tales of sorrow done,
Shoulder'd his crutch, and show'd how fields were won.
Pleas'd with his guests, the good man learned to glow,
And quite forgot their vices in their woe;
Careless their merits, or their faults to scan,
His pity gave ere charity began.

Thus to relieve the wretched was his pride,
And e'en his failings lean'd to Virtue's side;
But in his duty prompt at every call,
He watch'd and wept, he pray'd and felt, for all.
And, as a bird each fond endearment tries
To tempt its new-fledg'd offspring to the skies,
He tried each art, reprov'd each dull delay,
Allur'd to brighter worlds, and led the way.

[1] This has been identified with Catherine Geraghty, a familiar
personage at Lissoy in Goldsmith's boyhood.
[2] The character that follows is probably combined from the author's
father, his brother Henry, and his uncle Contarine, all clergymen.

Beside the bed where parting life was laid,
And sorrow, guilt, and pain, by turns dismay'd,
The reverend champion stood. At his control
Despair and anguish fled the struggling soul;
Comfort came down the trembling wretch to raise,
And his last faltering accents whisper'd praise.

At church with meek and unaffected grace,
H s looks adorn'd the venerable place;
Truth from his lips prevail'd with double sway,
And fools, who came to scoff, remain'd to pray.
The service pass'd, around the pious man,
With steady zeal, each honest rustic ran;
Even children follow'd with endearing wile,
And pluck'd his gown, to share the good man's smile.
His ready smile a parent's warmth express'd,
Their welfare pleas'd him, and their cares distress'd;
To them his heart, his love, his griefs were given,
But all his serious thoughts had rest in Heaven.
As some tall cliff, that lifts its awful form,
Swells from the vale, and midway leaves the storm,
Though round its breast the rolling clouds are spread,
Eternal sunshine settles on its head.

Beside yon straggling fence that skirts the way,
With blossom'd furze unprofitably gay,
There, in his noisy mansion, skill'd to rule,
The village master taught his little school;[1]
A man severe he was, and stern to view;
I knew him well, and every truant knew;
Well had the boding tremblers learn'd to trace
The day's disasters in his morning face;
Full well they laugh'd, with counterfeited glee,
At all his jokes, for many a joke had he;
Full well the busy whisper, circling round,
Convey'd the dismal tidings when he frown'd;
Yet he was kind: or if severe in aught,
The love he bore to learning was in fault;
The village all declar'd how much he knew;
'Twas certain he could write, and cypher too;

[1] Some of the traits of this portrait correspond with those of Goldsmith's master at Lissoy, one Byrne.

Lands he could measure, terms and tides presage,
And even the story ran that he could gauge.
In arguing too, the parson own'd his skill,
For e'en though vanquish'd, he could argue still;
While words of learned length and thundering sound
Amaz'd the gazing rustics rang'd around,
And still they gaz'd, and still the wonder grew,
That one small head could carry all he knew.

But past is all his fame. The very spot
Where many a time he triumph'd, is forgot.
Near yonder thorn, that lifts its head on high,
Where once the sign-post caught the passing eye,
Low lies that house where nut-brown draughts inspir'd,
Where grey-beard mirth and smiling toil retir'd,
Where village statesmen talk'd with looks profound,
And news much older than their ale went round.
Imagination fondly stoops to trace
The parlour splendours of that festive place;
The white-wash'd wall, the nicely sanded floor,
The varnish'd clock that click'd behind the door;
The chest contriv'd a double debt to pay,
A bed by night, a chest of drawers by day;
The pictures plac'd for ornament and use,
The twelve good rules,[1] the royal game of goose;[2]
The hearth, except when winter chill'd the day,
With aspen boughs, and flowers, and fennel gay;
While broken tea-cups, wisely kept for show,
Rang'd o'er the chimney, glisten'd in a row.

Vain transitory splendours! could not all
Reprieve the tottering mansion from its fall!
Obscure it sinks, nor shall it more impart
An hour's importance to the poor man's heart;
Thither no more the peasant shall repair
To sweet oblivion of his daily care;
No more the farmer's news, the barber's tale,
No more the wood-man's ballad shall prevail;
No more the smith his dusky brow shall clear,

---

[1] The well-known maxims "found in the study of King Charles the First, of Blessed Memory," and common in Goldsmith's day as a broadside.
[2] See Strutt's *Sports and Pastimes*, Bk. iv. ch. 2, § xxv.

Relax his ponderous strength, and lean to hear;
The host himself no longer shall be found
Careful to see the mantling bliss go round;
Nor the coy maid, half willing to be press'd,
Shall kiss the cup to pass it to the rest.

Yes! let the rich deride, the proud disdain,
These simple blessings of the lowly train;
To me more dear, congenial to my heart,
One native charm, than all the gloss of art;
Spontaneous joys, where Nature has its play,
The soul adopts, and owns their first-born sway;
Lightly they frolic o'er the vacant mind,
Unenvied, unmolested, unconfin'd:
But the long pomp, the midnight masquerade,
With all the freaks of wanton wealth array'd,
In these, ere triflers half their wish obtain,
The toiling pleasure sickens into pain;
And, even while fashion's brightest arts decoy,
The heart distrusting asks, if this be joy.

Ye friends to truth, ye statesmen, who survey
The rich man's joys increase, the poor's decay,
'Tis yours to judge, how wide the limits stand
Between a splendid and a happy land.
Proud swells the tide with loads of freighted ore,
And shouting Folly hails them from her shore;
Hoards, even beyond the miser's wish abound,
And rich men flock from all the world around.
Yet count our gains. This wealth is but a name
That leaves our useful products still the same.
Not so the loss. The man of wealth and pride
Takes up a space that many poor supplied;
Space for his lake, his park's extended bounds,
Space for his horses, equipage, and hounds;
The robe that wraps his limbs in silken sloth
Has robb'd the neighbouring fields of half their growth,
His seat, where solitary sports are seen,
Indignant spurns the cottage from the green;
Around the world each needful product flies,
For all the luxuries the world supplies:
While thus the land adorn'd for pleasure, all
In barren splendour feebly waits the fall.

As some fair female unadorn'd and plain,
Secure to please while youth confirms her reign,
Slights every borrow'd charm that dress supplies,
Nor shares with art the triumph of her eyes:
But when those charms are pass'd, for charms are frail,
When time advances and when lovers fail,
She then shines forth, solicitous to bless,
In all the glaring impotence of dress.
Thus fares the land, by luxury betray'd,
In nature's simplest charms at first array'd,
But verging to decline, its splendours rise,
Its vistas strike, its palaces surprise;
While, scourg'd by famine, from the smiling land
The mournful peasant leads his humble band;
And while he sinks, without one arm to save,
The country blooms—a garden, and a grave.

Where then, ah! where, shall poverty reside,
To 'scape the pressure of contiguous pride?
If to some common's fenceless limits stray'd,
He drives his flock to pick the scanty blade,
Those fenceless fields the sons of wealth divide,
And even the bare-worn common is denied.

If to the city sped—What waits him there?
To see profusion that he must not share;
To see ten thousand baneful arts combin'd
To pamper luxury, and thin mankind;
To see those joys the sons of pleasure know
Extorted from his fellow creature's woe.
Here, while the courtier glitters in brocade,
There the pale artist plies the sickly trade;
Here, while the proud their long-drawn pomps display,
There the black gibbet glooms beside the way.
The dome where Pleasure holds her midnight reign
Here, richly deck'd, admits the gorgeous train;
Tumultuous grandeur crowds the blazing square,
The rattling chariots clash, the torches glare.
Sure scenes like these no troubles e'er annoy!
Sure these denote one universal joy!
Are these thy serious thoughts?—Ah, turn thine eyes
Where the poor houseless shivering female lies.[1]

[1] Cf. *The Bee*, 27th October, 1759 (*A City Night-Piece*).

She once, perhaps, in village plenty bless'd,
Has wept at tales of innocence distress'd;
Her modest looks the cottage might adorn,
Sweet as the primrose peeps beneath the thorn;
Now lost to all; her friends, her virtue fled,
Near her betrayer's door she lays her head,
And, pinch'd with cold, and shrinking from the shower,
With heavy heart deplores that luckless hour,
When idly first, ambitious of the town,
She left her wheel and robes of country brown.

Do thine, sweet AUBURN, thine, the loveliest train,
Do thy fair tribes participate her pain?
E'en now, perhaps, by cold and hunger led,
At proud men's doors they ask a little bread!

Ah, no. To distant climes, a dreary scene,
Where half the convex world intrudes between,
Through torrid tracts with fainting steps they go,
Where wild Altama[1] murmurs to their woe.
Far different there from all that charm'd before,
The various terrors of that horrid shore;
Those blazing suns that dart a downward ray,
And fiercely shed intolerable day;
Those matted woods where birds forget to sing,
But silent bats in drowsy clusters cling;
Those poisonous fields with rank luxuriance crown'd,
Where the dark scorpion gathers death around;
Where at each step the stranger fears to wake
The rattling terrors of the vengeful snake;
Where crouching tigers wait their hapless prey,
And savage men more murderous still than they;
While oft in whirls the mad tornado flies,
Mingling the ravag'd landscape with the skies.
Far different these from every former scene,
The cooling brook, the grassy-vested green,
The breezy covert of the warbling grove,
That only shelter'd thefts of harmless love.

Good Heaven! what sorrows gloom'd that parting day,
That call'd them from their native walks away;

[1] Alatamaha, in Georgia, North America.

When the poor exiles, every pleasure pass'd,
Hung round their bowers, and fondly look'd their last,
And took a long farewell, and wish'd in vain
For seats like these beyond the western main;
And shuddering still to face the distant deep,
Return'd and wept, and still returned to weep.
The good old sire, the first prepar'd to go
To new-found worlds, and wept for others' woe;
But for himself, in conscious virtue brave,
He only wish'd for worlds beyond the grave.
His lovely daughter, lovelier in her tears,
The fond companion of his helpless years,
Silent went next, neglectful of her charms,
And left a lover's for a father's arms.
With louder plaints the mother spoke her woes,
And bless'd the cot where every pleasure rose;
And kiss'd her thoughtless babes with many a tear,
And clasp'd them close, in sorrow doubly dear;
Whilst her fond husband strove to lend relief
In all the silent manliness of grief.

O luxury! thou curs'd by Heaven's decree,
How ill exchang'd are things like these for thee!
How do thy potions, with insidious joy
Diffuse their pleasures only to destroy!
Kingdoms, by thee, to sickly greatness grown,
Boast of a florid vigour not their own;
At every draught more large and large they grow,
A bloated mass of rank unwieldy woe;
Till sapp'd their strength, and every part unsound,
Down, down they sink, and spread a ruin round.

Even now the devastation is begun,
And half the business of destruction done;
Even now, methinks, as pondering here I stand,
I see the rural virtues leave the land:
Down where yon anchoring vessel spreads the sail,
That idly waiting flaps with every gale,
Downward they move, a melancholy band,
Pass from the shore, and darken all the strand.
Contented toil, and hospitable care,
And kind connubial tenderness, are there;

And piety with wishes plac'd above,
And steady loyalty, and faithful love.
And thou, sweet Poetry, thou loveliest maid,
Still first to fly where sensual joys invade;
Unfit in these degenerate times of shame,
To catch the heart, or strike for honest fame:
Dear charming nymph, neglected and decried,
My shame in crowds, my solitary pride;
Thou source of all my bliss, and all my woe,
That found'st me poor at first, and keep'st me so;
Thou guide by which the nobler arts excel,
Thou nurse of every virtue, fare thee well!
Farewell, and Oh! where'er thy voice be tried,
On Torno's[1] cliffs, or Pambamarca's[2] side,
Whether where equinoctial fervours glow,
Or winter wraps the polar world in snow,
Still let thy voice, prevailing over time,
Redress the rigours of th' inclement clime;
Aid slighted truth; with thy persuasive strain
Teach erring man to spurn the rage of gain;
Teach him, that states of native strength possess'd,
Though very poor, may still be very bless'd;
That trade's proud empire hastes to swift decay,
As ocean sweeps the labour'd mole away;
While self-dependent power can time defy,
As rocks resist the billows and the sky.[3]

                    OLIVER GOLDSMITH.

[1] Tornea, a river falling into the Gulf of Bothnia.
[2] A mountain near Quito, South America.
[3] Johnson wrote the last four lines. (Birkbeck Hill's *Boswell*, 1887, ii. 7.)

A SONG TO DAVID

ARGUMENT. Invocation, i-iii. The excellence and lustre of David's character (in twelve points of view), proved from the history of his life, iv-xvi. He consecrates his genius for consolation and edification:—The subjects he made choice of—the Supreme Being—angels, men of renown, the works of nature in all directions, either particularly or collectively considered, xvii-xxvi. He obtains power over infernal spirits, and the malignity of his enemies; wins the heart of Michal, xxvii-xxix. Shows that the pillars of knowledge are the monuments of God's works in the first week, xxx-xxxvii.

An exercise upon the Decalogue, xl-xlix. The transcendent virtue of praise and adoration, l-li. An exercise upon the seasons and the right use of them, lii-lxiii. An exercise upon the senses, and how to subdue them, lxiv-lxxi. An amplification in five degrees, which is wrought up to this conclusion:—That the best poet who ever lived, was thought worthy of the highest honour which possibly can be conceived, as the Saviour of the world was ascribed to his house, and called his son in the body, lxxii. The End.

I

O Thou, that sitt'st upon a throne,
With harp of high, majestic tone,
    To praise the King of kings:
And voice of heaven-ascending swell,
Which, while its deeper notes excel,
    Clear as a clarion rings;

II

To bless each valley, grove, and coast,
And charm the cherubs to the post
    Of gratitude in throngs;
To keep the days on Zion's Mount,
And send the Year to his account,
    With dances and with songs:

III

O servant of God's holiest charge,
The minister of praise at large,
    Which thou mayst now receive;
From thy blest mansion hail and hear,
From topmost eminence appear
    To this the wreath I weave.

IV

Great, valiant, pious, good, and clean,
Sublime, contemplative, serene,
   Strong, constant, pleasant, wise!
Bright effluence of exceeding grace;
Best man! the swiftness and the race,
   The peril and the prize!

V

Great—from the lustre of his crown,
From Samuel's horn, and God's renown,
   Which is the people's voice;
For all the host, from rear to van,
Applauded and embraced the man—
   The man of God's own choice.

VI

Valiant—the word, and up he rose:
The fight—he triumphed o'er the foes
   Whom God's just laws abhor;
And, armed in gallant faith, he took
Against the boaster, from the brook,
   The weapons of the war.

VII

Pious—magnificent and grand,
'Twas he the famous temple plann'd,
   (The seraph in his soul:)
Foremost to give the Lord his dues,
Foremost to bless the welcome news,
   And foremost to condole.

VIII

Good—from Jehudah's genuine vein,
From God's best nature, good in grain,

His aspect and his heart:
To pity, to forgive, to save,
Witness En-gedi's conscious cave,
    And Shimei's blunted dart.

IX

Clean—if perpetual prayer be pure,
And love, which could itself inure
    To fasting and to fear—
Clean in his gestures, hands and feet,
To smite the lyre, the dance complete,
    To play the sword and spear.

X

Sublime—invention ever young,
Of vast conception, tow'ring tongue,
    To God the eternal theme;
Notes from yon exaltations caught,
Unrivall'd royalty of thought,
    O'er meaner strains supreme.

XI

Contemplative—on God to fix
His musings, and above the six
    The Sabbath-day he blessed;
'Twas then his thoughts self-conquest pruned,
And heavenly melancholy tuned,
    To bless and bear the rest.

XII

Serene—to sow the seeds of peace,
Remembering, when he watched the fleece,
    How sweetly Kidron purled—
To further knowledge, silence vice,
And plant perpetual paradise,
    When God had calmed the world.

XIII

Strong—in the Lord, who could defy
Satan, and all his powers that lie
   In sempiternal night;
And hell, and horror, and despair
Were as the lion and the bear
   To his undaunted might.

XIV

Constant—in love to God, THE TRUTH,
Age, manhood, infancy, and youth:
   To Jonathan his friend
Constant, beyond the verge of death;
And Ziba, and Mephibosheth,
   His endless fame attend.

XV

Pleasant—and various as the year;
Man, soul, and angel without Peer,
   Priest, champion, sage, and boy;
In armour or in ephod clad,
His pomp, his piety was glad;
   Majestic was his joy.

XVI

Wise—in recovery from his fall,
Whence rose his eminence o'er all,
   Of all the most reviled;
The light of Israel in his ways,
Wise are his precepts, prayer, and praise,
   And counsel to his child.

XVII

His muse, bright angel of his verse,
Gives balm for all the thorns that pierce,

For all the pangs that rage:
Blest light, still gaining on the gloom,
The more than Michal of his bloom,
    The Abishag of his age.

XVIII

He sang of God—the mighty source
Of all things—the stupendous force
    On which all strength depends;
From Whose right arm, beneath Whose eyes,
All period, power, and enterprise
    Commences, reigns, and ends.

XIX

Angels—their ministry and meed,
Which to and fro with blessings speed,
    Or with their citterns wait;
Where Michael, with his millions, bows,
Where dwells the seraph and his spouse,
    The cherub and her mate.

XX

Of man—the semblance and effect
Of God and love—the saint elect
    For infinite applause—
To rule the land, and briny broad,
To be laborious in his laud,
    And heroes in his cause.

XXI

The world—the clustering spheres He made,
The glorious light, the soothing shade,
    Dale, champaign, grove, and hill;
The multitudinous abyss,
Where Secrecy remains in bliss,
    And Wisdom hides her skill.

XXII

Trees, plants, and flowers—of virtuous root;
Gem yielding blossom, yielding fruit,
    Choice gums and precious balm;
Bless ye the nosegay in the vale,
And with the sweetness of the gale
    Enrich the thankful psalm.

XXIII

Of fowl—even every beak and wing
Which cheer the winter, hail the spring,
    That live in peace or prey;
They that make music, or that mock,
The quail, the brave domestic cock,
    The raven, swan, and jay.

XXIV

Of fishes—every size and shape,
Which nature frames of light escape,
    Devouring man to shun:
The shells are in the wealthy deep,
The shoals upon the surface leap,
    And love the glancing sun.

XXV

Of beasts—the beaver plods his task;
While the sleek tigers roll and bask,
    Nor yet the shades arouse;
Her cave the mining coney scoops;
Where o'er the mead the mountain stoops,
    The kids exult and browse.

XXVI

Of gems—their virtue and their price,
Which, hid in earth from man's device,

Their darts of lustre sheathe;
The jasper of the master's stamp,
The topaz blazing like a lamp,
   Among the mines beneath.

XXVII

Blest was the tenderness he felt,
When to his graceful harp he knelt,
   And did for audience call;
When Satan with his hand he quelled,
And in serene suspense he held
   The frantic throes of Saul.

XXVIII

His furious foes no more maligned
As he such melody divined,
   And sense and soul detained;
Now striking strong, now soothing soft,
He sent the godly sounds aloft,
   Or in delight refrained.

XXIX

When up to heaven his thoughts he piled
From fervent lips fair Michal smiled,
   As blush to blush she stood;
And chose herself the queen, and gave
Her utmost from her heart—" so brave,
   And plays his hymns so good."

XXX

The pillars of the Lord are seven,
Which stand from earth to topmost heaven;
   His wisdom drew the plan;
His Word accomplished the design,
From brightest gem to deepest mine,
   From CHRIST enthroned to Man.

XXXI

Alpha, the cause of causes, first
In station, fountain, whence the burst
  Of light and blaze of day;
Whence bold attempt, and brave advance,
Have motion, life, and ordinance,
  And heaven itself its stay.

XXXII

Gamma supports the glorious arch
On which angelic legions march,
  And is with sapphires paved;
Thence the fleet clouds are sent adrift,
And thence the painted folds that lift
  The crimson veil, are waved.

XXXIII

Eta with living sculpture breathes,
With verdant carvings, flowery wreaths,
  Of never-wasting bloom;
In strong relief his goodly base
All instruments of labour grace,
  The trowel, spade, and loom.

XXXIV

Next Theta stands to the Supreme—
Who formed in number, sign, and scheme,
  The illustrious lights that are;
And one addressed his saffron robe,
And one, clad in a silver globe,
  Held rule with every star.

XXXV

Iota's tuned to choral hymns
Of those that fly, while he that swims

In thankful safety lurks;
And foot, and chapiter, and niche,
The various histories enrich
  Of God's recorded works.

XXXVI

Sigma presents the social droves
With him that solitary roves,
  And man of all the chief;
Fair on whose face, and stately frame,
Did God impress His hallowed name,
  For ocular belief.

XXXVII

OMEGA! GREATEST and the BEST,
Stands sacred to the day of rest,
  For gratitude and thought;
Which blessed the world upon his pole,
And gave the universe his goal,
  And closed the infernal draught.

XXXVIII

O DAVID, scholar of the Lord!
Such is thy science, whence reward,
  And infinite degree;
O strength, O sweetness, lasting ripe!
God's harp thy symbol, and thy type
  The lion and the bee!

XXXIX

There is but One who ne'er rebelled,
But One by passion unimpelled,
  By pleasures unenticed;
He from himself hath semblance sent,
Grand object of his own content,
  And saw the God in CHRIST.

XL

Tell them, I Am, Jehovah said
To Moses; while earth heard in dread,
   And, smitten to the heart,
At once above, beneath, around,
All Nature, without voice or sound,
   Replied, "O Lord, Thou Art."

XLI

Thou art—to give and to confirm,
For each his talent and his term;
   All flesh thy bounties share:
Thou shalt not call thy brother fool:
The porches of the Christian school
   Are meekness, peace, and prayer.

XLII

Open and naked of offence,
Man's made of mercy, soul, and sense:
   God armed the snail and wilk;
Be good to him that pulls thy plough;
Due food and care, due rest allow
   For her that yields thee milk.

XLIII

Rise up before the hoary head,
And God's benign commandment dread,
   Which says thou shalt not die:
"Not as I will, but as Thou wilt,"
Prayed He, whose conscience knew no guilt;
   With Whose blessed pattern vie.

XLIV

Use all thy passions! love is thine,
And joy, and jealousy divine;

Thine hope's eternal fort,
And care thy leisure to disturb
With fear concupiscence to curb,
    And rapture to transport.

XLV

Act simply, as occasion asks;
Put mellow wine in seasoned casks;
    Till not with ass and bull:
Remember thy baptismal bond;
Keep from commixtures foul and fond,
    Nor work thy flax with wool.

XLVI

Distribute; pay the Lord His tithe,
And make the widow's heart-strings blithe;
    Resort with those that weep:
As you from all and each expect,
For all and each thy love direct,
    And render as you reap.

XLVII

The slander and its bearer spurn,
And propagating praise sojourn,
    To make thy welcome last;
Turn from old Adam to the New:
By hope futurity pursue:
    Look upwards to the past.

XLVIII

Control thine eye, salute success,
Honour the wiser, happier bless,
    And for their neighbour feel;
Grutch not of mammon and his leaven,
Work emulation up to heaven
    By knowledge and by zeal.

XLIX

O DAVID, highest in the list
Of worthies, on God's ways insist,
    The genuine word repeat!
Vain are the documents of men,
And vain the flourish of the pen
    That keeps the fool's conceit.

L

Praise above all—for praise prevails;
Heap up the measure, load the scales,
    And good to goodness add:
The generous soul her Saviour aids,
But peevish obloquy degrades;
    The Lord is great and glad.

LI

For ADORATION all the ranks
Of Angels yield eternal thanks,
    And David in the midst:
With God's good poor, which, last and least
In man's esteem, Thou to Thy feast,
    O blessèd Bridegroom, bidst.

LII

For ADORATION seasons change,
And order, truth, and beauty range,
    Adjust, attract, and fill:
The grass the polyanthus checks;
And polished porphyry reflects,
    By the descending rill.

LIII

Rich almonds colour to the prime
For ADORATION; tendrils climb,

And fruit-trees pledge their gems;
And Ivis, with her gorgeous vest,
Builds for her eggs her cunning nest,
   And bell-flowers bow their stems.

LIV

With vinous syrup cedars spout;
From rocks pure honey gushing out,
   For ADORATION springs:
All scenes of painting crowd the map
Of nature; to the mermaid's pap
   The scalèd infant clings.

LV

The spotted ounce and playsome cubs
Run rustling 'mong the flowering shrubs,
   And lizards feed the moss;
For ADORATION beasts embark,
While waves upholding halcyon's ark
   No longer roar and toss.

LVI

While Israel sits beneath his fig,
With coral root and amber sprig
   The weaned adventurer sports;
Where to the palm the jasmine cleaves,
For ADORATION 'mong the leaves
   The gale his peace reports.

LVII

Increasing days their reign exalt,
Nor in the pink and mottled vault
   The opposing spirits tilt;
And by the coasting reader spied,
The silverlings and crusions glide
   For ADORATION gilt.

LVIII

For ADORATION ripening canes,
And cocoa's purest milk detains
    The western pilgrim's staff;
Where rain in clasping boughs enclosed,
And vines with oranges disposed,
    Embower the social laugh.

LIX

Now labour his reward receives,
For ADORATION counts his sheaves,
    To peace, her bounteous prince;
The nect'rine his strong tint imbibes,
And apples of ten thousand tribes,
    And quick peculiar quince.

LX

The wealthy crops of whitening rice
'Mongst thyine woods and groves of spice,
    For ADORATION grow;
And, marshalled in the fencèd land,
The peaches and pomegranates stand,
    Where wild carnations blow.

LXI

The laurels with the winter strive;
The crocus burnishes alive
    Upon the snow-clad earth;
For ADORATION myrtles stay
To keep the garden from dismay,
    And bless the sight from dearth.

LXII

The pheasant shows his pompous neck;
And ermine, jealous of a speck,

With fear eludes offence:
The sable, with his glossy pride,
For ADORATION is descried,
    Where frosts the waves condense.

LXIII

The cheerful holly, pensive yew,
And holy thorn, their trim renew;
    The squirrel hoards his nuts;
All creatures batten o'er their stores,
And careful nature all her doors
    For ADORATION shuts.

LXIV

For ADORATION, DAVID's Psalms
Lift up the heart to deeds of alms;
    And he, who kneels and chants,
Prevails his passions to control,
Finds meat and medicine to the soul,
    Which for translation pants.

LXV

For ADORATION, beyond match,
The scholar bullfinch aims to catch
    The soft flute's ivory touch;
And, careless, on the hazel spray
The daring redbreast keeps at bay
    The damsel's greedy clutch.

LXVI

For ADORATION, in the skies
The Lord's philosopher espies
    The dog, the ram, and rose;
The planet's ring, Orion's sword;
Nor is his greatness less adored
    In the vile worm that glows.

LXVII

For ADORATION, on the strings
The western breezes work their wings,
  The captive ear to soothe—
Hark! 'tis a voice—how still, and small—
That makes the cataracts to fall,
  Or bids the sea be smooth!

LXVIII

For ADORATION, incense comes
From bezoar, and Arabian gums,
  And from the civet's fur:
But as for prayer, or e'er it faints,
Far better is the breath of saints
  Than galbanum or myrrh.

LXIX

For ADORATION, from the down
Of damsons to th' anana's crown,
  God sends to tempt the taste;
And while the luscious zest invites
The sense, that in the scene delights,
  Commands desire be chaste.

LXX

For ADORATION, all the paths
Of grace are open, all the baths,
  Of purity refresh;
And all the rays of glory beam
To deck the man of God's esteem,
  Who triumphs o'er the flesh.

LXXI

For ADORATION, in the dome
Of CHRIST, the sparrows find a home;

And on his olives perch;
The swallow also dwells with thee,
O man of God's humility,
    Within his Saviour's CHURCH.

LXXII

Sweet is the dew that falls betimes,
And drops upon the leafy limes;
    Sweet, Hermon's fragrant air:
Sweet is the lily's silver bell,
And sweet the wakeful tapers' smell
    That watch for early prayer.

LXXIII

Sweet the young nurse, with love intense,
Which smiles o'er sleeping innocence;
    Sweet when the lost arrive:
Sweet the musician's ardour beats,
While his vague mind's in quest of sweets,
    The choicest flowers to hive.

LXXIV

Sweeter, in all the strains of love,
The language of thy turtle-dove,
    Paired to thy swelling chord;
Sweeter, with every grace endued,
The glory of thy gratitude
    Respired unto the Lord.

LXXV

Strong is the horse upon his speed;
Strong in pursuit the rapid glede,
    Which makes at once his game:
Strong the tall ostrich on the ground;
Strong through the turbulent profound
    Shoots Xiphias to his aim.

LXXVI

Strong is the lion—like a coal
His eyeball—like a bastion's mole
  His chest against the foes:
Strong the gier-eagle on his sail,
Strong against tide the enormous whale
  Emerges as he goes.

LXXVII

But stronger still in earth and air,
And in the sea, the man of prayer,
  And far beneath the tide:
And in the seat to faith assigned,
Where ask is have, where seek is find,
  Where knock is open wide.

LXXVIII

Beauteous the fleet before the gale;
Beauteous the multitudes in mail,
  Ranked arms, and crested heads;
Beauteous the garden's umbrage mild,
Walk, water, meditated wild,
  And all the bloomy beds.

LXXIX

Beauteous the moon full on the lawn;
And beauteous when the veil's withdrawn,
  The virgin to her spouse:
Beauteous the temple, decked and filled,
When to the heaven of heavens they build
  Their heart-directed vows.

LXXX

Beauteous, yea beauteous more than these,
The Shepherd King upon his knees,

For his momentous trust;
With wish of infinite conceit,
For man, beast, mute, the small and great,
And prostrate dust to dust.

LXXXI

Precious the bounteous widow's mite;
And precious, for extreme delight,
The largess from the churl:
Precious the ruby's blushing blaze,
And alba's blest imperial rays,
And pure cerulean pearl.

LXXXII

Precious the penitential tear;
And precious is the sigh sincere;
Acceptable to God:
And precious are the winning flowers,
In gladsome Israel's feast of bowers,
Bound on the hallowed sod.

LXXXIII

More precious that diviner part
Of David, even the Lord's own heart,
Great, beautiful, and new;
In all things where it was intent,
In all extremes, in each event,
Proof—answering true to true.

LXXXIV

Glorious the sun in mid career;
Glorious th' assembled fires appear;
Glorious the comet's train:
Glorious the trumpet and alarm;
Glorious th' Almighty's stretched-out arm;
Glorious th' enraptured main:

LXXXV

Glorious the northern lights a-stream;
Glorious the song, when God's the theme;
  Glorious the thunder's roar:
Glorious Hosannah from the den;
Glorious the catholic Amen;
  Glorious the martyr's gore:

LXXXVI

Glorious,—more glorious, is the crown
Of Him that brought salvation down,
  By meekness called thy Son:
Thou that stupendous truth believed;—
And now the matchless deed's achieved,
  DETERMINED, DARED, and DONE.

CHRISTOPHER SMART.

TAM O' SHANTER

A TALE

Of Brownyis and of Bogillis full is this Buke.
GAWIN DOUGLAS.

This poem was first published in 1791, in a book entitled *Antiquties of Scotland*, by Captain Grose. In the preface the author said: " To my ingenious friend, Mr. Robert Burns, I have been variously obligated; he was not only at the pains of marking out what was worthy of notice in Ayrshire, the county honoured by his birth, but he also wrote expressly for the work, the *pretty tale* annexed to Alloway Church." The *pretty tale* was *Tam o' Shanter*. The poem was composed one afternoon in October, 1790, whilst the poet was walking by the banks of the river Ellisland. Of it Sir Walter Raleigh says: " This is in many ways the strongest and maturest of all his works. . . . In *Tam o' Shanter* Burns surpasses himself: no masterpiece of narrative so concise, so various, so telling, is to be found even in Chaucer. Is it not a strange thing that the king of poetic story-tellers told only one story ? "

WHEN chapman billies leave the street,
And drouthy neibors neibors meet;
As market days are wearing late,
And folk begin to tak the gate,
While we sit bousing at the nappy,
An' getting fou and unco happy,

We think na on the lang Scots miles,
The mosses, waters, slaps and stiles,
That lie between us and our hame,
Where sits our sulky, sullen dame,
Gathering her brows like gathering storm,
Nursing her wrath to keep it warm.

This truth fand honest TAM O' SHANTER,
As he frae Ayr ae night did canter:
(Auld Ayr, wham ne'er a town surpasses,
For honest men and bonie lasses).

O Tam! had'st thou but been sae wise,
As taen thy ain wife Kate's advice!
She tauld thee weel thou was a skellum,
A blethering, blustering, drunken blellum;
That frae November till October,
Ae market-day thou was na sober;
That ilka melder wi' the Miller,
Thou sat as lang as thou had siller;
That ev'ry naig was ca'd a shoe on,
The Smith and thee gat roarin fou on;
That at the Lord's house, ev'n on Sunday,
Thou drank wi' Kirkton Jean till Monday;
She prophesied that late or soon,
Thou wad be found, deep drown'd in Doon,
Or catch'd wi' warlocks in the mirk,
By Alloway's auld, haunted kirk.

Ah, gentle dames! it gars me greet,
To think how mony counsels sweet,
How mony lengthen'd, sage advices,
The husband frae the wife despises!

But to our tale:—Ae market night,
Tam had got planted unco right,
Fast by an ingle, bleezing finely,
Wi' reaming swats that drank divinely;
And at his elbow, Souter Johnie,
His ancient, trusty, drouthy crony:
Tam lo'ed him like a very brither;
They had been fou for weeks thegither.
The night drave on wi sangs an' clatter;

And aye the ale was growing better:
The Landlady and Tam grew gracious,
Wi' favours secret, sweet and precious:
The Souter tauld his queerest stories;
The Landlord's laugh was ready chorus:
The storm without might rair and rustle,
Tam did na mind the storm a whistle.

Care, mad to see a man sae happy,
E'en drown'd himsel amang the nappy.
As bees flee hame wi' lades o' treasure,
The minutes wing'd their way wi' pleasure:
Kings may be blest, but Tam was glorious,
O'er a' the ills o' life victorious!

But pleasures are like poppies spread,
You seize the flow'r, its bloom is shed;
Or like the snow falls in the river,
A moment white—then melts for ever;
Or like the Borealis race,
That flit ere you can point their place;
Or like the Rainbow's lovely form
Evanishing amid the storm.—
Nae man can tether Time nor Tide,
The hour approaches Tam maun ride;
That hour, o' night's black arch the key-stane,
That dreary hour he mounts his beast in;
And sic a night he taks the road in,
As ne'er poor sinner was abroad in.

The wind blew as 'twad blawn its last;
The rattling showers rose on the blast;
The speedy gleams the darkness swallow'd;
Loud, deep, and lang the thunder bellow'd:
That night, a child might understand,
The deil had business on his hand.

Weel-mounted on his grey mare Meg,
A better never lifted leg,
Tam skelpit on thro' dub and mire,
Despising wind, and rain, and fire;

Whiles holding fast his gude blue bonnet,
Whiles crooning o'er some auld Scots sonnet,
Whiles glow'rin round wi' prudent cares,
Lest bogles catch him unawares;
Kirk-Alloway was drawing nigh,
Where ghaists and houlets nightly cry.

By this time he was cross the ford,
Where in the snaw the chapman smoor'd;
And past the birks and meikle stane,
Where drunken Charlie brak 's neck-bane;
And thro' the whins, and by the cairn,
Where hunters fand the murder'd bairn;
And near the thorn, aboon the well,
Where Mungo's mither hang'd hersel'.
Before him Doon pours all his floods,
The doubling storm roars thro' the woods,
The lightnings flash from pole to pole,
Near and more near the thunders roll,
When, glimmering thro' the groaning trees,
Kirk-Alloway seem'd in a bleeze,
Thro' ilka bore the beams were glancing,
And loud resounded mirth and dancing.

Inspiring bold John Barleycorn!
What dangers thou canst make us scorn!
Wi' tippenny, we fear nae evil:
Wi' usquabae, we'll face the devil!
The swats sae ream'd in Tammie's noddle,
Fair play, he car'd na deils a boddle,
But Maggie stood, right sair astonish'd,
Till, by the heel and hand admonish'd,
She ventur'd forward on the light;
And, wow! Tam saw an unco sight!
Warlocks and witches in a dance:
Nae cotillon, brent new frae France,
But hornpipes, jigs, strathspeys, and reels,
Put life and mettle in their heels.
A winnock-bunker in the east,
There sat auld Nick, in shape o' beast;
A tousie tyke, black, grim, and large,
To gie them music was his charge:

He screw'd the pipes and gart them skirl,
Till roof and rafters a' did dirl.—
Coffins stood round, like open presses,
That shaw'd the Dead in their last dresses;
And (by some devilish cantraip sleight)
Each in its cauld hand held a light.
By which heroic Tam was able
To note upon the haly table,
A murderer's banes, in gibbet-airns;
Twa span-lang, wee, unchristened bairns;
A thief, new-cutted frae a rape,
Wi' his last gasp his gab did gape;
Five tomahawks, wi' blude red-rusted;
Five scimitars, wi' murder crusted;
A garter which a babe had strangled;
A knife, a father's throat had mangled,
Whom his ain son of life bereft,
The grey hairs yet stack to the heft;
Wi' mair of horrible and awfu',
Which even to name wad be unlawfu'.

As Tammie glowr'd, amaz'd and curious,
The mirth and fun grew fast and furious;
The Piper loud and louder blew,
The dancers quick and quicker flew,
They reel'd, they set, they cross'd, they cleekit,
Till ilka carlin swat and reekit,
And coost her duddies to the wark,
And linkit at it in her sark!

Now Tam, O Tam! had they been queans,
A' plump and strapping in their teens!
Their sarks, instead o' creeshie flainen,
Been snaw-white seventeen-hunder linen!—
Thir breeks o' mine, my only pair,
That aince were plush, o' guid blue hair,
I wad hae gien them off my hurdies,
For ae blink o' the bonie burdies!
But wither'd beldams, auld and droll,
Rigwoodie hags wad spean a foal,
Louping an' flinging on a crummock,
I wonder did na turn thy stomach.

But Tam kent what was what fu' brawlie:
There was ae winsome wench and waulie
That night enlisted in the core,
Lang after ken'd on Carrick shore
(For mony a beast to dead she shot,
And perish'd mony a bonie boat,
And shook baith meikle corn and bear,
And kept the country-side in fear);
Her cutty sark, o' Paisley harn,
That while a lassie she had worn,
In longitude tho' sorely scanty,
It was her best, and she was vauntie.
Ah! little ken'd thy reverend grannie,
That sark she coft for her wee Nannie,
Wi' twa pund Scots ('twas a' her riches),
Wad ever grac'd a dance of witches!

But here my Muse her wing maun cour,
Sic flights are far beyond her power;
To sing how Nannie lap and flang
(A souple jade she was and strang),
And how Tam stood, like ane bewitch'd,
And thought his very een enrich'd:
Even Satan glowr'd, and fidg'd fu' fain,
And hotch'd and blew wi' might and main:
Till first ae caper, syne anither,
Tam tint his reason a' thegither,
And roars out, " Weel done, Cutty-sark! "
And in an instant all was dark:
And scarcely had he Maggie rallied,
When out the hellish legion sallied.

As bees bizz out wi' angry fyke,
When plundering herds assail their byke;
As open pussie's mortal foes,
When, pop! she starts before their nose;
As eager runs the market-crowd,
When " Catch the thief! " resounded aloud;
So Maggie runs, the witches follow,
Wi' mony an eldritch skreich and hollo.

Ah, Tam! Ah, Tam! thou'll get thy fairin!
In hell they'll roast thee like a herrin!

In vain thy Kate awaits thy comin!
Kate soon will be a woefu' woman!
Now, do thy speedy utmost, Meg,
And win the key-stane o' the brig;
There, at them thou thy tail may toss,
A running stream they dare na cross,
But ere the key-stane she could make,
The fient a tail she had to shake!
For Nannie, far before the rest,
Hard upon noble Maggie prest,
And flew at Tam wi' furious ettle;
But little wist she Maggie's mettle!
Ae spring brought off her master hale,
But left behind her ain grey tail:
The carlin claught her by the rump,
And left poor Maggie scarce a stump.

Now, wha this tale o' truth shall read,
Ilk man, and mother's son, take heed:
Whene'er to Drink you are inclin'd,
Or Cutty-sarks rin in your mind,
Think ye may buy the joys o'er dear;
Remember Tam o' Shanter's mare.

(Ellisland, 1790)

PHŒBE DAWSON

Two summers since, I saw at Lammas fair,
The sweetest flower that ever blossomed there;
When Phœbe Dawson gaily crossed the green,
In haste to see and happy to be seen;
Her air, her manners, all who saw, admired,
Courteous though coy, and gentle though retired;
The joy of youth and health her eyes displayed,
And ease of heart her every look conveyed;
A native skill her simple robes expressed,
As with untutored elegance she dressed;
The lads around admired so fair a sight,
And Phœbe felt, and felt she gave, delight.

Admirers soon of every age she gained,
Her beauty won them and her worth retained;
Envy itself could no contempt display,
They wished her well, whom yet they wished away;
Correct in thought, she judged a servant's place
Preserved a rustic beauty from disgrace;
But yet on Sunday-eve, in freedom's hour,
With secret joy she felt that beauty's power;
When some proud bliss upon the heart would steal,
That, poor or rich, a beauty still must feel.

At length, the youth ordained to move her breast,
Before the swains with bolder spirit pressed;
With looks less timid made his passion known,
And pleased by manners, most unlike her own;
Loud though in love, and confident though young;
Fierce in his air, and voluble of tongue;
By trade a tailor, though, in scorn of trade,
He served the squire, and brushed the coat he made;
Yet now, would Phœbe her consent afford,
Her slave alone, again he'd mount the board;
With her should years of growing love be spent,
And growing wealth: she sighed and looked consent.

Now, through the lane, up hill, and cross the green—
Seen by but few, and blushing to be seen—
Dejected, thoughtful, anxious, and afraid—
Led by the lover, walked the silent maid:
Slow through the meadows roved they many a mile,
Toyed by each bank and trifled at each stile;
Where, as he painted every blissful view,
And highly coloured what he strongly drew,
The pensive damsel, prone to tender fears,
Dimmed the false prospect with prophetic tears:
Thus passed the allotted hours, till, lingering late,
The lover loitered at the master's gate;
There he pronounced adieu! and yet would stay,
Till chidden—soothed—entreated—forced away!
He would of coldness, though indulged, complain,
And oft retire and oft return again;
When, if his teasing vexed her gentle mind,
The grief assumed compelled her to be kind!
For he would proof of plighted kindness crave,
That she resented first, and then forgave,
And to his grief and penance yielded more

Than his presumption had required before:
    Ah! fly temptation, youth; refrain! refrain!
    Each yielding maid and each presuming swain!
Lo! now with red rent cloak and bonnet black,
And torn green gown loose hanging at her back,
One who an infant in her arms sustains,
And seems in patience striving with her pains;
Pinched are her looks, as one who pines for bread,
Whose cares are growing and whose hopes are fled;
Pale her parched lips, her heavy eyes sunk low,
And tears unnoticed from their channels flow;
Serene her manner, till some sudden pain
Frets the meek soul, and then she's calm again;
Her broken pitcher to the pool she takes,
And every step with cautious terror makes;
For not alone that infant in her arms,
But nearer cause her anxious soul alarms;
With water burdened then she picks her way,
Slowly and cautious, in the clinging clay;
Till, in mid-green, she trusts a place unsound,
And deeply plunges in the adhesive ground;
Thence, but with pain, her slender foot she takes,
While hope the mind as strength the frame forsakes;
For when so full the cup of sorrow grows,
Add but a drop, it instantly o'erflows.
And now her path but not her peace she gains,
Safe from her task, but shivering with her pains;
Her home she reaches, open leaves the door,
And placing first her infant on the floor,
She bares her bosom to the wind, and sits,
And sobbing struggles with the rising fits;
In vain, they come, she feels the inflating grief,
That shuts the swelling bosom from relief;
That speaks in feeble cries a soul distressed,
Or the sad laugh that cannot be repressed;
The neighbour-matron leaves her wheel, and flies
With all her aid her poverty supplies;
Unfee'd, the calls of nature she obeys,
Not led by profit, not allured by praise;
And waiting long, till these contentions cease,
She speaks of comfort, and departs in peace.
    Friend of distress! the mourner feels thy aid,
She cannot pay thee, but thou wilt be paid.

But who this child of weakness, want, and care?
'Tis Phœbe Dawson, pride of Lammas fair;
Who took her lover for his sparkling eyes,
Expressions warm, and love-inspiring lies:
Compassion first assailed her gentle heart
For all his suffering, all his bosom's smart:
" And then his prayers! they would a savage move,
And win the coldest of the sex to love: "
But ah! too soon his looks success declared,
Too late her loss the marriage-rite repaired;
The faithless flatterer then his vows forgot,
A captious tyrant or a noisy sot:
If present, railing till he saw her pained;
If absent, spending what their labours gained;
Till that fair form in want and sickness pined,
And hope and comfort fled that gentle mind.

   Then fly temptation, youth; resist! refrain!
   Nor let me preach for ever and in vain!

         GEORGE CRABBE.

MICHAEL

A PASTORAL POEM[1]

IF from the public way you turn your steps
Up the tumultuous brook of Greenhead Ghyll,
You will suppose that with an upright path
Your feet must struggle; in such bold ascent
The pastoral mountains front you, face to face.
But, courage! for around that boisterous brook
The mountains have all opened out themselves,
And made a hidden valley of their own.
No habitation can be seen; but they

---

[1] Written at Town-end, Grasmere, about the same time as " The
Brothers." The Sheepfold, on which so much of the poem turns,
remains, or rather the ruins of it. The character and circumstances
of Luke were taken from a family to whom had belonged, many years
before, the house we lived in at Town-end, along with some fields and
woodlands on the eastern shore of Grasmere. The name of the Evening
Star was not in fact given to this house, but to another on the same
side of the valley, more to the north.

Who journey thither find themselves alone
With a few sheep, with rocks and stones, and kites
That overhead are sailing in the sky.
It is in truth an utter solitude;
Nor should I have made mention of this Dell
But for one object which you might pass by,
Might see and notice not. Beside the brook
Appears a straggling heap of unhewn stones!
And to that simple object appertains
A story—unenriched with strange events,
Yet not unfit, I deem, for the fireside,
Or for the summer shade. It was the first
Of those domestic tales that spake to me
Of shepherds, dwellers inthe valleys, men
Whom I already loved; not verily
For their own sakes, but for the fields and hills
Where was their occupation and abode.
And hence this Tale, while I was yet a Boy
Careless of books, yet having felt the power
Of Nature, by the gentle agency
Of natural objects, led me on to feel
For passions that were not my own, and think
(At random and imperfectly indeed)
On man, the heart of man, and human life.
Therefore, although it be a history
Homely and rude, I will relate the same
For the delight of a few natural hearts;
And, with yet fonder feeling, for the sake
Of youthful Poets, who among these hills
Will be my second self when I am gone.

    Upon the forest-side in Grasmere Vale
There dwelt a Shepherd, Michael was his name;
An old man, stout of heart, and strong of limb.
His bodily frame had been from youth to age
Of an unusual strength: his mind was keen,
Intense, and frugal, apt for all affairs,
And in his shepherd's calling he was prompt
And watchful more than ordinary men.
Hence had he learned the meaning of all winds,
Of blasts of every tone; and, oftentimes,
When others heeded not, He heard the South
Make subterraneous music, like the noise
Of bagpipers on distant Highland hills.

The Shepherd, at such warning, of his flock
Bethought him, and he to himself would say,
" The winds are now devising work for me ! "
And, truly, at all times, the storm, that drives
The traveller to a shelter, summoned him
Up to the mountains : he had been alone
Amid the heart of many thousand mists,
That came to him, and left him, on the heights.
So lived he till his eightieth year was past.
And grossly that man errs, who should suppose
That the green valleys, and the streams and rocks,
Were things indifferent to the Shepherd's thoughts.
Fields, where with cheerful spirits he had breathed
The common air; hills, which with vigorous step
He had so often climbed; which had impressed
So many incidents upon his mind
Of hardship, skill or courage, joy or fear;
Which, like a book, preserved the memory
Of the dumb animals, whom he had saved,
Had fed or sheltered, linking to such acts
The certainty of honourable gain;
Those fields, those hills—what could they less? had laid
Strong hold on his affections, were to him
A pleasurable feeling of blind love,
The pleasure which there is in life itself.
    His days had not been passed in singleness.
His Helpmate was a comely matron, old—
Though younger than himself full twenty years.
She was a woman of a stirring life,
Whose heart was in her house : two wheels she had
Of antique form; this large, for spinning wool;
That small, for flax; and if one wheel had rest
It was because the other was at work.
The Pair had but one inmate in their house,
An only Child, who had been born to them
When Michael, telling o'er his years, began
To deem that he was old,—in shepherd's phrase.
With one foot in the grave. This only Son,
With two brave sheep-dogs tried in many a storm,
The one of an inestimable worth,
Made all their household. I may truly say,
That they were as a proverb in the vale
For endless industry. When day was gone,

And from their occupations out of doors
The Son and Father were come home, even then,
Their labour did not cease; unless when all
Turned to the cleanly supper-board, and there,
Each with a mess of pottage and skimmed milk,
Sat round the basket piled with oaten cakes,
And their plain home-made cheese. Yet when the meal
Was ended, Luke (for so the Son was named)
And his old Father both betook themselves
To such convenient work as might employ
Their hands by the fireside; perhaps to card
Wool for the Housewife's spindle, or repair
Some injury done to sickle, flail, or scythe,
Or other implement of house or field.

  Down from the ceiling, by the chimney's edge,
That in our ancient uncouth country style
With huge and black projection overbrowed
Large space beneath, as duly as the light
Of day grew dim the Housewife hung a lamp;
An aged utensil, which had performed
Service beyond all others of its kind.
Early at evening did it burn—and late,
Surviving comrade of uncounted hours,
Which, going by from year to year, had found,
And left, the couple neither gay perhaps
Nor cheerful, yet with objects and with hopes,
Living a life of eager industry.
And now, when Luke had reached his eighteenth year,
There by the light of this old lamp they sate,
Father and Son, while far into the night
The Housewife plied her own peculiar work,
Making the cottage through the silent hours
Murmur as with the sound of summer flies.
This light was famous in its neighbourhood,
And was a public symbol of the life
That thrifty Pair had lived. For, as it chanced,
Their cottage on a plot of rising ground
Stood single, with large prospect, north and south,
High into Easedale, up to Dunmail-Raise,
And westward to the village near the lake;
And from this constant light, so regular
And so far seen, the House itself, by all
Who dwelt within the limits of the vale,

Both old and young, was named THE EVENING STAR.
　Thus living on through such a length of years,
The Shepherd, if he loved himself, must needs
Have loved his Helpmate; but to Michael's heart
This son of his old age was yet more dear—
Less from instinctive tenderness, the same
Fond spirit that blindly works in the blood of all—
Than that a child, more than all other gifts
That earth can offer to declining man,
Brings hope with it, and forward-looking thoughts,
And stirrings of inquietude, when they
By tendency of nature needs must fail.
Exceeding was the love he bare to him,
His heart and his heart's joy! For oftentimes
Old Michael, while he was a babe in arms,
Had done him female service, not alone
For pastime and delight, as is the use
Of fathers, but with patient mind enforced
To acts of tenderness; and he had rocked
His cradle, as with a woman's gentle hand.
　And, in a later time, ere yet the Boy
Had put on boy's attire, did Michael love,
Albeit of a stern unbending mind,
To have the Young-one in his sight, when he
Wrought in the field, or on his shepherd's stool
Sate with a fettered sheep before him stretched
Under the large old oak, that near his door
Stood single, and, from matchless depth of shade,
Chosen for the Shearer's covert from the sun,
Thence in our rustic dialect was called
The CLIPPING TREE,[1] a name which yet it bears.
There, while they two were sitting in the shade,
With others round them, earnest all and blithe,
Would Michael exercise his heart with looks
Of fond correction and reproof bestowed
Upon the Child, if he disturbed the sheep
By catching at their legs, or with his shouts
Scared them, while they lay still beneath the shears.
　And when by Heaven's good grace the boy grew up
A healthy Lad, and carried in his cheek
Two steady roses that were five years old;
Then Michael from a winter coppice cut

---

[1] Clipping is the word used in the North of England for shearing.

With his own hand a sapling, which he hooped
With iron, making it throughout in all
Due requisites a perfect shepherd's staff,
And gave it to the Boy; wherewith equipt
He as a watchman oftentimes was placed
At gate or gap, to stem or turn the flock;
And, to his office prematurely called,
There stood the urchin, as you will divine,
Something between a hindrance and a help;
And for this cause not always, I believe,
Receiving from his Father hire of praise;
Though nought was left undone which staff, or voice,
Or looks, or threatening gestures, could perform.

But soon as Luke, full ten years old, could stand
Against the mountain blasts; and to the heights,
Not fearing toil, nor length of weary ways,
He with his Father daily went, and they
Were as companions, why should I relate
That objects which the Shepherd loved before
Were dearer now? that from the Boy there came
Feelings and emanations—things which were
Light to the sun and music to the wind;
And that the old Man's heart seemed born again?

Thus in his Father's sight the Boy grew up:
And now, when he had reached his eighteenth year,
He was his comfort and his daily hope.

While in this sort the simple household lived
From day to day, to Michael's ear there came
Distressful tidings. Long before the time
Of which I speak, the Shepherd had been bound
In surety for his brother's son, a man
Of an industrious life, and ample means;
But unforeseen misfortunes suddenly
Had prest upon him; and old Michael now
Was summoned to discharge the forfeiture,
A grievous penalty, but little less
Than half his substance. This unlooked-for claim,
At the first hearing, for a moment took
More hope out of his life than he supposed
That any old man ever could have lost.
As soon as he had armed himself with strength
To look his trouble in the face, it seemed
The shepherd's sole resource to sell at once

A portion of his patrimonial fields.
Such was his first resolve; he thought again,
And his heart failed him. " Isabel," said he,
Two evenings after he had heard the news,
" I have been toiling more than seventy years,
And in the open sunshine of God's love
Have we all lived: yet if these fields of ours
Should pass into a stranger's hand, I think
That I could not lie quiet in my grave.
Our lot is a hard lot; the sun himself
Has scarcely been more diligent than I;
And I have lived to be a fool at last
To my own family. An evil man
That was, and made an evil choice, if he
Were false to us; and if he were not false,
There are ten thousand to whom loss like this
Had been no sorrow. I forgive him;—but
'Twere better to be dumb than to talk thus.

    When I began, my purpose was to speak
Of remedies and of a cheerful hope.
Our Luke shall leave us, Isabel; the land
Shall not go from us, and it shall be free;
He shall possess it, free as is the wind
That passes over it. We have, thou know'st,
Another kinsman—he will be our friend
In this distress. He is a prosperous man,
Thriving in trade—and Luke to him shall go,
And with his kinsman's help and his own thrift
He quickly will repair this loss, and then
He may return to us. If here he stay,
What can be done? Where every one is poor,
What can be gained? "

                          At this the old Man paused.
And Isabel sat silent, for her mind
Was busy, looking back into past times.
There's Richard Bateman, thought she to herself,
He was a parish-boy—at the church-door
They made a gathering for him, shillings, pence
And halfpennies, wherewith the neighbours bought
A basket, which they filled with pedlar's wares;
And, with this basket on his arm, the lad
Went up to London, found a master there,
Who, out of many, chose the trusty boy

To go and overlook his merchandise
Beyond the seas; where he grew wondrous rich,
And left estates and monies to the poor.
And, at his birth-place, built a chapel, floored
With marble which he sent from foreign lands.
These thoughts, and many others of like sort,
Passed quickly through the mind of Isabel,
And her face brightened. The old Man was glad,
And thus resumed:—" Well, Isabel! this scheme
These two days, has been meat and drink to me.
Far more than we have lost is left us yet.
—We have enough—I wish indeed that I
Were younger;—but this hope is a good hope.
—Make ready Luke's best garments, of the best
Buy for him more, and let us send him forth
To-morrow, or the next day, or to-night:
—If he *could* go, the Boy should go to-night."
    Here Michael ceased, and to the fields went forth
With a light heart. The Housewife for five days
Was restless morn and night, and all day long
Wrought on with her best fingers to prepare
Things needful for the journey of her son.
But Isabel was glad when Sunday came
To stop her in her work: for, when she lay
By Michael's side, she through the last two nights,
Heard him, how he was troubled in his sleep:
And when they rose at morning she could see
That all his hopes were gone. That day at noon
She said to Luke, while they two by themselves
Were sitting at the door, " Thou must not go;
We have no other Child but thee to lose,
None to remember—do not go away,
For if thou leave thy Father he will die."
The Youth made answer with a jocund voice;
And Isabel, when she had told her fears,
Recovered heart. That evening her best fare
Did she bring forth, and all together sat
Like happy people round a Christmas fire.
    With daylight Isabel resumed her work;
And all the ensuing week the house appeared
As cheerful as a grove in Spring; at length
The expected letter from their kinsman came,
With kind assurances that he would do

His utmost for the welfare of the Boy;
To which, requests were added, that forthwith
He might be sent to him. Ten times or more
The letter was read over; Isabel
Went forth to show it to the neighbours round;
Nor was there at that time on English land
A prouder heart than Luke's. When Isabel
Had to her house returned, the old Man said,
" He shall depart to-morrow." To this word
The Housewife answered, talking much of things
Which, if at such short notice he should go,
Would surely be forgotten. But at length
She gave consent, and Michael was at ease.

Near the tumultuous brook of Greenhead Ghyll,
In that deep valley, Michael had designed
To build a Sheepfold; and, before he heard
The tidings of his melancholy loss,
For this same purpose he had gathered up
A heap of stones, which by the streamlet's edge
Lay thrown together, ready for the work.
With Luke that evening thitherward he walked:
And soon as they had reached the place he stopped,
And thus the old Man spake to him:—" My Son,
To-morrow thou wilt leave me: with full heart
I look upon thee, for thou art the same
That wert a promise to me ere thy birth,
And all thy life hast been my daily joy.
I will relate to thee some little part
Of our two histories; 'twill do thee good
When thou art from me, even if I should touch
On things thou canst not know of.——After thou
First cam'st into the world—as oft befalls
To new-born infants—thou didst sleep away
Two days, and blessings from thy Father's tongue
Then fell upon thee. Day by day passed on,
And still I loved thee with increasing love.
Never to living ear came sweeter sounds
Than when I heard thee by our own fireside
First uttering, without words, a natural tune;
While thou, a feeding babe, didst in thy joy
Sing at thy Mother's breast. Month followed month,
And in the open fields my life was passed
And on the mountains; else I think that thou

Hadst been brought up upon thy Father's knees.
But we were playmates, Luke: among these hills,
As well thou knowest, in us the old and young
Have played together, nor with me didst thou
Lack any pleasure which a boy can know."
Luke had a manly heart; but at these words
He sobbed aloud. The old Man grasped his hand,
And said, " Nay, do not take it so—I see
That these are things of which I need not speak.
—Even to the utmost I have been to thee
A kind and a good Father: and herein
I but repay a gift which I myself
Received at others' hands; for, though now old
Beyond the common life of man, I still
Remember them who loved me in my youth.
Both of them sleep together: here they lived,
As all their Forefathers had done; and when
At length their time was come, they were not loth
To give their bodies to the family mould.
I wished that thou should'st live the life they lived:
But 'tis a long time to look back, my Son,
And see so little gain from threescore years.
These fields were burthened when they came to me;
Till I was forty years of age, not more
Than half of my inheritance was mine.
I toiled and toiled; God blessed me in my work,
And till these three weeks past the land was free.
—It looks as if it never could endure
Another Master. Heaven forgive me, Luke,
If I judge ill for thee, but it seems good
That thou should'st go."
                        At this the old Man paused;
Then pointing to the stones near which they stood,
Thus, after a short silence, he resumed:
" This was a work for us; and now, my Son,
It is a work for me. But, lay one stone—
Here, lay it for me, Luke, with thine own hands.
Nay, Boy, be of good hope;—we both may live
To see a better day. At eighty-four
I still am strong and hale;—do thou thy part;
I will do mine.—I will begin again
With many tasks that were resigned to thee:
Up to the heights, and in among the storms,

Will I without thee go again, and do
All works which I was wont to do alone,
Before I knew thy face.—Heaven bless thee, Boy!
Thy heart these two weeks has been beating fast
With many hopes; it should be so—yes—yes—
I knew that thou could'st never have a wish
To leave me, Luke: thou hast been bound to me
Only by links of love: when thou art gone,
What will be left to us!—But, I forget
My purposes. Lay now the corner-stone,
As I requested; and hereafter, Luke,
When thou art gone away, should evil men
Be thy companions, think of me, my Son,
And of this moment; hither turn thy thoughts,
And God will strengthen thee: amid all fear
And all temptation, Luke, I pray that thou
May'st bear in mind the life thy Fathers lived,
Who, being innocent, did for that cause
Bestir them in good deeds. Now, fare thee well—
When thou return'st, thou in this place wilt see
A work which is not here: a covenant
'Twill be between us; but, whatever fate
Befall thee, I shall love thee to the last,
And bear thy memory with me to the grave."

   The Shepherd ended here; and Luke stooped down,
And, as his Father had requested, laid
The first stone of the Sheepfold. At the sight
The old Man's grief broke from him; to his heart
He pressed his Son, he kissèd him and wept;
And to the house together they returned.
—Hushed was that House in peace, or seeming peace,
Ere the night fell:—with morrow's dawn the Boy
Began his journey, and when he had reached
The public way, he put on a bold face;
And all the neighbours, as he passed their doors,
Came forth with wishes and with farewell prayers,
That followed him till he was out of sight.

   A good report did from their Kinsman come,
Of Luke and his well-doing: and the Boy
Wrote loving letters, full of wondrous news,
Which, as the Housewife phrased it, were throughout
" The prettiest letters that were ever seen."
Both parents read them with rejoicing hearts.

So, many months passed on: and once again
The Shepherd went about his daily work
With confident and cheerful thoughts; and now
Sometimes when he could find a leisure hour
He to that valley took his way, and there
Wrought at the Sheepfold. Meantime Luke began
To slacken in his duty; and, at length,
He in the dissolute city gave himself
To evil courses: ignominy and shame
Fell on him, so that he was driven at last
To seek a hiding-place beyond the seas.

There is a comfort in the strength of love;
'Twill make a thing endurable, which else
Would overset the brain, or break the heart:
I have conversed with more than one who well
Remember the old Man, and what he was
Years after he had heard this heavy news.
His bodily frame had been from youth to age
Of an unusual strength. Among the rocks
He went, and still looked up to sun and cloud,
And listened to the wind; and, as before,
Performed all kinds of labour for his sheep,
And for the land, his small inheritance.
And to that hollow dell from time to time
Did he repair, to build the Fold of which
His flock had need. 'Tis not forgotten yet
The pity which was then in every heart
For the old Man—and 'tis believed by all
That many and many a day he thither went,
And never lifted up a single stone.

There, by the Sheepfold, sometimes was he seen
Sitting alone, or with his faithful Dog,
Then old, beside him, lying at his feet.
The length of full seven years, from time to time,
He at the building of this Sheepfold wrought,
And left the work unfinished when he died.
Three years, or little more, did Isabel
Survive her Husband: at her death the estate
Was sold, and went into a stranger's hand.
The Cottage which was named the EVENING STAR
Is gone—the ploughshare has been through the ground
On which it stood; great changes have been wrought
In all the neighbourhood:—yet the oak is left

That grew beside their door; and the remains
Of the unfinished Sheepfold may be seen
Beside the boisterous brook of Greenhead Ghyll.

WILLIAM WORDSWORTH.

(1800)

LINES COMPOSED A FEW MILES ABOVE
TINTERN ABBEY, ON REVISITING THE
BANKS OF THE WYE DURING A TOUR.
JULY 13, 1798[1]

FIVE years have past; five summers, with the length
Of five long winters! and again I hear
These waters, rolling from their mountain-springs
With a soft inland murmur.[2]—once again
Do I behold these steep and lofty cliffs,
That on a wild secluded scene impress
Thoughts of more deep seclusion; and connect
The landscape with the quiet of the sky.
The day is come when I again repose
Here, under this dark sycamore, and view
These plots of cottage-ground, these orchard-tufts,
Which at this season, with their unripe fruits,
Are clad in one green hue, and lose themselves
'Mid groves and copses. Once again I see
These hedge-rows, hardly hedge-rows, little lines
Of sportive wood run wild: these pastoral farms,
Green to the very door; and wreaths of smoke
Sent up, in silence, from among the trees!
With some uncertain notice, as might seem
Of vagrant dwellers in the houseless woods,
Or of some Hermit's cave, where by his fire
The Hermit sits alone.

[1] No poem of mine was composed under circumstances more pleasant
for me to remember than this. I began it upon leaving Tintern, after
crossing the Wye, and concluded it just as I was entering Bristol in the
evening, after a ramble of four or five days, with my Sister. Not a
line of it was altered, and not any part of it written down till I reached
Bristol. It was published almost immediately after in the Lyrical
Ballads.

[2] The river is not affected by the tides a few miles above Tintern.

These beauteous forms,
Through a long absence, have not been to me
As is a landscape to a blind man's eye:
But oft, in lonely rooms, and 'mid the din
Of towns and cities, I have owed to them
In hours of weariness, sensations sweet,
Felt in the blood, and felt along the heart;
And passing even into my purer mind,
With tranquil restoration:—feelings too
Of unremembered pleasure: such, perhaps,
As have no slight or trivial influence
On that best portion of a good man's life,
His little, nameless, unremembered, acts
Of kindness and of love. Nor less, I trust,
To them I may have owed another gift,
Of aspect more sublime; that blessed mood,
In which the burthen of the mystery,
In which the heavy and the weary weight
Of all this unintelligible world,
Is lightened:—that serene and blessed mood,
In which the affections gently lead us on,—
Until, the breath of this corporeal frame
And even the motion of our human blood
Almost suspended, we are laid asleep
In body, and become a living soul:
While with an eye made quiet by the power
Of harmony, and the deep power of joy,
We see into the life of things.
                          If this
Be but a vain belief, yet, oh! how oft—
In darkness and amid the many shapes
Of joyless daylight; when the fretful stir
Unprofitable, and the fever of the world,
Have hung upon the beatings of my heart—
How oft, in spirit, have I turned to thee,
O sylvan Wye! thou wanderer thro' the woods,
How often has my spirit turned to thee!
    And now, with gleams of half-extinguished thought
With many recognitions dim and faint,
And somewhat of a sad perplexity,
The picture of the mind revives again:
While here I stand, not only with the sense
Of present pleasure, but with pleasing thoughts

That in this moment there is life and food
For future years. And so I dare to hope,
Though changed, no doubt, from what I was when
   first
I came among these hills; when like a roe
I bounded o'er the mountains, by the sides
Of the deep rivers, and the lonely streams,
Wherever nature led: more like a man
Flying from something that he dreads, than one
Who sought the thing he loved. For nature then
(The coarser pleasures of my boyish days,
And their glad animal movements all gone by)
To me was all in all.—I cannot paint
What then I was. The sounding cataract
Haunted me like a passion: the tall rock,
The mountain, and the deep and gloomy wood,
Their colours and their forms, were then to me
An appetite; a feeling and a love,
That had no need of a remoter charm,
By thought supplied, nor any interest
Unborrowed from the eye.—That time is past,
And all its aching joys are now no more,
And all its dizzy raptures. Not for this
Faint I, nor mourn nor murmur; other gifts
Have followed; for such loss, I would believe,
Abundant recompence. For I have learned
To look on nature, not as in the hour
Of thoughtless youth; but hearing oftentimes
The still, sad music of humanity,
Nor harsh nor grating, though of ample power
To chasten and subdue. And I have felt
A presence that disturbs me with the joy
Of elevated thoughts; a sense sublime
Of something far more deeply interfused,
Whose dwelling is the light of setting suns,
And the round ocean and the living air,
And the blue sky, and in the mind of man;
A motion and a spirit, that impels
   All thinking things, all objects of all thought,
And rolls through all things. Therefore am I still
A lover of the meadows and the woods,
And mountains; and of all that we behold
From this green earth; of all the mighty world

Of eye, and ear,—both what they half create,[1]
And what perceive; well pleased to recognise
In nature and the language of the sense,
The anchor of my purest thoughts, the nurse,
The guide, the guardian of my heart, and soul
Of all my moral being.
                              Nor perchance,
If I were not thus taught, should I the more
Suffer my genial spirits to decay:
For thou art with me here upon the banks
Of this fair river; thou my dearest Friend,
My dear, dear Friend; and in thy voice I catch
The language of my former heart, and read
My former pleasures in the shooting lights
Of thy wild eyes. Oh! yet a little while
May I behold in thee what I was once,
My dear, dear Sister! and this prayer I make,
Knowing that Nature never did betray
The heart that loved her; 'tis her privilege,
Through all the years of this our life, to lead
From joy to joy: for she can so inform
The mind that is within us, so impress
With quietness and beauty, and so feed
With lofty thoughts, that neither evil tongues,
Rash judgments, nor the sneers of selfish men,
Nor greetings where no kindness is, nor all
The dreary intercourse of daily life,
Shall e'er prevail against us, or disturb
Our cheerful faith, that all which we behold
Is full of blessings. Therefore let the moon
Shine on thee in thy solitary walk;
And let the misty mountain-winds be free
To blow against thee: and, in after years,
When these wild ecstasies shall be matured
Into a sober pleasure; when thy mind
Shall be a mansion for all lovely forms,
Thy memory be as a dwelling-place
For all sweet sounds and harmonies; oh! then,
If solitude, or fear, or pain, or grief,
Should be thy portion, with what healing thoughts
Of tender joy wilt thou remember me,

[1] This line has a close resemblance to an admirable line of Young's, the exact expression of which I do not recollect.

And these my exhortations! Nor, perchance—
If I should be where I no more can hear
Thy voice, nor catch from thy wild eyes these gleams
Of past existence—wilt thou then forget
That on the banks of this delightful stream
We stood together; and that I, so long
A worhipper of Nature, hither came
Unwearied in that service: rather say
With warmer love—oh! with far deeper zeal
Of holier love. Nor wilt thou then forget,
That after many wanderings, many years
Of absence, these steep woods and lofty cliffs,
And this green pastoral landscape, were to me
More dear, both for themselves and for thy sake!

WILLIAM WORDSWORTH.

(1798)

CHRISTABEL

PART THE FIRST

'Tɪs the middle of night by the castle clock,
And the owls have awakened the crowing cock,
Tu—whit!——To—whoo!
And hark, again! the crowing cock,
How drowsily it crew.

Sir Leoline, the Baron rich,
Hath a toothless mastiff, which
From her kennel beneath the rock
Maketh answer to the clock,
Four for the quarters, and twelve for the hour;
Ever and aye, by shine and shower,
Sixteen short howls, not over loud;
Some say, she sees my lady's shroud.

Is the night chilly and dark?
The night is chilly, but not dark.
The thin grey cloud is spread on high,
It covers but not hides the sky.

The moon is behind, and at the full;
And yet she looks both small and dull.
The night is chill, the cloud is grey:
'Tis a month before the month of May,
And the Spring comes slowly up this way.

The lovely lady, Christabel,
Whom her father loves so well,
What makes her in the wood so late,
A furlong from the castle gate?
She had dreams all yesternight
Of her own betrothèd knight;
And she in the midnight wood will pray
For the weal of her lover that's far away.

She stole along, she nothing spoke,
The sighs she heaved were soft and low,
And nought was green upon the oak
But moss and rarest mistletoe:
She kneels beneath the huge oak tree,
And in silence prayeth she.

The lady sprang up suddenly,
The lovely lady, Christabel!
It moaned as near, as near can be,
But what it is she cannot tell.—
On the other side it seems to be,
Of the huge, broad-breasted, old oak tree.

The night is chill; the forest bare;
Is it the wind that moaneth bleak?
There is not wind enough in the air
To move away the ringlet curl
From the lovely lady's cheek—
There is not wind enough to twirl
The one red leaf, the last of its clan,
That dances as often as dance it can,
Hanging so light, and hanging so high,
On the topmost twig that looks up at the sky.

Hush, beating heart of Christabel!
Jesu, Maria, shield her well!

She folded her arms beneath her cloak,
And stole to the other side of the oak.
    What sees she there?

There she sees a damsel bright,
Drest in a silken robe of white,
That shadowy in the moonlight shone:
The neck that made that white robe wan,
Her stately neck, and arms were bare;
Her blue-veined feet unsandal'd were,
And wildly glittered here and there
The gems entangled in her hair.
I guess, 'twas frightful there to see
A lady so richly clad as she—
Beautiful exceedingly!

Mary mother, save me now!
(Said Christabel,) And who art thou?

The lady strange made answer meet,
And her voice was faint and sweet:—
Have pity on my sore distress,
I scarce can speak for weariness:
Stretch forth thy hand, and have no fear!
Said Christabel, How camest thou here?
And the lady, whose voice was faint and sweet
Did thus pursue her answer meet:—

My sire is of a noble line,
And my name is Geraldine:
Five warriors seized me yestermorn,
Me, even me, a maid forlorn:
They choked my cries with force and fright,
And tied me on a palfrey white.
The palfrey was as fleet as wind,
And they rode furiously behind.
They spurred amain, their steeds were white:
And once we crossed the shade of night.
As sure as Heaven shall rescue me,
I have no thought what men they be;
Nor do I know how long it is
(For I have lain entranced I wis)

Since one, the tallest of the five,
Took me from the palfrey's back,
A weary woman, scarce alive.
Some muttered words his comrades spoke:
He placed me underneath this oak;
He swore they would return with haste;
Whither they went I cannot tell—
I thought I heard, some minutes past,
Sounds as of a castle bell.
Stretch forth thy hand (thus ended she),
And help a wretched maid to flee.

Then Christabel stretched forth her hand,
And comforted fair Geraldine:
O well, bright dame! may you command
The service of Sir Leoline;
And gladly our stout chivalry
Will he send forth and friends withal
To guide and guard you safe and free
Home to your noble father's hall.

She rose: and forth with steps they passed
That strove to be, and were not, fast.
Her gracious stars the lady blest,
And thus spake on sweet Christabel:
All our household are at rest,
The hall as silent as the cell;
Sir Leoline is weak in health,
And may not well awakened be,
But we will move as if in stealth,
And I beseech your courtesy,
This night, to share your couch with me.

They crossed the moat, and Christabel
Took the key that fitted well;
A little door she opened straight,
All in the middle of the gate;
The gate that was ironed within and without,
Where an army in battle array had marched out.
The lady sank, belike through pain,
And Christabel with might and main

Lifted her up, a weary weight,
Over the threshold of the gate:
Then the lady rose again,
And moved, as she were not in pain.

So free from danger, free from fear,
They crossed the court: right glad they were.
And Christabel devoutly cried
To the lady by her side,
Praise we the Virgin all divine
Who hath rescued thee from thy distress!
Alas, alas! said Geraldine,
I cannot speak for weariness.
So free from danger, free from fear,
They crossed the court: right glad they were.

Outside her kennel, the mastiff old
Lay fast asleep, in moonshine cold.
The mastiff old did not awake,
Yet she an angry moan did make!
And what can ail the mastiff bitch?
Never till now she uttered yell
Beneath the eye of Christabel.
Perhaps it is the owlet's scritch:[1]
For what can ail the mastiff bitch?

They passed the hall, that echoes still,
Pass as lightly as you will!
The brands were flat, the brands were dying,
Amid their own white ashes lying;
But when the lady passed, there came
A tongue of light, a fit of flame;
And Christabel saw the lady's eye,
And nothing else saw she thereby,
Save the boss of the shield of Sir Leoline tall,
Which hung in a murky old niche in the wall.
O softly tread, said Christabel,
My father seldom sleepeth well.

Sweet Christabel her feet doth bare,
And jealous of the listening air

[1] Screech.

They steal their way from stair to stair,
Now in glimmer, and now in gloom,
And now they pass the Baron's room,
As still as death, with stifled breath!
And now have reached her chamber door;
And now doth Geraldine press down
The rushes of the chamber floor.

The moon shines dim in the open air,
And not a moonbeam enters here.
But they without its light can see
The chamber carved so curiously,
Carved with figures strange and sweet,
All made out of the carver's brain,
For a lady's chamber meet:
The lamp with twofold silver chain
Is fastened to an angel's feet.

The silver lamp burns dead and dim;
But Christabel the lamp will trim.
She trimmed the lamp, and made it bright,
And left it swinging to and fro,
While Geraldine, in wretched plight,
Sank down upon the floor below.

O weary lady, Geraldine,
I pray you, drink this cordial wine!
It is a wine of virtuous powers;
My mother made it of wild flowers.

And will your mother pity me,
Who am a maiden most forlorn?
Christabel answered—Woe is me!
She died the hour that I was born.
I have heard the grey-haired friar tell
How on her death-bed she did say,
That she should hear the castle-bell
Strike twelve upon my wedding-day.
O mother dear! that thou wert here!
I would, said Geraldine, she were!

But soon with altered voice, said she—
" Off, wandering mother! Peak and pine!
I have power to bid thee flee."
Alas! what ails poor Geraldine?
Why stares she with unsettled eye?
Can she the bodiless dead espy?
And why with hollow voice cries she,
" Off, woman, off! this hour is mine—
Though thou her guardian spirit be,
Off, woman, off! 'tis given to me."

Then Christabel knelt by the lady's side,
And raised to heaven her eyes so blue—
Alas! said she, this ghastly ride—
Dear lady! it hath wildered you!
The lady wiped her moist cold brow,
And faintly said, " 'tis over now!"

Again the wild-flower wine she drank:
Her fair large eyes 'gan glitter bright,
And from the floor whereon she sank,
The lofty lady stood upright:
She was most beautiful to see,
Like a lady of a far countree.

And thus the lofty lady spake—
" All they who live in the upper sky,
Do love you, holy Christabel!
And you love them, and for their sake
And for the good which me befel,
Even I in my degree will try,
Fair maiden, to requite you well.
But now unrobe yourself; for I
Must pray, ere yet in bed I lie."

Quoth Christabel, So let it be!
And as the lady bade, did she.
Her gentle limbs did she undress,
And lay down in her loveliness.

But through her brain of weal and woe
So many thoughts moved to and fro,

That vain it were her lids to close;
So half-way from the bed she rose,
And on her elbow did recline
To look at the lady Geraldine.

Beneath the lamp the lady bowed,
And slowly rolled her eyes around;
Then drawing in her breath aloud,
Like one that shuddered, she unbound
The cincture from beneath her breast:
Her silken robe, and inner vest,
Dropt to her feet, and full in view,
Behold! her bosom and half her side——
A sight to dream of, not to tell!
O shield her! shield sweet Christabel!

Yet Geraldine nor speaks nor stirs;
Ah! what a striken look was hers!
Deep from within she seems half-way
To lift some weight with sick assay,[1]
And eyes the maid and seeks delay;
Then suddenly, as one defied,
Collects herself in scorn and pride,
And lay down by the Maiden's side!—
And in her arms the maid she took,
    Ah well-a-day!
And with low voice and doleful look
These words did say:
" In the touch of this bosom there worketh a spell,
Which is lord of thy utterance, Christabel!
Thou knowest to-night, and wilt know to-morrow,
This mark of my shame, this seal of my sorrow;
    But vainly thou warrest,
      For this is alone in
    Thy power to declare,
      That in the dim forest
    Thou heard'st a low moaning,
And found'st a bright lady, surpassingly fair;
And didst bring her home with thee in love and in charity,
To shield her and shelter her from the damp air."

---

[1] Attempt.

THE CONCLUSION TO PART THE FIRST

It was a lovely sight to see
The lady Christabel, when she
Was praying at the old oak tree.
    Amid the jaggèd shadows
    Of mossy leafless boughs,
    Kneeling in the moonlight,
    To make her gentle vows;
Her slender palms together prest,
Heaving sometimes on her breast;
Her face resigned to bliss or bale—
Her face, oh call it fair not pale,
And both blue eyes more bright than clear,
Each about to have a tear.
With open eyes (ah woe is me!)
Asleep, and dreaming fearfully,
Fearfully dreaming, yet, I wis,
Dreaming that alone, which is—
O sorrow and shame! Can this be she,
The lady, who knelt at the old oak tree?
And lo! the worker of these harms,
That holds the maiden in her arms,
Seems to slumber still and mild,
As a mother with her child.

A star hath set, a star hath risen,
O Geraldine! since arms of thine
Have been the lovely lady's prison.
O Geraldine! one hour was thine—
Thou'st had thy will! By tairn and rill,
The night-birds all that hour were still.
But now they are jubilant anew,
From cliff and tower, tu—whoo! tu—whoo!
Tu—whoo! tu—whoo! from wood and fell!

And see! the lady Christabel
Gathers herself from out her trance;
Her limbs relax, her countenance
Grows sad and soft; the smooth thin lids
Close o'er her eyes; and tears she sheds—

Large tears that leave the lashes bright!
And oft while she seems to smile
As infants at a sudden light!
Yea, she doth smile, and she doth weep,
Like a youthful hermitess,
Beauteous in a wilderness,
Who, praying always, prays in sleep.
And, if she move unquietly,
Perchance, 'tis but the blood so free
Comes back and tingles in her feet.
No doubt, she hath a vision sweet.
What if her guardian spirit 'twere,
What if she knew her mother near?
But this she knows, in joys and woes,
That saints will aid if men will call:
For the blue sky bends over all!

(1797)

PART THE SECOND

Each matin bell, the Baron saith,
Knells us back to a world of death.
These words Sir Leoline first said,
When he rose and found his lady dead:
These words Sir Leoline will say
Many a morn to his dying day!

And hence the custom and law began
That still at dawn the sacristan,
Who duly pulls the heavy bell,
Five and forty beads must tell
Between each stroke—a warning knell,
Which not a soul can choose but hear
From Bratha Head to Wyndermere.
Saith Bracy the bard, So let it knell!
And let the drowsy sacristan
Still count as slowly as he can!
There is no lack of such, I ween,
As well fill up the space between.
In Langdale Pike and Witch's Lair,
And Dungeon-ghyll so foully rent,
With ropes of rock and bells of air

Three sinful sextons' ghosts are pent,
Who all give back, one after t'other,
The death-note to their living brother;
And oft too, by the knell offended,
Just as their one! two! three! is ended,
The devil mocks the doleful tale
With a merry peal from Borrowdale.

The air is still! through mist and cloud
That merry peal comes ringing loud;
And Geraldine shakes off her dread,
And rises lightly from the bed;
Puts on her silken vestments white,
And tricks her hair in lovely plight,
And nothing doubting of her spell
Awakens the lady Christabel.
" Sleep you, sweet lady Christabel?
I trust that you have rested well."

And Christabel awoke and spied
The same who lay down by her side—
O rather say, the same whom she
Raised up beneath the old oak tree!
Nay, fairer yet! and yet more fair!
For she belike hath drunken deep
Of all the blessedness of sleep!
And while she spake, her looks, her air,
Such gentle thankfulness declare,
That (so it seemed) her girded vests
Grew tight beneath her heaving breasts.
" Sure I have sinn'd!" said Christabel,
" Now heaven be praised if all be well!"
And in low faltering tones, yet sweet,
Did she the lofty lady greet
With such perplexity of mind
As dreams too lively leave behind.

So quickly she rose, and quickly arrayed
Her maiden limbs, and having prayed
That He, who on the cross did groan,
Might wash away her sins unknown,
She forthwith led fair Geraldine
To meet her sire, Sir Leoline.

The lovely maid and the lady tall
Are pacing both into the hall,
And pacing on through page and groom,
Enter the Baron's presence-room.

The Baron rose, and while he prest
His gentle daughter to his breast,
With cheerful wonder in his eyes
The lady Geraldine espies,
And gave such welcome to the same,
As might beseem so bright a dame!

But when he heard the lady's tale,
And when she told her father's name,
Why waxed Sir Leoline so pale,
Murmuring o'er the name again,
Lord Roland de Vaux of Tryermaine?

Alas! they had been friends in youth;
But whispering tongues can poison truth
And constancy lives in realms above;
And life is thorny; and youth is vain;
And to be wroth with one we love
Doth work like madness in the brain.
And thus it chanced, as I divine,
With Roland and Sir Leoline.
Each spake words of high disdain
And insult to his heart's best brother:
They parted—ne'er to meet again!
But never either found another
To free the hollow heart from paining—
They stood aloof, the scars remaining,
Like cliffs which had been rent asunder;
A dreary sea now flows between.
But neither heat, nor frost, nor thunder,
Shall wholly do away, I ween,
The marks of that which once hath been.

Sir Leoline, a moment's space,
Stood gazing on the damsel's face:
And the youthful Lord of Tryermaine
Came back upon his heart again.

O then the Baron forgot his age,
His noble heart swelled high with rage;
He swore by the wounds in Jesu's side
He would proclaim it far and wide,
With trump and solemn heraldry,
That they, who thus had wronged the dame,
Were base as spotted infamy!
" And if they dare deny the same,
My herald shall appoint a week,
And let the recreant traitors seek
My tourney court—that there and then
I may dislodge their reptile souls
From the bodies and forms of men! "
He spake: his eye in lightning rolls!
For the lady was ruthlessly seized; and he kenned
In the beautiful lady the child of his friend!

And now the tears were on his face,
And fondly in his arms he took
Fair Geraldine, who met the embrace,
Prolonging it with joyous look.
Which when she viewed, a vision fell
Upon the soul of Christabel,
The vision of fear, the touch and pain!
She shrunk and shuddered, and saw again—
(Ah, woe is me! Was it for thee,
Thou gentle maid! such sights to see?)
Again she saw that bosom old,
Again she felt that bosom cold,
And drew in her breath with a hissing sound:
Whereat the Knight turned wildly round,
And nothing saw, but his own sweet maid
With eyes upraised, as one that prayed.

The touch, the sight, had passed away,
And in its stead that vision blest,
Which comforted her after-rest,
While in the lady's arms she lay,
Had put a rapture in her breast,
And on her lips and o'er her eyes
Spread smiles like light!
                 With new surprise,

" What ails then my belovèd child? "
The Baron said—His daughter mild
Made answer, " All will yet be well! "
I ween, she had no power to tell
Aught else : so mighty was the spell.

Yet he, who saw this Geraldine,
Had deemed her sure a thing divine.
Such sorrow with such grace she blended,
As if she feared she had offended
Sweet Christabel, that gentle maid!
And with such lowly tones she prayed
She might be sent without delay
Home to her father's mansion.
                              " Nay!
Nay, by my soul! " said Leoline.
" Ho! Bracy the bard, the charge be thine!
Go thou, with music sweet and loud,
And take two steeds with trappings proud,
And take the youth whom thou lov'st best
To bear thy harp, and learn thy song,
And clothe you both in solemn vest,
And over the mountains haste along,
Lest wandering folk, that are abroad,
Detain you on the valley road.

" And when he has crossed the Irthing flood,
My merry bard! he hastes, he hastes
Up Knorren Moor, through Halegarth Wood,
And reaches soon that castle good
Which stands and threatens Scotland's wastes.

" Bard Bracy! bard Bracy! your horses are fleet,
Ye must ride up the hall, your music so sweet,
More loud than your horses' echoing feet!
And loud and loud to Lord Roland call,
Thy daughter is safe in Langdale hall!
Thy beautiful daughter is safe and free—
Sir Leoline greets thee thus through me.
He bids thee come without delay
With all thy numerous array ;

And take thy lovely daughter home:
And he will meet thee on the way
With all his numerous array
White with their panting palfreys' foam:
And, by mine honour! I will say,
That I repent me of the day
When I spake words of fierce disdain
To Roland de Vaux of Tryermaine!—
—For since the evil hour hath flown,
Many a summer's sun hath shone;
Yet ne'er found I a friend again
Like Roland de Vaux of Tryermaine."

The lady fell, and clasped his knees,
Her face upraised, her eyes o'erflowing;
And Bracy replied, with faltering voice,
His gracious hail on all bestowing;
" Thy words, thou sire of Christabel,
Are sweeter than my harp can tell;
Yet might I gain a boon of thee,
This day my journey should not be,
So strange a dream hath come to me;
That I had vowed with music loud
To clear yon wood from thing unblest,
Warn'd by a vision in my rest!
For in my sleep I saw that dove,
That gentle bird, whom thou dost love,
And call'st by thy own daughter's name—
Sir Leoline! I saw the same,
Fluttering, and uttering fearful moan,
Among the green herbs in the forest alone,
Which when I saw and when I heard,
I wonder'd what might ail the bird;
For nothing near it could I see,
Save the grass and green herbs underneath the old tree.

" And in my dream, methought, I went
To search out what might there be found;
And what the sweet bird's trouble meant,
That thus lay fluttering on the ground.
I went and peered, and could descry
No cause for her distressful cry;

But yet for her dear lady's sake
I stooped, methought, the dove to take,
When lo! I saw a bright green snake
Coiled around its wings and neck,
Green as the herbs on which it couched,
Close by the dove's its head it crouched;
And with the dove it heaves and stirs,
Swelling its neck as she swelled hers!
I woke; it was the midnight hour,
The clock was echoing in the tower;
But though my slumber was gone by,
This dream it would not pass away—
It seems to live upon my eye!
And thence I vowed this self-same day
With music strong and saintly song
To wander through the forest bare,
Lest aught unholy loiter there."
Thus Bracy said: the Baron, the while,
Half-listening heard him with a smile;
Then turned to Lady Geraldine,
His eyes made up of wonder and love;
And said in courtly accents fine,
" Sweet maid, Lord Roland's beauteous dove,
With arms more strong than harp or song,
Thy sire and I will crush the snake! "
He kissed her forehead as he spake,
And Geraldine in maiden wise
Casting down her large bright eyes,
With blushing cheek and courtesy fine
She turned her from Sir Leoline;
Softly gathering up her train,
That o'er her right arm fell again;
And folded her arms across her chest,
And couched her head upon her breast,
And looked askance at Christabel——
Jesu, Maria, shield her well!

A snake's small eye blinks dull and shy,
And the lady's eyes they shrunk in her head,
Each shrunk up to a serpent's eye,
And with somewhat of malice, and more of dread,
At Christabel she look'd askance!—

One moment—and the sight was fled!
But Christabel in dizzy trance
Stumbling on the unsteady ground
Shuddered aloud, with a hissing sound;
And Geraldine again turned round,
And like a thing, that sought relief,
Full of wonder and full of grief,
She rolled her large bright eyes divine
Wildly on Sir Leoline.

The maid, alas! her thoughts are gone,
She nothing sees—no sight but one!
The maid, devoid of guile and sin,
I know not how, in fearful wise,
So deeply had she shrunken in
That look, those shrunken serpent eyes,
That all her features were resigned
To this sole image in her mind:
And passively did imitate
That look of dull and treacherous hate!
And thus she stood, in dizzy trance,
Still picturing that look askance
With forced unconscious sympathy
Full before her father's view——
As far as such a look could be
In eyes so innocent and blue!

And when the trance was o'er, the maid
Paused awhile, and inly prayed:
Then falling at the Baron's feet,
" By my mother's soul do I entreat
That thou this woman send away! "
She said: and more she could not say:
For what she knew she could not tell,
O'er-mastered by the mighty spell.

Why is thy cheek so wan and wild,
Sir Leoline? Thy only child
Lies at thy feet, thy joy, thy pride,
So fair, so innocent, so mild;
The same, for whom thy lady died!
O, by the pangs of her dear mother

Think thou no evil of thy child!
For her, and thee, and for no other,
She prayed the moment ere she died:
Prayed that the babe for whom she died,
Might prove her dear lord's joy and pride!
That prayer her deadly pangs beguiled,
    Sir Leoline!
And wouldst thou wrong thy only child,
    Her child and thine?

Within the Baron's heart and brain
If thoughts, like these, had any share,
They only swelled his rage and pain,
And did but work confusion there.
His heart was cleft with pain and rage,
His cheeks they quivered, his eyes were wild,
Dishonour'd thus in his old age;
Dishonour'd by his only child,
And all his hospitality
To the insulted daughter of his friend
By more than woman's jealousy
Brought thus to a disgraceful end—
He rolled his eye with stern regard
Upon the gentle minstrel bard,
And said in tones abrupt, austere—
"Why, Bracy! dost thou loiter here?
I bade thee hence!" The bard obeyed;
And turning from his own sweet maid,
The agèd knight, Sir Leoline,
Led forth the lady Geraldine!

(1801)

THE CONCLUSION TO PART THE SECOND

A little child, a limber elf,
Singing, dancing to itself,
A fairy thing with red round cheeks,
That always finds, and never seeks,
Makes such a vision to the sight
As fills a father's eyes with light;

And pleasures flow in so thick and fast
Upon his heart, that he at last
Must needs express his love's excess
With words of unmeant bitterness.
Perhaps 'tis pretty to force together
Thought so all unlike each other;
To mutter and mock a broken charm,
To dally with wrong that does no harm.
Perhaps 'tis tender too and pretty
At each wild word to feel within
A sweet recoil of love and pity.
And what, if in a world of sin
(O sorrow and shame should this be true!)
Such giddiness of heart and brain
Comes seldom save from rage and pain,
So talks as it's most used to do.

                                        S. T. COLERIDGE.

(? 1801)

GLENFINLAS; OR, LORD RONALD'S CORONACH[1]

The simple tradition, upon which the following stanzas are founded,
runs thus: While two Highland hunters were passing the night in a
solitary *bothy* (a hut, built for the purpose of hunting), and making
merry over their venison and whisky, one of them expressed a wish
that they had pretty lasses to complete their party. The words were
scarcely uttered, when two beautiful young women, habited in green,
entered the hut, dancing and singing. One of the hunters was seduced
by the siren who attached herself particularly to him, to leave the hut:
the other remained, and, suspicious of the fair seducers, continued to
play upon a trump, or Jew's harp, some strain, consecrated to the
Virgin Mary. Day at length came, and the temptress vanished. Searching in the forest, he found the bones of his unfortunate friend, who had
been torn to pieces and devoured by the fiend into whose toils he had
fallen. The place was from thence called the Glen of the Green Women.
    Glenfinlas is a tract of forest-ground, lying in the Highlands of
Perthshire, not far from Callender in Menteith. It was formerly a royal
forest, and now belongs to the Earl of Moray. This country, as well as
the adjacent district of Balquidder, was, in times of yore, chiefly
inhabited by the Macgregors. To the west of the Forest of Glenfinlas
lies Loch Katrine and its romantic avenue, called the Trossachs.
Benledi, Benmore, and Benvoirlich, are mountains in the same district,
and at no great distance from Glenfinlas. The river Teith passes Callender and the Castle of Doune, and joins the Forth near Stirling. The
pass of Lenny is immediately above Callender, and is the principal

---

[1] *Coronach* is the lamentation for a deceased warrior, sung by the
aged of the clan.

access to the Highlands from that town. Glenartney is a forest, near
Benvoirlich. The whole forms a sublime tract of Alpine scenery.
This ballad first appeared in the *Tales of Wonder*.

> For them the viewless forms of air obey,
> Their bidding heed, and at their beck repair;
> They know what spirit brews the stormful day,
> And heartless oft, like moody madness stare,
> To see the phantom-train their secret work prepare.
>
> COLLINS.

" O HONE a rie'! O hone a rie'!
　　The pride of Albin's line is o'er,
And fall'n Glenartney's stateliest tree;
　　We ne'er shall see Lord Ronald more! "

O, sprung from great Macgillianore,
　　The chief that never fear'd a foe,
How matchless was thy broad claymore,
　　How deadly thine unerring bow!

Well can the Saxon[1] widows tell,
　　How, on the Teith's resounding shore,
The boldest Lowland warriors fell,
　　As down from Lenny's pass you bore.

But o'er his hills, in festal day,
　　How blazed Lord Ronald's beltane-tree,
While youths and maids the light strathspey
　　So nimbly danced with Highland glee!

Cheer'd by the strength of Ronald's shell,
　　E'en age forgot his tresses hoar;
But now the loud lament we swell,
　　O ne'er to see Lord Ronald more!

From distant isles a chieftain came,
　　The joys of Ronald's halls to find,
And chase with him the dark-brown game,
　　That bounds o'er Albin's hills of wind.

'Twas Moy; whom in Columba's isle
　　The seer's prophetic spirit found,
As, with a minstrel's fire the while,
　　He waked his harp's harmonious sound.

[1] The term Sassenach, or Saxon, is applied by the Highlanders to
their Low-Country neighbours.

Full many a spell to him was known,
  Which wandering spirits shrink to hear;
And many a lay of potent tone,
  Was never meant for mortal ear.

For there, 'tis said, in mystic mood,
  High converse with the dead they hold,
And oft espy the fated shroud,
  That shall the future corpse enfold.

O so it fell, that on a day,
  To rouse the red deer from their den,
The Chiefs have ta'en their distant way,
  And scour'd the deep Glenfinlas glen.

No vassals wait their sports to aid,
  To watch their safety, deck their board;
Their simple dress, the Highland plaid,
  Their trusty guard, the Highland sword.

Three summer days, through brake and dell,
  Their whistling shafts successful flew;
And still, when dewy evening fell,
  The quarry to their hut they drew.

In grey Glenfinlas' deepest nook
  The solitary cabin stood,
Fast by Moneira's sullen brook,
  Which murmurs through that lonely wood.

Soft fell the night, the sky was calm,
  When three successive days had flown;
And summer mist in dewy balm
  Steep'd heathy bank, and mossy stone.

The moon, half-hid in silvery flakes,
  Afar her dubious radiance shed,
Quivering on Katrine's distant lakes,
  And resting on Benledi's head.

Now in their hut, in social guise,
   Their silvan fare the Chiefs enjoy;
And pleasure laughs in Ronald's eyes,
   As many a pledge he quaffs to Moy.

" What lack we here to crown our bliss,
   While thus the pulse of joy beats high ?
What, but fair woman's yielding kiss,
   Her panting breath and melting eye ?

" To chase the deer of yonder shades,
   This morning left their father's pile
The fairest of our mountain maids,
   The daughters of the proud Glengyle.

" Long have I sought sweet Mary's heart,
   And dropp'd the tear, and heaved the sigh:
But vain the lover's wily art,
   Beneath a sister's watchful eye.

" But thou mayst teach that guardian fair,
   While far with Mary I am flown,
Of other hearts to cease her care,
   And find it hard to guard her own.

" Touch but thy harp, thou soon shalt see
   The lovely Flora of Glengyle,
Unmindful of her charge and me,
   Hang on thy notes, 'twixt tear and smile.

" Or, if she choose a melting tale,
   All underneath the greenwood bough,
Will good St. Oran's rule prevail,
   Stern huntsman of the rigid brow ? "—

" Since Enrick's fight, since Morna's death,
   No more on me shall rapture rise,
Responsive to the panting breath,
   Or yielding kiss, or melting eyes.

" E'en then, when o'er the heath of woe,
  Where sunk my hopes of love and fame,
I bade my harp's wild wailings flow,
  On me the Seer's sad spirit came.

" The last dread curse of angry heaven,
  With ghastly sights and sounds of woe,
To dash each glimpse of joy was given—
  The gift, the future ill to know.

" The bark thou saw'st, yon summer morn,
  So gaily part from Oban's bay,
My eye beheld her dash'd and torn,
  Far on the rocky Colonsay.

" Thy Fergus too—thy sister's son,
  Thou saw'st, with pride, the gallant's power,
As marching 'gainst the Lord of Downe,
  He left the skirts of huge Benmore.

" Thou only saw'st their tartans wave,
  As down Benvoirlich's side they wound,
Heard'st but the pibroch, answering brave
  To many a target clanking round.

" I heard the groans, I mark'd the tears,
  I saw the wound his bosom bore,
When on the serried Saxon spears
  He pour'd his clan's resistless roar.

" And thou, who bidst me think of bliss,
  And bidst my heart awake to glee,
And court, like thee, the wanton kiss—
  That heart, O Ronald, bleeds for thee!

" I see the death-damps chill thy brow;
  I hear thy Warning Spirit cry;
The corpse-lights dance—they're gone, and now—
  No more is given to gifted eye! "—

" Alone enjoy thy dreary dreams,
   Sad prophet of the evil hour!
Say, should we scorn joy's transient beams,
   Because to-morrow's storm may lour?

" Or false, or sooth, thy words of woe,
   Clangillian's Chieftain ne'er shall fear;
His blood shall bound at rapture's glow,
   Though doom'd to stain the Saxon spear.

" E'en now, to meet me in yon dell,
   My Mary's buskins brush the dew."
He spoke, nor bade the Chief farewell,
   But called his dogs, and gay withdrew.

Within an hour return'd each hound;
   In rush'd the rousers of the deer;
They howl'd in melancholy sound,
   Then closely couch'd beside the Seer.

No Ronald yet; though midnight came,
   And sad were Moy's prophetic dreams,
As, bending o'er the dying flame,
   He fed the watch-fire's quivering gleams.

Sudden the hounds erect their ears,
   And sudden cease their moaning howl;
Close press'd to Moy, they mark their fears
   By shivering limbs and stifled growl.

Untouch'd, the harp began to ring,
   As softly, slowly, oped the door;
And shook responsive every string,
   As light a footstep press'd the floor.

And by the watch-fire's glimmering light
   Close by the minstrel's side was seen
An huntress maid, in beauty bright,
   All dropping wet her robes of green.

All dropping wet her garments seem;
  Chill'd was her cheek, her bosom bare,
As, bending o'er the dying gleam,
  She wrung the moisture from her hair.

With maiden blush, she softly said,
  " O gentle hunstman, hast thou seen,
In deep Glenfinlas' moonlight glade,
  A lovely maid in vest of green:

" With her a Chief in Highland pride;
  His shoulders bear the hunter's bow,
The mountain dirk adorns his side,
  Far on the wind his tartans flow ? "—

" And who art thou ? and who are they ?
  All ghastly gazing, Moy replied:
" And why, beneath the moon's pale ray,
  Dare ye thus roam Glenfinlas' side ? "—

" Where wild Loch Katrine pours her tide,
  Blue, dark, and deep, round many an isle,
Our father's towers o'erhang her side,
  The castle of the bold Glengyle.

" To chase the dun Glenfinlas deer,
  Our woodland course this morn we bore,
And haply met, while wandering here,
  The son of great Macgillianore.

" O aid me, then, to seek the pair,
  Whom, loitering in the woods, I lost;
Alone, I dare not venture there,
  Where walks, they say, the shrieking ghost."—

" Yes, many a shrieking ghost walks there;
  Then, first, my own sad vow to keep,
Here will I pour my midnight prayer,
  Which still must rise when mortals sleep."—

" O first, for pity's gentle sake,
   Guide a lone wanderer on her way!
For I must cross the haunted brake,
   And reach my father's towers ere day."—

" First, three times tell each Ave-bead,
   And thrice a Pater-noster say;
Then kiss with me the holy rede;
   So shall we safely wend our way."—

" O shame to knighthood, strange and foul!
   Go, doff the bonnet from thy brow,
And shroud thee in the monkish cowl,
   Which best befits thy sullen vow.

" Not so, by high Dunlathmon's fire,
   Thy heart was froze to love and joy,
When gaily rung thy raptured lyre
   To wanton Moran's melting eye."

Wild stared the minstrel's eyes of flame,
   And high his sable locks arose,
And quick his colour went and came,
   As fear and rage alternate rose.

" And thou! when by the blazing oak
   I lay, to her and love resign'd,
Say, rode ye on the eddying smoke,
   Or sail'd ye on the midnight wind?

" Not thine a race of mortal blood,
   Nor old Glengyle's pretended line;
Thy dame, the Lady of the Flood—
   Thy sire, the Monarch of the Mine."

He mutter'd thrice St. Oran's rhyme,
   And thrice St. Fillan's powerful prayer;
Then turn'd him to the eastern clime,
   And sternly shook his coal-black hair.

And, bending o'er his harp, he flung
  His wildest witch-notes on the wind;
And loud, and high, and strange, they rung,
  As many a magic change they find.

Tall wax'd the Spirit's altering form,
  Till to the roof her stature grew;
Then, mingling with the rising storm,
  With one wild yell away she flew.

Rain beats, hail rattles, whirlwinds tear:
  The slender hut in fragments flew;
But not a lock of Moy's loose hair
  Was waved by wind, or wet by dew.

Wild mingling with the howling gale,
  Loud bursts of ghastly laughter rise;
High o'er the minstrel's head they sail,
  And die amid the northern skies.

The voice of thunder shook the wood,
  As ceased the more than mortal yell;
And, spattering foul, a shower of blood
  Upon the hissing firebrands fell.

Next dropp'd from high a mangled arm;
  The fingers strain'd an half-drawn blade.
And last, the life-blood streaming warm,
  Torn from the trunk, a gasping head.

Oft o'er that head, in battling field,
  Stream'd the proud crest of high Benmore;
That arm the broad claymore could wield,
  Which dyed the Teith with Saxon gore.

Woe to Moneira's sullen rills!
  Woe to Glenfinlas' dreary glen!
There never son of Albin's hills
  Shall draw the hunter's shaft agen.

E'en the tired pilgrim's burning feet
  At noon shall shun that sheltering den,
Lest, journeying in their rage, he meet
  The wayward Ladies of the Glen.

SIR WALTER SCOTT 241

And we—behind the Chieftain's shield,
No more shall we in safety dwell;
None leads the people to the field—
And we the loud lament must swell.

O hone a rie'! O hone a rie'!
The pride of Albin's line is o'er!
And fall'n Glenartney's stateliest tree;
We ne'er shall see Lord Ronald more!

SIR WALTER SCOTT.

THE SIEGE OF CORINTH

"The grand army of the Turks (in 1715), under the Prime Vizier, to open to themselves a way into the heart of the Morea, and to form the siege of Napoli di Romania, the most considerable place in all that country,[1] thought it best in the first place to attack Corinth, upon which they made several storms. The garrison being weakened, and the governor seeing it was impossible to hold out against so mighty a force, thought it fit to beat a parley: but while they were treating about the articles, one of the magazines in the Turkish camp, wherein they had six hundred barrels of powder, blew up by accident, whereby six or seven hundred men were killed; which so enraged the infidels, that they would not grant any capitulation, but stormed the place with so much fury, that they took it, and put most of the garrison, with Signior Minotti, the governor, to the sword. The rest, with Antonio Bembo, proveditor extraordinary, were made prisoners of war."—*History of the Turks*, vol. iii. p. 151.

In the year since Jesus died for men,
Eighteen hundred years and ten,
We were a gallant company,
Riding o'er land, and sailing o'er sea.
Oh! but we went merrily!
We forded the river, and clomb the high hill,
Never our steeds for a day stood still;

[1] Napoli di Romania is not now the most considerable place in the Morea, but Tripolitza, where the Pacha resides, and maintains his government. Napoli is near Argos. I visited all three in 1801–11; and, in the course of journeying through the country from my first arrival in 1809, I crossed the Isthmus eight times in my way from Attica to the Morea, over the mountains, or in the other direction, when passing from the Gulf of Athens to that of Lepanto. Both the routes are picturesque and beautiful, though very different: that by sea has more sameness; but the voyage being always within sight of land, and often very near it, presents many attractive views of the islands Salamis, Ægina, Poro, etc., and the coast of the Continent.

Whether we lay in the cave or the shed,
Our sleep fell soft on the hardest bed;
Whether we couch'd in our rough capote,
On the rougher plank of our gliding boat,
Or stretch'd on the beach, or our saddles spread
As a pillow beneath the resting head,
Fresh we woke upon the morrow:
All our thoughts and words had scope,
We had health, and we had hope,
Toil and travel, but no sorrow.
We were of all tongues and creeds;—
Some were those who counted beads,
Some of mosque, and some of church,
And some, or I mis-say, of neither;
Yet through the wide world might ye search,
Nor find a motlier crew nor blither.
But some are dead, and some are gone,
And some are scatter'd and alone,
And some are rebels on the hills[1]
That look along Epirus' valleys,
Where freedom still at moments rallies,
And pays in blood oppression's ills;
And some are in a far countree,
And some are restlessly at home;
But never more, oh! never, we
Shall meet to revel and to roam.

But those hardy days flew cheerily,
And when they now fall drearily,
My thoughts, like swallows, skim the main,
And bear my spirit back again
Over the earth, and through the air,
A wild bird and a wanderer.
'Tis this that ever wakes my strain,
And oft, too oft, implores again
The few who may endure my lay,
To follow me so far away.
Stranger—wilt thou follow now,
And sit with me on Acro-Corinth's brow?

[1] The last tidings recently heard of Dervish (one of the Arnaouts who followed me) state him to be in revolt upon the mountains, at the head of some of the bands common in that country in times of trouble.

I

Many a vanish'd year and age,
And tempest's breath, and battle's rage,
Have swept o'er Corinth; yet she stands,
A fortress form'd to Freedom's hands.[1]
The whirlwind's wrath, the earthquake's shock,
Have left untouch'd her hoary rock,
The keystone of a land, which still,
Though fall'n, looks proudly on that hill,
The landmark to the double tide
That purpling rolls on either side,
As if their waters chafed to meet,
Yet pause and crouch beneath her feet.
But could the blood before her shed
Since first Timoleon's brother bled,[2]
Or baffled Persia's despot fled,
Arise from out the earth which drank
The stream of slaughter as it sank,
That sanguine ocean would o'erflow
Her isthmus idly spread below:
Or could the bones of all the slain,
Who perish'd there, be piled again,
That rival pyramid would rise
More mountain-like, through those clear skies,
Than yon tower-capp'd Acropolis,
Which seems the very clouds to kiss.

II

On dun Cithæron's ridge appears
The gleam of twice ten thousand spears;
And downward to the Isthmian plain,
From shore to shore of either main,
The tent is pitch'd, the crescent shines
Along the Moslem's leaguering lines
And the dusk Spahi's bands[3] advance

[1] In the original MS.: "A marvel from her Moslem bands."
[2] Timoleon, who had saved the life of his brother Timophanes in battle, afterwards killed him for aiming at the supreme power in Corinth, preferring his duty to his country to all the obligations of blood.
[3] Turkish holders of military fiefs, which oblige them to join the army, mounted at their own expense.

Beneath each bearded pacha's glance;
And far and wide as eye can reach
The turbaned cohorts throng the beach;
And there the Arab's camel kneels,
And there his steed the Tartar wheels;
The Turcoman hath left his herd,[1]
The sabre round his loins to gird;
And there the volleying thunders pour
Till waves grow smoother to the roar.
The trench is dug, the cannon's breath
Wings the far hissing globe of death;
Fast whirl the fragments from the wall,
Which crumbles with the ponderous ball;
And from that wall the foe replies,
O'er dusty plain and smoky skies,
With fires that answer fast and well
The summons of the Infidel.

III

But near and nearest to the wall
Of those who wish and work its fall,
With deeper skill in war's black art,
Than Othman's sons, and high of heart
As any chief that ever stood
Triumphant in the fields of blood;
From post to post, and deed to deed,
Fast spurring on his reeking steed,
Where sallying ranks the trench assail,
And make the foremost Moslem quail;
Or where the battery, guarded well,
Remains as yet impregnable,
Alighting cheerly to inspire
The soldier slackening in his fire;
The first and freshest of the host
Which Stamboul's sultan there can boast,
To guide the follower o'er the field,
To point the tube, the lance to wield,
Or whirl around the bickering blade;—
Was Alp, the Adrian renegade!

[1] The life of the Turcomans is wandering and patriarchal: they
dwell in tents.

IV

From Venice—once a race of worth
His gentle sires—he drew his birth;
But late an exile from her shore
Against his countrymen he bore
The arms they taught to bear; and now
The turban girt his shaven brow.
Through many a change had Corinth pass'd
With Greece to Venice' rule at last;
And here, before her walls, with those
To Greece and Venice equal foes,
He stood a foe with all the zeal
Which young and fiery converts feel,
Within whose heated bosom throngs
The memory of a thousand wrongs.
To him had Venice ceased to be
Her ancient civic boast—" the Free ";
And in the palace of St. Mark
Unnamed accusers in the dark
Within the " Lion's mouth " had placed
A charge against him uneffaced:
He fled in time, and saved his life,
To waste his future years in strife,
That taught his land how great his loss
In him who triumphed o'er the Cross,
'Gainst which he rear'd the Crescent high,
And battled to avenge or die.

V

Coumourgi[1]—he whose closing scene
Adorn'd the triumph of Eugene,
When on Carlowitz' bloody plain,
The last and mightiest of the slain.

[1] Ali Coumourgi, the favourite of three sultans, and Grand Vizier to Achmet III., after recovering Peloponnesus from the Venetians in one campaign, was mortally wounded in the next, against the Germans, at the battle of Peterwardin (in the plain of Carlowitz), in Hungary, endeavouring to rally his guards. He died of his wounds next day. His last order was the decapitation of General Breuner, and some other German prisoners; and his last words, " O that I could thus serve all the Christian dogs! " a speech and act not unlike one of Caligula. He was a young man of great ambition and unbounded presumption: on being told that Prince Eugene, then opposed to him, " was a great general," he said, " I shall become a greater, and at his expense."

He sank, regretting not to die,
But cursed the Christian victory—
Coumourgi—can his glory cease,
That latest conqueror of Greece,
Till Christian hands to Greece restore
The freedom Venice gave of yore?
A hundred years have roll'd away
Since he refixed the Moslem's sway.
And now he led the Mussulman,
And gave the guidance of the van
To Alp, who well repaid the trust
By cities levell'd with the dust;
And proved, by many a deed of death,
How firm his heart in novel faith.

VI

The walls grew weak; and fast and hot
Against them pour'd the ceaseless shot,
With unabating fury sent
From battery to battlement;
And thunder-like the pealing din
Rose from each heated culverin;
And here and there some crackling dome
Was fired before the exploding bomb;
And as the fabric sank beneath
The shattering shell's volcanic breath,
In red and wreathing columns flash'd
The flame, as loud the ruin crash'd,
Or into countless meteors driven,
Its earth-stars melted into heaven;
Whose clouds that day grew doubly dun,
Impervious to the hidden sun,
With volumed smoke that slowly grew
To one wide sky of sulphurous hue.

VII

But not for vengeance, long delay'd,
Alone, did Alp, the renegade,
The Moslem warriors sternly teach
His skill to pierce the promised breach:

Within these walls a maid was pent
His hope would win without consent
Of that inexorable sire,
Whose heart refused him in its ire,
When Alp, beneath his Christian name,
Her virgin hand aspired to claim.
In happier mood, and earlier time,
While unimpeach'd for traitorous crime,
Gayest in gondola or hall,
He glitter'd through the Carnival;
And tuned the softest serenade
That e'er on Adria's waters play'd
At midnight to Italian maid.

VIII

And many deem'd her heart was won;
For sought by numbers, given to none,
Had young Francesca's hand remain'd
Still by the church's bonds unchain'd:
And when the Adriatic bore
Lanciotto to the Paynim shore,
Her wonted smiles were seen to fail,
And pensive wax'd the maid and pale;
More constant at confessional,
More rare at masque and festival;
Or seen at such, with downcast eyes,
Which conquer'd hearts they ceased to prize:
With listless look she seems to gaze:
With humbler care her form arrays;
Her voice less lively in the song;
Her step, though light, less fleet among
The pairs, on whom the Morning's glance
Breaks, yet unsated with the dance.

IX

Sent by the state to guard the land,
(Which, wrested from the Moslem's hand,
While Sobieski tamed his pride
By Buda's wall and Danube's side,

The chiefs of Venice wrung away
From Patra to Eubœa's bay,)
Minotti held in Corinth's towers
The Doge's delegated powers,
While yet the pitying eye of Peace
Smiled o'er her long-forgotten Greece;
And ere that faithless truce was broke
Which freed her from the unchristian yoke,
With him his gentle daughter came;
Nor there, since Menelaus' dame
Forsook her lord and land, to prove
What woes await on lawless love,
Had fairer form adorn'd the shore
Than she, the matchless stranger, bore.

X

The wall is rent, the ruins yawn;
And, with to-morrow's earliest dawn,
O'er the disjointed mass shall vault
The foremost of the fierce assault.
The bands are rank'd; the chosen van
Of Tartar and of Mussulman,
The full of hope, misnamed "forlorn,"
Who hold the thought of death in scorn,
And win their way with falchion's force,
Or pave the path with many a corse,
O'er which the following brave may rise,
Their stepping-stone—the last who dies!

XI

'Tis midnight: on the mountains brown
The cold, round moon shines deeply down;
Blue roll the waters, blue the sky
Spreads like an ocean hung on high,
Bespangled with those isles of light,
So wildly, spiritually bright;
Who ever gazed upon them shining
And turn'd to earth without repining,

Nor wish'd for wings to flee away,
And mix with their eternal ray?
The waves on either shore lay there
Calm, clear, and azure as the air;
And scarce their foam the pebbles shook,
But murmur'd meekly as the brook.
The winds were pillow'd on the waves;
The banners droop'd along their staves,
And, as they fell around them furling,
Above them shone the crescent curling;
And that deep silence was unbroke,
Save where the watch his signal spoke,
Save where the steed neigh'd oft and shrill,
And echo answer'd from the hill,
And the wide hum of that wild host,
Rustled like leaves from coast to coast,
As rose the Muezzin's voice in air
In midnight call to wonted prayer;
It rose, that chanted mournful strain,
Like some lone spirit's o'er the plain:
'Twas musical, but sadly sweet,
Such as when winds and harp-strings meet,
And take a long unmeasured tone,
To mortal minstrelsy unknown.
It seem'd to those within the wall
A cry prophetic of their fall:
It struck even the besieger's ear
With something ominous and drear,
An undefined and sudden thrill,
Which makes the heart a moment still,
Then beat with quicker pulse, ashamed
Of that strange sense its silence framed;
Such as a sudden passing-bell
Wakes, though but for a stranger's knell.

XII

The tent of Alp was on the shore;
The sound was hush'd, the prayer was o'er
The watch was set, the night-round made.
All mandates issued and obey'd:
'Tis but another anxious night,

His pains the morrow may requite
With all revenge and love can pay,
In guerdon for their long delay.
Few hours remain, and he hath need
Of rest, to nerve for many a deed
Of slaughter; but within his soul
The thoughts like troubled waters roll.
He stood alone among the host;
Not his the loud fanatic boast
To plant the crescent o'er the cross,
Or risk a life with little loss,
Secure in paradise to be
By Houris loved immortally:
Nor his, what burning patriots feel,
The stern exaltedness of zeal,
Profuse of blood, untired in toil,
When battling on the parent soil.
He stood alone—a renegade
Against the country he betray'd;
He stood alone amidst his band,
Without a trusted heart or hand:
They followed him, for he was brave,
And great the spoil he got and gave;
They crouch'd to him, for he had skill
To warp and wield the vulgar will:
But still his Christian origin
With them was little less than sin.
They envied even the faithless fame
He earn'd beneath a Moslem name;
Since he, their mightiest chief, had been
In youth a bitter Nazarene.
They did not know how pride can stoop,
When baffled feelings withering droop;
They did not know how hate can burn
In hearts once changed from soft to stern;
Nor all the false and fatal zeal
The convert of revenge can feel.
He ruled them—man may rule the worst,
By ever daring to be first;
So lions o'er the jackal sway;
The jackal points, he fells the prey,
Then on the vulgar yelling press,
To gorge the relics of success.

XIII

His head grows fever'd, and his pulse
The quick successive throbs convulse;
In vain from side to side he throws
His form, in courtship of repose;
Or if he dozed, a sound, a start
Awoke him with a sunken heart.
The turban on his hot brow press'd,
The mail weigh'd lead-like on his breast,
Though oft and long beneath its weight
Upon his eyes had slumber sate,
Without or couch or canopy,
Except a rougher field and sky
Than now might yield a warrior's bed,
Than now along the heaven was spread.
He could not rest, he could not stay
Within his tent to wait for day,
But walk'd him forth along the sand,
Where thousand sleepers strew'd the strand.
What pillow'd them? and why should he
More wakeful than the humblest be,
Since more their peril, worse their toil?
And yet they fearless dream of spoil;
While he alone, where thousands pass'd
A night of sleep, perchance their last,
In sickly vigil wander'd on,
And envied all he gazed upon.

XIV

He felt his soul become more light
Beneath the freshness of the night.
Cool was the silent sky, though calm,
And bathed his brow with airy balm:
Behind, the camp—before him lay,
In many a winding creek and bay,
Lepanto's gulf; and, on the brow
Of Delphi's hill, unshaken snow,
High and eternal, such as shone
Through thousand summers brightly gone,

Along the gulf, the mount, the clime;
It will not melt, like man, to time;
Tyrant and slave are swept away,
Less form'd to wear before the ray;
But that white veil, the lightest, frailest,
Which on the mighty mount thou hailest,
While tower and tree are torn and rent,
Shines o'er its craggy battlement;
In form a peak, in height a cloud,
In texture like a hovering shroud,
Thus high by parting Freedom spread,
As from her fond abode she fled,
And linger'd on the spot, where long
Her prophet spirit spake in song.
Oh! still her step at moments falters
O'er withered fields, and ruin'd altars,
And fain would wake, in souls too broken,
By pointing to each glorious token:
But vain her voice, till better days
Dawn in those yet remember'd rays
Which shone upon the Persian flying,
And saw the Spartan smile in dying.

xv

Not mindless of these mighty times
Was Alp, despite his flight and crimes;
And through this night, as on he wander'd,
And o'er the past and present ponder'd,
And thought upon the glorious dead
Who there in better cause had bled,
He felt how faint and feebly dim
The fame that could accrue to him
Who cheer'd the band, and waved the sword,
A traitor in a turban'd horde;
And led them to the lawless siege,
Whose best success were sacrilege.
Not so had those his fancy number'd,
The chiefs whose dust around him slumber'd;
Their phalanx marshall'd in the plain,
Whose bulwarks were not then in vain.
They fell devoted, but undying;

The very gale their names seem'd sighing:
The waters murmur'd of their name;
The woods were peopled with their fame;
The silent pillar, lone and grey,
Claim'd kindred with their sacred clay;
Their spirits wrapp'd the dusky mountain;
Their memory sparkled o'er the fountain;
The meanest rill, the mightiest river
Roll'd mingling with their fame for ever.
Despite of every yoke she bears,
That land is glory's still and theirs!
'Tis still a watchword to the earth:
When man would do a deed of worth
He points to Greece, and turns to tread,
So sanction'd, on the tyrant's head:
He looks to her, and rushes on
Where life is lost, or freedom won.

XVI

Still by the shore Alp mutely mused,
And woo'd the freshness Night diffused.
There shrinks no ebb in that tideless sea,[1]
Which changeless rolls eternally;
So that wildest of waves, in their angriest mood,
Scarce break on the bounds of the land for a rood;
And the powerless moon beholds them flow,
Heedless if she come or go:
Calm or high, in main or bay
On their course she hath no sway.
The rock unworn its base doth bare,
And looks o'er the surf, but it comes not there;
And the fringe of the foam may be seen below,
On the line that it left long ages ago:
A smooth short space of yellow sand
Between it and the greener land.

He wander'd on, along the beach,
Till within the range of a carbine's reach

---

[1] The reader need hardly be reminded that there are no perceptible tides in the Mediterranean.

Of the leaguer'd wall; but they saw him not,
Or how could he 'scape from the hostile shot?
Did traitors lurk in the Christians' hold?
Were their hands grown stiff, or their hearts wax'd cold?
I know not, in sooth; but from yonder wall
There flash'd no fire, and there hiss'd no ball,
Though he stood beneath the bastion's frown,
That flank'd the seaward gate of the town;
Though he heard the sound, and could almost tell
The sullen words of the sentinel,
As his measured step on the stone below
Clank'd, as he paced it to and fro;
And he saw the lean dogs beneath the wall
Hold o'er the dead their carnival,
Gorging and growling o'er carcass and limb;
They were too busy to bark at him!
From a Tartar's skull they had stripp'd the flesh,
As ye peel the fig when its fruit is fresh;
And their white tusks crunch'd o'er the whiter skull,[1]
As it slipp'd through their jaws, when their edge grew
    dull,
As they lazily mumbled the bones of the dead,
When they scarce could rise from the spot where they fed;
So well had they broken a lingering fast
With those who had fallen for that night's repast.
And Alp knew, by the turbans that roll'd on the sand,
The foremost of these were the best of his band:
Crimson and green were the shawls of their wear,
And each scalp had a single long tuft of hair,
All the rest was shaven and bare.
The scalps were in the wild dog's maw,
The hair was tangled round his jaw.
But close by the shore, on the edge of the gulf,
There sat a vulture flapping a wolf,
Who had stolen from the hills, but kept away,
Scared by the dogs, from the human prey;
But he seized on his share of a steed that lay,
Pick'd by the birds, on the sands of the bay.

[1] This spectacle I have seen, such as described, beneath the wall
of the Seraglio at Constantinople, in the little cavities worn by the
Bosphorus in the rock, a narrow terrace of which projects between
the wall and the water. I think the fact is also mentioned in Hob-
house's *Travels*. The bodies were probably those of some refractory
Janizaries.

XVII

Alp turn'd him from the sickening sight:
Never had shaken his nerves in fight;
But he better could brook to behold the dying,
Deep in the tide of their warm blood lying,
Scorch'd with the death-thirst, and writhing in vain,
Than the perishing dead who are past all pain.
There is something of pride in the perilous hour,
Whate'er be the shape in which death may lower;
For Fame is there to say who bleeds,
And Honour's eye on daring deeds!
But when all is past, it is humbling to tread
O'er the weltering field of the tombless dead,
And see worms of the earth, and fowls of the air,
Beasts of the forest, all gathering there;
All regarding man as their prey,
All rejoicing in his decay.

XVIII

There is a temple in ruin stands,
Fashion'd by long-forgotten hands;
Two or three columns, and many a stone,
Marble and granite, with grass o'ergrown!
Out upon Time! it will leave no more
Of the things to come than the things before!
Out upon Time! who for ever will leave
But enough of the past for the future to grieve
O'er that which hath been, and o'er that which must be:
What we have seen, our sons shall see;
Remnants of things that have pass'd away,
Fragments of stone, rear'd by creatures of clay!

XIX

He sate him down at a pillar's base,
And pass'd his hand athwart his face;
Like one in dreary musing mood,
Declining was his attitude;

His head was drooping on his breast,
Fever'd, throbbing, and oppress'd;
And o'er his brow, so downward bent,
Oft his beating fingers went,
Hurriedly, as you may see
Your own run over the ivory key,
Ere the measured tone is taken
By the chords you would awaken.
There he sate all heavily,
As he heard the night-wind sigh,
Was it the wind, through some hollow stone,
Sent that soft and tender moan?[1]
He lifted his head, and he look'd on the sea,
But it was unrippled as glass may be;
He look'd on the long grass—it waved not a blade;
How was that gentle sound convey'd?
He look'd to the banners—each flag lay still,
So did the leaves on Cithæron's hill,
And he felt not a breath come over his cheek;
What did that sudden sound bespeak?
He turn'd to the left—is he sure of sight?
There sate a lady, youthful and bright!

XX

He started up with more of fear
Than if an armèd foe were near.
" God of my fathers! what is here?
Who art thou, and wherefore sent
So near a hostile armament? "
His trembling hands refused to sign
The cross he deem'd no more divine:
He had resumed it in that hour,
But conscience wrung away the power.
He gazed, he saw: he knew the face
Of beauty, and the form of grace;

[1] I must here acknowledge a close, though unintentional, resemblance in these twelve lines to a passage in an unpublished poem of Mr. Coleridge, called " Christabel." It was not till after these lines were written that I heard that wild and singularly original and beautiful poem recited; and the MS. of that production I never saw till very recently, by the kindness of Mr. Coleridge himself, who, I hope, is convinced that I have not been a wilful plagiarist. The original idea undoubtedly pertains to Mr Coleridge, whose poem has been composed above fourteen years.

It was Francesca by his side,
The maid who might have been his bride.
The rose was yet upon her cheek,
But mellow'd with a tenderer streak;
Where was the play of her soft lips fled?
Gone was the smile that enliven'd their red.
The ocean's calm within their view
Beside her eye had less of blue;
But like that cold wave it stood still,
And its glance, though clear, was chill.
Around her form a thin robe twining,
Nought conceal'd her bosom shining;
Through the parting of her hair,
Floating darkly downward there,
Her rounded arm show'd white and bare:
And ere yet she made reply,
Once she raised her hand on high;
It was so wan, and transparent of hue,
You might have seen the moon shine through.

XXI

" I come from my rest to him I love best,
That I may be happy, and he may be bless'd.
I have pass'd the guards, the gate, the wall;
Sought thee in safety through foes and all.
'Tis said the lion will turn and flee
From a maid in the pride of her purity;
And the Power on high, that can shield the good
Thus from the tyrant of the wood,
Hath extended its mercy to guard me as well
From the hands of the leaguering infidel.
I come—and if I come in vain,
Never, oh never, we meet again!
Thou hast done a fearful deed
In falling away from thy father's creed:
But dash that turban to earth, and sign
The sign of the cross, and for ever be mine;
Wring the black drop from thy heart,
And to-morrow unites us no more to part."

" And where should our bridal couch be spread?
In the midst of the dying and the dead?

For to-morrow we give to the slaughter and flame
The sons and the shrines of the Christian name.
None, save thou and thine, I've sworn,
Shall be left upon the morn:
But thee will I bear to a lovely spot,
Where our hands shall be join'd, and our sorrow forgot.
There thou yet shalt be my bride,
When once again I've quell'd the pride
Of Venice; and her hated race
Have felt the arm they would debase
Scourge, with a whip of scorpions, those
Whom vice and envy made my foes."

Upon his hand she laid her own—
Light was the touch, but it thrill'd to the bone,
And shot a chillness to his heart,
Which fix'd him beyond the power to start.
Though slight was that grasp so mortal cold,
He could not loose him from its hold;
But never did clasp of one so dear
Strike on the pulse with such feeling of fear,
As those thin fingers, long and white,
Froze through his blood by their touch that night.
The feverish glow of his brow was gone,
And his heart sank so still that it felt like stone,
As he look'd on the face, and beheld its hue,
So deeply changed from what he knew:
Fair but faint—without the ray
Of mind, that made each feature play
Like sparkling waves on a sunny day;
And her motionless lips lay still as death,
And her words came forth without her breath,
And there rose not a heave o'er her bosom's swell,
And there seem'd not a pulse in her veins to dwell.
Though her eye shone out, yet the lids were fix'd,
And the glance that it gave was wild and unmix'd
With aught of change, as the eyes may seem
Of the restless who walk in a troubled dream;
Like the figures on arras, that gloomily glare,
Stirr'd by the breath of the wintry air,
So seen by the dying lamp's fitful light,
Lifeless, but life-like, and awful to sight;
As they seem, through the dimness, about to come down

From the shadowy wall where their images frown;
Fearfully flitting to and fro,
As the gusts on the tapestry come and go.
" If not for love of me be given
Thus much, then, for the love of heaven,—
Again I say—that turban tear
From off thy faithless brow, and swear
Thy injured country's sons to spare,
Or thou art lost; and never shalt see—
Not earth—that's past—but heaven or me.
If this thou dost accord, albeit
A heavy doom 'tis thine to meet,
That doom shall half absolve thy sin,
And mercy's gate may receive thee within:
But pause one moment more, and take
The curse of Him thou didst forsake;
And look once more to heaven, and see
Its love for ever shut from thee.
There is a light cloud by the moon—
'Tis passing, and will pass full soon—
If, by the time its vapoury sail
Hath ceased her shaded orb to veil,
Thy heart within thee is not changed,
Then God and man are both avenged;
Dark will thy doom be, darker still
Thine immortality of ill."

Alp look'd to heaven, and saw on high
The sign she spake of in the sky;
But his heart was swollen, and turn'd aside
By deep interminable pride.
This first false passion of his breast
Roll'd like a torrent o'er the rest.
He sue for mercy! *He* dismay'd
By wild words of a timid maid!
He, wrong'd by Venice, vow to save
Her sons, devoted to the grave!
No—though that cloud were thunder's worst,
And charged to crush him—let it burst!

He look'd upon it earnestly
Without an accent of reply;

He watch'd it passing; it is flown:
Full on his eye the clear moon shone,
And thus he spake—" Whate'er my fate,
I am no changeling—'tis too late:
The reed in storms may bow and quiver,
Then rise again; the tree must shiver.
What Venice made me, I must be,
Her foe in all, save love to thee:
But thou art safe: oh, fly with me!"
He turn'd, but she is gone!
Nothing is there but the column stone.
Hath she sunk in the earth, or melted in air?
He saw not—he knew not—but nothing is there.

XXII

The night is past, and shines the sun
As if that morn were a jocund one.
Lightly and brightly breaks away
The Morning from her mantle grey,
And the Noon will look on a sultry day.
Hark to the trump, and the drum,
And the mournful sound of the barbarous horn,
And the flap of the banners, that flit as they're borne,
And the neigh of the steed, and the multitude's hum,
And the clash, and the shout, "They come! they come!"
The horsetails are pluck'd from the ground, and the sword
From its sheath; and they form and but wait for the word.
Tartar, and Spahi, and Turcoman,
Strike your tents, and throng to the van;
Mount ye, spur ye, skirr the plain,
That the fugitive may flee in vain,
When he breaks from the town; and none escape,
Aged or young, in the Christian shape;
While your fellows on foot, in a fiery mass,
Bloodstain the breach through which they pass.
The steeds are all bridled, and snort to the rein;
Curved is each neck, and flowing each mane;
White is the foam of their champ on the bit:
The spears are uplifted; the matches are lit;
The cannon are pointed, and ready to roar,
And crush the wall they have crumbled before:

Forms in his phalanx each Janizar;
Alp at their head; his right arm is bare,
So is the blade of his scimitar;
The khan and the pachas are all at their post;
The vizier himself at the head of the host.
When the culverin's signal is fired, then on;
Leave not in Corinth a living one—
A priest at her altars, a chief in her halls,
A hearth in her mansions, a stone on her walls.
God and the prophet—Alla Hu!
Up to the skies with that wild halloo!
" There the breach lies for passage, the ladder to scale;
And your hands on your sabres, and how should ye fail?
He who first downs with the red cross may crave
His heart's dearest wish; let him ask it, and have! "
Thus utter'd Coumourgi, the dauntless vizier;
The reply was the brandish of sabre and spear,
And the shout of fierce thousands in joyous ire:
Silence—hark to the signal—fire!

XXIII

As the wolves, that headlong go
On the stately buffalo,
Though with fiery eyes, and angry roar,
And hoofs that stamp, and horns that gore,
He tramples on earth, or tosses on high
The foremost, who rush on his strength but to die:
Thus against the wall they went,
Thus the first were backward bent;
Many a bosom, sheathed in brass,
Strew'd the earth like broken glass,
Shiver'd by the shot, that tore
The ground whereon they moved no more:
Even as they fell, in files they lay,
Like the mower's grass at the close of day,
When his work is done on the levell'd plain;
Such was the fall of the foremost slain.

XXIV

As the spring-tides, with heavy plash,
From the cliffs invading dash

Huge fragments, sapp'd by the ceaseless flow,
Till white and thundering down they go,
Like the avalanche's snow
On the Alpine vales below;
Thus at length, outbreathed and worn,
Corinth's sons were downward borne
By the long and oft renew'd
Charge of the Moslem multitude,
In firmness they stood, and in masses they fell,
Heap'd by the host of the infidel
Hand to hand, and foot to foot:
Nothing there, save death, was mute;
Stroke, and thrust, and flash, and cry
For quarter, or for victory,
Mingle there with the volleying thunder,
Which makes the distant cities wonder
How the sounding battle goes,
If with them, or for their foes;
If they must mourn, or may rejoice
In that annihilating voice,
Which pierces the deep hills through and through
With an echo dread and new:
You might have heard it, on that day,
O'er Salamis and Megara;
(We have heard that hearers say,)
Even unto Piræus' bay.

XXV

From the point of encountering blades to the hilt,
Sabres and swords with blood were gilt;
But the rampart is won, and the spoil begun,
And all but the after carnage done.
Shriller shrieks now mingling come
From within the plunder'd dome:
Hark to the haste of flying feet,
That splash in the blood of the slippery street;
But here and there, where 'vantage ground
Against the foe may still be found,
Desperate groups, of twelve or ten,
Make a pause, and turn again—
With banded backs against the wall,
Fiercely stand, or fighting fall.

There stood an old man—his hairs were white,
But his veteran arm was full of might:
So gallantly bore he the brunt of the fray,
The dead before him, on that day,
In a semicircle lay;
Still he combated unwounded,
Though retreating, unsurrounded.
Many a scar of former fight
Lurk'd beneath his corslet bright;
But of every wound his body bore,
Each and all had been ta'en before:
Though aged, he was so iron of limb,
Few of our youth could cope with him;
And the foes, whom he singly kept at bay,
Outnumber'd his thin hairs of silver grey.
From right to left his sabre swept:
Many an Othman mother wept
Sons that were unborn, when dipp'd
His weapon first in Moslem gore,
Ere his years could count a score.
Of all he might have been the sire
Who fell that day beneath his ire:
For, sonless left long years ago,
His wrath made many a childless foe;
And since the day, when in the strait
His only boy had met his fate,
His parent's iron hand did doom
More than a human hecatomb.
If shades by carnage be appeased,
Patroclus' spirit less was pleased
Than his, Minotti's son, who died
Where Asia's bounds and ours divide.
Buried he lay, where thousands before
For thousands of years were inhumed on the shore;
What of them is left, to tell
Where they lie, and how they fell?
Not a stone on their turf, nor a bone in their graves;
But they live in the verse that immortally saves.

XXVI

Hark to the Allah shout! a band
Of the Mussulman bravest and best is at hand:

Their leader's nervous arm is bare,
Swifter to smite, and never to spare—
Uncloth'd to the shoulder it waves them on:
Thus in the fight is he ever known:
Others a gaudier garb may show,
To tempt the spoil of the greedy foe;
Many a hand's on a richer hilt,
But none on a steel more ruddily gilt;
Many a loftier turban may wear,—
Alp is but known by the white arm bare;
Look through the thick of the fight, 'tis there!
There is not a standard on that shore
So well advanced the ranks before;
There is not a banner in Moslem war
Will lure the Delhis half so far;
It glances like a falling star!
Where'er that mighty arm is seen,
The bravest be, or late have been;
There the craven cries for quarter
Vainly to the vengeful Tartar;
Or the hero, silent lying,
Scorns to yield a groan in dying,
Mustering his last feeble blow
'Gainst the nearest levell'd foe,
Though faint beneath the mutual wound,
Grappling on the gory ground.

XXVII

Still the old man stood erect,
And Alp's career a moment check'd.
" Yield thee, Minotti; quarter take,
For thine own, thy daughter's sake."
" Never, renegado, never!
Though the life of thy gift would last for ever."

" Francesca!—Oh, my promised bride!
Must she too perish by thy pride ? "
" She is safe "—" Where? where? "—" in heaven;
From whence thy traitor soul is driven—
Far from thee, and undefiled."
Grimly then Minotti smiled,
As he saw Alp staggering bow
Before his words, as with a blow.

" Oh God! when died she ? "—" Yesternight—
Nor weep I for her spirit's flight:
None of my pure race shall be
Slaves to Mahomet and thee—
Come on! "—That challenge is in vain—
Alp's already with the slain!
While Minotti's words were wreaking
More revenge in bitter speaking
Than his falchion's point had found,
Had the time allow'd to wound,
From within the neighbouring porch
Of a long-defended church,
Where the last and desperate few
Would the failing fight renew,
The sharp shot dash'd Alp to the ground;
Ere an eye could view the wound
That crash'd through the brain of the infidel,
Round he spun, and down he fell;
A flash like fire within his eyes
Blazed, as he bent no more to rise,
And then eternal darkness sunk
Through all the palpitating trunk;
Nought of life left, save a quivering
Where his limbs were slightly shivering:
They turn'd him on his back; his breast
And brow were stain'd with gore and dust,
And through his lips the life-blood oozed,
From its deep veins lately loosed;
But in his pulse there was no throb,
Nor on his lips one dying sob;
Sigh, nor word, nor struggling breath
Heralded his way to death:
Ere his very thought could pray,
Unaneled he pass'd away,
Without a hope from mercy's aid
To the last—a Renegade.

XXVIII

Fearfully the yell arose
Of his followers, and his foes;
These in joy, in fury those:
Then again in conflict mixing,

Clashing swords, and spears transfixing,
Interchanged the blow and thrust,
Hurling warriors in the dust.
Street by street, and foot by foot,
Still Minotti dares dispute
The latest portion of the land
Left beneath his high command;
With him, aiding heart and hand,
The remnant of his gallant band.
Still the church is tenable,
Whence issued late the fated ball
That half avenged the city's fall,
When Alp, her fierce assailant, fell:
Thither bending sternly back,
They leave before a bloody track;
And, with their faces to the foe,
Dealing wounds with every blow,
The chief, and his retreating train,
Join to those within the fane;
There they yet may breathe awhile,
Shelter'd by the massy pile.

XXIX

Brief breathing-time! the turban'd host,
With adding ranks and raging boast,
Press onwards with such strength and heat,
Their numbers balk their own retreat;
For narrow the way that led to the spot
Where still the Christians yielded not;
And the foremost, if fearful, may vainly try
Through the massy column to turn and fly;
They perforce must do or die.
They die; but ere their eyes could close,
Avengers o'er their bodies rose;
Fresh and furious, fast they fill
The ranks unthinn'd, though slaughter'd still;
And faint the weary Christians wax
Before the still renew'd attacks:
And now the Othmans gain the gate;
Still resists its iron weight,
And still, all deadly aim'd and hot,
From every crevice comes the shot;

From every shatter'd window pour
The volleys of the sulphurous shower:
But the portal wavering grows and weak—
The iron yields, the hinges creak—
It bends—it falls—and all is o'er:
Lost Corinth may resist no more!

XXX

Darkly, sternly, and all alone,
Minotti stood o'er the altar stone;
Madonna's face upon him shone,
Painted in heavenly hues above,
With eyes of light and looks of love;
And placed upon that holy shrine
To fix our thoughts on things divine,
When pictured there, we kneeling see
Her, and the boy-God on her knee,
Smiling sweetly on each prayer
To heaven, as if to waft it there.
Still she smiled; even now she smiles,
Though slaughter streams along her aisles:
Minotti lifted his aged eyes,
And made the sign of a cross with a sigh,
Then seized a torch which blazed thereby;
And still he stood, while, with steel and flame,
Inward and onward the Mussulman came.

XXXI

The vaults beneath the mosaic stone
Contain'd the dead of ages gone;
Their names were on the graven floor,
But now illegible with gore;
The carvèd crests, and curious hues
The varied marble's veins diffuse,
Were smear'd and slippery—stain'd, and strown
With broken swords, and helms o'erthrown:
There were dead above, and the dead below
Lay cold in many a coffin'd row;
You might see them piled in sable state,
By a pale light through a gloomy grate;

But War had enter'd their dark caves,
And stored along the vaulted graves
Her sulphurous treasures, thickly spread
In masses by the fleshless dead:
Here, throughout the siege, had been
The Christian's chiefest magazine;
To these a late-form'd train now led,
Minotti's last and stern resource
Against the foe's o'erwhelming force.

XXXII

The foe came on, and few remain
To strive, and those must strive in vain:
For lack of further lives, to slake
The thirst of vengeance now awake,
With barbarous blows they gash the dead,
And lop the already lifeless head,
And fell the statues from their niche,
And spoil the shrines of offerings rich,
And from each other's rude hands wrest
The silver vessels saints had bless'd.
To the high altar on they go;
Oh, but it made a glorious show!
On its table still behold
The cup of consecrated gold;
Massy and deep, a glittering prize,
Brightly it sparkles to plunderers' eyes:
That morn it held the holy wine,
Converted by Christ to His blood so divine,
Which His worshippers drank at the break of day,
To shrive their souls ere they joined in the fray.
Still a few drops within it lay;
And round the sacred table glow
Twelve lofty lamps, in splendid row,
From the purest metal cast;
A spoil—the richest and the last.

XXXIII

So near they came, the nearest stretch'd
To grasp the spoil he almost reach'd,
When old Minotti's hand

Touch'd with the torch the train—
'Tis fired!
Spire, vaults, the shrine, the spoil, the slain,
The turban'd victors, the Christian band,
All that of living or dead remain,
Hurl'd on high with the shiver'd fane,
In one wild roar expired!
The shatter'd town—the walls thrown down—
The waves a moment backward bent—
The hills that shake, although unrent,
As if an earthquake pass'd—
The thousand shapeless things all driven
In cloud and flame athwart the heaven,
By that tremendous blast—
Proclaim'd the desperate conflict o'er
On that too long afflicted shore:
Up to the sky like rockets go
All that mingled there below:
Many a tall and goodly man,
Scorch'd and shrivell'd to a span,
When he fell to earth again
Like a cinder strew'd the plain:
Down the ashes shower like rain;
Some fell in the gulf, which received the sprinkles
With a thousand circling wrinkles;
Some fell on the shore, but, far away,
Scatter'd o'er the isthmus lay;
Christian or Moslem, which be they?
Let their mothers see and say!
When in cradled rest they lay,
And each nursing mother smiled
On the sweet sleep of her child,
Little deem'd she such a day
Would rend those tender limbs away.
Not the matrons that them bore
Could discern their offspring more;
That one moment left no trace
More of human form or face
Save a scatter'd scalp or bone:
And down came blazing rafters, strown
Around, and many a falling stone,
Deeply dinted in the clay,
All blacken'd there and reeking lay.

All the living things that heard
That deadly earth-shock disappear'd:
The wild birds flew; the wild dogs fled,
And howling left the unburied dead;
The camels from their keepers broke;
The distant steer forsook the yoke—
The nearer steer plunged o'er the plain,
And burst his girth, and tore his rein;
The bull-frog's note, from out the marsh
Deep-mouth'd arose, and doubly harsh;
The wolves yell'd on the cavern'd hill
Where echo roll'd in thunder still;
The jackal's troop, in gather'd cry,
Bay'd from afar complainingly,
With a mix'd and mournful sound,
Like crying babe, and beaten hound:
With sudden wing, and ruffled breast,
The eagle left his rocky nest,
And mounted nearer to the sun,
The clouds beneath him seem'd so dun:
Their smoke assail'd his startled beak,
And made him higher soar and shriek—
Thus was Corinth lost and won!

LORD BYRON.

ADONAIS

AN ELEGY ON THE DEATH OF JOHN KEATS, AUTHOR OF "ENDYMION," "HYPERION," ETC.

Ἀστὴρ πρὶν μὲν ἔλαμπες ἐνὶ ζωοῖσιν Ἑῷος·
νῦν δὲ θανὼν λάμπεις Ἕσπερος ἐν φθιμένοις.—PLATO.

[Comp. at Pisa during the early days of June, 1821, and printed, with the author's name, at Pisa, "with the types of Didot," by 13th July, 1821.]

PREFACE

Φάρμακον ἦλθε, Βίων, ποτὶ σὸν στόμα, φάρμακον εἶδες·
πῶς τευ τοῖς χείλεσσι ποτέδραμε, κοὐκ ἐγλυκάνθη;
τίς δὲ βροτὸς τοσσοῦτον ἀνάμερος, ἢ κεράσαι τοι,
ἢ δοῦναι λαλέοντι τὸ φάρμακον; ἔκφυγεν ᾠδάν.

MOSCHUS, *Epitaph. Bion.*

IT is my intention to subjoin to the London edition of this poem a criticism upon the claims of its lamented object to be classed among the writers of the highest genius who have adorned our age. My known repugnance to the narrow principles of taste on which several of his earlier compositions were modelled prove at least that I am an impartial judge. I consider the fragment of *Hyperion* as second to nothing that was ever produced by a writer of the same years.

John Keats died at Rome of a consumption in his twenty-fourth year, on the —— of —— 1821; and was buried in the romantic and lonely cemetery of the Protestants in that city, under the pyramid which is the tomb of Cestius, and the massy walls and towers, now mouldering and desolate, which formed the circuit of ancient Rome. The cemetery is an open space among the ruins, covered in winter with violets and daisies. It might make one in love with death, to think that one should be buried in so sweet a place.

The genius of the lamented person to whose memory I have dedicated these unworthy verses was not less delicate and fragile than it was beautiful; and where cankerworms abound, what wonder if its young flower was blighted in the bud? The savage criticism on his *Endymion*, which appeared in the *Quarterly Review*, produced the most violent effect on his susceptible mind; the agitation thus originated ended in the rupture of a blood-vessel in the lungs; a rapid consumption ensued, and the succeeding acknowledgments from more candid critics of the true greatness of his powers were ineffectual to heal the wound thus wantonly inflicted.

It may be well said that these wretched men know not what they do. They scatter their insults and their slanders without heed as to whether the poisoned shaft lights on a heart made callous by many blows or one like Keats's composed of more penetrable stuff. One of their associates is, to my knowledge, a most base and unprincipled calumniator. As to *Endymion*, was it a poem, whatever might be its defects, to be treated contemptuously by those who had celebrated, with various degrees of complacency and panegyric, *Paris*, and *Woman*, and a *Syrian Tale*, and Mrs. Lefanu, and Mr. Barrett, and Mr. Howard Payne, and a long list of the illustrious obscure? Are these the men who in their venal good nature presumed to draw a parallel between the Rev. Mr. Milman and Lord Byron? What gnat did they strain at here, after having swallowed all those camels? Against what woman taken in adultery dares the foremost of these literary prostitutes to cast his opprobrious stone? Miserable man! you, one of the meanest, have wantonly defaced one of the noblest specimens of the workmanship of God. Nor shall it be your excuse, that, murderer as you are, you have spoken daggers, but used none.

The circumstances of the closing scene of poor Keats's life were not made known to me until the *Elegy* was ready for the press. I am given to understand that the wound which his sensitive spirit had received from the criticism of *Endymion* was exasperated by the bitter sense of unrequited benefits; the poor fellow seems to have been hooted from the stage of life, no less by those on whom he had wasted the promise of genius, than those on whom he had lavished his fortune and his care. He was accompanied to Rome, and attended in his last illness by Mr. Severn, a young artist of the highest promise, who, I have been informed, "almost risked his own life, and sacrificed every prospect to unwearied attendance upon his dying friend." Had I known these circumstances before the completion of my poem, I should have been tempted to add my feeble tribute of applause to the more solid recompense which the virtuous man finds in the recollection of his own motives. Mr. Severn can dispense with a reward from "such stuff as dreams are made of." His conduct is a golden augury of the success of his future career—may the unextinguished Spirit of his illustrious friend animate the creations of his pencil, and plead against Oblivion for his name!

ADONAIS

I

I WEEP for Adonais—he is dead!
Oh, weep for Adonais! though our tears
Thaw not the frost which binds so dear a head!
And thou, sad Hour, selected from all years
To mourn our loss, rouse thy obscure compeers,
And teach them thine own sorrow, say: "With me
Died Adonais; till the Future dares
Forget the Past, his fate and fame shall be
An echo and a light unto eternity!"

II

Where wert thou, mighty Mother, when he lay,
When thy Son lay, pierced by the shaft which flies
In darkness? where was lorn Urania
When Adonais died? With veilèd eyes,
'Mid listening Echoes, in her Paradise
She sate, while one, with soft enamoured breath,
Rekindled all the fading melodies,
With which, like flowers that mock the corse beneath,
He had adorned and hid the coming bulk of Death.

III

Oh, weep for Adonais—he is dead!
Wake, melancholy Mother, wake and weep!
Yet wherefore? Quench within their burning bed
Thy fiery tears, and let thy loud heart keep,
Like his, a mute and uncomplaining sleep;
For he is gone, where all things wise and fair
Descend;—oh, dream not that the amorous Deep
Will yet restore him to the vital air;
Death feeds on his mute voice, and laughs at our despair.

IV

Most musical of mourners, weep again
Lament anew, Urania!—he died,
Who was the Sire of an immortal strain,
Blind, old, and lonely, when his country's pride,

The priest, the slave, and the liberticide,
Trampled and mocked with many a loathèd rite
Of lust and blood; he went unterrified,
Into the gulf of death; but his clear Sprite
Yet reigns o'er earth; the third among the sons of light.

v

Most musical of mourners, weep anew!
Not all to that bright station dared to climb;
And happier they their happiness who knew,
Whose tapers yet burn through that night of time
In which suns perished; others more sublime,
Struck by the envious wrath of man or god,
Have sunk, extinct in their refulgent prime;
And some yet live, treading the thorny road,
Which leads, through toil and hate, to Fame's serene abode.

VI

But now, thy youngest, dearest one, has perished—
The nursling of thy widowhood, who grew,
Like a pale flower by some sad maiden cherished,
And fed with true-love tears, instead of dew;
Most musical of mourners, weep anew!
Thy extreme hope, the loveliest and the last,
The bloom, whose petals nipped before they blew
Died, on the promise of the fruit, is waste;
The broken lily lies—the storm is overpast.

VII

To that high Capital, where kingly Death
Keeps his pale court in beauty and decay,
He came; and bought, with price of purest breath,
A grave among the eternal.—Come away!
Haste, while the vault of blue Italian day
Is yet his fitting charnel-roof! while still
He lies, as if in dewy sleep he lay;
Awake him not! surely he takes his fill
Of deep and liquid rest, forgetful of all ill.

VIII

He will awake no more, oh, never more!—
Within the twilight chamber spreads apace
The shadow of white Death, and at the door
Invisible Corruption waits to trace
His extreme way to her dim dwelling-place;
The eternal Hunger sits, but pity and awe
Soothe her pale rage, nor dares she to deface
So fair a prey, till darkness, and the law
Of change, shall o'er his sleep the mortal curtain draw.

IX

Oh, weep for Adonais!—The quick Dreams,
The passion-wingèd Ministers of thought,
Who were his flocks, whom near the living streams
Of his young spirit he fed, and whom he taught
The love which was its music, wander not,—
Wander no more, from kindling brain to brain,
But droop there, whence they sprung; and mourn their lot
Round the cold heart, where, after their sweet pain,
They ne'er will gather strength, or find a home again.

X

And one with trembling hands clasps his cold head,
And fans him with her moonlight wings, and cries;
" Our love, our hope, our sorrow, is not dead;
See, on the silken fringe of his faint eyes,
Like dew upon a sleeping flower, there lies
A tear some Dream has loosened from his brain."
Lost Angel of a ruined Paradise !
She knew not 'twas her own; as with no stain
She faded, like a cloud which had outwept its rain.

XI

One from a lucid urn of starry dew
Washed his light limbs as if embalming them;
Another clipped her profuse locks, and threw
The wreath upon him, like an anadem,
Which frozen tears instead of pearls begem;

Another in her wilful grief would break
Her bow and wingèd reeds, as if to stem
A greater loss with one which was more weak;
And dull the barbèd fire against his frozen cheek.

XII

Another Splendour on his mouth alit,
That mouth, whence it was wont to draw the breath
Which gave it strength to pierce the guarded wit,
And pass into the panting heart beneath
With lightning and with music: the damp death
Quenched its caress upon his icy lips;
And, as a dying meteor stains a wreath
Of moonlight vapour, which the cold night clips,
It flushed through his pale limbs, and passed to its eclipse.

XIII

And others came . . . Desires and Adorations,
Wingèd Persuasions and veiled Destinies,
Splendours, and Glooms, and glimmering Incarnations
Of hopes and fears, and twilight Phantasies;
And Sorrow, with her family of Sighs,
And Pleasure, blind with tears, led by the gleam
Of her own dying smile instead of eyes,
Came in slow pomp;—the moving pomp might seem
Like pageantry of mist on an autumnal stream.

XIV

All he had loved, and moulded into thought,
From shape, and hue, and odour, and sweet sound,
Lamented Adonais.   Morning sought
Her eastern watch-tower, and her hair unbound,
Wet with the tears which should adorn the ground,
Dimmed by the aëreal eyes that kindle day;
Afar the melancholy thunder moaned,
Pale Ocean in unquiet slumber lay,
And the wild Winds flew round, sobbing in their dismay.

XV

Lost Echo sits amid the voiceless mountains,
And feeds her grief with his remembered lay,
And will no more reply to winds or fountains,
Or amorous birds perched on the young green spray,
Or herdsman's horn, or bell at closing day;
Since she can mimic not his lips, more dear
Than those for whose disdain she pined away
Into a shadow of all sounds:—a drear
Murmur, between their songs, is all the woodmen hear.

XVI

Grief made the young Spring wild, and she threw down
Her kindling buds, as if she Autumn were,
Or they dead leaves; since her delight is flown,
For whom should she have waked the sullen year?
To Phœbus was not Hyacinth so dear
Nor to himself Narcissus, as to both
Thou, Adonais: wan they stand and sere
Amid the faint companions of their youth,
With dew all turned to tears; odour, to sighing ruth.

XVII

Thy spirit's sister, the lorn nightingale
Mourns not her mate with such melodious pain;
Not so the eagle, who like thee could scale
Heaven, and could nourish in the sun's domain
Her mighty youth with morning, doth complain,
Soaring and screaming round her empty nest,
As Albion wails for thee: the curse of Cain
Light on his head who pierced thy innocent breast,
And scared the angel soul that was its earthly guest!

XVIII

Ah, woe is me! Winter is come and gone,
But grief returns with the revolving year;
The airs and streams renew their joyous tone;
The ants, the bees, the swallows reappear;
Fresh leaves and flowers deck the dead Season's bier;
The amorous birds now pair in every brake,

And build their mossy homes in field and brere;
And the green lizard, and the golden snake,
Like unimprisoned flames, out of their trance awake.

XIX

Through wood and stream and field and hill and Ocean
A quickening life from the Earth's heart has burst
As it has ever done, with change and motion,
From the great morning of the world when first
God dawned on Chaos; in its stream immersed,
The lamps of Heaven flash with a softer light;
All baser things pant with life's sacred thirst;
Diffuse themselves; and spend in love's delight,
The beauty and the joy of their renewèd might.

XX

The leprous corpse, touched by this spirit tender,
Exhales itself in flowers of gentle breath;
Like incarnations of the stars, when splendour
Is changed to fragrance, they illumine death
And mock the merry worm that wakes beneath;
Nought we know, dies. Shall that alone which knows
Be as a sword consumed before the sheath
By sightless lightning?—the intense atom glows
A moment, then is quenched in a most cold repose.

XXI

Alas! that all we loved of him should be,
But for our grief, as if it had not been,
And grief itself be mortal! Woe is me!
Whence are we, and why are we? of what scene
The actors or spectators? Great and mean
Meet massed in death, who lends what life must borrow.
As long as skies are blue, and fields are green,
Evening must usher night, night urge the morrow,
Month follow month with woe, and year wake year to sorrow.

XXII

He will awake no more, oh, never more!
"Wake thou," cried Misery, "childless Mother, rise
Out of thy sleep, and slake, in thy heart's core

A wound more fierce than his, with tears and sighs."
And all the Dreams that watched Urania's eyes,
And all the Echoes whom their sister's song
Had held in holy silence, cried: " Arise! "
Swift as a Thought by the snake Memory stung
From her ambrosial rest the fading Splendour sprung.

XXIII

She rose like an autumnal Night, that springs
Out of the East, and follows wild and drear
The golden Day, which, on eternal wings,
Even as a ghost abandoning a bier,
Had left the Earth a corpse. Sorrow and fear
So struck, so roused, so rapt Urania;
So saddened round her like an atmosphere
Of stormy mist; so swept her on her way
Even to the mournful place where Adonais lay.

XXIV

Out of her secret Paradise she sped,
Through camps and cities rough with stone, and steel,
And human hearts, which to her aery tread
Yielding not, wounded the invisible
Palms of her tender feet where'er they fell:
And barbèd tongues, and thoughts more sharp than they,
Rent the soft Form they never could repel,
Whose sacred blood, like the young tears of May,
Paved with eternal flowers that undeserving way.

XXV

In the death-chamber for a moment Death,
Shamed by the presence of that living Might,
Blushed to annihilation, and the breath
Revisited those lips, and Life's pale light
Flashed through those limbs, so late her dear delight.
" Leave me not wild and drear and comfortless,
As silent lightning leaves the starless night!
Leave me not! " cried Urania: her distress
Roused Death: Death rose and smiled, and met her vain
    caress.

XXVI

" Stay yet awhile! speak to me once again;
Kiss me, so long but as a kiss may live;
And in my heartless breast and burning brain
That word, that kiss, shall all thoughts else survive.
With food of saddest memory kept alive,
Now thou art dead, as if it were a part
Of thee, my Adonais! I would give
All that I am to be as thou now art!
But I am chained to Time, and cannot thence depart!

XXVII

" O gentle child, beautiful as thou wert,
Why didst thou leave the trodden paths of men
Too soon, and with weak hands though mighty heart
Dare the unpastured dragon in his den ?
Defenceless as thou wert, oh, where was then
Wisdom the mirrored shield, or scorn the spear?
Or hadst thou waited the full cycle, when
Thy spirit should have filled its crescent sphere,
The monsters of life's waste had fled from thee like deer.

XXVIII

" The herded wolves, bold only to pursue;
The obscene ravens, clamorous o'er the dead;
The vultures to the conqueror's banner true
Who feed where Desolation first has fed,
And whose wings rain contagion;—how they fled,
When, like Apollo, from his golden bow
The Pythian of the age one arrow sped
And smiled!—The spoilers tempt no second blow,
They fawn on the proud feet that spurn them lying low.

XXIX

" The sun comes forth, and many reptiles spawn;
He sets, and each ephemeral insect then
Is gathered into death without a dawn,
And the immortal stars awake again;
So is it in the world of living men:

A godlike mind soars forth, in its delight
Making earth bare and veiling heaven, and when
It sinks, the swarms that dimmed or shared its light
Leave to its kindred lamps the spirit's awful night."

XXX

Thus ceased she: and the mountain shepherds came,
Their garlands sere, their magic mantles rent;
The Pilgrim of Eternity, whose fame
Over his living head like Heaven is bent,
An early but enduring monument,
Came, veiling all the lightnings of his song
In sorrow; from her wilds Ierne sent
The sweetest lyrist of her saddest wrong,
And Love taught Grief to fall like music from his tongue.

XXXI

Midst others of less note, came one frail Form,
A phantom among men; companionless
As the last cloud of an expiring storm
Whose thunder is its knell; he, as I guess,
Had gazed on Nature's naked loveliness,
Actæon-like, and now he fled astray
With feeble steps o'er the world's wilderness,
And his own thoughts, along that rugged way,
Pursued, like raging hounds, their father and their prey.

XXXII

A pardlike Spirit beautiful and swift—
A Love in desolation masked;—a Power
Girt round with weakness;—it can scarce uplift
The weight of the superincumbent hour;
It is a dying lamp, a falling shower,
A breaking billow;—even whilst we speak
Is it not broken? On the withering flower
The killing sun smiles brightly: on a cheek
The life can burn in blood, even while the heart may break.

XXXIII

His head was bound with pansies overblown,
And faded violets, white, and pied and blue;

And a light spear topped with a cypress cone,
Round whose rude shaft dark ivy-tresses grew
Yet dripping with the forest's noonday dew,
Vibrated, as the ever-beating heart
Shook the weak hand that grasped it; of that crew
He came the last, neglected and apart;
A herd-abandoned deer struck by the hunter's dart.

XXXIV

All stood aloof, and at his partial moan
Smiled through their tears; well knew that gentle band
Who in another's fate now wept his own,
As in the accents of an unknown land
He sung new sorrow; sad Urania scanned
The Stranger's mien, and murmured: "Who art thou?"
He answered not, but with a sudden hand
Made bare his branded and ensanguined brow,
Which was like Cain's or Christ's—oh! that it should be so!

XXXV

What softer voice is hushed over the dead?
Athwart what brow is that dark mantle thrown?
What form leans sadly o'er the white death-bed,
In mockery of monumental stone,
The heavy heart heaving without a moan?
If it be He, who, gentlest of the wise,
Taught, soothed, loved, honoured the departed one,
Let me not vex, with inharmonious sighs,
The silence of that heart's accepted sacrifice.

XXXVI

Our Adonais has drunk poison—oh!
What deaf and viperous murderer could crown
Life's early cup with such a draught of woe!
The nameless worm would now itself disown:
It felt, yet could escape, the magic tone
Whose prelude held all envy, hate, and wrong,
But what was howling in one breast alone,
Silent with expectation of the song,
Whose master's hand is cold, whose silver lyre unstrung.

XXXVII

Live thou, whose infamy is not thy fame!
Live! fear no heavier chastisement from me,
Thou noteless blot on a remembered name
But be thyself, and know thyself to be!
And ever at thy season be thou free
To spill the venom when thy fangs o'erflow:
Remorse and Self-contempt shall cling to thee;
Hot Shame shall burn upon thy secret brow,
And like a beaten hound tremble thou shalt—as now.

XXXVIII

Nor let us weep that our delight is fled
Far from those carrion kites that scream below;
He wakes or sleeps with the enduring dead;
Thou canst not soar where he is sitting now.—
Dust to the dust! but the pure spirit shall flow
Back to the burning fountain whence it came,
A portion of the Eternal, which must glow
Through time and change, unquenchably the same,
Whilst thy cold embers choke the sordid hearth of shame.

XXXIX

Peace, peace! he is not dead, he doth not sleep—
He hath awakened from the dream of life—
'Tis we, who lost in stormy visions, keep
With phantoms an unprofitable strife,
And in mad trance, strike with our spirit's knife
Invulnerable nothings.—*We* decay
Like corpses in a charnel; fear and grief
Convulse us and consume us day by day,
And cold hopes swarm like worms within our living clay.

XL

He has outsoared the shadow of our night;
Envy and calumny and hate and pain,
And that unrest which men miscall delight,
Can touch him not and torture not again;
From the contagion of the world's slow stain

He is secure, and now can never mourn
A heart grown cold, a head grown grey in vain;
Nor, when the spirit's self has ceased to burn,
With sparkless ashes load an unlamented urn.

XLI

He lives, he wakes—'tis Death is dead, not he;
Mourn not for Adonais.—Thou young Dawn,
Turn all thy dew to splendour, for from thee
The spirit thou lamentest is not gone;
Ye caverns and ye forests, cease to moan!
Cease, ye faint flowers and fountains, and thou Air,
Which like a mourning veil thy scarf hadst thrown
O'er the abandoned Earth, now leave it bare
Even to the joyous stars which smile on its despair!

XLII

He is made one with Nature: there is heard
His voice in all her music, from the moan
Of thunder, to the song of night's sweet bird;
He is a presence to be felt and known
In darkness and in light, from herb and stone,
Spreading itself where'er that Power may move
Which has withdrawn his being to its own;
Which wields the world with never-wearied love,
Sustains it from beneath, and kindles it above.

XLIII

He is a portion of the loveliness
Which once he made more lovely: he doth bear
His part, while the one Spirit's plastic stress
Sweeps through the dull dense world, compelling there,
All new successions to the forms they wear;
Torturing th' unwilling dross that checks its fligh
To its own likeness, as each mass may bear;
And bursting in its beauty and its might
From trees and beasts and men into the Heaven's light.

XLIV

The splendours of the firmament of time
May be eclipsed, but are extinguished not;

Like stars to their appointed height they climb,
And death is a low mist which cannot blot
The brightness it may veil. When lofty thought
Lifts a young heart above its mortal lair,
And love and life contend in it, for what
Shall be its earthly doom, the dead live there
And move like winds of light on dark and stormy air.

XLV

The inheritors of unfulfilled renown
Rose from their thrones, built beyond mortal thought,
Far in the Unapparent. Chatterton
Rose pale,—his solemn agony had not
Yet faded from him; Sidney, as he fought
And as he fell and as he lived and loved
Sublimely mild, a Spirit without spot,
Arose; and Lucan, by his death approved:
Oblivion as they rose shrank like a thing reproved.

XLVI

And many more, whose names on Earth are dark,
But whose transmitted effluence cannot die
So long as fire outlives the parent spark,
Rose, robed in dazzling immortality.
" Thou art become as one of us," they cry,
" It was for thee yon kingless sphere has long
Swung blind in unascended majesty,
Silent alone amid an Heaven of Song.
Assume thy wingèd throne, thou Vesper of our throng! "

XLVII

Who mourns for Adonais? Oh, come forth,
Fond wretch! and know thyself and him aright.
Clasp with thy panting soul the pendulous Earth;
As from a centre, dart thy spirit's light
Beyond all worlds, until its spacious might
Satiate the void circumference: then shrink
Even to a point within our day and night;
And keep thy heart light lest it make thee sink
When hope has kindled hope, and lured thee to the brink.

XLVIII

Or go to Rome, which is the sepulchre,
Oh, not of him, but of our joy: 'tis nought
That ages, empires, and religions there
Lie buried in the ravage they have wrought;
For such as he can lend,—they borrow not
Glory from those who made the world their prey;
And he is gathered to the kings of thought
Who waged contention with their time's decay,
And of the past are all that cannot pass away.

XLIX

Go thou to Rome,—at once the Paradise,
The grave, the city, and the wilderness;
And where its wrecks like shattered mountains rise,
And flowering weeds, and fragrant copses dress
The bones of Desolation's nakedness
Pass, till the spirit of the spot shall lead
Thy footsteps to a slope of green access
Where, like an infant's smile, over the dead
A light of laughing flowers along the grass is spread;

L

And grey walls moulder round, on which dull Time
Feeds, like slow fire upon a hoary brand;
And one keen pyramid with wedge sublime,
Pavilioning the dust of him who planned
This refuge for his memory, doth stand
Like flame transformed to marble; and beneath,
A field is spread, on which a newer band
Have pitched in Heaven's smile their camp of death,
Welcoming him we lose with scarce extinguished breath.

LI

Here pause: these graves are all too young as yet
To have outgrown the sorrow which consigned
Its charge to each; and if the seal is set,
Here, on one fountain of a mourning mind,
Break it not thou! too surely shalt thou find

Thine own well full, if thou returnest home,
Of tears and gall.   From the world's bitter wind
Seek shelter in the shadow of the tomb.
What Adonais is, why fear we to become?

LII

The One remains, the many change and pass;
Heaven's light forever shines, Earth's shadows fly;
Life, like a dome of many-coloured glass,
Stains the white radiance of Eternity,
Until Death tramples it to fragments.—Die,
If thou wouldst be with that which thou dost seek!
Follow where all is fled!—Rome's azure sky,
Flowers, ruins, statues, music, words are weak
The glory they transfuse with fitting truth to speak.

LIII

Why linger, why turn back, why shrink, my Heart?
Thy hopes are gone before: from all things here
They have departed; thou shouldst now depart!
A light is passed from the revolving year,
And man, and woman; and what still is dear
Attracts to crush, repels to make thee wither.
The soft sky smiles,—the low wind whispers near:
'Tis Adonais calls! oh, hasten thither,
No more let Life divide what Death can join together.

LIV

That Light whose smile kindles the Universe,
That Beauty in which all things work and move,
That Benediction which the eclipsing Curse
Of birth can quench not, that sustaining Love
Which through the web of being blindly wove
By man and beast and earth and air and sea,
Burns bright or dim, as each are mirrors of
The fire for which all thirst; now beams on me,
Consuming the last clouds of cold mortality.

LV

The breath whose might I have invoked in song
Descends on me; my spirit's bark is driven,
Far from the shore, far from the trembling throng

Whose sails were never to the tempest given;
The massy earth and spherèd skies are riven!
I am borne darkly, fearfully, afar;
Whilst, burning through the inmost veil of Heaven,
The soul of Adonais, like a star,
Beacons from the abode where the Eternal are.

P. B. SHELLEY.

THE SENSITIVE PLANT

[Pisa, March? 1820. Publ. 1820.]

PART FIRST

A SENSITIVE PLANT in a garden grew,
And the young winds fed it with silver dew,
And it opened its fan-like leaves to the light,
And closed them beneath the kisses of Night.

And the Spring arose on the garden fair,
Like the Spirit of Love felt everywhere;
And each flower and herb on Earth's dark breast
Rose from the dreams of its wintry rest.

But none ever trembled and panted with bliss
In the garden, the field, or the wilderness,
Like a doe in the noontide with love's sweet want,
As the companionless Sensitive Plant.

The snowdrop, and then the violet,
Arose from the ground with warm rain wet,
And their breath was mixed with fresh odour, sent
From the turf, like the voice and the instrument.

Then the pied wind-flowers and the tulip tall,
And narcissi, the fairest among them all,
Who gaze on their eyes in the stream's recess,
Till they die of their own dear loveliness;

And the Naiad-like lily of the vale,
Whom youth makes so fair and passion so pale
That the light of its tremulous bells is seen
Through their pavilions of tender green:

And the hyacinth purple, and white, and blue,
Which flung from its bells a sweet peal anew
Of music so delicate, soft, and intense,
It was felt like an odour within the sense;

And the rose like a nymph to the bath addressed
Which unveiled the depth of her glowing breast,
Till, fold after fold, to the fainting air
The soul of her beauty and love lay bare:

And the wand-like lily, which lifted up,
As a mænad, its moonlight-coloured cup,
Till the fiery star, which is its eye,
Gazed through clear dew on the tender sky;

And the jessamine faint, and the sweet tuberose,
The sweetest flower for scent that blows;
And all rare blossoms from every clime
Grew in that garden in perfect prime.

And on the stream whose inconstant bosom
Was pranked, under boughs of embowering blossom,
With golden and green light, slanting through
Their heaven of many a tangled hue,

Broad water-lilies lay tremulously,
And starry river-buds glimmered by,
And around them the soft stream did glide and dance
With a motion of sweet sound and radiance.

And the sinuous paths of lawn and of moss,
Which led through the garden along and across,
Some open at once to the sun and the breeze,
Some lost among bowers of blossoming trees,

Were all paved with daisies and delicate bells
As fair as the fabulous asphodels,
And flow'rets which, drooping as day drooped too,
Fell into pavilions, white, purple, and blue,
To roof the glow-worm from the evening dew.

And from this undefilèd Paradise
The flowers (as an infant's awakening eyes
Smile on its mother, whose singing sweet
Can first lull, and at last must awaken it),

When Heaven's blithe winds had unfolded them,
As mine-lamps enkindle a hidden gem,
Shone smiling to Heaven, and every one
Shared joy in the light of the gentle sun;

For each one was interpenetrated
With the light and the odour its neighbour shed,
Like young lovers whom youth and love make dear
Wrapped and filled by their mutual atmosphere.

But the Sensitive Plant which could give small fruit
Of the love which it felt from the leaf to the root,
Received more than all, it loved more than ever,
Where none wanted but it, could belong to the giver:

For the Sensitive Plant has no bright flower;
Radiance and odour are not its dower;
It loves, even like Love, its deep heart is full,
It desires what it has not, the Beautiful!

The light winds which from unsustaining wings
Shed the music of many murmurings;
The beams which dart from many a star
Of the flowers whose hues they bear afar;

The plumèd insects swift and free,
Like golden boats on a sunny sea,
Laden with light and odour, which pass
Over the gleam of the living grass;

The unseen clouds of the dew, which lie
Like fire in the flowers till the sun rides high,
Then wander like spirits among the spheres,
Each cloud faint with the fragrance it bears;

The quivering vapours of dim noontide,
Which like a sea o'er the warm earth glide,
In which every sound, and odour and beam,
Move, as reeds in a single stream;

Each and all like ministering angels were
For the Sensitive Plant sweet joy to bear,
Whilst the lagging hours of the day went by
Like windless clouds o'er a tender sky.

And when evening descended from Heaven above,
And the Earth was all rest, and the air was all love,
And delight, though less bright, was far more deep,
And the day's veil fell from the world of sleep,

And the beasts, and the birds, and the insects were drowned
In an ocean of dreams without a sound;
Whose waves never mark, though they ever impress
The light sand which paves it, consciousness;

(Only overhead the sweet nightingale
Ever sang more sweet as the day might fail,
And snatches of its Elysian chant
Were mixed with the dreams of the Sensitive Plant);—

The Sensitive Plant was the earliest
Upgathered into the bosom of rest;
A sweet child weary of its delight,
The feeblest and yet the favourite,
Cradled within the embrace of Night.

PART SECOND

There was a Power in this sweet place,
An Eve in this Eden; a ruling Grace
Which to the flowers, did they waken or dream,
Was as God is to the starry scheme.

A Lady, the wonder of her kind
Whose form was upborne by a lovely mind
Which, dilating, had moulded her mien and motion
Like a sea-flower unfolded beneath the ocean,

Tended the garden from morn to even:
And the meteors of that sublunar Heaven,
Like the lamps of the air when the Night walks forth,
Laughed round her footsteps up from the Earth!

She had no companion of mortal race,
But her tremulous breath and her flushing face
Told, whilst the morn kissed the sleep from her eyes,
That her dreams were less slumber than Paradise:

As if some bright Spirit for her sweet sake
Had deserted Heaven while the stars were awake,
As if yet around her he lingering were,
Though the veil of daylight concealed him from her.

Her step seemed to pity the grass it pressed;
You might hear by the heaving of her breast,
That the coming and going of the wind
Brought pleasure there and left passion behind.

And wherever her aery footstep trod,
Her trailing hair from the grassy sod
Erased its light vestige, with shadowy sweep;
Like a sunny storm o'er the dark green deep.

I doubt not the flowers of that garden sweet
Rejoiced in the sound of her gentle feet;
I doubt not they felt the spirit that came
From her glowing fingers through all their frame.

She sprinkled bright water from the stream
On those that were faint with the sunny beam;
And out of the cups of the heavy flowers
She emptied the rain of the thunder-showers.

She lifted their head with her tender hands,
And sustained them with rods and osier-bands;
If the flowers had been her own infants, she
Could never have nursed them more tenderly.

And all killing insects and gnawing worms,
And things of obscene and unlovely forms,
She bore, in a basket of Indian woof,
Into the rough woods far aloof,—

In a basket, of grasses and wild-flowers full,
The freshest her gentle hands could pull
For the poor banished insects, whose intent,
Although they did ill, was innocent.

But the bee and the beamlike ephemeris
Whose path is the lightning's, and soft moths that kiss
The sweet lips of the flowers, and harm not, did she
Make her attendant angels be.

And many an antenatal tomb,
Where butterflies dream of the life to come,
She left clinging round the smooth and dark
Edge of the odorous cedar bark.

This fairest creature from earliest Spring
Thus moved through the garden ministering
All the sweet season of Summertide,
And ere the first leaf looked brown—she died!

PART THIRD

Three days the flowers of the garden fair,
Like stars when the moon is awakened, were,
Or the waves of Baiæ, ere luminous
She floats up through the smoke of Vesuvius.

And on the fourth, the Sensitive Plant
Felt the sound of the funeral chant,
And the steps of the bearers heavy and slow,
And the sobs of the mourners, deep and low;

The weary sound and the heavy breath,
And the silent motions of passing death,
And the smell, cold, oppressive, and dank,
Sent through the pores of the coffin-plank;

The dark grass, and the flowers among the grass,
Were bright with tears as the crowd did pass;
From their sighs the wind caught a mournful tone,
And sate in the pines, and gave groan for groan.

The garden, once fair, became cold and foul,
Like the corpse of her who had been its soul,
Which at first was lovely as if in sleep,
Then slowly changed till it grew a heap
To make men tremble who never weep.

Swift Summer into the Autumn flowed,
And frost in the mist of the morning rode,
Though the noonday sun looked clear and bright
Mocking the spoil of the secret night.

The rose-leaves, like flakes of crimson snow,
Paved the turf and the moss below.
The lilies were drooping, and white, and wan,
Like the head and the skin of a dying man.

And Indian plants, of scent and hue
The sweetest that ever were fed on dew,
Leaf after leaf, day after day,
Were massed into the common clay.

And the leaves, brown, yellow, and gray, and red,
And white with the whiteness of what is dead,
Like troops of ghosts on the dry wind passed;
Their whistling noise made the birds aghast.

And the gusty winds waked the wingèd seeds,
Out of their birthplace of ugly weeds,
Till they clung round many a sweet flower's stem,
Which rotted into the earth with them.

The water-blooms under the rivulet
Fell from the stalks on which they were set;
And the eddies drove them here and there,
As the winds did those of the upper air.

Then the rain came down, and the broken stalks
Were bent and tangled across the walks;
And the leafless network of parasite bowers
Massed into ruin; and all sweet flowers.

Between the time of the wind and the snow
All loathliest weeds began to grow,
Whose coarse leaves were splashed with many a speck
Like the water-snake's belly and the toad's back.

And thistles, and nettles, and darnels rank,
And the dock, and henbane, and hemlock dank,
Stretched out its long and hollow shank,
And stifled the air till the dead wind stank.

And plants, at whose names the verse feels loath,
Filled the place with a monstrous undergrowth,
Prickly, and pulpous, and blistering, and blue,
Livid, and starred with a lurid dew.

Their moss rotted off them, flake by flake,
Till the thick stalk stuck like a murderer's stake,
Where rags of loose flesh yet tremble on high,
Infecting the winds that wander by.[1]

And agarics, and fungi, with mildew and mould
Started like mist from the wet ground cold;
Pale, fleshy, as if the decaying dead
With a spirit of growth had been animated!

Spawn, weeds, and filth, a leprous scum,
Made the running rivulet thick and dumb,
And at its outlet flags huge as stakes
Dammed it up with roots knotted like water-snakes.

And hour by hour, when the air was still,
The vapours arose which have strength to kill;
At morn they were seen, at noon they were felt,
At night they were darkness no star could melt.

And unctuous meteors from spray to spray
Crept and flitted in broad noonday
Unseen; every branch on which they alit
By a venomous blight was burned and bit.

The Sensitive Plant, like one forbid,
Wept, and the tears within each lid
Of its folded leaves, which together grew,
Were changed to a blight of frozen glue.

For the leaves soon fell, and the branches soon
By the heavy axe of the blast were hewn;
The sap shrank to the root through every pore
As blood to a heart that will beat no more.

For Winter came: the wind was his whip:
One choppy finger was on his lip:
He had torn the cataracts from the hills
And they clanked at his girdle like manacles;

His breath was a chain which without a sound
The earth, and the air, and the water bound;
He came, fiercely driven, in his chariot-throne
By the tenfold blasts of the Arctic zone.

[1] This stanza was suppressed in later editions.

Then the weeds which were forms of living death
Fled from the frost to the earth beneath.
Their decay and sudden flight from frost
Was but like the vanishing of a ghost!

And under the roots of the Sensitive Plant
The moles and the dormice died for want:
The birds dropped stiff from the frozen air
And were caught in the branches naked and bare.

First there came down a thawing rain
And its dull drops froze on the boughs again;
Then there steamed up a freezing dew
Which to the drops of the thaw-rain grew;

And a northern whirlwind, wandering about
Like a wolf that had smelt a dead child out,
Shook the boughs thus laden, and heavy, and stiff,
And snapped them off with his rigid griff.

When Winter had gone and Spring came back
The Sensitive Plant was a leafless wreck;
But the mandrakes, and toadstools, and docks, and darnels,
Rose like the dead from their ruined charnels.

CONCLUSION

Whether the Sensitive Plant, or that
Which within its boughs like a Spirit sat,
Ere its outward form had known decay,
Now felt this change, I cannot say.

Whether that Lady's gentle mind,
No longer with the form combined
Which scattered love, as stars do light,
Found sadness, where it left delight,

I dare not guess; but in this life
Of error, ignorance, and strife,
Where nothing is, but all things seem,
And we the shadows of the dream,

It is a modest creed, and yet
Pleasant if one considers it,
To own that death itself must be,
Like all the rest, a mockery.

That garden sweet, that lady fair,
And all sweet shapes and odours there,
In truth have never passed away:
'Tis we, 'tis ours, are changed; not they.

For love, and beauty, and delight,
There is no death nor change: their might
Exceeds our organs, which endure
No light, being themselves obscure.

P. B. SHELLEY.

THE EVE OF ST. AGNES

ST. AGNES' EVE—ah, bitter chill it was!
The owl, for all his feathers, was a-cold;
The hare limp'd trembling through the frozen grass,
And silent was the flock in woolly fold:
Numb were the Beadsman's fingers while he told
His rosary, and while his frosted breath,
Like pious incense from a censer old,
Seem'd taking flight for heaven without a death,
Past the sweet Virgin's picture, while his prayer he saith.

His prayer he saith, this patient, holy man;
Then takes his lamp, and riseth from his knees,
And back returneth, meagre, barefoot, wan,
Along the chapel aisle by slow degrees:
The sculptured dead, on each side, seem to freeze
Emprison'd in black, purgatorial rails:
Knights, ladies, praying in dumb orat'ries,
He passeth by, and his weak spirit fails
To think how they may ache in icy hoods and mails.

Northward he turneth through a little door,
And scarce three steps, ere Music's golden tongue
Flatter'd to tears this aged man and poor.

But no—already had his death-bell rung;
The joys of all his life were said and sung;
His was harsh penance on St. Agnes' Eve:
Another way he went, and soon among
Rough ashes sat he for his soul's reprieve,
And all night kept awake, for sinners' sake to grieve.

That ancient Beadsman heard the prelude soft;
And so it chanced, for many a door was wide,
From hurry to and fro. Soon, up aloft,
The silver, snarling trumpets 'gan to chide:
The level chambers, ready with their pride,
Were glowing to receive a thousand guests:
The carved angels, ever eager-eyed,
Stared, where upon their heads the cornice rests,
With hair blown back, and wings put crosswise on their
    breasts.

At length burst in the argent revelry,
With plume, tiara, and all rich array,
Numerous as shadows haunting fairily
The brain new-stuff'd, in youth, with triumphs gay
Of old romance. These let us wish away,
And turn, sole-thoughted, to one Lady there,
Whose heart had brooded, all that wintry day,
On love, and wing'd St. Agnes' saintly care,
As she had heard old dames full many times declare.

They told her how, upon St. Agnes' Eve,
Young virgins might have visions of delight,
And soft adorings from their loves receive
Upon the honey'd middle of the night,
If ceremonies due they did aright;
As, supperless to bed they must retire,
And couch supine their beauties, lily white;
Nor look behind, nor sideways, but require
Of Heaven with upward eyes for all that they desire.

Full of this whim was thoughtful Madeline:
The music, yearning like a God in pain,
She scarcely heard; her maiden eyes divine,
Fix'd on the floor, saw many a sweeping train
Pass by—she heeded not at all: in vain

Came many a tiptoe, amorous cavalier,
And back retir'd; not cool'd by high disdain,
But she saw not: her heart was otherwhere;
She sigh'd for Agnes' dreams, the sweetest of the year.

She danced along with vague, regardless eyes,
Anxious her lips, her breathing quick and short;
The hallow'd hour was near at hand, she sighs:
Amid the timbrels, and the throng'd resort
Of whisperers in anger or in sport;
'Mid looks of love, defiance, hate, and scorn,
Hoodwink'd with faery fancy; all amort,
Save to St. Agnes and her lambs unshorn,
And all the bliss to be before to-morrow morn.

So, purposing each moment to retire,
She linger'd still. Meantime, across the moors,
Had come young Porphyro, with heart on fire
For Madeline. Beside the portal doors,
Buttress'd from moonlight, stands he, and implores
All saints to give him sight of Madeline,
But for one moment in the tedious hours,
That he might gaze and worship all unseen;
Perchance speak, kneel, touch, kiss—in sooth such things
    have been.

He ventures in: let no buzz'd whisper tell,
All eyes be muffled, or a hundred swords
Will storm his heart, Love's feverous citadel:
For him, those chambers held barbarian hordes.
Hyena foemen, and hot-blooded lords
Whose very dogs would execration howl
Against his lineage; not one breast affords
Him any mercy in that mansion foul,
Save one old beldame, weak in body and in soul.

Ah, happy chance! the aged creature came,
Shuffling along with ivory-headed wand,
To where he stood, hid from the torch's flame,
Behind a broad hall pillar, far beyond
The sound of merriment and chorus bland.
He startled her: but soon she knew his face,
And grasp'd his fingers in her palsied hand,

Saying, " Mercy Porphyro! hie thee from this place;
They are all here to-night, the whole blood-thirsty race!

" Get hence! get hence! there's dwarfish Hildebrand:
He had a fever late, and in the fit
He cursed thee and thine, both house and land:
Then there's that old Lord Maurice, not a whit
More tame for his grey hairs—Alas me! flit!
Flit like a ghost away."—" Ah, Gossip dear,
We're safe enough; here in this arm-chair sit,
And tell me how "—" Good saints! not here, not here;
Follow me, child, or else these stones will be thy bier."

He followed through a lowly arched way,
Brushing the cobwebs with his lofty plume;
And as she mutter'd " Well-a—well-a-day! "
He found him in a little moonlight room,
Pale, latticed, chill, and silent as a tomb.
" Now tell me where is Madeline," said he,
" O tell me, Angela, by the holy loom
Which none but secret sisterhood may see,
When they St. Agnes' wool are weaving piously."

" St. Agnes! Ah! it is St. Agnes' Eve—
Yet men will murder upon holy days.
Thou must hold water in a witch's sieve,
And be liege-lord of all the Elves and Fays
To venture so: it fills me with amaze
To see thee, Porphyro!—St. Agnes' Eve!
God's help! my lady fair the conjurer plays
This very night: good angels her deceive!
But let me laugh awhile,—I've mickle time to grieve."

Feebly she laugheth in the languid moon,
While Porphyro upon her face doth look,
Like puzzled urchin on an aged crone
Who keepeth closed a wondrous riddle-book,
As spectacled she sits in chimney nook.
But soon his eyes grew brilliant, when she told
His lady's purpose; and he scarce could brook
Tears, at the thought of those enchantments cold,
And Madeline asleep in lap of legends old.

Sudden a thought came like a full-blown rose,
Flushing his brow, and in his pained heart
Made purple riot: then doth he propose
A stratagem, that makes the beldame start:
" A cruel man and impious thou art!
Sweet lady! let her pray, and sleep and dream
Alone with her good angels, far apart
From wicked men like thee. Go, go! I deem
Thou canst not surely be the same that thou didst seem."

" I will not harm her, by all saints I swear! "
Quoth Porphyro: " O may I ne'er find grace
When my weak voice shall whisper its last prayer,
If one of her soft ringlets I displace,
Or look with ruffian passion in her face.
Good Angela, believe me, by these tears;
Or I will, even in a moment's space,
Awake, with horrid shout, my foemen's ears,
And beard them, though they be more fang'd than wolves
    and bears."

" Ah! why wilt thou affright a feeble soul?
A poor, weak, palsy-stricken, churchyard thing,
Whose passing-bell may ere the midnight toll;
Whose prayers for thee, each morn and evening,
Were never miss'd." Thus plaining, doth she bring
A gentler speech from burning Porphyro;
So woeful, and of such deep sorrowing,
That Angela gives promise she will do
Whatever he shall wish, betide her weal or woe.

Which was, to lead him, in close secrecy,
Even to Madeline's chamber, and there hide
Him in a closet, of such privacy
That he might see her beauty unespied,
And win perhaps that night a peerless bride,
While legion'd fairies paced the coverlet,
And pale enchantment held her sleepy-eyed.
Never on such a night have lovers met,
Since Merlin paid his Demon all the monstrous debt.

" It shall be as thou wishest," said the Dame:
" All cates and dainties shall be stored there

Quickly on this feast-night: by the tambour frame
Her own lute thou wilt see: no time to spare,
For I am slow and feeble, and scarce dare
On such a catering trust my dizzy head.
Wait here, my child, with patience; kneel in prayer
The while. Ah! thou must needs the lady wed,
Or may I never leave my grave among the dead."

So saying she hobbled off with busy fear.
The lover's endless minutes slowly pass'd;
The dame return'd, and whisper'd in his ear
To follow her; with aged eyes aghast
From fright of dim espial. Safe at last
Through many a dusky gallery, they gain
The maiden's chamber, silken, hush'd and chaste;
Where Porphyro took covert, pleased amain.
His poor guide hurried back with agues in her brain.

Her faltering hand upon the balustrade,
Old Angela was feeling for the stair,
When Madeline, St. Agnes' charmed maid,
Rose, like a mission'd spirit, unaware:
With silver taper's light, and pious care,
She turn'd, and down the aged gossip led
To a safe level matting. Now prepare,
Young Prophyro, for gazing on that bed;
She comes, she comes again, like ring-dove fray'd and fled.

Out went the taper as she hurried in;
Its little smoke, in pallid moonshine, died:
She closed the door, she panted, all akin
To spirits of the air, and visions wide:
No utter'd syllable, or, woe betide!
But to her heart, her heart was voluble,
Paining with eloquence her balmy side;
As though a tongueless nightingale should swell
Her throat in vain, and die, heart-stifled, in her dell.

A casement high and triple-arch'd there was,
All garlanded with carven imageries,
Of fruits and flowers, and bunches of knot-grass,
And diamonded with panes of quaint device,
Innumerable of stains and splendid dyes,

As are the tiger-moth's deep-damask'd wings;
And in the midst, 'mong thousand heraldries,
And twilight saints, and dim emblazonings,
A shielded scutcheon blush'd with blood of queens and kings.

Full on this casement shone the wintry moon,
And threw warm gules on Madeline's fair breast,
As down she knelt for Heaven's grace and boon;
Rose-bloom fell on her hands, together prest,
And on her silver cross soft amethyst,
And on her hair a glory, like a saint:
She seem'd a splendid angel, newly drest,
Save wings, for heaven:—Porphyro grew faint:
She knelt, so pure a thing, so free from mortal taint.

Anon his heart revives: her vespers done,
Of all its wreathed pearls her hair she frees;
Unclasps her warmed jewels one by one;
Loosens her fragrant boddice; by degrees
Her rich attire creeps rustling to her knees:
Half-hidden, like a mermaid in sea-weed,
Pensive awhile she dreams awake, and sees,
In fancy, fair St. Agnes in her bed,
But dares not look behind, or all the charm is fled.

Soon, trembling in her soft and chilly nest,
In sort of wakeful swoon, perplex'd she lay,
Until the poppied warmth of sleep oppress'd
Her soothed limbs, and soul fatigued away;
Flown, like a thought, until the morrow-day;
Blissfully haven'd both from joy and pain;
Clasp'd like a missal where swart Paynims pray;
Blinded alike from sunshine and from rain,
As though a rose should shut, and be a bud again.

Stolen to this paradise, and so entranced,
Porphyro gazed upon her empty dress,
And listen'd to her breathing, if it chanced
To wake into a slumberous tenderness;
Which when he heard, that minute did he bless,
And breath'd himself: then from the closet crept,
Noiseless as fear in a wide wilderness,
And over the hush'd carpet, silent, stept,
And 'tween the curtains peep'd, where, lo!—how fast she slept!

Then by the bed-side, where the faded moon
Made a dim, silver twilight, soft he set
A table, and, half anguish'd, threw thereon
A cloth of woven crimson, gold, and jet:—
O for some drowsy Morphean amulet!
The boisterous, midnight, festive clarion,
The kettle-drum, and far-heard clarionet,
Affray his ears, though but in dying tone:—
The hall-door shuts again, and all the noise is gone.

And still she slept an azure-lidded sleep,
In blanched linen, smooth, and lavender'd,
While he from forth the closet brought a heap
Of candied apple, quince, and plum, and gourd;
With jellies soother than the creamy curd,
And lucent syrops, tinct with cinnamon;
Manna and dates, in argosy transferr'd
From Fez; and spiced dainties, every one,
From silken Samarcand to cedar'd Lebanon.

These delicates he heap'd with glowing hand
On golden dishes and in baskets bright
Of wreathed silver: sumptuous they stand
In the retired quiet of the night,
Filling the chilly room with perfume light.—
" And now, my love, my seraph fair, awake!
Thou art my heaven, and I thine eremite:
Open thine eyes, for meek St. Agnes' sake,
Or I shall drowse beside thee, so my soul doth ache."

Thus whispering, his warm, unnerved arm
Sank in her pillow. Shaded was her dream
By the dusk curtains:—'twas a midnight charm
Impossible to melt as iced stream:
The lustrous salvers in the moonlight gleam;
Broad golden fringe upon the carpet lies:
It seem'd he never, never could redeem
From such a steadfast spell his lady's eyes;
So mused awhile, entoil'd in woofed phantasies.

Awakening, up he took her hollow lute,—
Tumultuous,—and, in chords that tenderest be,
He play'd an ancient ditty, long since mute,

In Provence call'd " La belle dame sans mercy ";
Close to her ear touching the melody;—
Wherewith disturb'd, she utter'd a soft moan:
He ceased—she panted quick—and suddenly
Her blue affrayed eyes wide open shone:
Upon his knees he sank, pale as smooth-sculptured stone.

Her eyes were open, but she still beheld,
Now wide awake, the vision of her sleep:
There was a painful change, that nigh expell'd
The blisses of her dream so pure and deep.
At which fair Madeline began to weep,
And moan forth witless words with many a sigh,
While still her gaze on Porphyro would keep;
Who knelt, with joined hands and piteous eye,
Fearing to move or speak, she look'd so dreamingly.

" Ah, Porphyro ! " said she, " but even now
Thy voice was at sweet tremble in mine ear,
Made tunable with every sweetest vow;
And those sad eyes were spiritual and clear:
How changed thou art ! how pallid, chill, and drear !
Give me that voice again, my Porphyro,
Those looks immortal, those complainings dear !
Oh leave me not in this eternal woe,
For if thou diest, my Love, I know not where to go."

Beyond a mortal man impassion'd far
At these voluptuous accents, he arose,
Ethereal, flush'd, and like a throbbing star
Seen 'mid the sapphire heaven's deep repose;
Into her dream he melted, as the rose
Blendeth its odour with the violet,—
Solution sweet: meantime the frost-wind blows
Like Love's alarum, pattering the sharp sleet
Against the window-panes; St. Agnes' moon hath set.

'Tis dark: quick pattereth the flaw-blown sleet.
" This is no dream, my bride, my Madeline ! "
'Tis dark: the iced gusts still rave and beat:
" No dream, alas ! alas ! and woe is mine !
Porphyro will leave me here to fade and pine.
Cruel ! what traitor could thee hither bring?

I curse not, for my heart is lost in thine,
Though thou forsakest a deceived thing;—
A dove forlorn and lost with sick unpruned wing."

"My Madeline! sweet dreamer! lovely bride!
Say, may I be for aye thy vassal blest?
Thy beauty's shield, heart-shaped and vermeil-dyed?
Ah, silver shrine, here will I take my rest
After so many hours of toil and quest,
A famish'd pilgrim,—saved by miracle.
Though I have found, I will not rob thy nest,
Saving of thy sweet self; if thou think'st well
To trust, fair Madeline, to no rude infidel.

"Hark! 'tis an elfin storm from faery land,
Of haggard seeming, but a boon indeed:
Arise—arise! the morning is at hand;—
The bloated wassailers will never heed;—
Let us away, my love, with happy speed;
There are no ears to hear, or eyes to see,—
Drown'd all in Rhenish and the sleepy mead.
Awake! arise! my love, and fearless be,
For o'er the southern moors I have a home for thee."

She hurried at his words, beset with fears,
For there were sleeping dragons all around
At glaring watch, perhaps, with ready spears.
Down the wide stairs a darkling way they found;
In all the house was heard no human sound.
A chain-droop'd lamp was flickering by each door;
The arras, rich with horsemen, hawk, and hound,
Flutter'd in the besieging wind's uproar;
And the long carpets rose along the gusty floor.

They glide, like phantoms, into the wide hall;
Like phantoms to the iron porch they glide,
Where lay the Porter, in uneasy sprawl,
With a huge empty flagon by his side:
The wakeful bloodhound rose, and shook his hide,
But his sagacious eye an inmate owns:
By one, and one, the bolts full easy slide:—
The chains lie silent on the footworn stones;
The key turns, and the door upon its hinges groans.

And they are gone: ay, ages long ago
These lovers fled away into the storm.
That night the Baron dreamt of many a woe,
And all his warrior-guests with shade and form
Of witch, and demon, and large coffin-worm,
Were long be-nightmared. Angela the old
Died palsy-twitch'd, with meagre face deform;
The Beadsman, after thousand aves told,
For aye unsought-for slept among his ashes cold.

JOHN KEATS.

THE LOTOS-EATERS

" Courage! " he said, and pointed toward the land,
" This mounting wave will roll us shoreward soon."
In the afternoon they came unto a land,
In which it seemed always afternoon.
All round the coast the languid air did swoon,
Breathing like one that hath a weary dream.
Full-faced above the valley stood the moon;
And like a downward smoke, the slender stream
Along the cliff to fall and pause and fall did seem.

A land of streams! some, like a downward smoke,
Slow-dropping veils of thinnest lawn, did go;
And some thro' wavering lights and shadows broke,
Rolling a slumbrous sheet of foam below.
They saw the gleaming river seaward flow
From the inner land: far off, three mountain-tops,
Three silent pinnacles of aged snow,
Stood sunset-flush'd: and, dew'd with showery drops,
Up-clomb the shadowy pine above the woven copse.

The charmed sunset linger'd low adown
In the red West: thro' mountain clefts the dale
Was seen far inland, and the yellow down
Border'd with palm, and many a winding vale
And meadow, set with slender galingale;
A land where all things always seem'd the same!
And round about the keel with faces pale,
Dark faces pale against that rosy flame,
The mild-eyed melancholy Lotos-eaters came.

Branches they bore of that enchanted stem,
Laden with flower and fruit, whereof they gave
To each, but whoso did receive of them,
And taste, to him the gushing of the wave
Far far away did seem to mourn and rave
On alien shores; and if his fellow spake,
His voice was thin, as voices from the grave;
And deep-asleep he seem'd, yet all awake,
And music in his ears his beating heart did make.

They sat them down upon the yellow sand,
Between the sun and moon upon the shore;
And sweet it was to dream of Father-land,
Of child, and wife, and slave; but evermore
Most weary seem'd the sea, weary the oar,
Weary the wandering fields of barren foam.
Then some one said, " We will return no more ";
And all at once they sang, " Our island home
Is far beyond the wave; we will no longer roam."

CHORIC SONG

I

THERE is sweet music here that softer falls
Than petals from blown roses on the grass,
Or night-dews on still waters between walls
Of shadowy granite, in a gleaming pass;
Music that gentlier on the spirit lies,
Than tir'd eyelids upon tir'd eyes;
Music that brings sweet sleep down from the blissful skies.
Here are cool mosses deep,
And thro' the moss the ivies creep,
And in the stream the long-leaved flowers weep,
And from the craggy ledge the poppy hangs in sleep.

II

Why are we weigh'd upon with heaviness,
And utterly consumed with sharp distress,
While all things else have rest from weariness?
All things have rest: why should we toil alone,
We only toil, who are the first of things,

And make perpetual moan,
Still from one sorrow to another thrown:
Nor ever fold our wings,
And cease from wanderings,
Nor steep our brows in slumber's holy balm;
Nor harken what the inner spirit sings,
" There is no joy but calm! "
Why should we only toil, the roof and crown of things?

III

Lo! in the middle of the wood,
The folded leaf is woo'd from out the bud
With winds upon the branch, and there
Grows green and broad, and takes no care,
Sun-steep'd at noon, and in the moon
Nightly dew-fed; and turning yellow
Falls, and floats adown the air.
Lo! sweeten'd with the summer light,
The full-juiced apple, waxing over-mellow,
Drops in a silent autumn night.
All its allotted length of days,
The flower ripens in its place,
Ripens and fades, and falls, and hath no toil,
Fast-rooted in the fruitful soil.

IV

Hateful is the dark-blue sky,
Vaulted o'er the dark-blue sea.
Death is the end of life; ah, why
Should life all labour be?
Let us alone. Time driveth onward fast,
And in a little while our lips are dumb.
Let us alone. What is it that will last?
All things are taken from us, and become
Portions and parcels of the dreadful Past.
Let us alone. What pleasure can we have
To war with evil? Is there any peace
In ever climbing up the climbing wave?
All things have rest, and ripen toward the grave
In silence; ripen, fall and cease:
Give us long rest or death, dark death, or dreamful ease.

v

How sweet it were, hearing the downward stream,
With half-shut eyes ever to seem
Falling asleep in a half-dream!
To dream and dream, like yonder amber light,
Which will not leave the myrrh-bush on the height;
To hear each other's whisper'd speech;
Eating the Lotos day by day,
To watch the crisping ripples on the beach,
And tender curving lines of creamy spray;
To lend our hearts and spirits wholly
To the influence of mild-minded melancholy;
To muse and brood and live again in memory,
With those old faces of our infancy
Heap'd over with a mound of grass,
Two handfuls of white dust, shut in an urn of brass!

vi

Dear is the memory of our wedded lives,
And dear the last embraces of our wives
And their warm tears: but all hath suffer'd change;
For surely now our household hearths are cold:
Our sons inherit us: our looks are strange:
And we should come like ghosts to trouble joy.
Or else the island princes over-bold
Have eat our substance, and the minstrel sings
Before them of the ten-years' war in Troy,
And our great deeds, as half-forgotten things.
Is there confusion in the little isle?
Let what is broken so remain.
The Gods are hard to reconcile:
'Tis hard to settle order once again.
There *is* confusion worse than death,
Trouble on trouble, pain on pain,
Long labour unto aged breath,
Sore task to hearts worn out with many wars
And eyes grown dim with gazing on the pilot-stars.

vii

But, propt on beds of amaranth and moly,
How sweet (while warm airs lull us, blowing lowly)

With half-dropt eyelids still,
Beneath a heaven dark and holy,
To watch the long bright river drawing slowly
His waters from the purple hill—
To hear the dewy echoes calling
From cave to cave thro' the thick-twined vine—
To watch the emerald-colour'd water falling
Thro' many a wov'n acanthus-wreath divine!
Only to hear and see the far-off sparkling brine,
Only to hear were sweet, stretch'd out beneath the pine.

VIII

The Lotos blooms below the barren peak:
The Lotos blows by every winding creek:
All day the wind breathes low with mellower tone:
Thro' every hollow cave and alley lone
Round and round the spicy downs the yellow Lotos-dust is
    blown.
We have had enough of action, and of motion we,
Roll'd to starboard, roll'd to larboard, when the surge was
    seething free,
Where the wallowing monster spouted his foam-fountains in
    the sea.
Let us swear an oath, and keep it with an equal mind,
In the hollow Lotos-land to live and lie reclined
On the hills like Gods together, careless of mankind.
For they lie beside their nectar, and the bolts are hurl'd
Far below them in the valleys, and the clouds are lightly
    curl'd
Round their golden houses, girdled with the gleaming world:
Where they smile in secret, looking over wasted lands,
Blight and famine, plague and earthquake, roaring deep
    and fiery sands,
Clanging fights, and flaming towns, and sinking ships, and
    praying hands.
But they smile, they find a music centred in a doleful song
Steaming up, a lamentation and an ancient tale of wrong,
Like a tale of little meaning tho' the words are strong;
Chanted from an ill-used race of men that cleave the soil,
Sow the seed, and reap the harvest with enduring toil,
Storing yearly little dues of wheat, and wine and oil:

Till they perish and they suffer—some, 'tis whisper'd—down
    in hell
Suffer endless anguish, others in Elysian valleys dwell,
Resting weary limbs at last on beds of asphodel.
Surely, surely, slumber is more sweet than toil, the shore
Than labour in the deep mid-ocean, wind and wave and oar;
Oh rest ye, brother mariners, we will not wander more.

                                  LORD TENNYSON.

(1853)

ABT VOGLER

(AFTER HE HAS BEEN EXTEMPORISING UPON THE INSTRUMENT OF HIS INVENTION)

I

WOULD that the structure brave, the manifold music I build,
    Bidding my organ obey, calling its keys to their work,
Claiming each slave of the sound, at a touch, as when Solomon
    willed
    Armies of angels that soar, legions of demons that lurk,
Man, brute, reptile, fly,—alien of end and of aim,
    Adverse, each from the other heaven-high, hell-deep
    removed,—
Should rush into sight at once as he named the ineffable Name,
    And pile him a palace straight, to pleasure the princess he
    loved!

II

Would it might tarry like his, the beautiful building of mine,
    This which my keys in a crowd pressed and importuned
    to raise!
Ah, one and all, how they helped, would dispart now and
    now combine,
    Zealous to hasten the work, heighten their master his
    praise!
And one would bury his brow with a blind plunge down to
    hell,
    Burrow awhile and build, broad on the roots of things,
Then up again swim into sight, having based me my palace
    well,
    Founded it, fearless of flame, flat on the nether springs.

III

And another would mount and march, like the excellent
    minion he was,
    Ay, another and yet another, one crowd but with many a
        crest,
Raising my rampired walls of gold as transparent as glass,
    Eager to do and die, yield each his place to the rest:
For higher still and higher (as a runner tips with fire,
    When a great illumination surprises a festal night—
    Outlining round and round Rome's dome from space to spire)
        Up, the pinnacled glory reached, and the pride of my soul
        was in sight.

IV

In sight? Not half! for it seemed, it was certain, to match
    man's birth,
    Nature in turn conceived, obeying an impulse as I;
And the emulous heaven yearned down, made effort to reach
    the earth,
    As the earth had done her best, in my passion, to scale the
        sky:
Novel splendours burst forth, grew familiar and dwelt with
    mine,
    Not a point nor peak but found and fixed its wandering star;
Meteor-moons, balls of blaze: and they did not pale nor pine,
    For earth had attained to heaven, there was no more near
    nor far.

V

Nay, more; for there wanted not who walked in the glare
    and glow,
    Presences plain in the place; or, fresh from the Protoplast,
Furnished for ages to come, when a kindlier wind should blow,
    Lured now to begin and live, in a house to their liking at
    last;
Or else the wonderful Dead who have passed through the
    body and gone,
    But were back once more to breathe in an old world worth
    their new;
What never had been, was now; what was, as it shall be anon;
    And what is—shall I say, matched both? for I was made
    perfect too.

VI

All through my keys that gave their sounds to a wish of my
    soul,
    All through my soul that praised as its wish flowed visibly
        forth,
All through music and me! For think, had I painted the
    whole,
    Why, there it had stood, to see, nor the process so wonder-
        worth;
Had I written the same, made verse—still, effect proceeds
    from cause,
    Ye know why the forms are fair, ye hear how the tale is
        told;
It is all triumphant art, but art in obedience to laws,
    Painter and poet are proud in the artist-list enrolled:—

VII

But here is the finger of God, a flash of the will that can,
    Existent behind all laws, that made them and, lo, they are!
And I know not if, save in this, such gift be allowed to man,
    That out of three sounds he frame, not a fourth sound,
        but a star.
Consider it well: each tone of our scale in itself is nought;
    It is everywhere in the world—loud, soft, and all is said:
Give it to me to use! I mix it with two in my thought:
    And, there! Ye have heard and seen: consider and bow
        the head!

VIII

Well, it is gone at last, the palace of music I reared;
    Gone! and the good tears start, the praises that come too
        slow;
For one is assured at first, one scarce can say that he feared,
    That he even gave it a thought, the gone thing was to go.
Never to be again! But many more of the kind
    As good, nay, better perchance: is this your comfort to me?
To me, who must be saved because I cling with my mind
    To the same, same self, same love, same God: ay, what
        was, shall be.

IX

Therefore to whom turn I but to thee, the ineffable Name?
  Builder and maker, thou, of houses not made with hands!
What, have fear of change from thee who art ever the same?
  Doubt that thy power can fill the heart that thy power
    expands?
There shall never be one lost good! What was, shall live as
    before;
  The evil is null, is nought, is silence implying sound;
What was good shall be good, with, for evil, so much good
    more;
  On the earth the broken arcs; in the heaven, a perfect
    round.

X

All we have willed or hoped or dreamed of good shall exist;
  Not its semblance, but itself; no beauty, nor good, nor
    power
Whose voice has gone forth, but each survives for the melodist
  When eternity affirms the conception of an hour.
The high that proved too high, the heroic for earth too hard,
  The passion that left the ground to lose itself in the sky,
Are music sent up to God by the lover and the bard;
  Enough that he heard it once: we shall hear it by-and-by.

XI

And what is our failure here but a triumph's evidence
  For the fulness of the days? Have we withered or
    agonised?
Why else was the pause prolonged but that singing might
    issue thence?
  Why rushed the discords in but that harmony should be
    prized?
Sorrow is hard to bear, and doubt is slow to clear,
  Each sufferer says his say, his scheme of the weal and woe:
But God has a few of us whom he whispers in the ear;
  The rest may reason and welcome: 'tis we musicians know.

XII

Well, it is earth with me; silence resumes her reign:
   I will be patient and proud, and soberly acquiesce.
Give me the keys. I feel for the common chord again,
   Sliding by semitones, till I sink to the minor,—yes,
And I blunt it into a ninth, and I stand on alien ground,
   Surveying awhile the heights I rolled from into the deep;
Which, hark, I have dared and done, for my resting-place is
     found,
   The C major of this life: so, now I will try to sleep.

                       ROBERT BROWNING.

A DEATH IN THE DESERT

[SUPPOSED of Pamphylax the Antiochene:
It is a parchment, of my rolls the fifth,
Hath three skins glued together, is all Greek
And goeth from *Epsilon* down to *Mu*:
Lies second in the surnamed Chosen Chest,
Stained and conserved with juice of terebinth,
Covered with cloth of hair, and lettered *Xi*,
From Xanthus, my wife's uncle, now at peace:
Mu and *Epsilon* stand for my own name.
I may not write it, but I make a cross
To show I wait His coming, with the rest,
And leave off here: beginneth Pamphylax.]

I said, " If one should wet his lips with wine,
And slip the broadest plantain-leaf we find,
Or else the lappet of a linen robe,
Into the water-vessel, lay it right,
And cool his forehead just above the eyes,
The while a brother, kneeling either side,
Should chafe each hand and try to make it warm,—
He is not so far gone but he might speak."

This did not happen in the outer cave,
Nor in the secret chamber of the rock
Where, sixty days since the decree was out,
We had him, bedded on a camel-skin,

And waited for his dying all the while;
But in the midmost grotto: since noon's light
Reached there a little, and we would not lose
The last of what might happen on his face.

I at the head, and Xanthus at the feet,
With Valens and the Boy, had lifted him,
And brought him from the chamber in the depths,
And laid him in the light where we might see:
For certain smiles began about his mouth,
And his lids moved, presageful of the end.

Beyond, and half way up the mouth o' the cave,
The Bactrian convert, having his desire,
Kept watch, and made pretence to graze a goat
That gave us milk, on rags of various herb,
Plantain and quitch, the rocks' shade keeps alive:
So that if any thief or soldier passed,
(Because the persecution was aware)
Yielding the goat up promptly with his life,
Such man might pass on, joyful at a prize,
Nor care to pry into the cool o' the cave.
Outside was all noon and the burning blue.

" Here is wine," answered Xanthus,—dropped a drop;
I stooped and placed the lap of cloth aright,
Then chafed his right hand, and the Boy his left:
But Valens had bethought him, and produced
And broke a ball of nard, and made perfume.
Only, he did—not so much wake, as—turn
And smile a little, as a sleeper does
If any dear one call him, touch his face—
And smiles and loves, but will not be disturbed.

Then Xanthus said a prayer, but still he slept:
It is the Xanthus that escaped to Rome,
Was burned, and could not write the chronicle.

Then the Boy sprang up from his knees, and ran,
Stung by the splendour of a sudden thought,
And fetched the seventh plate of graven lead
Out of the secret chamber, found a place,
Pressing with finger on the deeper dints,

And spoke, as 'twere his mouth proclaiming first,
" I am the Resurrection and the Life."

Whereat he opened his eyes wide at once,
And sat up of himself, and looked at us;
And thenceforth nobody pronounced a word;
Only, outside, the Bactrian cried his cry
Like the lone desert-bird that wears the ruff,
As signal we were safe, from time to time.

First he said, " If a friend declared to me,
This my son Valens, this my other son,
Were James and Peter,—nay, declared as well
This lad was very John,—I could believe!
—Could, for a moment, doubtlessly believe:
So is myself withdrawn into my depths,
The soul retreated from the perished brain
Whence it was wont to feel and use the world
Through these dull members, done with long ago.
Yet I myself remain; I feel myself:
And there is nothing lost. Let be, awhile! "

[This is the doctrine he was wont to teach,
How divers persons witness in each man,
Three souls which make up one soul: first, to wit,
A soul of each and all the bodily parts,
Seated therein, which works, and is what Does,
And has the use of earth, and ends the man
Downward: but, tending upward for advice,
Grows into, and again is grown into
By the next soul, which, seated in the brain,
Useth the first with its collected use,
And feeleth, thinketh, willeth,—is what Knows:
Which, duly tending upward in its turn,
Grows into, and again is grown into
By the last soul, that uses both the first,
Subsisting whether they assist or no,
And, constituting man's self, is what Is—
And leans upon the former, makes it play,
As that played off the first: and, tending up,
Holds, is upheld by, God, and ends the man
Upward in that dread point of intercourse,
Nor needs a place, for it returns to Him.

What Does, what Knows, what Is; three souls, one man.
I give the glossa of Theotypas.]

And then, " A stick, once fire from end to end;
Now, ashes save that tip that holds a spark!
Yet, blow the spark, it runs back, spreads itself
A little where the fire was: thus I urge
The soul that served me, till it task once more
What ashes of my brain have kept their shape,
And these make effort on the last o' the flesh,
Trying to taste again the truth of things—"
(He smiled)—" their very superficial truth;
As that ye are my sons, that it is long
Since James and Peter had release by death,
And I am only he, your brother John,
Who saw and heard, and could remember all.
Remember all! It is not much to say.
What if the truth broke on me from above
As once and oft-times? Such might hap again:
Doubtlessly He might stand in presence here,
With head wool-white, eyes flame, and feet like brass,
The sword and the seven stars, as I have seen—
I who now shudder only and surmise
' How did your brother bear that sight and live!'

" If I live yet, it is for good, more love
Through me to men: be nought but ashes here
That keep awhile my semblance, who was John,—
Still, when they scatter, there is left on earth
No one alive who knew (consider this!)
—Saw with his eyes and handled with his hands
That which was from the first, the Word of Life.
How will it be when none more saith ' I saw '?

" Such ever was love's way: to rise, it stoops.
Since I, whom Christ's mouth taught, was bidden teach,
I went, for many years, about the world,
Saying ' It was so; so I heard and saw,'
Speaking as the case asked: and men believed.
Afterward came the message to myself
In Patmos isle; I was not bidden teach,
But simply listen, take a book and write,
Nor set down other than the given word,

With nothing left to my arbitrament
To choose or change: I wrote, and men believed.
Then, for my time grew brief, no message more.
No call to write again, I found a way,
And, reasoning from my knowledge, merely taught
Men should, for love's sake, in love's strength believe;
Or I would pen a letter to a friend
And urge the same as friend, nor less nor more:
Friends said I reasoned rightly, and believed.
But at the last, why, I seemed left alive
Like a sea-jelly weak on Patmos strand,
To tell dry sea-beach gazers how I fared
When there was mid-sea, and the mighty things:
Left to repeat, ' I saw, I heard, I knew,'
And go all over the old ground again,
With Antichrist already in the world,
And many Antichrists, who answered prompt
' Am I not Jasper as thyself art John?
Nay, young, whereas through age thou mayest forget;
Wherefore, explain, or how shall we believe?'
I never thought to call down fire on such,
Or, as in wonderful and early days,
Pick up the scorpion, tread the serpent dumb;
But patient stated much of the Lord's life
Forgotten or misdelivered, and let it work:
Since much that at the first, in deed and word,
Lay simply and sufficiently exposed,
Had grown (or else my soul was grown to match,
Fed through such years, familiar with such light,
Guarded and guided still to see and speak)
Of new significance and fresh result;
What first were guessed as points, I now knew stars,
And named them in the Gospel I have writ.
For men said, ' It is getting long ago:
Where is the promise of His coming?'—asked
These young ones in their strength, as loth to wait,
Of me who, when their sires were born, was old.
I, for I loved them, answered, joyfully,
Since I was there, and helpful in my age;
And, in the main, I think such men believed.
Finally, thus endeavouring, I fell sick,
Ye brought me here, and I supposed the end,
And went to sleep with one thought that, at least,

Though the whole earth should lie in wickedness,
We had the truth, might leave the rest to God.
Yet now I wake in such decrepitude
As I had slidden down and fallen afar,
Past even the presence of my former self,
Grasping the while for stay at facts which snap,
Till I am found away from my own world,
Feeling for foot-hold through a blank profound,
Along with unborn people in strange lands,
Who say—I hear said or conceive they say—
' Was John at all, and did he say he saw ?
Assure us, ere we ask what he might see ! '

" And how shall I assure them ?   Can they share
—They, who have flesh, a veil of youth and strength
About each spirit, that needs must bide its time,
Living and learning still as years assist
Which wear the thickness thin, and let man see—
With me who hardly am withheld at all,
But shudderingly, scarce a shred between,
Lie bare to the universal prick of light?
Is it for nothing we grow old and weak,
We whom God loves ? When pain ends, gain ends too.
To me, that story—ay, that Life and Death
Of which I wrote ' it was '—to me, it is;
—Is, here and now: I apprehend nought else.
Is not God now i' the world His power first made?
Is not His love at issue still with sin,
Visibly when a wrong is done on earth ?
Love, wrong, and pain, what see I else around ?
Yea, and the Resurrection and Uprise
To the right hand of the throne—what is it beside,
When such truth, breaking bounds, o'erfloods my soul,
And, as I saw the sin and death, even so
See I the need yet transiency of both,
The good and glory consummated thence?
I saw the power; I see the Love, once weak,
Resume the Power: and in this word ' I see,'
Lo, there is recognised the Spirit of both
That moving o'er the spirit of man, unblinds
His eye and bids him look. These are, I see;
But ye, the children, His beloved ones too,
Ye need,—as I should use an optic glass

I wondered at erewhile, somewhere i' the world,
It had been given a crafty smith to make;
A tube, he turned on objects brought too close,
Lying confusedly insubordinate
For the unassisted eye to master once:
Look through his tube, at distance now they lay,
Become succinct, distinct, so small, so clear!
Just thus, ye needs must apprehend what truth
I see, reduced to plain historic fact,
Diminished into clearness, proved a point
And far away: ye would withdraw your sense
From out eternity, strain it upon time,
Then stand before that fact, that Life and Death
Stay there at gaze, till it dispart, dispread,
As though a star should open out, all sides,
Grow the world on you, as it is my world.

" For life, with all it yields of joy and woe,
And hope and fear,—believe the aged friend,—
Is just our chance o' the prize of learning love,
How love might be, hath been indeed, and is;
And that we hold thenceforth to the uttermost
Such prize despite the envy of the world,
And, having gained truth, keep truth: that is all.
But see the double way wherein we are led,
How the soul learns diversely from the flesh!
With flesh, that hath so little time to stay,
And yields mere basement for the soul's emprise,
Expect prompt teaching. Helpful was the light,
And warmth was cherishing and food was choice
To every man's flesh, thousand years ago,
As now to yours and mine; the body sprang
At once to the height, and stayed: but the soul,—no!
Since sages who, this noontide, meditate
In Rome or Athens, may descry some point
Of the eternal power, hid yestereve;
And, as thereby the power's whole mass extends,
So much extends the æther floating o'er,
The love that tops the might, the Christ in God.
Then, as new lessons shall be learned in these
Till earth's work stop and useless time run out,
So duly, daily, needs provision be
For keeping the soul's prowess possible,

Building new barriers as the old decay,
Saving us from evasion of life's proof,
Putting the question ever, ' Does God love,
And will ye hold that truth against the world ? '
Ye know there needs no second proof with good
Gained for our flesh from any earthly source:
We might go freezing, ages,—give us fire,
Thereafter we judge fire at its full worth,
And guard it safe through every chance, ye know!
That fable of Prometheus and his theft,
How mortals gained Jove's fiery flower, grows old
(I have been used to hear the pagans own)
And out of mind; but fire, howe'er its birth,
Here is it, precious to the sophist now
Who laughs the myth of Æschylus to scorn,
As precious to those satyrs of his play,
Who touched it in gay wonder at the thing.
While were it so with the soul,—this gift of truth
Once grasped, were this our soul's gain safe, and sure
To prosper as the body's gain is wont,—
Why, man's probation would conclude, his earth
Crumble; for he both reasons and decides,
Weighs first, then chooses: will he give up fire
For gold or purple once he knows its worth?
Could he give Christ up were His worth as plain?
Therefore, I say, to test man, the proofs shift,
Nor may he grasp that fact like other fact,
And straightway in his life acknowledge it,
As, say, the indubitable bliss of fire.
Sigh ye, ' It had been easier once than now ' ?
To give you answer I am left alive;
Look at me who was present from the first!
Ye know what things I saw; then came a test,
My first, befitting me who so had seen:
' Forsake the Christ thou sawest transfigured, Him
Who trod the sea and brought the dead to life?
What should wring this from thee ! '—ye laugh and ask.
What wrung it? Even a torchlight and a noise,
The sudden Roman faces, violent hands,
And fear of what the Jews might do! Just that,
And it is written, ' I forsook and fled ':
There was my trial, and it ended thus.
Ay, but my soul had gained its truth, could grow:

Another year or two,—what little child,
What tender woman that had seen no least
Of all my sights, but barely heard them told,
Who did not clasp the cross with a light laugh,
Or wrap the burning robe round, thanking God?
Well, was truth safe for ever, then? Not so.
Already had begun the silent work
Whereby truth, deadened of its absolute blaze,
Might need love's eye to pierce the o'erstretched doubt.
Teachers were busy, whispering ' All is true
As the aged ones report; but youth can reach
Where age gropes dimly, weak with stir and strain,
And the full doctrine slumbers till to-day.'
Thus, what the Roman's lowered spear was found,
A bar to me who touched and handled truth,
Now proved the glozing of some new shrewd tongue,
This Ebion, this Cerinthus or their mates,
Till imminent was the outcry ' Save our Christ! '
Whereon I stated much of the Lord's life
Forgotten or misdelivered, and let it work.
Such work done, as it will be, what comes next?
What do I hear say, or conceive men say,
' Was John at all, and did he say he saw?
Assure us, ere we ask what he might see! '

" Is this indeed a burthen for late days,
And may I help to bear it with you all,
Using my weakness which becomes your strength?
For if a babe were born inside this grot,
Grew to a boy here, heard us praise the sun,
Yet had but yon sole glimmer in light's place,—
One loving him and wishful he should learn,
Would much rejoice himself was blinded first
Month by month here, so made to understand
How eyes, born darkling, apprehend amiss:
I think I could explain to such a child
There was more glow outside than gleams he caught,
Ay, nor need urge ' I saw it, so believe! '
It is a heavy burthen you shall bear
In latter days, new lands, or old grown strange,
Left without me, which must be very soon.
What is the doubt, my brothers? Quick with it!
I see you stand conversing, each new face,

Either in fields, of yellow summer eves,
On islets yet unnamed amid the sea;
Or pace for shelter 'neath a portico
Out of the crowd in some enormous town
Where now the larks sing in a solitude;
Or muse upon blank heaps of stone and sand
Idly conjectured to be Ephesus:
And no one asks his fellow any more
' Where is the promise of His coming? ' but
' Was he revealed in any of His lives,
As Power, as Love, as Influencing Soul? '

" Quick, for time presses, tell the whole mind out,
And let us ask and answer and be saved!
My book speaks on, because it cannot pass;
One listens quietly, nor scoffs but pleads
' Here is a tale of things done ages since;
What truth was ever told the second day?
Wonders, that would prove doctrine, go for nought.
Remains the doctrine, love; well, we must love,
And what we love most, power and love in one,
Let us acknowledge on the record here,
Accepting these in Christ: must Christ then be?
Has He been? Did not we ourselves make Him?
Our mind receives but what it holds, no more.
First of the love, then; we acknowledge Christ—
A proof we comprehend His love, a proof
We had such love already in ourselves,
Knew first what else we should not recognise.
'Tis mere projection from man's inmost mind,
And, what he loves, thus falls reflected back,
Becomes accounted somewhat out of him;
He throws it up in air, it drops down earth's,
With shape, name, story added, man's old way.
How prove you Christ came otherwise at least?
Next try the power: He made and rules the world:
Certes there is a world once made, now ruled,
Unless things have been ever as we see.
Our sires declared a charioteer's yoked steeds
Brought the sun up the east and down the west,
Which only of itself now rises, sets,
As if a hand impelled it and a will,—
Thus they long thought, they who had will and hands:

But the new question's whisper is distinct,
Wherefore must all force needs be like ourselves?
We have the hands, the will; what made and drives
The sun is force, is law, is named, not known,
While will and love we do know; marks of these,
Eye-witnesses attest, so books declare—
As that, to punish or reward our race,
The sun at undue times arose or set
Or else stood still: what do not men affirm?
But earth requires as urgently reward
Or punishment to-day as years ago,
And none expects the sun will interpose:
Therefore it was mere passion and mistake,
Or erring zeal for right, which changed the truth.
Go back, far, farther, to the birth of things;
Ever the will, the intelligence, the love,
Man's!—which he gives, supposing he but finds,
As late he gave head, body, hands and feet,
To help these in what forms he called his gods.
First, Jove's brow, Juno's eyes were swept away
But Jove's wrath, Juno's pride continued long;
As last, will, power, and love discarded these,
So law in turn discards power, love, and will.
What proveth God is otherwise at least?
All else, projection from the mind of man!'

" Nay, do not give me wine, for I am strong,
But place my gospel where I put my hands.

" I say that man was made to grow, not stop;
That help, he needed once, and needs no more,
Having grown but an inch by, is withdrawn:
For he hath new needs, and new helps to these.
This imports solely, man should mount on each
New height in view; the help whereby he mounts,
The ladder-rung his foot has left, may fall,
Since all things suffer change save God the Truth.
Man apprehends Him newly at each stage
Whereat earth's ladder drops, its service done;
And nothing shall prove twice what once was proved.
You stick a garden-plot with ordered twigs
To show inside lie germs of herbs unborn,
And check the careless step would spoil their birth,

But when herbs wave, the guardian twigs may go,
Since should ye doubt of virtues, question kinds,
It is no longer for old twigs ye look,
Which proved once underneath lay store of seed,
But to the herb's self, by what light ye boast,
For what fruit's signs are. This book's fruit is plain,
Nor miracles need prove it any more.
Doth the fruit show? Then miracles bade 'ware
At first of root and stem, saved both till now
From trampling ox, rough boar and wanton goat.
What? Was man made a wheelwork to wind up,
And be discharged, and straight wound up anew?
No!—grown, his growth lasts; taught, he ne'er forgets:
May learn a thousand things, not twice the same.

" This might be pagan teaching: now hear mine.

" I say, that as the babe, you feed awhile,
Becomes a boy and fit to feed himself,
So, minds at first must be spoon-fed with truth:
When they can eat, babe's-nurture is withdrawn.
I fed the babe whether it would or no:
I bid the boy or feed himself or starve.
I cried once, ' That ye may believe in Christ,
Behold this blind man shall receive his sight! '
I cry now, ' Urgest thou, *for I am shrewd
And smile at stories how John's word could cure—
Repeat that miracle and take my faith ? '*
I say, that miracle was duly wrought
When, save for it, no faith was possible.
Whether a change were wrought i' the shows o' the world,
Whether the change came from our minds which see
Of shows o' the world so much as and no more
Than God wills for His purpose,—(what do I
See now, suppose you, there where you see rock
Round us?)—I know not; such was the effect,
So faith grew, making void more miracles
Because too much: they would compel, not help.
I say, the acknowledgment of God in Christ
Accepted by thy reason, solves for thee
All questions in the earth and out of it,
And has so far advanced thee to be wise.
Wouldst thou unprove this to re-prove the proved,

In life's mere minute, with power to use that proof,
Leave knowledge and revert to how it sprung?
Thou hast it: use it and forthwith, or die!

" For I say, this is death and the sole death,
When a man's loss comes to him from his gain,
Darkness from light, from knowledge ignorance,
And lack of love from love made manifest;
A lamp's death when, replete with oil, it chokes:
A stomach's when, surcharged with food, it starves.
With ignorance was surety of a cure.
When man, appalled at nature, questioned first
' What if there lurk a might behind this might? '
He needed satisfaction God could give,
And did give, as ye have the written word:
But when he finds might still redouble might,
Yet asks, ' Since all is might, what use of will? '
—Will, the one source of might,—he being man
With a man's will and a man's might, to teach
In little how the two combine in large,—
That man has turned round on himself and stands,
Which in the course of nature is, to die.

" And when man questioned, ' What if there be love
Behind the will and might, as real as they? '—
He needed satisfaction God could give,
And did give, as ye have the written word:
But when, beholding that love everywhere,
He reasons, ' Since such love is everywhere,
And since ourselves can love and would be loved,
We ourselves make the love, and Christ was not,'—
How shall ye help this man who knows himself,
That he must love and would be loved again,
Yet, owning his own love that proveth Christ,
Rejecteth Christ through very need of Him?
The lamp o'erswims with oil, the stomach flags
Loaded with nurture, and that man's soul dies.

" If he rejoin, ' But this was all the while
A trick; the fault was, first of all, in thee,
Thy story of the places, names and dates,
Where, when and how the ultimate truth had rise.
—Thy prior truth, at last discovered none,
Whence now the second suffers detriment.

What good of giving knowledge if, because
O' the manner of the gift, its profit fail?
And why refuse what modicum of help
Had stopped the after-doubt, impossible
I' the face of truth—truth absolute, uniform?
Why must I hit of this and miss of that,
Distinguish just as I be weak or strong,
And not ask of thee and have answer prompt,
Was this once, was it not once?—then and now
And evermore, plain truth from man to man.
Is John's procedure just the heathen bard's?
Put question of his famous play again
How for the ephemerals' sake Jove's fire was filched,
And carried in a cane and brought to earth;
The fact is in the fable, cry the wise,
Mortals obtained the boon, so much is fact,
Though fire be spirit and produced on earth.
As with the Titan's, so now with thy tale:
Why breed in us perplexity, mistake,
Nor tell the whole truth in the proper words?'

" I answer, Have ye yet to argue out
The very primal thesis, plainest law,
—Man is not God but hath God's end to serve,
A master to obey, a course to take,
Somewhat to cast off, somewhat to become?
Grant this, then man must pass from old to new,
From vain to real, from mistake to fact,
From what once seemed good, to what now proves best.
How could man have progression otherwise?
Before the point was mooted ' What is God?'
No savage man inquired ' What am myself?'
Much less replied, ' First, last, and best of things.'
Man takes that title now if he believes
Might can exist with neither will nor love,
In God's case—what he names now Nature's Law—
While in himself he recognises love
No less than might and will: and rightly takes.
Since if man prove the sole existent thing
Where these combine, whatever their degree,
However weak the might or will or love,
So they be found there, put in evidence,—
He is as surely higher in the scale

Than any might with neither love nor will,
As life, apparent in the poorest midge,
(When the faint dust-speck flits, ye guess its wing)
Is marvellous beyond dead Atlas' self—
Given to the nobler midge for resting-place!
Thus, man proves best and highest—God, in fine,
And thus the victory leads but to defeat,
The gain to loss, best rise to the worst fall,
His life becomes impossible, which is death.

" But if, appealing thence, he cower, avouch
He is mere man, and in humility
Neither may know God nor mistake himself;
I point to the immediate consequence
And say, by such confession straight he falls
Into man's place, a thing nor God nor beast,
Made to know that he can know and not more:
Lower than God who knows all and can all,
Higher than beasts which know and can so far
As each beast's limit, perfect to an end,
Nor conscious that they know, nor craving more;
While man knows partly but conceives beside,
Creeps ever on from fancies to the fact,
And in this striving, this converting air
Into a solid he may grasp and use,
Finds progress, man's distinctive mark alone,
Not God's, and not the beasts': God is, they are,
Man partly is and wholly hopes to be.
Such progress could not more attend his soul
Were all it struggles after found at first
And guesses changed to knowledge absolute,
Than motion wait his body, were all else
Than it the solid earth on every side,
Where now through space he moves from rest to rest.
Man, therefore, thus conditioned, must expect
He could not, what he knows now, know at first;
What he considers that he knows to-day,
Come but to-morrow, he will find misknown;
Getting increase of knowledge, since he leans
Because he lives, which is to be a man,
Set to instruct himself by his past self:
First, like the brute, obliged by facts to learn,
Next, as man may, obliged by his own mind,

Bent, habit, nature, knowledge turned to law.
God's gift was that man should conceive of truth
And yearn to gain it, catching at mistake,
As midway help till he reach fact indeed.
The statuary ere he mould a shape
Boasts a like gift, the shape's idea, and next
The aspiration to produce the same;
So, taking clay, he calls his shape thereout,
Cries ever ' Now I have the thing I see ':
Yet all the while goes changing what was wrought,
From falsehood like the truth, to truth itself.
How were it had he cried ' I see no face,
No breast, no feet i' the ineffectual clay ' ?
Rather commend him that he clapped his hands,
And laughed ' It is my shape and lives again! '
Enjoyed the falsehood, touched it on to truth,
Until yourselves applaud the flesh indeed
In what is still flesh-imitating clay.
Right in you, right in him, such way be man's!
God only makes the live shape at a jet.
Will ye renounce this pact of creatureship?
The pattern on the Mount subsists no more,
Seemed awhile, then returned to nothingness;
But copies, Moses strove to make thereby,
Serve still and are replaced as time requires:
By these, make newest vessels, reach the type!
If ye demur, this judgment on your head,
Never to reach the ultimate, angels' law,
Indulging every instinct of the soul
There where law, life, joy, impulse are one thing!

" Such is the burthen of the latest time.
I have survived to hear it with my ears,
Answer it with my lips: does this suffice?
For if there be a further woe than such,
Wherein my brothers struggling need a hand,
So long as any pulse is left in mine,
May I be absent even longer yet,
Plucking the blind ones back from the abyss,
Though I should tarry a new hundred years! "

But he was dead; 'twas about noon, the day
Somewhat declining: we five buried him

That eve, and then, dividing, went five ways,
And I, disguised, returned to Ephesus.

By this, the cave's mouth must be filled with sand.
Valens is lost, I know not of his trace;
The Bactrian was but a wild childish man,
And could not write nor speak, but only loved:
So, lest the memory of this go quite,
Seeing that I to-morrow fight the beasts,
I tell the same to Phœbas, whom believe.
For many look again to find that face,
Beloved John's to whom I ministered,
Somewhere in life about the world; they err:
Either mistaking what was darkly spoke
At ending of his book, as he relates,
Or misconceiving somewhat of this speech
Scattered from mouth to mouth, as I suppose.
Believe ye will not see him any more
About the world with his divine regard!
For all was as I say, and now the man
Lies as he lay once, breast to breast with God.

———

[Cerinthus read and mused; one added this:

" If Christ, as thou affirmest, be of men
Mere man, the first and best but nothing more,—
Account Him, for reward of what He was,
Now and for ever, wretchedest of all.
For see; Himself conceived of life as love,
Conceived of love as what must enter in,
Fill up, make one with His each soul He loved:
Thus much for man's joy, all men's joy for Him.
Well, He is gone, thou sayest, to fit reward.
But by this time are many souls set free,
And very many still retained alive:
Nay, should His coming be delayed awhile,
Say, ten years longer (twelve years, some compute)
See if, for every finger of thy hands,
There be not found, that day the world shall end,
Hundreds of souls, each holding by Christ's word
That He will grow incorporate with all,
With me as Pamphylax, with him as John,

Groom for each bride! Can a mere man do this?
Yet Christ saith, this He lived and died to do.
Call Christ, then, the illimitable God,
Or lost!"

              But 'twas Cerinthus that is lost.]

                    ROBERT BROWNING.

THE SCHOLAR GIPSY

Go, for they call you, shepherd, from the hill;
  Go, shepherd, and untie the wattled cotes!
    No longer leave thy wistful flock unfed,
  Nor let thy bawling fellows rack their throats,
    Nor the cropp'd grasses shoot another head.
      But when the fields are still,
  And the tired men and dogs all gone to rest,
    And only the white sheep are sometimes seen
    Cross and recross the strips of moon-blanch'd green,
Come, shepherd, and again renew the quest!

Here, where the reaper was at work of late—
  In this high field's dark corner, where he leaves
    His coat, his basket, and his earthen cruse,
  And in the sun all morning binds the sheaves,
    Then here, at noon, comes back his stores to use—
      Here will I sit and wait,
  While to my ear from uplands far away
    The bleating of the folded flocks is borne,
    With distant cries of reapers in the corn—
All the live murmur of a summer's day.

Screen'd is this nook o'er the high, half-reap'd field,
  And here till sun-down, shepherd! will I be.
    Through the thick corn the scarlet poppies peep,
  And round green roots and yellowing stalks I see
    Pale pink convolvulus in tendrils creep;
      And air-swept lindens yield
  Their scent, and rustle down their perfumed showers
    Of bloom on the bent grass where I am laid,
    And bower me from the August sun with shade;
And the eye travels down to Oxford's towers.

And near me on the grass lies Glanvil's book—
  Come, let me read the oft-read tale again!
  The story of that Oxford scholar poor,
Of pregnant parts and quick inventive brain,
  Who, tired of knocking at preferment's door,
    One summer-morn forsook
His friends, and went to learn the gipsy-lore,
  And roam'd the world with that wild brotherhood,
  And came, as most men deem'd, to little good,
But came to Oxford and his friends no more.

But once, years after, in the country-lanes,
  Two scholars, whom at college erst he knew,
  Met him, and of his way of life enquired;
Whereat he answer'd, that the gipsy-crew,
  His mates, had arts to rule as they desired
    The workings of men's brains,
And they can bind them to what thoughts they will.
  " And I," he said, " the secret of their art,
  When fully learn'd, will to the world impart;
But it needs heaven-sent moments for this skill."

This said, he left them, and return'd no more.—
  But rumours hung about the country-side,
  That the lost Scholar long was seen to stray,
Seen by rare glimpses, pensive and tongue-tied,
  In hat of antique shape, and cloak of grey,
    The same the gipsies wore.
Shepherds had met him on the Hurst in spring;
  At some lone alehouse in the Berkshire moors,
  On the warm ingle-bench, the smock-frock'd boors
Had found him seated at their entering.

But, 'mid their drink and clatter, he would fly.
  And I myself seem half to know thy looks,
  And put the shepherds, wanderer! on thy trace;
And boys who in lone wheatfields scare the rooks
  I ask if thou hast pass'd their quiet place;
    Or in my boat I lie
Moor'd to the cool bank in the summer-heats,
  'Mid wide grass meadows which the sunshine fills,
  And watch the warm, green-muffled Cumner hills,
And wonder if thou haunt'st their shy retreats.

For most, I know, thou lov'st retired ground!
  Thee at the ferry Oxford riders blithe,
    Returning home in summer-nights, have met
  Crossing the stripling Thames at Bab-lock-hithe,
    Trailing in the cool stream thy fingers wet,
      As the slow punt swings round;
  And leaning backward in a pensive dream,
    And fostering in thy lap a heap of flowers
    Pluck'd in shy fields and distant Wychwood bowers,
  And thine eyes resting on the moonlit stream,

And then they land, and thou art seen no more!—
  Maidens, who from the distant hamlets come
    To dance around the Fyfield elm in May,
  Oft through the darkening fields have seen thee roam,
    Or cross a stile into the public way.
      Oft thou hast given them store
  Of flowers—the frail-leaf'd, white anemone,
    Dark bluebells drench'd with dews of summer eves,
    And purple orchises with spotted leaves—
  But none has words she can report of thee.

And, above Godstow Bridge, when hay-time's here
  In June, and many a scythe in sunshine flames,
    Men who through those wide fields of breezy grass
  Where black-wing'd swallows haunt the glittering Thames
    To bathe in the abandon'd lasher pass,
      Have often pass'd thee near
  Sitting upon the river bank o'ergrown;
    Mark'd thine outlandish garb, thy figure spare,
    Thy dark vague eyes, and soft abstracted air—
  But, when they came from bathing, thou wert gone!

At some lone homestead in the Cumner hills,
  Where at her open door the housewife darns,
    Thou hast been seen, or hanging on a gate
  To watch the threshers in the mossy barns.
    Children who early range these slopes and late
      For cresses from the rills,
  Have known thee watching, all an April-day,
    The springing pastures and the feeding kine;
    And mark'd thee, when the stars come out and shine,
  Through the long dewy grass move slow away.

In autumn, on the skirts of Bagley Wood—
  Where most the gipsies by the turf-edged way
    Pitch their smoked tents, and every bush you see
  With scarlet patches tagg'd and shreds of grey,
    Above the forest-ground called Thessaly—
      The blackbird, picking food,
  Sees thee, nor stops his meal, nor fears at all;
    So often has he known thee past him stray,
    Rapt, twirling in thy hand a wither'd spray,
  And waiting for the spark from heaven to fall.

And once, in winter, on the causeway chill
  Where home through flooded fields foot-travellers go,
    Have I not pass'd thee on the wooden bridge,
  Wrapt in thy cloak and battling with the snow,
    Thy face tow'rd Hinksey and its wintry ridge?
      And thou hast climb'd the hill,
  And gain'd the white brow of the Cumner range;
    Turn'd once to watch, while thick the snowflakes fall,
    The line of festal light in Christ-Church hall—
  Then sought thy straw in some sequester'd grange.

But what—I dream! Two hundred years are flown
  Since first thy story ran through Oxford halls,
    And the grave Glanvil did the tale inscribe
  That thou wert wander'd from the studious walls
    To learn strange arts, and join a gipsy-tribe;
      And thou from earth art gone
  Long since, and in some quiet churchyard laid—
    Some country-nook, where o'er thy unknown grave
    Tall grasses and white flowering nettles wave,
  Under a dark, red-fruited yew-tree's shade.

—No, no, thou hast not felt the lapse of hours!
  For what wears out the life of mortal men?
    'Tis that from change to change their being rolls;
  'Tis that repeated shocks, again, again,
    Exhaust the energy of strongest souls
      And numb the elastic powers,
  Till having used our nerves with bliss and teen,
    And tired upon a thousand schemes our wit,
    To the just-pausing Genius we remit
  Our worn-out life, and are—what we have been.

Thou hast not lived, why should'st thou perish, so?
  Thou hadst *one* aim, *one* business, *one* desire;
    Else wert thou long since numbered with the dead!
  Else hadst thou spent, like other men, thy fire!
    The generations of thy peers are fled,
      And we ourselves shall go;
  But thou possessest an immortal lot,
    And we imagine thee exempt from age
    And living as thou liv'st on Glanvil's page,
  Because thou hadst—what we, alas! have not.

For early didst thou leave the world, with powers
  Fresh, undiverted to the world without,
    Firm to their mark, not spent on other things;
  Free from the sick fatigue, the languid doubt,
    Which much to have tried, in much been baffled, brings.
      O life unlike to ours!
  Who fluctuate idly without term or scope,
    Of whom each strives, nor knows for what he strives,
    And each half lives a hundred different lives;
  Who wait like thee, but not, like thee, in hope.

Thou waitest for the spark from heaven! and we,
  Light half-believers of our casual creeds,
    Who never deeply felt, nor clearly will'd,
  Whose insight never has borne fruit in deeds,
    Whose vague resolves never have been fulfill'd;
      For whom each year we see
  Breeds new beginnings, disappointments new;
    Who hesitate and falter life away,
    And lose to-morrow the ground won to-day—
  Ah! do not we, wanderer! await it too?

Yes, we await it!—but it still delays,
  And then we suffer! and amongst us one,
    Who most has suffer'd, takes dejectedly
  His seat upon the intellectual throne; .
    And all his store of sad experience he
      Lays bare of wretched days;
  Tells us his misery's birth and growth and signs,
    And how the dying spark of hope was fed,
    And how the breast was soothed, and how the head,
  And all his hourly varied anodynes.

This for our wisest! and we others pine,
  And wish the long unhappy dream would end,
    And waive all claim to bliss, and try to bear;
  With close-lipp'd patience for our only friend
    Sad patience, too near neighbour to despair—
      But none has hope like thine!
  Thou through the fields and through the woods dost stray,
    Roaming the country-side, a truant boy,
    Nursing thy project in unclouded joy,
  And every doubt long blown by time away.

O born in days when wits were fresh and clear,
  And life ran gaily as the sparkling Thames;
    Before this strange disease of modern life,
  With its sick hurry, its divided aims,
    Its heads o'ertaxed, its palsied hearts, was rife—
      Fly hence, our contact fear!
  Still fly, plunge deeper in the bowering wood!
    Averse, as Dido did with gesture stern
    From her false friend's approach in Hades turn,
  Wave us away, and keep thy solitude!

Still nursing the unconquerable hope,
  Still clutching the inviolable shade,
    With a free, onward impulse brushing through,
  By night, the silver'd branches of the glade—
    Far on the forest-skirts, where none pursue,
      On some mild pastoral slope
  Emerge, and resting on the moonlit pales
    Freshen thy flowers as in former years
    With dew, or listen with enchanted ears,
  From the dark dingles, to the nightingales!

But fly our paths, our feverish contact fly!
  For strong the infection of our mental strife,
    Which, though it gives no bliss, yet spoils for rest;
  And we should win thee from thy own fair life,
    Like us distracted, and like us unblest.
      Soon, soon thy cheer would die,
  Thy hopes grow timorous, and unfix'd thy powers,
    And thy clear aims be cross and shifting made;
    And then thy glad perennial youth would fade,
  Fade, and grow old at last, and die like ours.

Then fly our greetings, fly our speech and smiles!
  —As some grave Tyrian trader, from the sea,
    Descried at sunrise an emerging prow
  Lifting the cool-hair'd creepers stealthily,
    The fringes of a southward-facing brow
      Among the Ægæan isles;
And saw the merry Grecian coaster come,
    Freighted with amber grapes, and Chian wine,
    Green, bursting figs, and tunnies steep'd in brine—
And knew the intruders on his ancient home,

The young light-hearted masters of the waves—
    And snatch'd his rudder, and shook out more sail;
    And day and night held on indignantly
  O'er the blue Midland waters with the gale,
    Betwixt the Syrtes and soft Sicily,
      To where the Atlantic raves
Outside the western straits; and unbent sails
    There, where down cloudy cliffs, through sheets of foam,
    Shy traffickers, the dark Iberians come;
And on the beach undid his corded bales.

MATTHEW ARNOLD.

GOBLIN MARKET

MORNING and evening
Maids heard the goblins cry:
" Come buy our orchard fruits,
Come buy, come buy:
Apples and quinces,
Lemons and oranges,
Plump unpecked cherries,
Melons and raspberries,
Bloom-down-cheeked peaches,
Swart-headed mulberries,
Wild free-born cranberries,
Crab-apples, dewberries,
Pine-apples, blackberries,
Apricots, strawberries;—
All ripe together

In summer weather,—
Morns that pass by,
Fair eves that fly;
Come buy, come buy:
Our grapes fresh from the vine,
Pomegranates full and fine,
Dates and sharp bullaces,
Rare pears and greengages,
Damsons and bilberries,
Taste them and try:
Currants and gooseberries,
Bright-fire-like barberries,
Figs to fill your mouth,
Citrons from the South,
Sweet to tongue and sound to eye;
Come buy, come buy."

Evening by evening
Among the brookside rushes,
Laura bowed her head to hear,
Lizzie veiled her blushes:
Crouching close together
In the cooling weather,
With clasping arms and cautioning lips,
With tingling cheeks and finger tips.
" Lie close," Laura said,
Pricking up her golden head:
" We must not look at goblin men,
We must not buy their fruits:
" Who knows upon what soil they fed
Their hungry thirsty roots? "
" Come buy," call the goblins
Hobbling down the glen.
" Oh," cried Lizzie, "Laura, Laura,
You should not peep at goblin men."
Lizzie covered up her eyes,
Covered close lest they should look;
Laura reared her glossy head,
And whispered like the restless brook:
" Look Lizzie, look Lizzie,
Down the glen tramp little men.
One hauls a basket,
One bears a plate,

One lugs a golden dish
Of many pounds weight.
How fair the vine must grow
Whose grapes are so luscious;
How warm the wind must blow
Through those fruit bushes."
" No," said Lizzie; " No, no, no;
Their offers should not charm us,
Their evil gifts would harm us."
She thrust a dimpled finger
In each ear, shut eyes and ran:
Curious Laura chose to linger
Wondering at each merchant man.
One had a cat's face,
One whisked a tail,
One tramped at a rat's pace,
One crawled like a snail,
One like a wombat prowled obtuse and furry,
One like a ratel tumbled hurry skurry.
She heard a voice like voice of doves
Cooing all together:
They sounded kind and full of loves
In the pleasant weather.

Laura stretched her gleaming neck
Like a rush-embedded swan,
Like a lily from the þeck,
Like a moonlit poplar branch,
Like a vessel at the launch
When its last restraint is gone.

Backwards up the mossy glen
Turned and trooped the goblin men,
With their shrill repeated cry,
" Come buy, come buy."
When they reached where Laura was
They stood stock still upon the moss,
Leering at each other,
Brother with queer brother;
Signalling each other,
Brother with sly brother.

One set his basket down,
One reared his plate;
One began to weave a crown,
Of tendrils, leaves and rough nuts brown
(Men sell not such in any town);
One heaved the golden weight
Of dish and fruit to offer her:
" Come buy, come buy," was still their cry.
Laura stared but did not stir,
Longed but had no money:
The whisk-tailed merchant bade her taste
In tones as smooth as honey,
The cat-faced purr'd,
The rat-paced spoke a word
Of welcome, and the snail-paced even was heard;
One parrot-voiced and jolly
Cried " Pretty Goblin " still for " Pretty Polly ";—
One whistled like a bird.

But sweet-tooth Laura spoke in haste:
" Good folk, I have no coin;
To take were to purloin:
I have no copper in my purse,
I have no silver either,
And all my gold is on the furze
That shakes in windy weather
Above the rusty heather."
" You have much gold upon your head,"
They answered all together:
" Buy from us with a golden curl."
She clipped a precious golden lock,
She dropped a tear more rare than pearl,
Then sucked their fruit globes fair or red:
Sweeter than honey from the rock,
Stronger than man-rejoicing wine,
Clearer than water flowed that juice;
She never tasted such before,
How could it cloy with length of use?
She sucked and sucked and sucked the more
Fruits which that unknown orchard bore;
She sucked until her lips were sore;
Then flung the empty rinds away

But gathered up one kernel-stone,
And knew not was it night or day
As she turned home alone.

Lizzie met her at the gate
Full of wise upbraidings:
" Dear, you should not stay so late,
Twilight is not good for maidens;
Should not loiter in the glen
In the haunts of goblin men.
Do you not remember Jeanie,
How she met them in the moonlight,
Took their gifts both choice and many,
Ate their fruits and wore their flowers
Plucked from bowers
Where summer ripens at all hours?
But ever in the noonlight
She pined and pined away;
Sought them by night and day,
Found them no more but dwindled and grew grey;
Then fell with the first snow,
While to this day no grass will grow
Where she lies low:
I planted daisies there a year ago
That never blow.
You should not loiter so."
" Nay, hush," said Laura:
" Nay, hush, my sister:
I ate and ate my fill,
Yet my mouth waters still;
To-morrow night I will buy more ": and kissed her:
" Have done with sorrow;
I'll bring you plums to-morrow
Fresh on their mother twigs,
Cherries worth getting;
You cannot think what figs
My teeth have met in,
What melons icy-cold
Piled on a dish of gold
Too huge for me to hold,
What peaches with a velvet nap,
Pellucid grapes without one seed:
Odorous indeed must be the mead

Whereon they grow, and pure the wave they drink
  With lilies at the brink,
  And sugar-sweet their sap."

  Golden head by golden head,
Like two pigeons in one nest
Folded in each other's wings,
They lay down in their curtained bed:
Like two blossoms on one stem,
Like two flakes of new-fall'n snow,
Like two wands of ivory
Tipped with gold for awful kings.
Moon and stars gazed in at them,
Wind sang to them lullaby,
Lumbering owls forbore to fly,
Not a bat flapped to and fro
Round their rest:
Cheek to cheek and breast to breast
Locked together in one nest.

  Early in the morning
When the first cock crowed his warning,
Neat like bees, as sweet and busy,
Laura rose with Lizzie:
Fetched in honey, milked the cows,
Aired and set to rights the house,
Kneaded cakes of whitest wheat,
Cakes for dainty mouths to eat,
Next churned butter, whipped up cream,
Fed their poultry, sat and sewed;
Talked as modest maidens should:
Lizzie with an open heart,
Laura in an absent dream,
One content, one sick in part;
One warbling for the mere bright day's delight,
One longing for the night.

  At length slow evening came:
They went with pitchers to the reedy brook;
Lizzie most placid in her look,
Laura most like a leaping flame.
They drew the gurgling water from its deep;
Lizzie plucked purple and rich golden flags,
Then turning homewards said: " The sunset flushes

Those furthest loftiest crags;
Come, Laura, not another maiden lags,
No wilful squirrel wags,
The beasts and birds are fast asleep."
But Laura loitered still among the rushes
And said the bank was steep.

And said the hour was early still,
The dew not fall'n, the wind not chill:
Listening ever, but not catching
The customary cry,
" Come buy, come buy,"
With its iterated jingle
Of sugar-baited words:
Not for all her watching
Once discerning even one goblin
Raving, whisking, tumbling, hobbling;
Let alone the herds
That used to tramp along the glen,
In groups or single,
Of brisk fruit-merchant men.

Till Lizzie urged, " O Laura, come;
I hear the fruit-call but I dare not look:
You should not loiter longer at this brook:
Come with me home.
The stars rise, the moon bends her arc,
Each glowworm winks her spark,
Let us get home before the night grows dark:
For clouds may gather
Though this is summer weather,
Put out the lights and drench us through;
Then if we lost our way what should we do ? "

Laura turned cold as stone
To find her sister heard that cry alone,
That goblin cry,
" Come buy our fruits, come buy."
Must she then buy no more such dainty fruits ?
Most she no more that succous pasture find,
Gone deaf and blind ?
Her tree of life drooped from the root:
She said not one word in her heart's sore ache;

But peering thro' the dimness, nought discerning,
Trudged home, her pitcher dripping all the way;
So crept to bed, and lay
Silent till Lizzie slept;
Then sat up in a passionate yearning,
And gnashed her teeth for baulked desire, and wept
As if her heart would break.

Day after day, night after night,
Laura kept watch in vain
In sullen silence of exceeding pain.
She never caught again the goblin cry:
" Come buy, come buy ";—
She never spied the goblin men
Hawking their fruits along the glen:
But when the moon waxed bright
Her hair grew thin and grey;
She dwindled, as the fair full moon doth turn
To swift decay and burn
Her fire away.

One day remembering her kernel-stone
She set it by a wall that faced the south;
Dewed it with tears, hoped for a root,
Watched for a waxing shoot,
But there came none;
It never saw the sun,
It never felt the trickling moisture run:
While with sunk eyes and faded mouth
She dreamed of melons, as a traveller sees
False waves in desert drouth
With shade of leaf-crowned trees,
And burns the thirstier in the sandful breeze.

She no more swept the house,
Tended the fowls or cows,
Fetched honey, kneaded cakes of wheat,
Brought water from the brook:
But sat down listless in the chimney-nook
And would not eat.

Tender Lizzie could not bear
To watch her sister's cankerous care
Yet not to share.

She night and morning
Caught the goblins' cry:
" Come buy our orchard fruits,
Come buy, come buy: "—
Beside the brook, along the glen,
She heard the tramp of goblin men,
The voice and stir
Poor Laura could not hear;
Longed to buy fruit to comfort her,
But feared to pay too dear.
She thought of Jeanie in her grave,
Who should have been a bride;
But who for joys brides hope to have
Fell sick and died
In her gay prime,
In earliest Winter time,
With the first glazing rime,
With the first snow-fall of crisp Winter time.

Till Laura dwindling
Seemed knocking at Death's door:
Then Lizzie weighed no more
Better and worse;
But put a silver penny in her purse,
Kissed Laura, crossed the heath with clumps of furze
At twilight, halted by the brook:
And for the first time in her life
Began to listen and look.

Laughed every goblin
When they spied her peeping:
Come towards her hobbling,
Flying, running, leaping,
Puffing and blowing,
Chuckling, clapping, crowing,
Clucking and gobbling,
Mopping and mowing,
Full of airs and graces,
Pulling wry faces,
Demure grimaces,
Cat-like and rat-like,
Ratel- and wombat-like,
Snail-paced in a hurry,

Parrot-voiced and whistler,
Helter skelter, hurry skurry,
Chattering like magpies,
Fluttering like pigeons,
Gliding like fishes,—
Hugged her and kissed her,
Squeezed and caressed her:
Stretched up their dishes,
Panniers and plates:
" Look at our apples
Russet and dun,
Bob at our cherries,
Bite at our peaches,
Citrons and dates,
Grapes for the asking,
Pears red with basking
Out in the sun,
Plums on their twigs;
Pluck them and suck them,
Pomegranates, figs."—

" Good folk," said Lizzie,
Mindful of Jeanie:
" Give me much and many ":—
Held out her apron,
Tossed them her penny.
" Nay, take a seat with us,
Honour and eat with us; "
They answered grinning:
" Our feast is but beginning.
Night is yet early,
Warm and dew-pearly,
Wakeful and starry:
Such fruits as these
No man can carry;
Half their bloom would fly,
Half their dew would dry,
Half their flavour would pass by.
Sit down and feast with us,
Be welcome guest with us,
Cheer you and rest with us."—
" Thank you," said Lizzie: " But one waits
At home alone for me:

So without further parleying,
If you will not sell me any
Of your fruits though much and many,
Give me back my silver penny
I tossed you for a fee."—
They began to scratch their pates,
No longer wagging, purring,
But visibly demurring,
Grunting and snarling.
One called her proud,
Cross-grained, uncivil;
Their tones waxed loud,
Their looks were evil.
Lashing their tails
They trod and hustled her,
Elbowed and jostled her,
Clawed with their nails,
Barking, mewing, hissing, mocking,
Tore her gown and soiled her stockings,
Twitched her hair out by the roots,
Stamped upon her tender feet,
Held her hands and squeezed their fruits
Against her mouth to make her eat.

White and golden Lizzie stood,
Like a lily in a flood,—
Like a rock of blue-veined stone
Lashed by tides obstreperously,—
Like a beacon left alone
In a hoary roaring sea,
Sending up a golden fire,—
Like a fruit-crowned orange-tree
White with blossoms honey-sweet
Sore beset by wasp and bee,—
Like a royal virgin town
Topped with gilded dome and spire
Close beleaguered by a fleet
Mad to tug her standard down.

One may lead a horse to water,
Twenty cannot make him drink.
Though the goblins cuffed and caught her,
Coaxed and fought her,

Bullied and besought her,
Scratched her, pinched her black as ink,
Kicked and knocked her,
Mauled and mocked her,
Lizzie uttered not a word;
Would not open lip from lip
Lest they should cram a mouthful in:
But laughed in heart to feel the drip
Of juice that syrupped all her face,
And lodged in dimples of her chin,
And streaked her neck which quaked like curd.
At last the evil people
Worn out by her resistance
Flung back her penny, kicked their fruit
Along whichever road they took,
Not leaving root or stone or shoot;
Some writhed into the ground,
Some dived into the brook
With ring and ripple,
Some scudded on the gale without a sound,
Some vanished in the distance.

In a smart, ache, tingle,
Lizzie went her way:
Knew not was it night or day;
Sprang up the bank, tore thro' the furze,
Threaded copse and dingle,
And heard her penny jingle
Bouncing in her purse,—
Its bounce was music to her ear.
She ran and ran
As if she feared some goblin man
Dogged her with gibe or curse
Or something worse:
But not one goblin scurried after,
Nor was she pricked by fear;
The kind heart made her windy-paced
That urged her home quite out of breath with haste
And inward laughter.

She cried " Laura," up the garden,
" Did you miss me?
Come and kiss me.

Never mind my bruises,
Hug me, kiss me, suck my juices
Squeezed from goblin fruits for you,
Goblin pulp and goblin dew.
Eat me, drink me, love me;
Laura, make much of me:
For your sake I have braved the glen
And had to do with goblin merchant men."

Laura started from her chair,
Flung her arms up in the air,
Clutched her hair:
" Lizzie, Lizzie, have you tasted
For my sake the fruit forbidden ?
Must your light like mine be hidden,
Your young life like mine be wasted,
Undone in mine undoing
And ruined in my ruin,
Thirsty, cankered, goblin-ridden ? "—
She clung about her sister,
Kissed and kissed and kissed her:
Tears once again
Refreshed her sunken eyes,
Dropping like rain
After long sultry drouth;
Shaking with aguish fear, and pain,
She kissed and kissed her with a hungry mouth.

Her lips began to scorch,
That juice was wormwood to her tongue,
She loathed the feast:
Writhing as one possessed she leaped and sung,
Rent all her robe, and wrung
Her hands in lamentable haste,
And beat her breast.
Her locks streamed like the torch
Borne by a racer at full speed,
Or like the mane of horses in their flight,
Or like an eagle when he stems the light
Straight toward the sun,
Or like a caged thing freed,
Or like a flying flag when armies run.

Swift fire spread through her veins, knocked at her heart,
Met the fire smouldering there
And overbore its lesser flame;
She gorged on bitterness without a name:
Ah! fool, to choose such part
Of soul-consuming care!
Sense failed in the mortal strife:
Like the watch-tower of a town
Which an earthquake shatters down,
Like a lightning-stricken mast,
Like a wind-uprooted tree
Spun about,
Like a foam-topped waterspout
Cast down headlong in the sea,
She fell at last;
Pleasure past and anguish past,
Is it death or is it life?

Life out of death.
That night long Lizzie watched by her,
Counted her pulse's flagging stir,
Felt for her breath,
Held water to her lips, and cooled her face
With tears and fanning leaves:
But when the first birds chirped about their eaves,
And early reapers plodded to the place
Of golden sheaves,
And dew-wet grass
Bowed in the morning winds so brisk to pass,
And new buds with new day
Opened of cup-like lilies on the stream,
Laura awoke as from a dream,
Laughed in the innocent old way,
Hugged Lizzie but not twice or thrice;
Her gleaming locks showed not one thread of grey,
Her breath was sweet as May
And light danced in her eyes.

Days, weeks, months, years,
Afterwards, when both were wives
With children of their own;
Their mother-hearts beset with fears,
Their lives bound up in tender lives;

Laura would call the little ones
And tell them of her early prime,
Those pleasant days long gone
Of not-returning time:
Would talk about the haunted glen,
The wicked, quaint fruit-merchant men,
Their fruits like honey to the throat
But poison in the blood;
(Men sell not such in any town:)
Would tell them how her sister stood
In deadly peril to do her good,
And win the fiery antidote:
Then joining hands to little hands
Would bid them cling together,
" For there is no friend like a sister
In calm or stormy weather;
To cheer one on the tedious way,
To fetch one if one goes astray,
To lift one if one totters down,
To strengthen whilst one stands."

CHRISTINA ROSSETTI.

THE BLESSED DAMOZEL

THE blessed Damozel lean'd out
    From the gold bar of Heaven:
Her blue grave eyes were deeper much
    Than a deep water, even.
She had three lilies in her hand,
    And the stars in her hair were seven.

Her robe, ungirt from clasp to hem,
    No wrought flowers did adorn,
But a white rose of Mary's gift
    On the neck meetly worn;
And her hair, lying down her back,
    Was yellow like ripe corn.

Herseem'd she scarce had been a day
    One of God's choristers;
The wonder was not yet quite gone
    From that still look of hers;

Albeit, to them she left, her day
  Had counted as ten years.

(To *one* it is ten years of years:
  . . . Yet now, here in this place,
Surely she lean'd o'er me,—her hair
  Fell all about my face. . . .
Nothing: the Autumn-fall of leaves.
  The whole year sets apace.)

It was the terrace of God's house
  That she was standing on,—
By God built over the sheer depth
  In which Space is begun;
So high, that looking downward thence,
  She scarce could see the sun.

It lies from Heaven across the flood
  Of ether, as a bridge.
Beneath, the tides of day and night
  With flame and darkness ridge
The void, as low as where this earth
  Spins like a fretful midge.

But in those tracts, with her, it was
  The peace of utter light
And silence. For no breeze may stir
  Along the steady flight
Of seraphim; no echo there,
  Beyond all depth or height.

Heard hardly, some of her new friends,
  Playing at holy games,
Spake, gentle-mouth'd, among themselves,
  Their virginal chaste names;
And the souls, mounting up to God,
  Went by her like thin flames.

And still she bow'd herself, and stoop'd
  Into the vast waste calm;
Till her bosom's pressure must have made
  The bar she lean'd on warm,
And the lilies lay as if asleep
  Along her bended arm.

From the fixt lull of Heaven, she saw
  Time, like a pulse, shake fierce
Through all the worlds. Her gaze still strove,
  In that steep gulf, to pierce
The swarm; and then she spoke, as when
  The stars sang in their spheres.

" I wish that he were come to me,
  For he will come," she said.
" Have I not pray'd in solemn Heaven?
  On earth has he not pray'd?
Are not two prayers a perfect strength?
  And shall I feel afraid?

" When round his head the aureole clings,
  And he is clothed in white,
I'll take his hand, and go with him
  To the deep wells of light,
And we will step down as to a stream
  And bathe there in God's sight.

" We two will stand beside that shrine,
  Occult, withheld, untrod,
Whose lamps tremble continually
  With prayer sent up to God;
And where each need, reveal'd, expects
  Its patient period.

" We two will lie i' the shadow of
  That living mystic tree
Within whose secret growth the Dove
  Sometimes is felt to be,
While every leaf that His plumes touch
  Saith his name audibly.

" And I myself will teach to him,—
  I myself, lying so,—
The songs I sing here; which his mouth
  Shall pause in, hush'd and slow,
Finding some knowledge at each pause,
  And some new thing to know."

(Alas! to *her* wise simple mind
    These things were all but known
Before: they trembled on her sense,—
    Her voice had caught their tone.
Alas, for lonely Heaven! Alas,
    For life wrung out alone!

Alas, and though the end were reach'd? . . .
    Was *thy* part understood
Or borne in trust? And for her sake
    Shall this too be found good?—
May the close lips that knew not prayer
    Praise ever, though they would?)

" We two," she said, " will seek the groves
    Where the lady Mary is,
With her five handmaidens, whose names
    Are five sweet symphonies:—
Cecily, Gertrude, Magdalen,
    Margaret and Rosalys.

" Circle-wise sit they, with bound locks
    And bosoms covered:
Into the fine cloth, white like flame,
    Weaving the golden thread,
To fashion the birth-robes for them
    Who are just born, being dead.

" He shall fear haply, and be dumb.
    Then I will lay my cheek
To his, and tell about our love,
    Not once abash'd or weak:
And the dear Mother will approve
    My pride, and let me speak.

" Herself shall bring us, hand in hand,
    To Him round whom all souls
Kneel—the unnumber'd solemn heads
    Bow'd with their aureoles:
And Angels, meeting us, shall sing
    To their citherns and citoles.

" There will I ask of Christ the Lord
    Thus much for him and me:—
To have more blessing than on earth
    In nowise; but to be
As then we were;—being as then
    At peace. Yea, verily.

" Yea, verily; when he is come
    We will do thus and thus:
Till this my vigil seem quite strange
    And almost fabulous;
We two will live at once, one life;
    And peace shall be with us."

She gazed, and listen'd, and then said,
    Less sad of speech than mild,—
" All this is when he comes." She ceased:
    The light thrill'd past her, fill'd
With Angels, in strong level lapse.
    Her eyes pray'd, and she smiled.

(I saw her smile.) But soon their flight
    Was vague 'mid the poised spheres.
And then she cast her arms along
    The golden barriers,
And laid her face between her hands,
    And wept. (I heard her tears.)

DANTE GABRIEL ROSSETTI.

THE DEATH OF CUCHULAIN[1]

A MAN came slowly from the setting sun,
To Forgail's daughter, Emer, in her dun,[2]
And found her dyeing cloth with subtle care,
And said, casting aside his draggled hair:
" I am Aleel, the swineherd, whom you bid
Go dwell upon the sea cliffs, vapour-hid;
But now my years of watching are no more."

---

[1] Pronounce Coohóolan.
[2] Fortified residence of a chief.

Then Emer cast the web upon the floor,
And stretching out her arms, red with the dye,
Parted her lips with a loud sudden cry.

Looking on her, Aleel, the swineherd, said:
" Not any god alive, nor mortal dead,
Has slain so mighty armies, so great kings,
Nor won the gold that now Cuchulain brings."

" Why do you tremble thus from feet to crown ? "

Aleel, the swineherd, wept and cast him down
Upon the web-heaped floor, and thus his word:
" With him is one sweet-throated like a bird."

" Who bade you tell these things ? " and then she cried
To those about, " Beat him with thongs of hide
And drive him from the door." And thus it was;
And where her son, Finmole, on the smooth grass
Was driving cattle, came she with swift feet,
And called out to him, " Son, it is not meet
That you stay idling here with flocks and herds."

" I have long waited, mother, for those words;
But wherefore now ? "
                              " There is a man to die;
You have the heaviest arm under the sky."

" My father dwells among the sea-worn bands,
And breaks the ridge of battle with his hands."

" Nay, you are taller than Cuchulain, son."

" He is the mightiest man in ship or dun."

" Nay, he is old and sad with many wars,
And weary of the crash of battle cars."

" I only ask what way my journey lies,
For God, who made you bitter, made you wise."

" The Red Branch kings a tireless banquet keep,
Where the sun falls into the Western deep,

Go there, and dwell on the green forest rim;
But tell alone your name and house to him
Whose blade compels, and bid them send you one
Who has a like vow from their triple dun."

Between the lavish shelter of a wood
And the grey tide, the Red Branch multitude
Feasted, and with them old Cuchulain dwelt,
And his young dear one close beside him knelt,
And gazed upon the wisdom of his eyes,
More mournful than the depth of starry skies,
And pondered on the wonder of his days;
And all around the harp-string told his praise,
And Concobar,[1] the Red Branch king of kings,
With his own fingers touched the brazen strings.

At last Cuchulain spake, " A young man strays
Driving the deer along the woody ways.
I often hear him singing to and fro,
I often hear the sweet sound of his bow.
Seek out what man he is."
                         One went and came.
" He bade me let all know he gives his name
At the sword point, and bade me bring him one
Who had a like vow from our triple dun."

" I only of the Red Branch hosted now,"
Cuchulain cried, " have made and keep that vow."

After short fighting in the leafy shade,
He spake to the young man, " Is there no maid
Who loves you, no white arms to wrap you round,
Or do you long for the dim sleepy ground,
That you come here to meet this ancient sword ? "

" The dooms of men are in God's hidden hoard."

" Your head a while seemed like a woman's head
That I loved once."
                    Again the fighting sped,
But now the war rage in Cuchulain woke,
And through the other's shield his long blade broke,
And pierced him.
                " Speak before your breath is done."
                    [1] Connor.

" I am Finmole, mighty Cuchulain's son."

" I put you from your pain. I can no more."

While day its burden on to evening bore,
With head bowed on his knees Cuchulain stayed;
Then Concobar sent that sweet-throated maid,
And she, to win him, his grey hair caressed:
In vain her arms, in vain her soft white breast.
Then Concobar, the subtlest of all men,
Ranking his Druids round him ten by ten,
Spake thus, " Cuchulain will dwell there and brood,
For three days more in dreadful quietude,
And then arise, and raving slay us all.
Go, cast on him delusions magical,
That he may fight the waves of the loud sea."
And ten by ten under a quicken tree,[1]
The Druids chaunted, swaying in their hands
Tall wands of alder and white quicken wands.

In three days' time, Cuchulain with a moan
Stood up, and came to the long sands alone:
For four days warred he with the bitter tide;
And the waves flowed above him, and he died.

W. B. YEATS.

WORDSWORTH'S GRAVE

I

THE old rude church, with bare, bald tower, is here;
Beneath its shadow high-born Rotha flows;
Rotha, remembering well who slumbers near,
And with cool murmur lulling his repose.

Rotha, remembering well who slumbers near.
His hills, his lakes, his streams are with him yet.
Surely the heart that read her own heart clear
Nature forgets not soon: 'tis we forget.

We that with vagrant soul his fixity
Have slighted; faithless, done his deep faith wrong;
Left him for poorer loves, and bowed the knee
To misbegotten strange new gods of song.

---

[1] Mountain-ash; rowan.

Yet, led by hollow ghost or beckoning elf
Far from her homestead to the desert bourn,
The vagrant soul returning to herself
Wearily wise, must needs to him return.

To him and to the powers that with him dwell:
Inflowings that divulged not whence they came;
And that secluded spirit unknowable,
The mystery we make darker with a name;

The Somewhat which we name but cannot know,
Ev'n as we name a star and only see
His quenchless flashings forth, which ever show
And ever hide him, and which are not he.

II

Poet who sleepest by this wandering wave!
When thou wast born, what birth-gift hadst thou then?
To thee what wealth was that the Immortals gave,
The wealth thou gavest in thy turn to men?

Not Milton's keen, translunar music thine;
Not Shakespeare's cloudless, boundless human view;
Not Shelley's flush of rose on peaks divine;
Nor yet the wizard twilight Coleridge knew.

What hadst thou that could make so large amends
For all thou hadst not and thy peers possessed,
Motion and fire, swift means to radiant ends?—
Thou hadst, for weary feet, the gift of rest.

From Shelley's dazzling glow or thunderous haze,
From Byron's tempest-anger, tempest-mirth,
Men turned to thee and found—not blast and blaze,
Tumult of tottering heavens, but peace on earth.

Nor peace that grows by Lethe, scentless flower,
There in white languors to decline and cease;
But peace whose names are also rapture, power,
Clear sight, and love: for these are parts of peace.

III

I hear it vouched the Muse is with us still;—
If less divinely frenzied than of yore,
In lieu of feelings she has wondrous skill
To simulate emotion felt no more.

Not such the authentic Presence pure, that made
This valley vocal in the great days gone!—
In *his* great days, while yet the spring-time played
About him, and the mighty morning shone.

No word-mosaic artificer, he sang
A lofty song of lowly weal and dole.
Right from the heart, right to the heart it sprang,
Or from the soul leapt instant to the soul.

He felt the charm of childhood, grace of youth,
Grandeur of age, insisting to be sung.
The impassioned argument was simple truth
Half-wondering at its own melodious tongue.

Impassioned? ay, to the song's ecstatic core!
But far removed were clangour, storm and feud;
For plenteous health was his, exceeding store
Of joy, and an impassioned quietude.

IV

A hundred years ere he to manhood came,
Song from celestial heights had wandered down,
Put off her robe of sunlight, dew and flame,
And donned a modish dress to charm the Town.

Thenceforth she but festooned the porch of things;
Apt at life's lore, incurious what life meant.
Dextrous of hand, she struck her lute's few strings,
Ignobly perfect, barrenly content.

Unflushed with ardour and unblanched with awe,
Her lips in profitless derision curled,
She saw with dull emotion—if she saw—
The vision of the glory of the world.

The human masque she watched, with dreamless eyes
In whose clear shallows lurked no trembling shade:
The stars, unkenned by her, might set and rise,
Unmarked by her, the daisies bloom and fade.

The age grew sated with her sterile wit.
Herself waxed weary on her loveless throne.
Men felt life's tide, the sweep and surge of it,
And craved a living voice, a natural tone.

For none the less, though song was but half true,
The world lay common, one abounding theme.
Man joyed and wept, and fate was ever new,
And love was sweet, life real, death no dream.

In sad stern verse the rugged scholar-sage
Bemoaned his toil unvalued, youth uncheered.
His numbers wore the vesture of the age,
But, 'neath it beating, the great heart was heard.

From dewy pastures, uplands sweet with thyme,
A virgin breeze freshened the jaded day.
It wafted Collins' lonely vesper-chime,
It breathed abroad the frugal note of Gray.

It fluttered here and there, nor swept in vain
The dusty haunts where futile echoes dwell,—
Then, in a cadence soft as summer rain,
And sad from Auburn voiceless, drooped and fell.

It drooped and fell, and one 'neath northern skies,
With southern heart, who tilled his father's field,
Found Poesy a-dying, bade her rise
And touch quick nature's hem and go forth healed.

On life's broad plain the ploughman's conquering share
Upturned the fallow lands of truth anew,
And o'er the formal garden's trim parterre
The peasant's team a ruthless furrow drew.

Bright was his going forth, but clouds ere long
Whelmed him; in gloom his radiance set, and those
Twin morning stars of the new century's song,
Those morning stars that sang together, rose.

In elfish speech the *Dreamer* told his tale
Of marvellous oceans swept by fateful wings.—
The Seér strayed not from earth's human pale,
But the mysterious face of common things

He mirrored as the moon in Rydal Mere
Is mirrored, when the breathless night hangs blue:
Strangely remote she seems and wondrous near,
And by some nameless difference born anew.

V

Peace—peace—and rest! Ah, how the lyre is loth,
Or powerless now, to give what all men seek:
Either it deadens with ignoble sloth
Or deafens with shrill tumult, loudly weak.

Where is the singer whose large notes and clear
Can heal and arm and plenish and sustain?
Lo, one with empty music floods the ear,
And one, the heart refreshing, tires the brain.

And idly tuneful, the loquacious throng
Flutter and twitter, prodigal of time,
And little masters make a toy of song
Till grave men weary of the sound of rhyme.

And some go prankt in faded antique dress,
Abhorring to be hale and glad and free;
And some parade a conscious naturalness,
The scholar's not the child's simplicity,

Enough;—and wisest who from words forbear,
The kindly river rails not as it glides;
And suave and charitable, the winning air
Chides not at all, or only him who chides.

VI

Nature! we storm thine ear with choric notes.
Thou answerest through the calm great nights and days,
" Laud me who will: not tuneless are your throats;
Yet if ye paused I should not miss the praise."

We falter, half-rebuked, and sing again.
We chant thy desertness and haggard gloom,
Or with thy splendid wrath inflate the strain,
Or touch it with thy colour and perfume.

One, his melodious blood aflame for thee,
Wooed with fierce lust, his hot heart world-defiled.
One, with the upward eye of infancy,
Looked in thy face and felt himself thy child.

Thee he approached without distrust or dread—
Beheld thee throned, an awful queen, above—
Climbed to thy lap and merely laid his head
Against thy warm wild heart of mother-love.

He heard that vast heart beating—thou didst press
Thy child so close, and lov'dst him unaware.
Thy beauty gladdened him; yet he scarce less
Had loved thee, had he never found thee fair!

For thou wast not as legendary lands
To which with curious eyes and ears we roam.
Nor wast thou as a fane 'mid solemn sands,
Where palmers halt at evening. Thou wast home.

And here, at home, still bides he; but he sleeps;
Not to be wakened even at thy word;
Though we, vague dreamers, dream he somewhere keeps
An ear still open to thy voice still heard,—

Thy voice, as heretofore, about him blown,
For ever blown about his silence now;
Thy voice, though deeper, yet so like his own
That almost, when he sang, we dreamed 'twas thou!

VII

Behind Helm Crag and Silver Howe the sheen
Of the retreating day is less and less.
Soon will the lordlier summits, here unseen,
Gather the night about their nakedness.

The half-heard bleat of sheep comes from the hill.
Faint sounds of childish play are in the air.
The river murmurs past. All else is still.
The very graves seem stiller than they were.

Afar though nation be on nation hurled,
And life with toil and ancient pain depressed,
Here one may scarce believe the whole wide world
Is not at peace, and all man's heart at rest.

Rest! 'twas the gift he gave; and peace! the shade
He spread, for spirits fevered with the sun.
To him his bounties are come back—here laid
In rest, in peace, his labour nobly done.

WILLIAM WATSON.

AUTHOR'S NOTE, 1921.—*Wordsworth's Grave* was begun at Rydal, in May 1884, finished rather more than three years later, and first published in the *National Review* for September 1887. In other words it was written during a period when the " Æsthetic School " and the " New Euphuists " were very much in evidence, and notwithstanding its outwardly quiet air, it was really a most militant manifesto against them and all they stood for. Largely by accident it has received what anyone acquainted with my whole work would, I think, agree with me in considering a disproportionate amount of attention relative to the rest and it has certainly been the main, if not the only cause, of my having had the ridiculously misplaced label " Wordsworthian " affixed to me by some of the undiscerning who are still fairly numerous. Like everybody who possesses any literary judgment I am, as you know, a great lover of Wordsworth. But a " Wordsworthian "? Not in the least. I may quite possibly be the worst poet that ever lived, but am at any rate no man's disciple.

THE HOUND OF HEAVEN

I FLED Him, down the nights and down the days;
  I fled Him, down the arches of the years;
I fled Him, down the labyrinthine ways
  Of my own mind; and in the mist of tears
I hid from Him, and under running laughter.
    Up vistaed hopes, I sped;
    And shot, precipitated,
Adown Titanic glooms of chasmèd fears,
  From those strong Feet that followed followed after.

      But with unhurrying chase,
      And unperturbèd pace,
  Deliberate speed, majestic instancy,
      They beat—and a Voice beat
      More instant than the Feet—
" All things betray thee, who betrayest Me."

I pleaded, outlaw-wise,
By many a hearted casement, curtained red,
    Trellised with intertwining charities;
(For though I knew His love Who followèd,
            Yet was I sore adread
Lest, having Him, I must have naught beside).
But, if one little casement parted wide,
    The gust of His approach would clash it to.
Fear wist not to evade, as Love wist to pursue,
Across the margent of the world I fled,
    And troubled the gold gateways of the stars,
    Smiting for shelter on their clangèd bars;
            Fretted to dulcet jars
And silvern chatter the pale ports o' the moon.
I said to dawn: Be sudden; to eve: Be soon—
    With thy young skyey blossoms heap me over
            From this tremendous Lover!
Float thy vague veil about me, lest He see!
    I tempted all His servitors, but to find
My own betrayal in their constancy,
In faith to Him their fickleness to me,
    Their traitorous trueness, and their loyal deceit,
To all swift things for swiftness did I sue;
    Clung to the whistling mane of every wind.
            But whether they swept, smoothly fleet,
            The long savannahs of the blue;
            Or whether, Thunder-driven,
            They clanged His chariot 'thwart a heaven,
Plashy with flying lightnings round the spurn o' their feet—
Fear wist not to evade as Love wist to pursue.

            Still with unhurrying chase,
            And unperturbèd pace,
        Deliberate speed, majestic instancy,
            Came on the following Feet,
            And a Voice above their beat—
    " Naught shelters thee, who wilt not shelter Me."

I sought no more that after which I strayed
            In face of man or maid;
But still within the little children's eyes
            Seems something, something that replies,
    They at least are for me, surely for me!

I turned me to them very wistfully;
But just as their young eyes grew sudden fair
    With dawning answers there,
Their angel plucked them from me by the hair.
" Come then, ye other children, Nature's—share
With me " (said I) " your delicate fellowship;
    Let me greet you lip to lip,
    Let me twine with you caresses,
        Wantoning
    With our Lady-Mother's vagrant tresses,
        Banqueting
    With her in her wind-walled palace,
    Underneath her azured daïs,
    Quaffing, as your taintless way is,
        From a chalice
Lucent-weeping out of the dayspring."
        So it was done:
I in their delicate fellowship was one—
Drew the bolt of Nature's secrecies.
        I knew all the swift importings
    On the wilful face of skies;
    I knew how the clouds arise,
    Spumèd of the wild sea-snortings;
        All that's born or dies
    Rose and drooped with; made them shapers
Of mine own moods, or wailful or divine—
    With them joyed and was bereaven.
    I was heavy with the even,
    When she lit her glimmering tapers
    Round the day's dead sanctities.
    I laughed in the morning's eyes.
I triumphed and I saddened with all weather,
    Heaven and I wept together,
And its sweet tears were salt with mortal mine;
Against the red throb of its sunset-heart
    I laid my own to beat,
    And share commingling heat;
But not by that, by that, was eased my human smart.
In vain my tears were wet on Heaven's grey cheek.
For ah! we know not what each other says,
    These things and I; in sound *I* speak—
Their sound is but their stir, they speak by silences.
Nature, poor stepdame, cannot slake my drouth;

Let her, if she would owe me,
Drop yon blue bosom-veil of sky, and show me
The breasts o' her tenderness:
Never did any milk of hers once bless
My thirsting mouth.

Nigh and high draws the chase,
With unperturbèd pace,
Deliberate speed, majestic instancy,
And past those noisèd Feet
A Voice comes yet more fleet—
" Lo! naught contents thee, who content'st not Me."

Naked I wait Thy love's uplifted stroke!
My harness piece by piece Thou hast hewn from me,
And smitten me to my knee;
I am defenceless utterly.
I slept, methinks, and woke,
And, slowly gazing, find me stripped in sleep.
In the rash lustihead of my young powers,
I shook the pillaring hours
And pulled my life upon me; grimed with smears,
I stand amid the dust o' the mounded years—
My mangled youth lies dead beneath the heap.
My days have crackled and gone up in smoke,
Have puffed and burst as sun-starts on a stream.
Yea, faileth now even dream
The dreamer, and the lute the lutanist;
Even the linked fantasies, in whose blossomy twist
I swung the earth a trinket at my wrist,
Are yielding; cords of all too weak account
For earth, with heavy griefs so overplussed.
Ah! is Thy love indeed
A weed, albeit an amaranthine weed,
Suffering no flowers except its own to mount?
Ah! must—
Designer infinite!—
Ah! must Thou char the wood ere Thou canst limn with it?
My freshness spent its wavering shower i' the dust;
And now my heart is as a broken fount,
Wherein tear-drippings stagnate, spilt down ever
From the dank thoughts that shiver
Upon the sighful branches of my mind.
Such is; what is to be?

The pulp so bitter, how shall taste the rind?
I dimly guess what Time in mists confounds;
Yet ever and anon a trumpet sounds
  From the hid battlements of Eternity:
  Those shaken mists a space unsettle, then
Round the half-glimpsèd turrets slowly wash again;
      But not ere him who summoneth
      I first have seen, enwound
With glooming robes purpureal, cypress-crowned;
His name I know, and what his trumpet saith.
Whether man's heart or life it be which yields
      Thee harvest, must Thy harvest fields
      Be dunged with rotten death?

      Now of that long pursuit
      Comes on at hand the bruit;
That Voice is round me like a bursting sea:
    " And is thy earth so marred,
    Shattered in shard on shard?
Lo, all things fly thee, for thou fliest Me!
    Strange, piteous, futile thing!
Wherefore should any set thee love apart?
Seeing none but I makes much of naught " (He said),
" And human love needs human meriting:
    How hast thou merited—
Of all man's clotted clay the dingiest clot?
    Alack, thou knowest not
How little worthy of any love thou art!
Whom wilt thou find to love ignoble thee,
    Save Me, save only Me?

All which I took from thee I did but take,
    Not for thy harms,
But just that thou might'st seek it in My arms,
    All which thy child's mistake
Fancies as lost, I have stored for thee at home:
    Rise, clasp My hand, and come."

    Halts by me that footfall:
    Is my gloom, after all,
Shade of His hand, outstretched caressingly?
    " Ah, fondest, blindest, weakest,
    I am He Whom thou seekest!
Thou dravest love from thee, who dravest Me."

FRANCIS THOMPSON.

A LETTER FROM A GIRL TO HER OWN
OLD AGE

LISTEN, and when thy hand this paper presses,
O time-worn woman, think of her who blesses
What thy thin fingers touch, with her caresses.

O mother, for the weight of years that break thee!
O daughter, for slow time must yet awake thee!
And from the changes of my heart must make thee.

O fainting traveller, morn is grey in heaven.
Dost thou remember how the clouds were driven?
And are they calm about the fall of even?

Pause near the ending of thy long migration,
For this one sudden hour of desolation
Appeals to one hour of thy meditation.

Suffer, O silent one, that I remind thee
Of the great hills that stormed the sky behind thee,
Of the wild winds of power that have resigned thee.

Know that the mournful plain where thou must wander
Is but a grey and silent world, but ponder
The misty mountains of the morning yonder.

Listen:—the mountain winds with rain were fretting,
And sudden gleams the mountain-tops besetting.
I cannot let thee fade to death, forgetting.

What part of this wild heart of mine I know not
Will follow with thee where the great winds blow not,
And where the young flowers of the mountain grow not.

Yet let my letter with thy lost thoughts in it
Tell what the way was when thou didst begin it.
And win with thee the goal when thou shalt win it.

Oh, in some hour of thine my thoughts shall guide thee,
Suddenly, though time, darkness, silence hide thee,
This wind from thy lost country flits beside thee,—

Telling thee: all thy memories moved the maiden,
With thy regrets was morning over-shaden,
With sorrow thou hast left, her life was laden.

But whither shall my thoughts turn to pursue thee?
Life changes, and the years and days renew thee.
Oh, Nature brings my straying heart unto thee.

Her winds will join us, with their constant kisses
Upon the evening as the morning tresses,
Her summers breathe the same unchanging blisses.

And we, so altered in our shifting phases,
Track one another 'mid the many mazes
By the eternal child-breath of the daisies.

I have not writ this letter of divining
To make a glory of thy silent pining,
A triumph of thy mute and strange declining.

Only one youth, and the bright life was shrouded.
Only one morning, and the day was clouded.
And one old age with all regrets is crowded.

Oh, hush; oh, hush! Thy tears my words are steeping.
Oh, hush, hush, hush! So full, the fount of weeping?
Poor eyes, so quickly moved, so near to sleeping?

Pardon the girl; such strange desires beset her.
Poor woman, lay aside the mournful letter
That breaks thy heart; the one who wrote, forget her.

The one who now thy faded features guesses,
With filial fingers thy grey hair caresses,
With morning tears thy mournful twilight blesses.

ALICE MEYNELL.

THE RHYME OF THE THREE SEALERS

Away by the lands of the Japanee
Where the paper lanterns glow
And the crews of all the shipping drink
In the house of Blood Street Joe,
At twilight, when the landward breeze
Brings up the harbour noise,
And ebb of Yokohama Bay
Swigs chattering through the buoys,
In Cisco's Dewdrop Dining Rooms
They tell the tale anew
Of a hidden sea and a hidden fight,
When the Baltic *ran from the* Northern Light
And the Stralsund *fought the two.*

Now this is the Law of the Muscovite, that he proves with
shot and steel,
When ye come by his isles in the Smoky Sea ye must not
take the seal,
Where the grey sea goes nakedly between the weed-hung
shelves,
And the little blue fox he is bred for his skin and the seal
they breed for themselves;
For when the *matkas* seek the shore to drop their pups aland,
The great man-seal haul out of the sea, aroaring, band by
band;
And when the first September gales have slaked their
rutting-wrath,
The great man-seal haul back to the sea and no man knows
their path.
Then dark they lie and stark they lie—rookery, dune, and
floe,
And the Northern Lights come down o' nights to dance
with the houseless snow;
And God Who clears the grounding berg and steers the
grinding floe,
He hears the cry of the little kit-fox and the wind along the
snow.
But since our women must walk gay and money buys their
gear,
The sealing-boats they filch that way at hazard year by year.

English they be and Japanee that hang on the Brown Bear's
    flank,
And some be Scot, but the worst of the lot, and the boldest
    thieves, be Yank!

It was the sealer *Northern Light*, to the Smoky Seas she bore,
With a stovepipe stuck from a starboard port and the
    Russian flag at her fore.
(*Baltic*, *Stralsund*, and *Northern Light*—oh! they were birds of
    a feather—
Slipping away to the Smoky Seas, three seal-thieves
    together!)
And at last she came to a sandy cove and the *Baltic* lay
    therein,
But her men were up with the herding seal to drive and
    club and skin.
There were fifteen hundred skins abeach, cool pelt and
    proper fur,
When the *Northern Light* drove into the bight and the sea-
    mist drove with her.
The *Baltic* called her men and weighed—she could not
    choose but run—
For a stovepipe seen through the closing mist, it shows like
    a four-inch gun
(And loss it is that is sad as death to lose both trip and ship
And lie for a rotting contraband on Vladivostockslip).
She turned and dived in the sea-smother as a rabbit dives
    in the whins,
And the *Northern Light* sent up her boats to steal the stolen
    skins.
They had not brought a load to side or slid their hatches
    clear,
When they were aware of a sloop-of-war, ghost-white and
    very near.
Her flag she showed, and her guns she showed—three of
    them, black, abeam,
And a funnel white with the crusted salt, but never a show
    of steam.

There was no time to man the brakes, they knocked the
    shackle free,
And the *Northern Light* stood out again, goose-winged to
    open sea.

(For life it is that is worse than death, by force of Russian law
To work in the mines of mercury that loose the teeth in
    your jaw.)
They had not run a mile from shore—they heard no shots
    behind—
When the skipper smote his hand on his thigh and threw
    her up in the wind:
" Bluffed—raised out on a bluff," said he, " for if my
    name's Tom Hall,
You must set a thief to catch a thief—and a thief has caught
    us all!
By every butt in Oregon and every spar in Maine,
The hand that spilled the wind from her sail was the hand
    of Reuben Paine!
He has rigged and trigged her with paint and spar, and,
    faith, he has faked her well—
But I'd know the *Stralsund's* deckhouse yet from here to the
    booms o' Hell.
Oh, once we ha' met at Baltimore, and twice on Boston
    pier,
But the sickest day for you, Reuben Paine, was the day that
    you came here—
The day that you came here, my lad, to scare us from our
    seal
With your funnel made o' your painted cloth, and your
    guns o' rotten deal!
Ring and blow for the *Baltic* now, and head her back to
    the bay,
And we'll come into the game again—with a double deck
    to play! "

They rang and blew the sealers' call—the poaching cry of
    the sea—
And they raised the *Baltic* out of the mist, and an angrg
    ship was she:
And blind they groped through the whirling white and
    blind to the bay again,
Till they heard the creak of the *Stralsund's* boom and the
    clank of her mooring chain.
They laid them down by bitt and boat, their pistols in their
    belts,
And: " Will you fight for it, Reuben Paine, or will you
    share the pelts? "

A dog-toothed laugh laughed Reuben Paine, and bared his
flenching-knife.

" Yea, skin for skin, and all that he hath a man will give
for his life;

But I've six thousand skins below, and Yeddo Port to see,

And there's never a law of God or man runs north of
Fifty-Three:

So go in peace to the naked seas with empty holds to fill,

And I'll be good to your seal this catch, as many as I shall
kill! "

Answered the snap of a closing lock and the jar of a gun-
butt slid,

But the tender fog shut fold on fold to hide the wrong they
did.

The weeping fog rolled fold on fold the wrath of man to
cloak,

And the flame-spurts pale ran down the rail as the sealing-
rifles spoke.

The bullets bit on bend and butt, the splinter slivered free

(Little they trust to sparrow-dust that stop the seal in his
sea!),

The thick smoke hung and would not shift, leaden it lay
and blue,

But three were down on the *Baltic's* deck and two of the
Stralsund's crew.

An arm's length out and overside the banked fog held them
bound,

But, as they heard or groan or word, they fired at the sound.

For one cried out on the Name of God, and one to have
him cease,

And the questing volley found them both and bade them
hold their peace;

And one called out on a heathen joss and one on the
Virgin's Name,

And the schooling bullet leaped across and showed them
whence they came.

And in the waiting silences the rudder whined beneath,

And each man drew his watchful breath slow taken 'tween
the teeth—

Trigger and ear and eye acock, knit brow and hard-drawn
lips—

Bracing his feet by chock and cleat for the rolling of the ships.

Till they heard the cough of a wounded man that fought
    in the fog for breath,
Till they heard the torment of Reuben Paine that wailed
    upon his death:

" The tides they'll go through Fundy Race, but I'll go
    never more
And see the hogs from ebb-tide mark turn scampering back
    to shore.
No more I'll see the trawlers drift below the Bass Rock
    ground,
Or watch the tall Fall steamer lights tear blazing up the
    Sound.
Sorrow is me, in a lonely sea and a sinful fight I fall,
But if there's law o' God or man you'll swing for it yet,
    Tom Hall!"

Tom Hall stood up by the quarter-rail. " Your words in
    your teeth," said he.
" There's never a law of God or man runs north of Fifty-
    Three.
So go in grace with Him to face, and an ill-spent life behind,
And I'll be good to your widows, Rube, as many as I shall
    find."
A *Stralsund* man shot blind and large, and a warlock Finn
    was he,
And he hit Tom Hall with a bursting ball a hand's-breadth
    over the knee.
Tom Hall caught hold by the topping-lift, and sat him down
    with an oath,
" You'll wait a little Rube," he said, " the Devil has called
    for both.
The Devil is driving both this tide, and the killing-grounds
    are close,
And we'll go up to the Wrath of God as the holluschickie
    goes.
O men, put back your guns again and lay your rifles by,
We've fought our fight, and the best are down. Let up
    and let us die!
Quit firing, by the bow there—quit! Call off the *Baltic's*
    crew!
You're sure of Hell as me or Rube—but wait till we get
    through."

There went no word between the ships, but thick and quick
    and loud
The life-blood drummed on the dripping decks with the
    fog-dew from the shroud.
The sea-pull drew them side by side, gunnel to gunnel laid,
And they felt the sheerstrakes pound and clear, but never
    a word was said.

Then Reuben Paine cried out again before his spirit passed :
" Have I followed the sea for thirty years to die in the dark
    at last ?
Curse on her work that has nipped me here with a shifty
    truck unkind—
I have gotten my death where I got my bread, but I dare
    not face it blind.
Curse on the fog ! Is there never a wind of all the winds
    I knew
To clear the smother from off my chest, and let me look at
    the blue ? "
The good fog heard—like a splitten sail, to left and right
    she tore,
And they saw the sun-dogs in the haze and the seal upon
    the shore.
Silver and grey ran spit and bay to meet the steelbacked
    tide,
And pinched and white in the clearing light the crews
    stared overside.
O rainbow-gay the red pools lay that swilled and spilled
    and spread,
And gold, raw gold, the spent shell rolled between the
    careless dead—
The dead that rocked so drunkenwise to weather and to lee.
And they saw the work their hands had done as God had
    bade them see.

And a little breeze blew over the rail that made the head-
    sails lift,
But no man stood by wheel or sheet, and they let the
    schooners drift.
And the rattle rose in Reuben's throat and he cast his soul
    with a cry,
And " Gone already ? " Tom Hall he said. " Then it's
    time for me to die."

His eyes were heavy with great sleep and yearning for the land,
And he spoke as a man that talks in dreams, his wound beneath his hand.
" Oh, there comes no good o' the westering wind that backs against the sun ;
Wash down the decks—they're all too red—and share the skins and run,
Baltic, Stralsund, and *Northern Light*—clean share and share for all,
You'll find the fleets off Tolstoi Mees, but you will not find Tom Hall.
Evil he did in shoal-water and black sin on the deep,
But now he's sick of watch and trick and now he'll turn and sleep.
He'll have no more of the crawling sea that made him súffer so,
But he'll lie down on the killing-grounds where the hollus-chickie go.
And west you'll sail and south again, beyond the sea-fog's rim,
And tell the Yoshiwara girls to burn a stick for him.
And you'll not weight him by the heels and dump him overside,
But carry him up to the sand-hollows to die as Bering died,
And make a place for Reuben Paine that knows the fight was fair,
And leave the two that did the wrong to talk it over there ! "

Half-steam ahead by guess and lead, for the sun is mostly veiled—
Through fog to fog, by luck and log, sail ye as Bering sailed;
And if the light shall lift aright to give your landfall plain,
North and by west, from Zapne Crest, ye raise the Crosses Twain.
Fair marks are they to the inner bay, the reckless poacher knows
What time the scarred see-catchie lead their sleek seraglios.
Ever they hear the floe-pack clear, and the blast of the old bull-whale,
And the deep seal-roar that beats off-shore above the loudest gale.

Ever they wait the winter's hate as the thundering boorga calls,
Where northward look they to St. George, and westward to St.
 Paul's.
Ever they greet the hunted fleet—lone keels off headlands drear—
When the sealing-schooners flit that way at hazard year by
 year.
Ever in Yokohama port men tell the tale anew
 Of a hidden sea and a hidden fight,
 When the Baltic *ran from the* Northern Light
And the Stralsund *fought the two.*

RUDYARD KIPLING.

THE DEAD QUIRE

I

BESIDE the Mead of Memories,
 Where Church-way mounts to Moaning Hill,
The sad man sighed his phantasies:
  He seems to sigh them still.

II

" 'Twas the Birth-tide Eve, and the hamleteers
 Made merry with ancient Mellstock zest,
But the Mellstock quire of former years
  Had entered into rest.

III

" Old Dewy lay by the gaunt yew tree,
 And Reuben and Michael a pace behind,
And Bowman with his family
  By the wall that the ivies bind.

IV

" The singers had followed one by one,
Treble, and tenor, and thorough-bass;
And the worm that wasteth had begun
    To mine their mouldering place.

V

" For two-score years, ere Christ-day light,
Mellstock had throbbed to strains from these:
But now there echoed on the night
    No Christmas harmonies.

VI

" Three meadows off, at a dormered inn,
The youth had gathered in high carouse,
And, ranged on settles, some therein
    Had drunk them to a drowse.

VII

" Loud, lively, reckless, some had grown,
Each dandling on his jigging knee
Eliza, Dolly, Nance, or Joan—
    Livers in levity.

VIII

" The taper flames and hearthfire shine
Grew smoke-hazed to a lurid light,
And songs on subjects not divine
    Were warbled forth that night.

IX

" Yet many were sons and grandsons here
Of those who, on such eves gone by,
At that still hour had throated clear
    Their anthems to the sky.

X

" The clock belled midnight; and ere long
One shouted, ' Now 'tis Christmas morn;
Here's to our women old and young,
    And to John Barleycorn! '

XI

" They drink the toast and shout again;
The pewter-ware rings back the boom,
And for a breath-while follows then
    A silence in the room.

XII

" When nigh without, as in old days,
The ancient quire of voice and string
Seemed singing words of prayer and praise
    As they had used to sing:

XIII

" *While shepherds watch'd their flocks by night,*—
Thus swells the long familiar sound
In many a quaint symphonic flight—
    To, *Glory shone around.*

XIV

" The sons defined their fathers' tones,
The widow his whom she had wed,
And others in the minor moans
    The viols of the dead.

XV

" Something supernal has the sound
As verse by verse the strain proceeds,
And stilly staring on the gound
    Each roysterer holds and heeds.

XVI

" Towards its chorded closing bar
Plaintively, thinly, waned the hymn,
Yet lingered, like the notes afar
    Of banded seraphim.

XVII

" With brows abashed, and reverent tread,
The hearkeners sought the tavern door:
But nothing, save wan moonlight, spread
    The empty highway o'er.

XVIII

" While on their hearing fixed and tense
The aerial music seemed to sink,
As it were gently moving thence
    Along the river brink.

XIX

" Then did the Quick pursue the Dead
By crystal Froom that crinkles there;
And still the viewless quire ahead
　　Voiced the old holy air.

XX

" By Bank-walk wicket, brightly bleached,
It passed, and 'twixt the hedges twain,
Dogged by the living; till it reached
　　The bottom of Church Lane.

XXI

" There at the turning, it was heard
Drawing to where the churchyard lay:
But when they followed thitherward
　　It smalled, and died away.

XXII

" Each gravestone of the quire, each mound,
Confronted them beneath the moon;
But no more floated therearound
　　That ancient Birth-night tune.

XXIII

" There Dewy lay by the gaunt yew tree,
There Reuben and Michael, a pace behind,
And Bowman with his family
　　By the wall that the ivies bind. . . .

XXIV

" As from a dream each sobered son
Awoke, and musing reached his door;
'Twas said that of them all, not one
    Sat in a tavern more."

XXV

—The sad man ceased; and ceased to heed
His listener, and crossed the leaze
From Moaning Hill towards the mead—
    The Mead of Memories.

THOMAS HARDY.

THE OLD VICARAGE, GRANTCHESTER

(Café des Westens, Berlin, May 1912)

JUST now the lilac is in bloom,
All before my little room;
And in my flower-beds, I think,
Smile the carnation and the pink;
And down the borders, well I know,
The poppy and the pansy blow. . . .
Oh! there the chestnuts, summer through,
Beside the river make for you
A tunnel of green gloom, and sleep
Deeply above; and green and deep
The stream mysterious glides beneath,
Green as a dream and deep as death.
—Oh, damn! I know it! and I know
How the May fields all golden show,
And when the day is young and sweet,
Gild gloriously the bare feet
That run to bathe. . . .
            Du lieber Gott!

Here am I, sweating, sick, and hot,
And there the shadowed waters fresh
Lean up to embrace the naked flesh.
Temperamentvoll German Jews
Drink beer around;—and *there* the dews
Are soft beneath a morn of gold.
Here tulips bloom as they are told;
Unkempt about those hedges blows
An English unofficial rose;
And there the unregulated sun
Slopes down to rest when day is done,
And wakes a vague unpunctual star,
A slippered Hesper; and there are
Meads towards Haslingfield and Coton
Where *das Betreten's* not *verboten*.

εἴθε γενοίμην . . . would I were
In Grantchester, in Grantchester!—
Some, it may be, can get in touch
With Nature there, or Earth, or such,
And clever modern men have seen
A Faun a-peeping through the green,
And felt the Classics were not dead,
To glimpse a Naiad's reedy head,
Or hear the Goat-foot piping low: . . .
But these are things I do not know.
I only know that you may lie
Day long and watch the Cambridge sky,
And, flower-lulled in sleepy grass,
Hear the cool lapse of hours pass,
Until the centuries blend and blur
In Grantchester, in Grantchester. . . .
Still in the dawnlit waters cool
His ghostly Lordship swims his pool,
And tries the strokes, essays the tricks,
Long learnt on Hellespont, or Styx.
Dan Chaucer hears his river still
Chatter beneath a phantom mill.
Tennyson notes, with studious eye,
How Cambridge waters hurry by . . .
And in that garden, black and white,
Creep whispers through the grass all night;

And spectral dance, before the dawn,
A hundred Vicars down the lawn;
Curates, long dust, will come and go
On lissom, clerical, printless toe;
And oft between the boughs is seen
The sly shade of a Rural Dean . . .
Till, at a shiver in the skies,
Vanishing with Satanic cries,
The prim ecclesiastic rout
Leaves but a startled sleeper-out,
Grey heavens, the first bird's drowsy calls,
The falling house that never falls.

God! I will pack, and take a train,
And get me to England once again!
For England's the one land, I know,
Where men with Splendid Hearts may go;
And Cambridgeshire, of all England,
The shire for Men who Understand;
And of *that* district I prefer
The lovely hamlet Grantchester.
For Cambridge people rarely smile,
Being urban, squat, and packed with guile;
And Royston men in the far South
Are black and fierce and strange of mouth;
At Over they fling oaths at one,
And worse than oaths at Trumpington,
And Ditton girls are mean and dirty,
And there's none in Harston under thirty,
And folks in Shelford and those parts
Have twisted lips and twisted hearts,
And Barton men make Cockney rhymes,
And Coton's full of nameless crimes,
And things are done you'd not believe
At Madingley, on Christmas Eve.
Strong men have run for miles and miles,
When one from Cherry Hinton smiles;
Strong men have blanched, and shot their wives,
Rather than send them to St. Ives;
Strong men have cried like babes, bydam,
To hear what happened at Babraham.
But Grantchester! ah, Grantchester!

There's peace and holy quiet there,
Great clouds along pacific skies,
And men and women with straight eyes,
Lithe children lovelier than a dream,
A bosky wood, a slumbrous stream,
And little kindly winds that creep
Round twilight corners, half asleep.
In Grantchester their skins are white;
They bathe by day, they bathe by night;
The women there do all they ought;
The men observe the Rules of Thought.
They love the Good; they worship Truth;
They laugh uproariously in youth;
(And when they get to feeling old,
They up and shoot themselves, I'm told). . . .

Ah, God! to see the branches stir
Across the moon at Grantchester!
To smell the thrilling-sweet and rotten
Unforgettable, unforgotten
River-smell, and hear the breeze
Sobbing in the little trees.
Say, do the elm-clumps greatly stand
Still guardians of that holy land?
The chestnuts shade, in reverend dream,
The yet unacademic stream?
Is dawn a secret shy and cold
Anadyomene, silver-gold?
And sunset still a golden sea
From Haslingfield to Madingley?
And after, ere the night is born,
Do hares come out about the corn?
Oh, is the water sweet and cool,
Gentle and brown, above the pool?
And laughs the immortal river still
Under the mill, under the mill?
Say, is there Beauty yet to find?
And Certainty? and Quiet kind?
Deep meadows yet, for to forget
The lies, and truths, and pain? . . . Oh! yet
Stands the Church clock at ten to three?
And is there honey still for tea?

RUPERT BROOKE.

THE MAID OF ARC

(To Marie Sturge Moore)

In Domrèmy a maid
  Was born of peasant seed;
Not sly, cowed or afraid
As girls of famished breed
And servant blood can be,
Not proud, uncurbed and free
As maidens of degree,
She grew; a lily blade.

Before the first buds come
Stands unnoticed and still,
Pale with unfingered bloom,
As she stood straight to thrill
To the young life she drew
From hills, bird-glances, dew,
All new as she was new,
While she watched sheep at home.

Even her lack of shoes
Let closelier to her press
The power she did not choose,
Her land's live tenderness.
When France was gashed by war
Her flesh felt each quick scar
Though she was safe and far:
English men were her foes.

As a bud unfurls in fire
She opened, a lily of France
Her faith and her desire
Took voice; whether by trance
Those Voices spoke in her,
Or in the natural air,
Vivid and hushed they were
To waft her high thoughts higher.

They gave her spirit a sword,
They taught her to lead men;
Tall cities she restored
To France's breast again.
At her word great captains sped.
Great English captains fled
At her will. In fight she bled
She was revered, adored.

She bade her King be crowned.
Yet he, a weak vain King,
When his court-captains frowned
Hated her fostering,
Ashamed of a woman's aid.
By succour denied and stayed
And a King's man's trick the Maid
Was seized by foes and bound.

Let it be quickly told
A lord of Burgundy
Sold her to us for gold;
More than Judas had he.
And Nicholas Loyseleur,
Who lined his coat with our fur,
Heard confession from her
And her poor secrets sold.

Pierre Cauchon as well,
Of Beauvais bishop, decreed
Her Voices were of Hell,
Her witch's body must bleed.
But English men were they
Who took her clothes away
And swore her foul, all say.
And English man shames to tell.

English men blind and true
Burnt that marvellous one;
She bore the things men do,
As women have always done;

But our hold on France was lost:
That a peasant's life was the cost,
Though live flames over her tossed,
Was sweet to her if she knew.

O Maid, strong heart, clear soul,
Say now it is well done
In keeping your France whole
That son and daughter and son
Of your dead enemies
Stand next your legionaries
No more ashamed, with these,
Of women's aid and toll.

In your inheritance,
O Maid, of Paradise
When your young, morning glance
Beholds heroes arise
To you, for France being slain,
As your own race bless then
The pardoned English men
Who sleep in fields of France.

GORDON BOTTOMLEY.

THE SIRENS

III. 3

MYSTERY of Dawn, ere yet the glory streams
Risen over earth, and pauses in that hush
When far, as from an ecstasy, clouds flush,
And hills lift up their pureness into dreams
Of light that not yet colours the cold flower,
And the earth-clasping, heaven-desiring tree
Trembles in virginal expectancy—
What breath of the unknown Power
Is this that, spirit to spirit, as with a spousal kiss
Comes seeking us, even us, through shadow and dew,—
Seeking in this soiled flesh what undiscovered world
Beyond tears, beyond bliss, beyond wisdom, beyond
Time? what recaptured harmony of earth and heaven?
What world made new?

A world so strange, the spirit thrills to flame,
Transfigured in a wonder of release!
A world so near, it has no other name
Than light and breath! Where lost we, then, this peace?
Wanting what charm to cleanse
Our eyes? To see; is this the last of gifts,
That, as the scales drop, the heart so uplifts?
O world where no possession is of men's,
Where the will rages not with fever to destroy
Differing wills, or warp another life to its use,
But each lives in the light of its own joy!

In one wide vision all have share, and we in all,
Infinitely companioned with the stars, the dust,
Beasts of the field, and stones, and flowers that fall!

This body that we use seems in that air
Marvellous; secret from ourselves; a power
Without which were no speech, nor deed done anywhere,
Nor could thought range and tower,
Nor seed be sown for the unborn time to reap;
Whose natural motion was ordained to be
Beautiful as a wave out of a sea
Boundless as mind asleep;
So passionately shaped, in every part perfect,
Universes are wounded in its abasement,
Crying from stone to star;
The unimagined height, the immeasurable deep,
Hungers, abysses, heavens, millions of ghosts from far
Meet in this body born to laugh and weep.

Weep; not for the endured, ancestral ill,
Perils and plagues, that ambush all our ways,
Time's injury, and pain's deep-wandered maze;
These need not eyes to see, but only flesh to feel.
But of the eternal vision to partake,
And see what we have done, and what refused,
To what accepted blindness we grow used,
And what marred shapes of one another make,
This is to weep such tears as no flesh-throes have cost,
Weep for our loves, our loves, that we ourselves have slain,
The powers of loveliness that we have left forlorn.
Eyes we had and saw not, ears and we did not hear!
Ah, when the heart, full-visioned, breaks in shame and pain,
Then is the world's hope born.

The cry of desolation turns to praise.
If falsehood first enchant the eager mind,
And if desire be cruel, being blind,
Eacy by its own infirmity betrays,
And some profounder, more imperious need
Drives through all smart, whatever world to lose,
The pure vision to choose,
And tho' Truth kill, there in the end be freed.
Open, open, gates of deliverance, open!
See, liberated spirits, see, victorious ones,
For testimony of us from homes of glory shine,
Vindicators of this brief flesh, they mingle us,—
Soiled and despoiled,—with beauty and with felicity,
And sting us from afar with the Divine.

Hands of men stretched out in so dark a craving!
Baffled heart, clouded vision; filled with ache
To know you have maimed the world you sought to make
Your instrument and minister, enslaving
Powers of earth and air—Hands that have wrought
So glorious things, the thoughts of joy to house!
Heart that has pulsed so ardent for its vow's
Accomplishment,—O heart so hardly taught!
O stretched-out hands! of you Eternity has need.
Give but your sacred passion and your shaping art,
The hunger of Eternity is there,—
Barren else, barren: chaos and a wilderness
Of feud and everlasting greed devouring greed,
The unshapen dream's despair!

Spirit of Man, dear spirit, sore opprest
With self-estrangement, and mis-choosing will,
And all satiety of gainful skill,—
Possession that was never yet possessed,—
You that have been so great a lover, giving
In innocency all for sacrifice;
Whom neither Time nor earth's regions suffice—
You too are sought, where still your dream is living
Over the secret oceans of unchartered mind
Who knows what voyagers, what sails invisibly
Press on, for all the lost, the foundered hopes untrue?
Who knows, through ignorant mists and storm upon that sea
What Lover, what unweariable Adventurer,
Makes still his quest of you?

O world that is within us, yet must still
Out of the eternal mystery be wooed
Ere it be ours and, breathing in the blood,
Live in its beauty, as the miracle
Of the divine colour of flowers in night
Was not, and is not of themselves alone
Nor of the dawn-beam, but of both made one,—
A marriage-mystery of earth and light!
O undiscovered world that all about us lies
When spirit to Spirit surrenders, and like young Love sees
Heaven with human eyes!
World of radiant morning! Joy's untravelled region!
Why lies it solitary? and O why tarry we?
Why daily wander out from Paradise?

III. 4

World-besieging Storm, from horizon heaped and menacing
Rear up the walls of thunder, till they tower
Shattering over earth, and from heart to heart reverberate,
Lancing that bright fear through the ruin-shower !
Revel, Winds, severing the bough of leafy promises
With rages from returning chaos sent !
Mockers and Destroyers, come; here is Man, predestinate
To all your arrows at his bosom bent.
Strip him of his splendours, of his conquests and dominions,
His secure boast to be earth's lord enthroned,
Humble him: he stands forth greater in his nakedness
Than in the wealth and safety that he owned.
He that so loved peril in all experience,
He that has gone with Sorrow all her way,
Will not now refuse or shrink; prove him to the innermost,
With worse than worst confront him: come what may,
Lo, you awake, O Trumpets of Calamity,
Some fragment of old Darkness in his breast;
Lo, to him fraternal is the stony and the terrible place;

His stricken Genius out of deeps unguessed
Rises up, grappling his reality to reality,
And still the secret in himself explores,
Bound beyond fear, the discovered and discoverer,
And in his own soul touches farthest shores.
Though he be stript of all, Powers from far replenish
    him,
Powers of the streaming worlds that through him stream.
O throbbing heart, O lifted arms, O tenderness,
O only capable of grief supreme !
O earth for ever mingled with unearthliness
Because the eternal with the brief is twined !
Wonder of breath that is momentary and tremulous
Suffices him who breathes eternal mind.
Vision that dawns beyond knowledge shall deliver him
From all that flattered, threatened, foiled, betrayed
Lo, having nothing, he is free of all the universe,
And where light is, he enters unafraid.

                                LAURENCE BINYON.

FLANNAN ISLE

" Though three men dwell on Flannan Isle
To keep the lamp alight,
As we steer'd under the lee, we caught
No glimmer through the night."

A passing ship at dawn had brought
The news; and quickly we set sail,
To find out what strange thing might ail
The keepers of the deep-sea light.

The winter day broke blue and bright,
With glancing sun and glancing spray,
As o'er the swell our boat made way,
As gallant as a gull in flight.
But, as we near'd the lonely Isle;

And look'd up at the naked height;
And saw the lighthouse towering white,
With blinded lantern, that all night
Had never shot a spark
Of comfort through the dark,
So ghostly in the cold sunlight
It seem'd, that we were struck the while
With wonder all too dread for words.

And, as into the tiny creek
We stole beneath the hanging crag,
We saw three queer, black, ugly birds—
Too big, by far, in my belief,
For guillemot or shag[1]—
Like seamen sitting bolt-upright
Upon a half-tide reef:
But, as we near'd, they plunged from sight,
Without a sound, or spurt of white.

And still too 'mazed to speak,
We landed; and made fast the boat;
And climb'd the track in single file,
Each wishing he was safe afloat,
On any sea, however far,
So it be far from Flannan Isle:

[1] *Shag.* The crested cormorant.

And still we seem'd to climb, and climb,
As though we'd lost all count of time,
And so must climb for evermore.
Yet, all too soon, we reached the door—
The black, sun-blister'd lighthouse-door,
That gaped for us ajar.

As, on the threshold, for a spell,
We paused, we seem'd to breathe the smell
Of limewash and of tar,
Familiar as our daily breath,
As though 'twere some strange scent of death:
And so, yet wondering, side by side,
We stood a moment, still tongue-tied:
And each with black foreboding eyed
The door, ere we should fling it wide,
To leave the sunlight for the gloom:
Till, plucking courage up, at last,
Hard on each other's heels we pass'd
Into the living-room.

Yet, as we crowded through the door,
We only saw a table, spread
For dinner, meat and cheese and bread;
But all untouch'd; and no one there;
As though, when they sat down to eat,
Ere they could even taste,
Alarm had come; and they in haste
Had risen and left the bread and meat:
For at the table-head a chair
Lay tumbled on the floor.

We listen'd; but we only heard
The feeble cheeping of a bird
That starved upon its perch:
And, listening still, without a word,
We set about our hopeless search.
We hunted high, we hunted low;
And soon ransack'd the empty house;
Then o'er the Island, to and fro,
We ranged, to listen and to look
In every cranny, cleft or nook
That might have hid a bird or mouse;

But, though we search'd from shore to shore,
We found no sign in any place
And soon again stood face to face
Before the gaping door:
And stole into the room once more
As frighten'd children steal.

Aye: though we hunted high and low,
And hunted everywhere,
Of the three men's fate we found no trace
Of any kind in any place,
But a door ajar, and an untouch'd meal,
And an overtoppled chair.

And, as we listen'd in the gloom
Of that forsaken living-room—
A chill clutch on our breath—
We thought how ill-chance came to all
Who kept the Flannan Light:
And how the rock had been the death
Of many a likely lad:
How six had come to a sudden end,
And three had gone stark mad:
And one whom we'd all known as friend
Had leapt from the lantern one still night,
And fallen dead by the lighthouse wall:
And long we thought,
Of the three we sought,
And of what might yet befall.

Like curs, a glance has brought to heel,
We listen'd, flinching there:
And look'd, and look'd, on the untouch'd meal,
And the overtoppled chair.

We seem'd to stand for an endless while,
Though still no word was said,
Three men alive on Flannan Isle,
Who thought on three men dead.

                              WILFRID WILSON GIBSON.

THE SILVER BIRD OF HERNDYKE MILL

By Herndyke Mill there haunts, folks tell,
   A strange and silver-breasted bird,
Her call is like a silver bell,
   So sweet a bell was never heard,—
The Silver Bird of Herndyke Mill,
   That flies so fast against the blast,
   And scares the stoat with one soft note
To hear her makes a man's blood chill.

The Charnel Path behind the Church,
   When nights are blackest, makes me pause,
But there 'tis only magpies perch
   And churning owls and goistering daws,
I fear the churchyard spooks much less,
   For all their flaming, starving eyes,
   Than that same Silver Bird which flies
At times through Herndyke wilderness.

In summer time the carps and rudds
   Sun in their scores below the weir:
In winter time the hurtling floods
   Forbid a soul to venture near.
But summer time and winter time
   Few people dare to linger there—
   Though mushrooms spring in many a ring—
For fear the Silver Bird should chime.

The stranger hears me with a smile.
   Why should a man so fear a bird?
But listen to my words awhile,
   But listen till the whole is heard;
And if your conscience is apprest
   With shameful act or wicked will,
   You durst not go to Herndyke Mill
Where flits the bird with silver breast.

Below the pleasant meeting-place
　　Of deep main stream and dwindled leat,
Where flock and glint the faint-heart dace,
　　By banks deep-grown in rabbit's-meat,
A little footbridge used to be—
　　A single plank from bank to bank,
　　A hand-rail white to see at night—
That led into a shrubbery.

In spring the sunlight green and cool
　　Dries up the seething grounds, and makes
The kingcups yet more beautiful,
　　And ushers out the bright green snakes.
But no one loves the anguish mist
　　That writhes its way at eventide
　　Along the copse's waterside:
So rarely come they there to tryst.

No lovers loiter there; alone
　　The homeless man may break the bounds,
But in the years now fled and flown
　　The miller used to mind these grounds,
And sometimes on the bridge he stood
　　In twilight peace, at day's decease;
　　Wrapt in his thought, as one who sought
To seem at one with stream and wood.

Now as he leant upon the rail
　　One glimmering summer night, when glooms
Were hearkening to the nightingale
　　And lading with dim dew the blooms,
Out of the woodside quietly
　　An agèd woman came, not fair,
　　But crowned with shining silver hair,
And craved a little charity.

" Sir, I am faint with walking far,
And penniless, and very old,
　　And under my unlucky star
　　I have no home, come warm or cold.
I have no sons,—my splendid son
　　That was my pride and dear love died,
　　Died in the war against the Tsar;
And I am friendless, loved of none."

The miller did not answer her—
  A selfish man whose god was greed.
The wandering lady cried, " Good sir,
  I pray you help me in my need."
With that the miller scorned her : " Go,
  I care not if you go to die.
  God does not help you, and should I ?
Sure some great sin has brought you low."

For such harsh words she set on him
  A fearful curse, a dread reproach,
And while she said it, down the stream
  In darkness splashed a chub or roach.
" I go to die within your wood,
  My silver hair shall tarnish there ;
  And by God's word a silver bird
Shall spring therefrom, the bird of Good.

The silver locks that care has made
  Shall turn into a silver breast—
The bird of Good shall never fade,
  Here shall she fly, and here shall rest.
If evil men come near her grange
  And shall affright them with her sweet
  Monotony of notes, and beat
Her wings about them fair and strange.

The holy presence of God shall awe
  The evil-doer that passes here.
From your white mill, and your green shaw,
  Shall spring a rumour sped with fear.
The Silver Bird, God's messenger,
  Shall guard the shrine of things divine,
  And your foul lie shall never die
While men are left that looked on her."

Her words were keen and sharp as flints :
  The miller stood as carved in stone.
She ceased : the silence made him wince,
  He looked and found himself alone.
A rustling in the tenterhooks
  Of brambles told him where she went,
  And with that rustling softly blent
The ripple-cripple of the brooks.

The little greenish stars looked on,
  The rustling in the coppice died:
A bat swerved oddly and was gone,
  A half-awakened night-wind sighed,
The miller with his heavy tread
  Was nearly to his threshold yew,
  A dor flew by with crackling cry
And struck him with a sort of dread.

The morning trod the dews once more
  And led abroad the rookery:
The pigeons glistened round the door,
  The wheel rolled round contentedly.
Free went the miller's callous tongue:
  He had forgot the wanderer's curse,
  Or else found himself no worse;
And warm the sunlight was, and young.

And so he went his wonted ways
  And robbed the farmer when he could,
And it was many many days
  Before he walked into his wood.
But in the sighting of the year,
  The shocked-up sheaves and withered leaves,
  The mourning nooks and sullen brooks
Brought back the woman's menace clear.

The sallows, how they shake and swirl
  As chilled by Autumn's trembling hands,
Their yellowed leaves so spin and twirl
  That down they drop like wasted brands.
They clog and huddle in the stream
  That's ruffled with the dismal draught
  Until their golden foundered craft
Are jostled by the groping bream.

There seems no heart in wood or wide,
  The midday comes with twilight fears,
The winds along the coverside
  Pause like bewildered travellers—
The miller picked her gloomy way,
  Intent to hound from off his ground
  A travelling man whose caravan
In cover of the coppice lay.

The sighing of the year was borne
  Deep, deep into the miller's soul.
The very footbridge looked forlorn,
  And plop plunged in a startled vole.
What shadows made his fancy grim
  Born of the outcast woman's word—
  When suddenly a silver bird
Was hovering, calling over him.

Her chiming channelled through his brain,
  His bright eyes held him, spelled him there.
He struck at her, he struck in vain,
  She fluttered round him, strange and fair.
And with her was that holy power
  So pure-intense as stilled his sense
  And in his ears the voice of tears
Grew slowly like a mournful flower.

The daylight dwindled from his eyes,
  A haze grew on him filled with moan:
His dazed soul stumbled with surmise,
  He walked the wilds of fear alone.
O who can tell what dreadful days
  He seemed to pass in this wild spell,
  Through what intolerable hell
Of phantoms with their searching gaze !

At last from glooms the silver breast
  Took fashion, and the dull day's light
Was round him (never light so blest),
  And then the Silver Bird took flight.
O miller, see your punishment,
  Your golden gain has brought forth pain,
  Your spoutsman's-boy has more of joy
Whose poor wage means his mother's rent.

Now, many a month and many a year
  Has died away on holt and hill
Since that rich miser told his fear
  And fled away and shut the mill.
And such stark tales have come to me
  Whom neighbours call Poor poaching Jack
  As every time have turned me back
From footing Herndyke shrubbery.

I've shot down pheasants from their roost
  By moonlight in the woods of squires:
In open day I've often noosed
  The Vicar's pike with cunning wires.
I've fooled a hundred keepers round,
  Risked Redstone Gaol and did not fail;
  But yon woodside I never tried
For fear of that which guards the ground.

The waters underneath the weir
  Hold battening monstrous fish by shoals:
And if a man is conscience-clear
  He may well come with baits and trolls;
And sure his creel would soon be full
  If, fearless of the bird of good,
  He angled all along the wood,
And in the blackness of the pool.

And nettles bunch where pansies flowered
  Within the garden's gap-struck pale,
And where the mill-wheel's spouting showered
  The weedy waters well nigh fail:
And resolute wasps come year by year
  Through bank's warm clay to make their way
  And built their nests, whence on their guests
Throughout the little garth they steer.

Amongst those twisted apple trees
  The little sunlights do abound:
They burn along like yellow bees
  And chequer all the shadowy ground:
The golden nobs and pippins swell
  And all unnoticed waste their prime,
  For few folk love to hear the chime
That brings the world of woe pell-mell.

By Herndyke Mill there haunts, folks tell,
  A holy silver-breasted bird;
Her call is like a silver bell,
  So sweet a bell was never heard,
The Silver Bird of Herndyke Mill,
  That flies so fast, against the blast,
  And frights the stoat with one soft note—
To hear her makes a man's blood chill.

EDMUND BLUNDEN.

LEPANTO

WHITE founts falling in the courts of the sun,
And the Soldan of Byzantium is smiling as they run;
There is laughter like the fountains in that face of all men
     feared,
It stirs the forest darkness, the darkness of his beard,
It curls the blood-red crescent, the crescent of his lips,
For the inmost sea of all the earth is shaken with his ships.
They have dared the white republics up the capes of Italy,
They have dashed the Adriatic round the Lion of the Sea,
And the Pope has cast his arms abroad for agony and loss,
And called the kings of Christendom for swords about the
     Cross.
The cold Queen of England is looking in the glass;
The shadow of the Valois is yawning at the Mass;
From evening isles fantastical rings faint the Spanish gun,
And the Lord upon the Golden Horn is laughing in the
     sun.

Dim drums throbbing, in the hills half heard,
Where only on a nameless throne a crownless prince has
     stirred,
Where, risen from a doubtful seat and half attainted stall,
The last knight of Europe takes weapons from the wall,
The last and lingering troubadour to whom the bird has
     sung,
That once went singing southward when all the world was
     young.
In that enormous silence, tiny and unafraid,
Comes up along a winding road the noise of the Crusade.
Strong gongs groaning as the guns boom far,
Don John of Austria is going to the war;
Stiff flags straining in the night-blasts cold, ,
In the gloom black-purple, in the glint old-gold,
Torchlight crimson on the copper kettle-drums,
Then the tuckets, then the trumpets, then the cannon, and
     he comes.
Don John laughing in the brave beard curled,
Spurning of his stirrups like the thrones of all the world,

Holding his head up for a flag of all the free.
Love-light of Spain—hurrah!
Death-light of Africa !
Don John of Austria
Is riding to the sea.

Mahound is in his paradise above the evening star
(*Don John of Austria is going to the war*).
He moves a mighty turban on the timeless houri's knees,
His turban that is woven of the sunsets and the seas.
He shakes the peacock gardens as he rises from his ease,
And he strides among the tree-tops and is taller than the
    trees,
And his voice through all the garden is a thunder sent to
    bring
Black Azrael and Ariel and Ammon on the wing.
Giants and the Genii,
Multiplex of wing and eye,
Whose strong obedience broke the sky
When Solomon was king.

They rush in red and purple from the red clouds of the
    morn,
From temples where the yellow gods shut up their eyes in
    scorn;
They rise in green robes roaring from the green hells of the
    sea
Where fallen skies and evil hues and eyeless creatures be;
On them the sea-valves cluster and the grey sea-forests
    curl,
Splashed with a splendid sickness, the sickness of the pearl;
They swell in sapphire smoke out of the blue cracks of the
    ground,—
They gather and they wonder and give worship to Ma-
    hound.
And he saith, " Break up the mountains where the hermit-
    folk can hide,
And sift the red and silver sands lest bone of saint abide,
And chase the Giaours flying night and day, not giving
    rest,
For that which was our trouble comes again out of the
    West.

We have set the seal of Solomon on all things under sun,
Of knowledge and of sorrow and endurance of things done,
But a noise is in the mountains, in the mountains, and I
    know
The voice that shook our palaces—four hundred years ago;
It is he that saith not " Kismet "; it is he that knows not
    Fate;
It is Richard, it is Raymond, it is Godfrey in the gate !
It is he whose loss is laughter when he counts the wager
    worth,
Put down your feet upon him, that our peace be on the
    earth."
For he heard drums groaning and he heard guns jar
(*Don John of Austria is going to the war*).
Sudden and still—hurrah !
Bolt from Iberia !
Don John of Austria
Is gone by Alcalar.

St. Michael's on his Mountain in the sea-roads of the north
(*Don John of Austria is girt and going forth*).
Where the grey seas glitter and the sharp tides shift,
And the sea-folk labour and the red sails lift.
He shakes his lance of iron and he clasps his wings of stone;
The noise is gone through Normandy; the noise is gone
    alone;
The North is full of tangled things and texts and aching
    eyes,
And dead is all the innocence of anger and surprise,
And Christian killeth Christian in a narrow dusty room,
And Christian dreadeth Christ that hath a newer face of
    doom,
And Christian hateth Mary that God kissed in Galilee,
But Don John of Austria is riding to the sea.
Don John calling through the blast and the eclipse,
Crying with the trumpet, with the trumpet of his lips,
Trumpet that sayeth ha !
Domino Gloria !
Don John of Austria
Is shouting to the ships.

King Philip's in his closet with the Fleece about his neck
(*Don John of Austria is armed upon the deck*).

The walls are hung with velvet that is black and soft as sin,
And little dwarfs creep out of it and little dwarfs creep in.
He holds a crystal phial that has colours like the moon,
He touches, and it tingles, and he trembles very soon,
And his face is as a fungus of a leprous white and grey
Like plants in the high houses that are shuttered from the day,
And death is in the phial and the end of noble work,
But Don John of Austria has fired upon the Turk.
Don John's hunting, and his hounds have bayed—
Booms away past Italy the rumour of his raid.
Gun upon gun, ha ! ha !
Gun upon gun, hurrah !
Don John of Austria
Has loosed the cannonade.

The Pope was in his chapel before day or battle broke
(*Don John of Austria is hidden in the smoke*).
The hidden room in man's house where God sits all the
    year,
The secret window whence the world looks small and very
    dear.
He sees as in a mirror on the monstrous twilight sea
The crescent of the cruel ships whose name is mystery;
They fling great shadows foe-wards, making Cross and
    Castle dark,
They veil the plumèd lions on the galleys of St. Mark;
And above the ships are palaces of brown, black-bearded
    chiefs.
And below the ships are prisons, where with multitudinous
    griefs,
Christian captives sick and sunless, all a labouring race
    repines
Like a race in sunken cities, like a nation in the mines.
They are lost like slaves that swat, and in the skies of
    morning hung
The stairways of the tallest gods when tyranny was young.

They are countless, voiceless, hopeless as those fallen or
    fleeing on
Before the high Kings' horses in the granite of Babylon.
And many a one grows witless in his quiet room in hell,
Where a yellow face looks inward through the lattice of his
    cell,

And he finds his God forgotten, and he seeks no more a
    sign—
(*But Don John of Austria has burst the battle-line !*)
Don John pounding from the slaughter-painted poop,
Purpling all the ocean like a bloody pirate's sloop,
Scarlet running over on the silvers and the golds,
Breaking of the hatches up and bursting of the holds,
Thronging of the thousands up that labour under sea,
White for bliss and blind for sun and stunned for liberty.
Vivat Hispania !
Domino Gloria !
Don John of Austria
Has set his people free !

Cervantes on his galley sets the sword back in the sheath
(*Don John of Austria rides homeward with a wreath*).
And he sees across a weary land a straggling road in Spain,
Up which a lean and foolish knight for ever rides in vain,
And he smiles, but now as Sultans smile, and settles back
    the blade . . .
(*But Don John of Austria rides home from the Crusade*).

G. K. CHESTERTON.

SNAKE

A snake came to my water-trough
On a hot, hot day, and I in pyjamas for the heat,
To drink there.

In the deep, strange-scented shade of the great dark carob-
tree
I came down the steps with my pitcher
And must wait, must stand and wait, for there he was at
the trough before me.
He reached down from a fissure in the earth-wall in the
gloom
And trailed his yellow-brown slackness soft-bellied down,
over the edge of the stone trough
And rested his throat upon the stone bottom,
And where the water had dripped from the tap, in a small
clearness,
He sipped with his straight mouth,
Softly drank through his straight gums, into his slack long
body,
Silently.

Someone was before me at my water-trough,
And I, like a second comer, waiting.

He lifted his head from his drinking, as cattle do,
And looked at me vaguely, as drinking cattle do,
And flickered his two-forked tongue from his lips, and
mused a moment,
And stooped and drank a little more,
Being earth-brown, earth-golden from the burning, burning
bowels of the earth
On the day of Sicilian July, with Etna smoking.

The voice of my education said to me
He must be killed,
For in Sicily the black, black snakes are innocent, the gold
are venomous.
And voices in me said, If you were a man
You would take a stick and break him now, and finish him
off.

But I must confess how I liked him,
How glad I was he had come like a guest in quiet, to drink
    at my water-trough
And depart peaceful, pacified, and thankless,
Into the burning bowels of this earth?

Was it cowardice, that I dared not kill him?
Was it perversity, that I longed to talk to him?
Was it humility, to feel so honoured?
I felt so honoured.

And yet those voices:
If you were not afraid, you would kill him!
And truly I was afraid, I was most afraid,
But even so, honoured still more
That he should seek my hospitality
From out the dark door of the secret earth.

He drank enough
And lifted his head, dreamily, as one who has drunken,
And flickered his tongue like a forked night on the air, so
    black,
Seeming to lick his lips,
And looked around like a god, unseeing, into the air
And slowly turned his head,
And slowly, very slowly, as if thrice adream,
Proceeded to draw his slow length curving round
And climb again the broken bank of my wall-face.

And as he put his head into that dreadful hole,
And as he slowly drew up, snake-easing his shoulders, and
    entered farther,
A sort of horror, a sort of protest against his withdrawing
    into that horrid black hole,
Deliberately going into the blackness, and slowly drawing
    himself after,
Overcame me now his back was turned.

I looked round, I put down my pitcher,
I picked up a clumsy log
And threw it at the water-trough with a clatter.
I think it did not hit him.

But suddenly that part of him that was left behind con-
 vulsed in undignified haste,
Writhed like lightning, and was gone
Into the black hole, the earth-slipped fissure in the wall-
 front,
At which, in the intense still noon, I stared with fascination.

And immediately I regretted it.
I thought how paltry, how vulgar, what a mean act!
I despised myself and the voices of my accursed human
 education.
And I thought of the albatross,
And I wished he would come back, my snake.

For he seemed to me again like a king,
Like a king in exile, uncrowned in the underworld,
Now due to be crowned again.

And so, I missed my chance with one of the lords
Of life.
And I have something to expiate;
A pettiness.

D. H. LAWRENCE.

ELEGY

THE SUMMER-HOUSE ON THE MOUND

How well my eyes remember the dim path!
My homeing heart no happier playground hath.
I need not close my lids but it appears
Through the bewilderment of forty years
To tempt my feet, my childish feet, between
Its leafy walls, beneath its arching green;
Fairer than dream of sleep, than Hope more fair
Leading to dreamless sleep her sister Care.

There grew two fellow limes, two rising trees,
Shadowing the lawn, the summer haunt of bees,
Whose stems, engraved with many a russet scar
From the spear-hurlings of our mimic war,

Pillar'd the portico to that wide walk,
A mossy terrace of the native chalk
Fashion'd, that led thro' the dark shades around
Straight to the wooden temple on the mound.
There live the memories of my early days,
There still with childish heart my spirit plays;
Yea, terror-stricken by the fiend despair
When she hath fled me, I have found her there;
And there 'tis ever noon, and glad suns bring
Alternate days of summer and of spring,
With childish thought, and childish faces bright,
And all unknown save but the hour's delight.

High on the mound the ivied arbour stood,
A dome of straw upheld on rustic wood:
Hidden in fern the steps of the ascent,
Whereby unto the southern front we went,
And from the dark plantation climbing free,
Over a valley look'd out on the sea.
That sea is ever bright and blue, the sky
Serene and blue, and ever white ships lie
High on the horizon steadfast in full sail,
Or nearer in the roads pass within hail
Of naked brigs and barques that windbound ride
At their taut cables heading to the tide.

There many an hour I have sat to watch; nay, now
The brazen disk is cold against my brow,
And in my sight a circle of the sea
Enlarged to swiftness, where the salt waves flee,
And ships in stately motion pass so near
That what I see is speaking to my ear:
I hear the waves dash and the tackle strain,
The canvas flap, the rattle of the chain
That runs out thro' the hawse, the clank of the winch
Winding the rusty cable inch by inch,
Till half I wonder if they have no care,
Those sailors, that my glass is brought to bear
On all their doings, if I vex them not
On every pretty task of their rough lot
Prying and spying, searching every craft
From painted truck to gunnel, fore and aft,—

Thro' idle Sundays as I have watch'd them lean
Long hours upon the rail, or neath its screen
Prone on the deck to lie outstretch'd at length,
Sunk in renewal of their wearied strength.

But what a feast of joy to me, if some
Fast-sailing frigate to the Channel come
Back'd here her topsail, or brought gently up
Let from her bow the splashing anchor drop,
By faint contrary wind stay'd in her cruise,
The Phaeton or dancing Arethuse,
Or some immense three-decker of the line,
Romantic as the tale of Troy divine;
Ere yet our iron age had doom'd to fall
The towering freeboard of the wooden wall,
And for the engines of a mightier Mars
Clipp'd their wide wings, and dock'd their soaring spars.
The gale that in their tackle sang, the wave
That neath their gilded galleries dasht so brave
Lost then their merriment, nor look to play
With the heavy-hearted monsters of to-day.

One noon in March upon that anchoring ground
Came Napier's fleet unto the Baltic bound:
Cloudless the sky and calm and blue the sea,
As round Saint Margaret's cliff mysteriously,
Those murderous queens walking in Sabbath sleep
Glided in line upon the windless deep:
For in those days was first seen low and black
Beside the full-rigg'd mast the strange smoke-stack,
And neath their stern revolv'd the twisted fan.
Many I knew as soon as I might scan,
The heavy *Royal George*, the *Acre* bright,
The *Hogue* and *Ajax*, and could name aright
Others that I remember now no more;
But chief, her blue flag flying at the fore,
With fighting guns a hundred thirty and one,
The Admiral ship *The Duke of Wellington*,
Whereon sail'd George, who in her gig had flown
The silken ensign by our sisters sewn.
The iron Duke himself,—whose soldier fame
To England's proudest ship had given her name,

And whose white hairs in this my earliest scene
Had scarce more honour'd than accustom'd been,—
Was two years since to his last haven past:
I had seen his castle-flag to fall half-mast
One morn as I sat looking on the sea,
When thus all England's grief came first to me,
Who hold my childhood favour'd that I knew
So well the face that won at Waterloo.

But now 'tis other wars, and other men ;—
The year that Napier sail'd, my years were ten—
Yea, and new homes and loves my heart hath found :
A priest has there usurped the ivied mound,
The bell that call'd to horse calls now to prayers,
And silent nuns tread the familiar stairs.
Within the peach-clad walls that old outlaw,
The Roman wolf, scratches with privy paw.

ROBERT BRIDGES.

SPANISH WATERS

SPANISH waters, Spanish waters, you are ringing in my ears,
Like a slow sweet piece of music from the grey forgotten
    years ;
Telling tales, and beating tunes, and bringing weary
    thoughts to me
Of the sandy beach at Muertos, where I would that I could
    be.

There's a surf breaks on Los Muertos, and it never stops to
    roar,
And it's there we came to anchor, and it's there we went
    ashore,
Where the blue lagoon is silent amid snags of rotting trees,
Dropping like the clothes of corpses cast up by the seas.

We anchored at Los Muertos when the dipping sun was red,
We left her half-a-mile to sea, to west of Nigger Head ;
And before the mist was on the Cay, before the day was
    done,
We were all ashore on Muertos with the gold that we had
    won.

We bore it through the marshes in a half-score battered
  chests,
Sinking, in the sucking quagmires to the sunburn on our
  breasts,
Heaving over tree-trunks, gasping, damning at the flies
  and heat,
Longing for a long drink, out of silver, in the ship's cool
  lazareet.

The moon came white and ghostly as we laid the treasure
  down,
There was gear there'd make a beggarman as rich as Lima
  Town,
Copper charms and silver trinkets from the chests of
  Spanish crews,
Gold doubloons and double moidores, louis d'ors and
  portagues,

Clumsy yellow-metal earrings from the Indians of Brazil,
Uncut emeralds out of Rio, bezoar stones from Guayaquil;
Silver, in the crude and fashioned, pots of old Arica bronze,
Jewels from the bones of Incas desecrated by the Dons.

We smoothed the place with mattocks, and we took and
  blazed the tree,
Which marks yon where the gear is hid that none will ever
  see,
And we laid aboard the ship again, and south away we
  steers,
Through the loud surf of Los Muertos which is beating in
  my ears.

I'm the last alive that knows it. All the rest have gone their
  ways
Killed, or died, or come to anchor in the old Mulatas Cays,
And I go singing, fiddling, old and starved and in despair,
And I know where all that gold is hid, if I were only there.

It's not the way to end it all. I'm old, and nearly blind,
And an old man's past's a strange thing, for it never leaves
  his mind.

And I see in dreams, awhiles, the beach, the sun's disc
    dipping red,
And the tall ship, under topsails, swaying in past Nigger
    Head.

I'd be glad to step ashore there. Glad to take a pick and go
To the lone blazed coco-palm tree in the place no others
    know,
And lift the gold and silver that has mouldered there for years
By the loud surf of Los Muertos which is beating in my ears.

JOHN MASEFIELD.

MISS THOMPSON GOES SHOPPING

MISS THOMPSON AT HOME

In her lone cottage on the downs,
With winds and blizzards and great crowns
Of shining cloud, with wheeling plover
And short grass sweet with the small white clover,
Miss Thompson lived, correct and meek,
A lonely spinster, and every week
On market-day she used to go
Into the little town below,
Tucked in the great downs' hollow bowl,
Like pebbles gathered in a shoal.

SHE GOES A-MARKETING

So, having washed her plates and cup
And banked the kitchen fire up,
Miss Thompson slipped upstairs and dressed,
Put on her black (her second best),
The bonnet trimmed with rusty plush,
Peeped in the glass with simpering blush,
From camphor-smelling cupboard took
Her thicker jacket off the hook
Because the day might turn to cold.
Then, ready, slipped downstairs and rolled
The hearthrug back; then searched about,
Found her basket, ventured out,
Snecked the door and paused to lock it
And plunged the key in some deep pocket.

Then as she tripped demurely down
The steep descent, the little town
Spread wider till its sprawling street
Enclosed her and her footfalls beat
On hard stone pavement; and she felt
Those throbbing ecstasies that melt
Through heart and mind as, happy, free,
Her small, prim personality
Merged into the seething strife
Of auction-marts and city life.

SHE VISITS THE BOOTMAKER

Serenely down the busy stream
Miss Thompson floated in a dream.
Now, hovering beelike, she would stop
Entranced before some tempting shop,
Getting in people's way and prying
At things she never thought of buying;
Now wafted on without an arm.
And thus in course of time she came
To Watson's bootshop. Long she pries
At boots and shoes of every size,
Brown football boots, with bar and stud,
For boys that scuffle in the mud,
And dancing-pumps with pointed toes
Glassy as jet, and dull black bows;
Slim ladies' shoes with two-inch heel,
And sprinkled beads of gold and steel.
" How anyone can wear such things ! "
On either side the doorway springs
(As in a tropic jungle loom
Masses of strange thick-petaled bloom
And fruits misshapen) fold on fold
A growth of sandshoes rubber-soled,
Clambering the doorposts, branching, spawning
Their barbarous bunches like an awning
Over the windows and the doors.

IS TEMPTED

But, framed among the other stores,
Something has caught Miss Thompson's eye
(O worldliness, O vanity !)

A pair of slippers—scarlet plush.
Miss Thompson feels a conscious blush
Suffuse her face, as though her thought
Had ventured further than it ought.
But O that colour's rapturous singing
And the answer in her lone heart ringing!
She turns (O, Guardian Angels, stop her
From doing anything improper!).
She turns; and, see, she stoops and bungles
In through the sandshoes' hanging jungles,
Away from light and common-sense,
Into the shop dim-lit and dense
With smells of polish and tanned hide.
Soon from a dark recess inside
Fat Mrs. Watson comes, slip slop,
To mind the business of the shop.
She walks flat-footed with a roll—
A serviceable, homely soul,
With kindly, ugly face like dough,
Hair dull and colourless as tow.
A huge Scotch pebble fills the space
Between her bosom and her face.
One sees her making beds all day.
Miss Thompson lets her say her say
—" So chilly for the time of year.
It's ages since we saw you here "—
Then, heart a flutter, speech precise,
Describes the shoes and asks the price.
" Them, miss? Ah, them is six-and-nine "!

WRESTLES WITH THE TEMPTATION

Miss Thompson shudders down the spine
(Dream of impossible romance).
She eyes them with a wistful glance,
Torn between good and evil. Yes,
For half-a-minute, and no less,
Miss Thompson strives with seven devils,
Then, soaring over earthly levels,
Turns from the shoes with lingering touch—

AND IS SAVED

" Ah, six-and-nine is far too much!
Sorry to trouble you. Good-day! "

SHE VISITS THE FISHMONGER

A little further down the way
Stands Miles's fish shop, whence is shed
So strong a smell of fishes dead
That people of a subtler sense
Hold their breath and hurry thence.
Miss Thompson hovers there and gazes.
Her housewife's knowing eye appraises
Salt and fresh, severely cons
Kippers bright as tarnished bronze;
Great cods disposed upon the sill,
Chilly and wet with gaping gill,
Flat head, glazed eye, and mute, uncouth,
Shapeless, wan, old-woman's mouth.
Next, a row of soles and plaice,
With querulous and twisted face,
And red-eyed bloaters, golden-grey;
Smoked haddocks ranked in neat array;
A group of smelts that take the light
Like slips of rainbow, pearly bright;
Silver trout with rosy spots,
And coral shrimps with keen black dots
For eyes, and hard and jointed sheath
And crisp tails curving underneath.
But there upon the sanded floor,
More wonderful in all that store
Than anything on slab or shelf,
Stood Miles the fishmonger himself.
Foursquare he stood and filled the place.
His huge hands and his jolly face
Were red. He had a mouth to quaff
Pint after pint: a sounding laugh,
But wheezy at the end, and oft
His eyes bulged outwards and he coughed.
Aproned he stood from chin to toe.
The apron's vertical long flow
Warped grandly outwards to display
His hale, round belly hung midway,
Whose apex was securely bound
With apron-strings wrapped round and round.
Outside Miss Thompson, small and staid,
Felt, as she always felt, afraid

Of this huge man who laughed so loud
And drew the notice of the crowd.
Awhile she paused in timid thought,
Then promptly hurried in and bought
"Two kippers, please. Yes, lovely weather."
"Two kippers? Sixpence altogether."
And in her basket laid the pair
Wrapped face to face in newspaper.

RELAPSES INTO TEMPTATION

Then on she went, as one half blind,
For things were stirring in her mind.
Then turned about with fixed intent,
And, heading for the bootshop, went

AND FALLS

Straight in and bought the slippers,
And popped them in beside the kippers.

SHE VISITS THE CHEMIST

So much for that. From there she tacked,
Still flushed by this decisive act,
Westward, and came without a stop
To Mr. Wren the chemist's shop,
And paused outside a while to see
The tall, big-bellied bottles, three—
Red, blue, and emerald, richly bright,
Each with its burning core of light.
The bell chimed as she pushed the door,
Spotless the oilcloth on the floor,
Limpid as water each glass case,
Each thing precisely in its place.
Rows of small drawers, black-lettered each
With curious words of foreign speech,
Ranked high above the other ware.
The old strange fragrance filled the air,
A fragrance like the garden pink,
But tinged with a vague medicinal stink
Of camphor, soap, new sponges, blent
With chloroform and violet scent.
And Wren the chemist tall and spare
Stood gaunt behind his counter there.

Quiet and very wise he seemed,
With skull-like face, bald head that gleamed;
Through spectacles his eyes looked kind;
He wore a pencil tucked behind
His ear. And never he mistakes
The wildest signs the doctor makes
Prescribing drugs. Brown paper, string
He will not use for anything,
But all in neat white parcels packs
And sticks them up with sealing wax.
Miss Thompson bowed and blushed, and then
Undoubting bought of Mr. Wren,
Being free from modern scepticism,
A bottle for her rheumatism,
Also some peppermints to take
In case of wind; an oval cake
Of scented soap; a penny square
Of pungent naphthalene to scare
The moth. And after Wren had wrapped
And sealed the lot, Miss Thompson clapped
Them in beside the fish and shoes.
" Good-day," she says, and off she goes.

IS LED AWAY BY THE PLEASURE OF THE TOWN

Bee-like, Miss Thompson, whither next?
Outside you pause awhile, perplext,
Your bearing lost. Then all comes back
And round she wheels, hot on the track
Of Giles the grocer; and from there
To Emilie the milliner,
There to be tempted by the sight
Of hats and blouses fiercely bright.
(O guard Miss Thompson, Powers that Be,
From Crudeness and Vulgarity !)
Still on from shop to shop she goes
With sharp bird's eye, inquiring nose,
Prying and peering, entering some,
Oblivious of the thought of home.

IS CONVINCED OF INDISCRETION

The town brimmed up with deep-blue haze,
But still she stayed to flit and gaze,

Her eyes a-blur with rapturous sights,
Her small soul full of small delights,
Empty her purse, her basket filled.
The traffic in the town was stilled.
The clock struck six. Men thronged the inns.
Dear, dear, she should be home long since.

AND RETURNS HOME

Then as she climbed the misty down
The lamps were lighted in the town's
Small streets.   She saw them star by star
Multiplying from afar ;
Till, mapped beneath her, she could trace
Each street and the wide, square market place
Sunk deep and deeper as she went
Higher up the steep ascent.
And all that soul-uplifting stir
Step by step fell back from her,
The glory gone, the blossoming
Shrivelled, and she, a small, frail thing,
Carrying her laden basket. Till
Darkness and silence of the hill
Received her in their restful care
And stars came dropping through the air.

But loudly, sweetly sang the slippers
In the basket with the kippers.
And loud and sweet the answer thrills
From her lone heart on the hills.

MARTIN ARMSTRONG.

THE OLD ANGLER

TWILIGHT leaned mirrored in a pool
    Where willow boughs swept green and hoar,
Silk-clear the water, calm and cool,
    Silent and weedy shore :

There in abstracted, brooding mood
    One fishing sate.   His painted float
Motionless as a planet stood ;
    Motionless his boat.

A melancholy soul was this,
  With lantern jaw, gnarled hand, vague eye;
Huddled in pensive solitariness
  He had fished existence by.

Empty his creel; stolen his bait—
  Impassively he angled on,
Though mist now showed the evening late
  And daylight wellnigh gone.

Suddenly, like a tongueless bell,
  Downward his gaudy cork did glide;
A deep, low-gathering, gentle swell
  Spread slowly far and wide.

Wheeped out his tackle from noiseless winch,
  And furtive as a thief, his thumb,
With nerve intense, wound inch by inch
  A line no longer numb.

What fabulous spoil could this unplayed
  Gape upward to a mortal air?—
He stoops engrossed; his tanned cheek greyed;
  His heart stood still; for there,

Wondrously fairing, beneath the skin
  Of secretly bubbling water seen,
Swims, not the silver of scale and fin—
  But gold inmixt with green.

Deeply astir in oozy bed,
  The darkening mirror ripples and rocks:
And lo—a wan-pale, lovely head,
  Hook tangled in its locks!

Cold from her haunt—a Naiad slim.
  Shoulder and cheek gleamed ivory white;
Though how faint stars stood over him,
  The hour hard on night.

Her green eyes gazed like one half-blind
  In sudden radiance; her breast
Breathed the sweet air, while gently twined,
  'Gainst the cold water pressed,

Her lean webbed hands.   She floated there,
  Light as a scentless petalled flower,
Water-drops dewing from her hair
  In tinkling beadlike shower.

So circling sidelong, her tender throat
  Uttered a grieving, desolate wail ;
Shrill o'er the dark pool lapsed its note,
  Piteous as nightingale.

Ceased Echo.   And he ?—a life's remorse
  Welled to a tongue unapt to charm,
But never a word broke harsh and hoarse
  To quiet her alarm.

With infinite stealth his twitching thumb
  Tugged softly at the tautened gut,
Bubble-light, fair, her lips now dumb,
  She moved, and struggled not ;

But with set, wild, unearthly eyes
  Pale-gleaming, fixed as if in fear,
She couched in the water, with quickening sighs,
  And floated near.

In hollow heaven the stars were at play ;
  Wan glow-worms greened the pool-side grass ;
Dipped the wide-bellied boat.   His prey
  Gazed on ; nor breathed.   Alas !—

Long sterile years had come and gone ;
  Youth, like a distant dream, was sped ;
Heart, hope, and eyes had hungered on. . . .
  He turned a shaking head,

And clumsily groped amid the gold,
  Sleek with night dews, of that tangling hair,
Till pricked his finger keen and cold
  The barb imbedded there.

Teeth clenched, he drew his knife—" Snip, snip,"—
  Groaned, and sate shivering back ; and she,
Treading the water with birdlike dip,
  Shook her sweet shoulders free :

Drew backward, smiling, infatuate fair,
  His life's disasters in her eyes,
All longing and folly, grief, despair,
  Daydreams and mysteries.

She stooped her brow; laid low her cheek,
  And, steering on that silk-tressed craft,
Out from the listening, leaf-hung creek,
  Tossed up her chin, and laughed—

A mocking, icy, inhuman note.
  One instant flashed that crystal breast,
Leaned, and was gone.   Dead-still the boat:
  And the deep dark at rest.

Flits moth to flower.   A water-rat
  Noses the placid ripple.   And lo!
Streams a lost meteor.   Night is late,
  And daybreak zephyrs flow. . . .

And he—the cheated?   Dusk till morn,
  Insensate, even of hope forsook,
He muttering squats, aloof, forlorn,
  Dangling a baitless hook.

WALTER DE LA MARE.

From A TIME TO DANCE

Sing we the two lieutenants, Parer and M'Intosh,
After the War wishing to hie them home to Australia,
Planned they would take a high way, a hazardous crazy
    air-way:
Death their foregone conclusion, a flight headlong to failure,
We said.   For no silver posh
Plane was their pigeon, no dandy dancer quick-stepping
    through heaven,
But a craft of obsolete design, a condemned D.H. nine;
Sold for a song it was, patched up though to write an
    heroic
Line across the world as it reeled on its obstinate stoic
Course to that southern haven.

On January 8, 1920, their curveting wheels kissed
England goodbye. Over Hounslow in morning mist
They rose and circled like buzzards while we rubbed our
    sleepy eyes :
Like a bird scarce-fledged they flew, whose flying hours
    are few—
Still dear is the nest but deeper its desire unto the skies—
And they left us to our sleeping.
They felt earth's warning tug on their wings : vain to
    advance
Asking a thoroughfare through the angers of the air
On so flimsy a frame ; but they pulled up her nose and the
    earth went sloping
Away, and they aimed for France.

Fog first, a wet blanket, a kill-joy, the primrose-of-morning's
    blight.
Blotting out the dimpled sea, the ample welcome of land,
The gay glance from the bright
Cliff-face behind, snaring the sky with treachery, sneering
At hope's loss of height. But they charged it, flying blind ;
They took a compass-bearing against that dealer of doubt,
As a saint when the field of vision is fogged gloriously steels
His spirit against the tainter of air, the elusive taunter :
They climbed to win a way out,
Then downward dared till the moody waves snarled at
    their wheels.

Landing at last near Conteville, who had skimmed the crest
    of oblivion,
They could not rest, but rose and flew on to Paris, and
    there
Trivially were delayed—a defective petrol feed—
Three days: a time hung heavy on
Hand and heart, till they leapt again to the upper air,
Their element, their lover, their angel antagonist.
Would have taken a fall without fame, but the sinewy
    framework the wrist
Of steel the panting engine wrestled well : and they went
South while the going was good, as a swallow that guide
    nor goad
Needs on his sunny scent.

At Lyons the petrol pump failed again, and forty-eight
　　hours
They chafed to be off, the haughty champions whose
　　breathing-space
Was an horizon span and the four winds their fan.
Over Italy's shores
A reverse, the oil ran out and cursing they turned about
Losing a hundred miles to find a landing-place.
Not a coast for a castaway this, no even chance of alighting
On sward or wind-smooth sand :
A hundred miles without pressure they flew, the engine
　　fighting
For breath, and its heart nearly burst before they dropped
　　to land.

And now the earth they had spurned rose up against them
　　in anger
Tier upon tier it towered, the terrible Apennines :
No sanctuary there for wings, not flares nor landing-lines
No hope of floor and hangar.
Yet those ice-tipped spears that disputed the passage set
　　spurs
To their two hundred and forty horse power ; grimly they
　　gained
Altitude, though the hand of heaven was heavy upon them,
The downdraught from the mountains ; though desperate
　　eddies spun them
Like a coin, yet unkindly tossed their luck came uppermost
And mastery remained.

Air was all ambushes round them, was avalanche earth-
　　quake
Quicksand, a funnel deep as doom, till climbing steep
They crawled like a fly up the face of perpendicular night
And levelled, finding a break
At fourteen thousand feet. Here earth is shorn from sight
Deadweight a darkness hangs on their eyelids, and they
　　bruise
Their eyes against a void ; vindictive the cold airs close
Down like a trap of steel and numb them from head to heel ;
Yet they kept an even keel,
For their spirit reached forward and took the controls
　　while their fingers froze.

They had not heard the last of death. When the mountains
 were passed,
He raised another crest, the long crescendo of pain
Kindled to climax, the plane.
Took fire. Alone in the sky with the breath of their enemy
Hot in their face they fought: from three thousand feet
 they tilted
Over, side-slipped away—a trick for an ace, a race
And running duel with death: flame streamed out behind
A crimson scarf of, as life-blood out of a wound, but the
 wind
Of their downfall staunched it; death wilted,
Lagged and died out in smoke—he could not stay their
 pace.

A lull for a while. The powers of hell rallied their legions.
On Parer now fell the stress of the flight; for the plane had
 been bumped,
Buffeted, thrashed by the air almost beyond repair:
But he tinkered and coaxed, and they limped
Over the Adriatic on into warmer regions.
Erratic their course to Athens, to Crete; coolly they rode
 her
Like a tired horse at the water-jumps, they jockeyed her
 over seas,
Till they came at last to a land whose dynasties of sand
Had seen Alexander, Napoleon, many a straddling invader,
But never none like these.

England to Cairo, a joy-ride, a forty-hour journey at most,
Had cost them forty-four days. What centuried strata of life
Fuelled the fire that haled them to heaven, the power that
 held them
Aloft? For their plane was a laugh,
A patch, brittle as matchstick, a bubble, a lift for a ghost
Bolts always working loose of propeller, cylinder, bearer;
Instruments faulty, filter, magneto, each strut unsound.
Yet after four days, though we swore she never could leave
 the ground,
We saw her in headstrong haste diminish towards the
 east—
That makeshift, mad sky-farer.

Aimed they now for Baghdad, unwritten in air's annals
A voyage. But theirs the fate all flights of logic to refute,
Who obeyed no average law, who buoyed the viewless
    channels
Of sky with a courage steadfast, luminous. Safe they
    crossed
Sinai's desert, and daring
The Nejd, the unneighbourly waste of Arabia, yet higher
    soaring
(Final a fall there for birds of passage, limed and lost
In shifty the sand's embrace) all day they strove to climb
Through stormy rain : but they felt her shorten her stride
    and falter,
And they fell at evening time.
Slept that night beside their machine, and the next morning
Raider Arabs appeared reckoning this stranded bird
A gift : like cobras they struck, and their gliding shadows
    athwart
The sand were all their warning.
But the aeronauts, knowing iron coinage here, had brought
Mills bombs and revolvers, and M'Intosh held them off
While Parer fought for life—
A spark, the mechanic's right answer, and finally wrought
A miracle, for the dumb engine spoke and they rose
Convulsively out of the clutch of the desert, the clench of
    their foes.
Orchestrate this theme, artificer-poet. Imagine
The roll, crackling percussion, quickening tempo of
    engine
For a start : the sound as they soar, an octave-upward slur
Scale of sky ascending :
Hours-held note of level flight, a beat unhurried,
Sustaining undertone of movement never-ending :
Wind shrill on the ailerons, flutes and fifes in a flurry
Devilish when they dive, plucking of tense stays.
These hardly heard it, who were the voice, the heavenly air
That sings above always.

We have seen the extremes, the burning, the freezing, the
    outward face
Of their exploit ; heroic peaks, tumbling-to-zero depressions
Little our graph can show, the line they traced through
    space,

Of the heart's passionate patience.
How soft drifts of sleep piled on their senses deep
And they dug themselves out often : how the plane was a
weight that hung
And swung on their aching nerve : how din drilled through
the skull
And sight sickened—so slow earth filtered past below.
Yet nerve failed never, heart clung
To height, and the brain kept its course and the hand its
skill
Baghdad renewed a propeller damaged in desert. Arid
Baluchistan spared them that brought down and spoilt with
thirst
Armies of Alexander. To Karachi they were carried
On cloud-back : fragile as tinder their plane, but they were
tender
Now to their need, and nursed
Them along till teeming India made room for them to
alight.
Wilting her wings, the sweltering suns had moulted her
bright
Plumage, rotten with rain
The fabric : but they packed her with iron washers and
tacked her
Together, good for an hour, and took the air again.

Feats for a hundred flights, they were prodigal of : a fairest
Now to tell—how they foiled death when the engine failed
Above the Irrawaddy, over close-woven forest.
What shoals for a pilot there, what a snarled passage and
dark
Shelves down to doom and grip
Of green ! But look, balanced superbly, quick off the mark
Swooping like centre three-quarter whose impetus storms a
gap—
Defenders routed, rooted their feet, and their arms are mown
Aside, that high or low aim at his overthrow—
M'Intosh touched her down.
And they picked her up out of it somehow and put her at
the air, a
Sorry hack for such steeplechasing, to leap the sky.
" We'll fly this bloody crate till it falls to bits at our feet,"
Said the mechanic Parer.

And at Moulmein soon they crashed; and the plane by
    their spirit's high
Tension long pinned, girded and guarded from dissolution,
Fell to bits at their feet. Wrecked was the under-carriage,
Radiator cracked, in pieces, compasses crocked;
Fallen to confusion.
Their winged hope was a heap of scrap, but unsplintered
    their courage.

Six weeks they worked in sun-glare and jungle damps,
    assembling
Fragments to make airworthy what was worth not its
    weight in air.
As a surgeon, grafter of skin, as a setter of bones tumbling
Apart, they had power to repair
This good for naught but the grave: they livened her
    engine and gave
Fuselage faith to rise rejuvenated from ruin.
Went with them stowaways, not knowing what hazard
    they flew in—
Bear-cubs, a baby alligator, lizards and snakes galore;
Mascots maybe, for the plane though twice she was
    floored again
Always came up for more.
Till they came to the pitiless mountains of Timor. Yet
    these, untamed,
Nor timorous, against the gradient and Niagara of air they
    climbed
Scarce-skimming the summits; and over the shark-toothed
    Timor Sea
Lost their bearings, but shirked not the odds, the deaths
    that lurked
A million to one on their trail:
They reached out to the horizon and plucked their destiny.
On for eight hours they flew blindfold against the unknown,
And the oil began to fail
And their flying spirit waned—one pint of petrol remained
When the land stood up to meet them and they came into
    their own.

Southward still to Melbourne, the bourn of their flight, they
    pressed
Till at last near Culcairn, like a last fretted leaf
Falling from brave autumn into earth's breast,

D.H. nine, their friend that had seen them to the end,
Gave up her airy life.
The Southern Cross was splendid above the spot where she
    fell,
The end of her rainbow curve over our weeping day:
And the flyers glad to be home, unharmed by that dizzy
    fall
Dazed as the dead awoken from death, stepped out of the
    broken
Body and went away.

What happened then, the roar
    and rave of waving crowds
That feted them, was only
    an afterglow of glory
Reflected on the clouds
    where they had climbed alone,
Day's golden epilogue:
    and them, whose meteor path
Lightened our eyes, whose great
    spirit lifted the fog
That sours a doubtful earth,
    the stars commemorate.

C. DAY LEWIS.